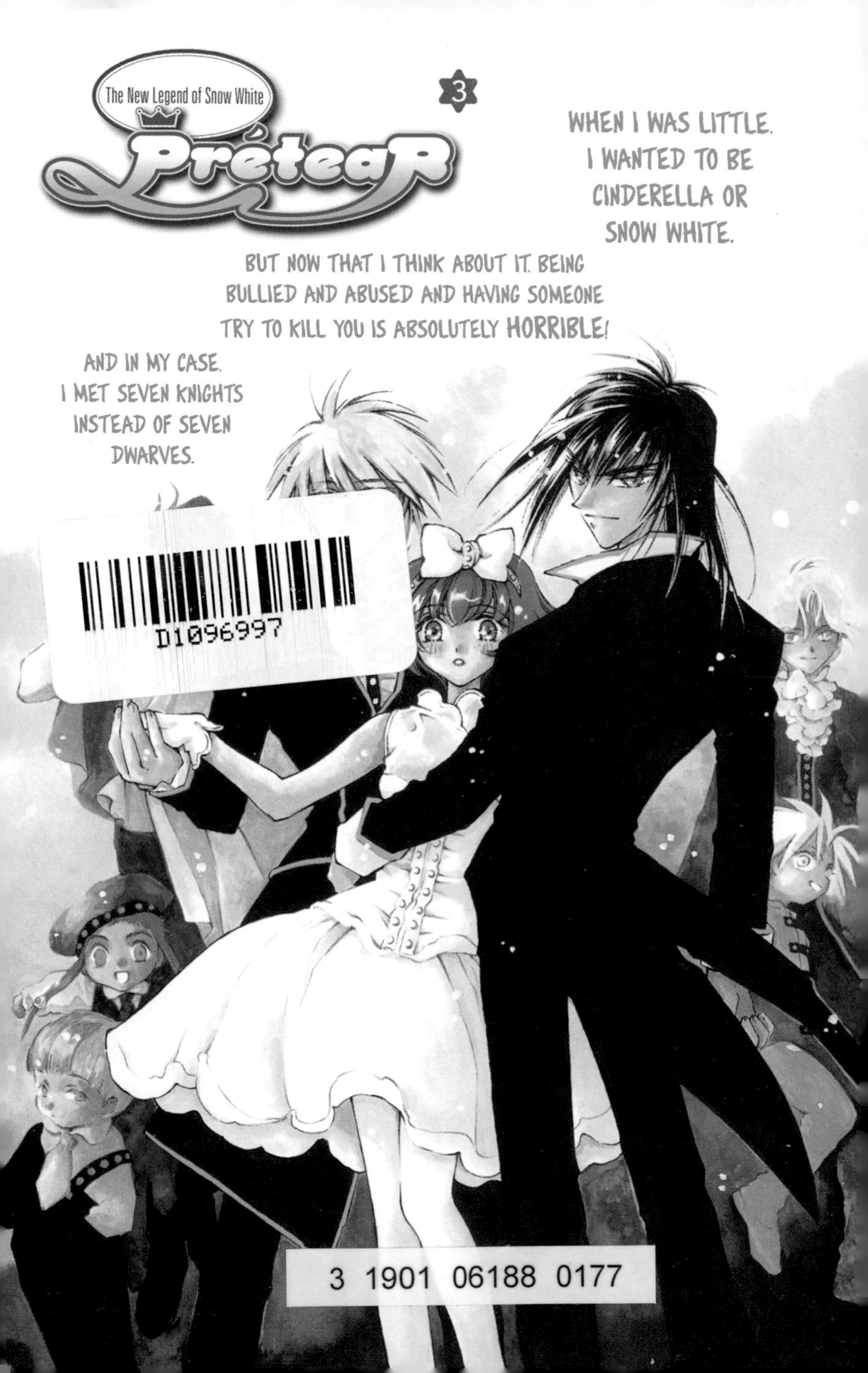
The New Legend of Snow White
Prétear
3
WHEN I WAS LITTLE, I WANTED TO BE CINDERELLA OR SNOW WHITE.
BUT NOW THAT I THINK ABOUT IT, BEING BULLIED AND ABUSED AND HAVING SOMEONE TRY TO KILL YOU IS ABSOLUTELY HORRIBLE!
AND IN MY CASE, I MET SEVEN KNIGHTS INSTEAD OF SEVEN DWARVES.

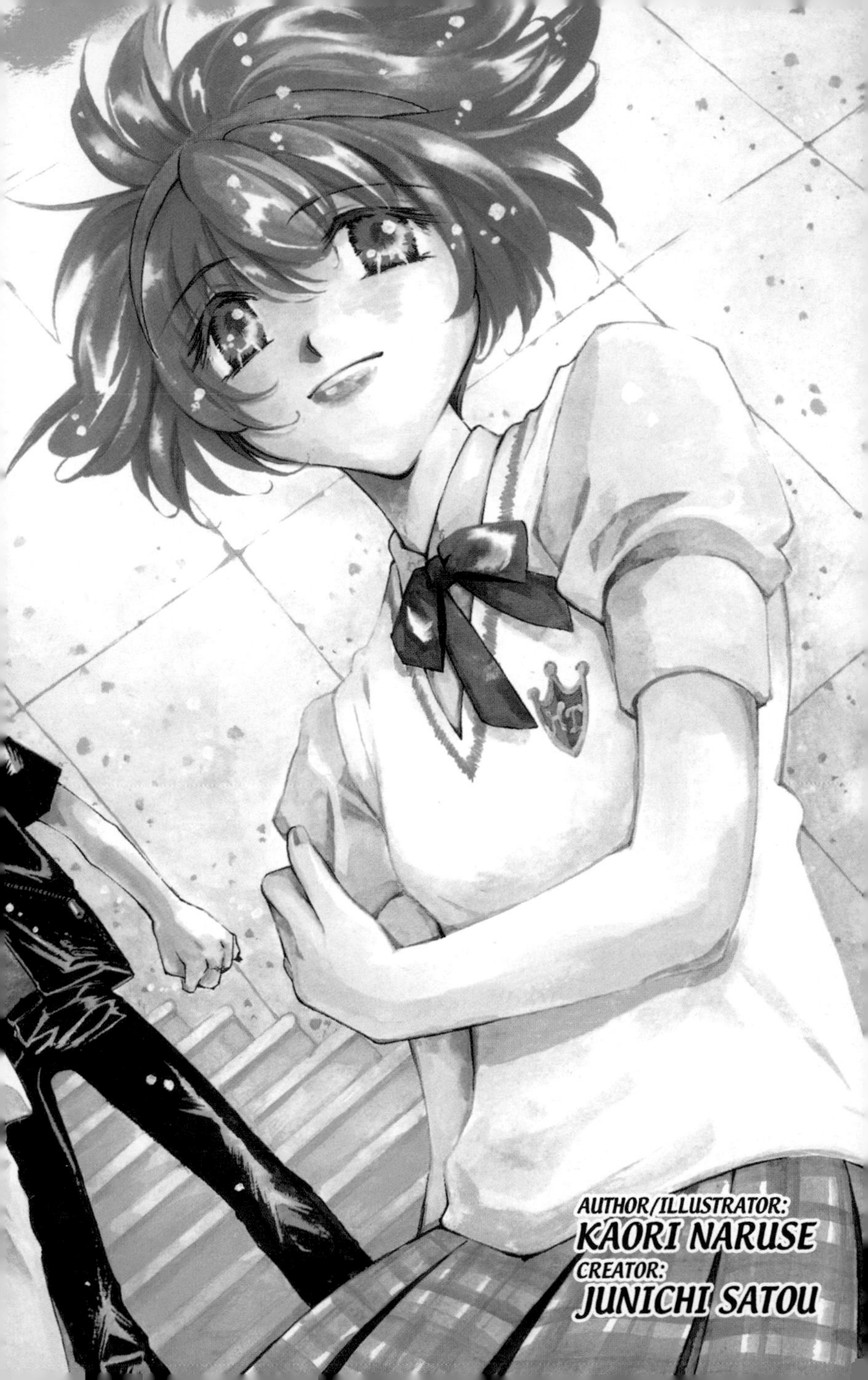
AUTHOR/ILLUSTRATOR:
KAORI NARUSE
CREATOR:
JUNICHI SATOU

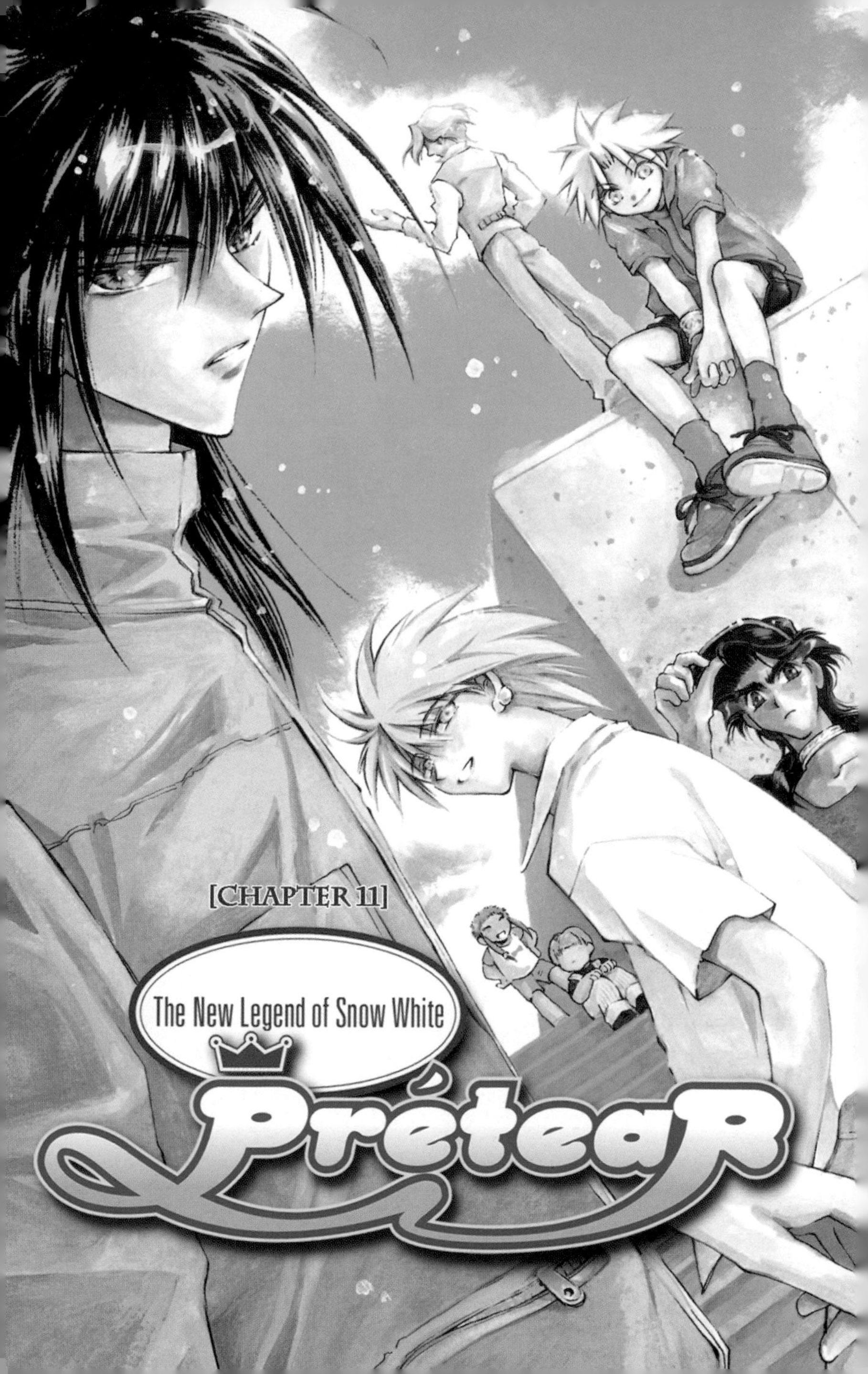
[CHAPTER 11]
The New Legend of Snow White
Prétear

CONTENTS

The Story Until Now: "We want you to become the Prétear, and save the world." That is what seven young men called the Leafe Knights asked of young Himeno. Thus began her battle with the Princess of Disaster, who steals the Leafe—the source of all life. However, Himeno finds out that the Prétear and the Princess of Disaster are essentially the same, and then discovers the real reason why the previous Prétear became the Princess of Disaster. Himeno can't hide her fear, but in the end she chooses to fight alongside the Knights, to protect the ones she loves.

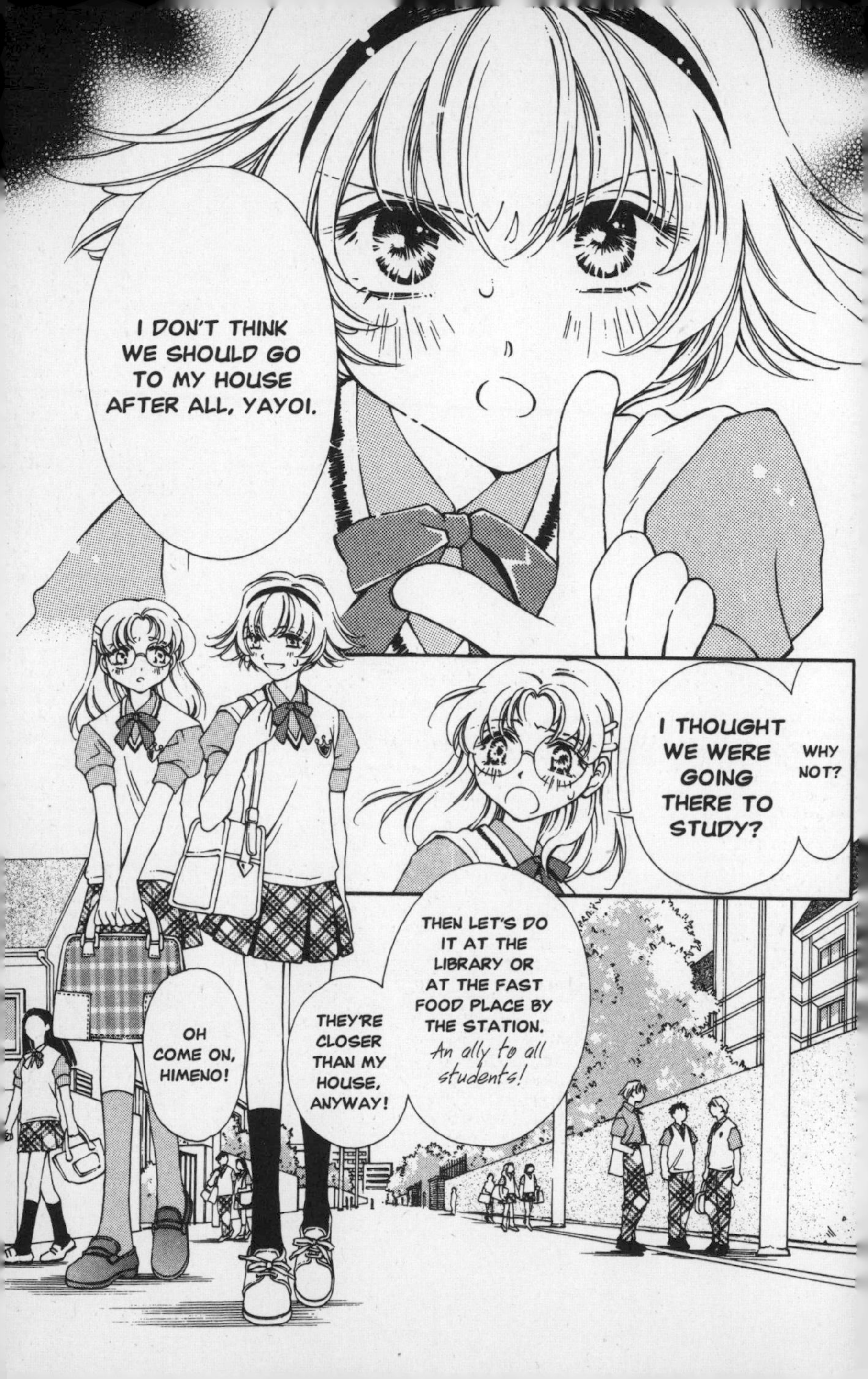
I DON'T THINK WE SHOULD GO TO MY HOUSE AFTER ALL, YAYOI.
WHY NOT?
I THOUGHT WE WERE GOING THERE TO STUDY?
THEN LET'S DO IT AT THE LIBRARY OR AT THE FAST FOOD PLACE BY THE STATION.
An ally to all students!
THEY'RE CLOSER THAN MY HOUSE, ANYWAY!
OH COME ON, HIMENO!

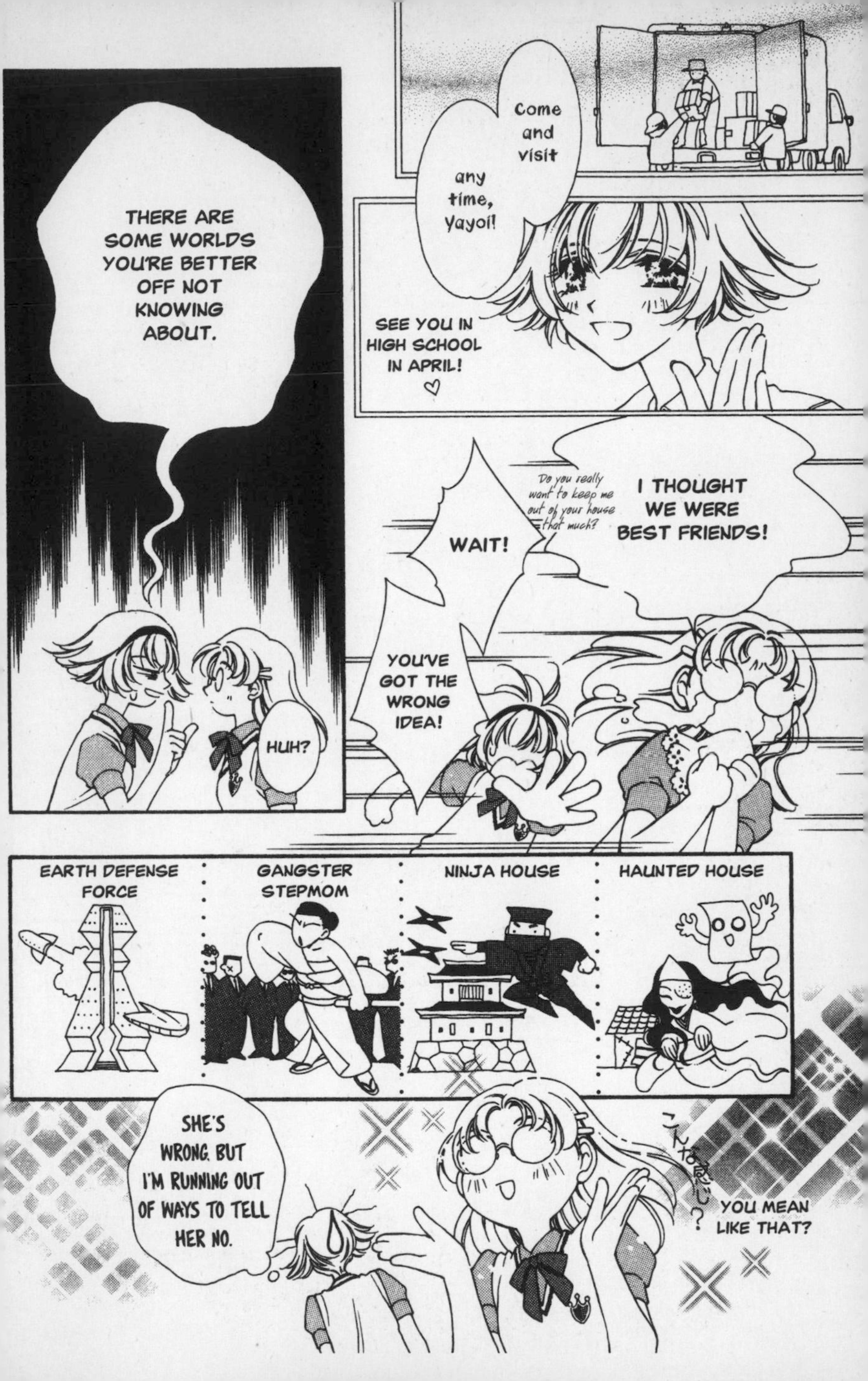
Come and visit
any time, Yayoi!
SEE YOU IN HIGH SCHOOL IN APRIL! ♡
I THOUGHT WE WERE BEST FRIENDS!
Do you really want to keep me out of your house that much?
WAIT!
YOU'VE GOT THE WRONG IDEA!
THERE ARE SOME WORLDS YOU'RE BETTER OFF NOT KNOWING ABOUT.
HUH?
HAUNTED HOUSE
NINJA HOUSE
GANGSTER STEPMOM
EARTH DEFENSE FORCE
こんな感じ?
YOU MEAN LIKE THAT?
SHE'S WRONG, BUT I'M RUNNING OUT OF WAYS TO TELL HER NO.

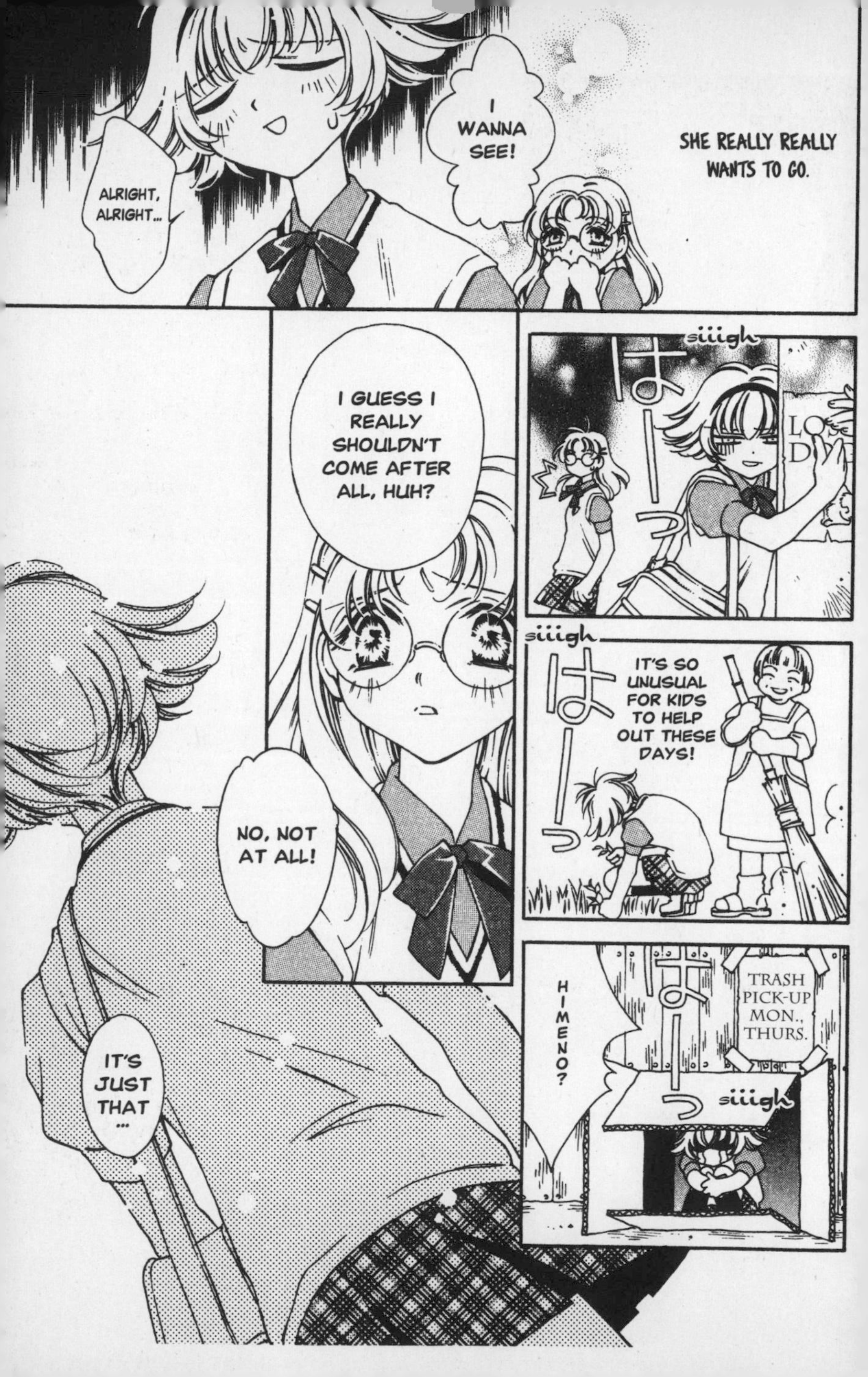
SHE REALLY REALLY WANTS TO GO.
I WANNA SEE!
ALRIGHT, ALRIGHT...
はーっ
siiigh
はーっ
siiigh
IT'S SO UNUSUAL FOR KIDS TO HELP OUT THESE DAYS!
TRASH PICK-UP MON., THURS.
はーっ
siiigh
HIMENO?
...
I GUESS I REALLY SHOULDN'T COME AFTER ALL, HUH?
NO, NOT AT ALL!
IT'S JUST THAT ...

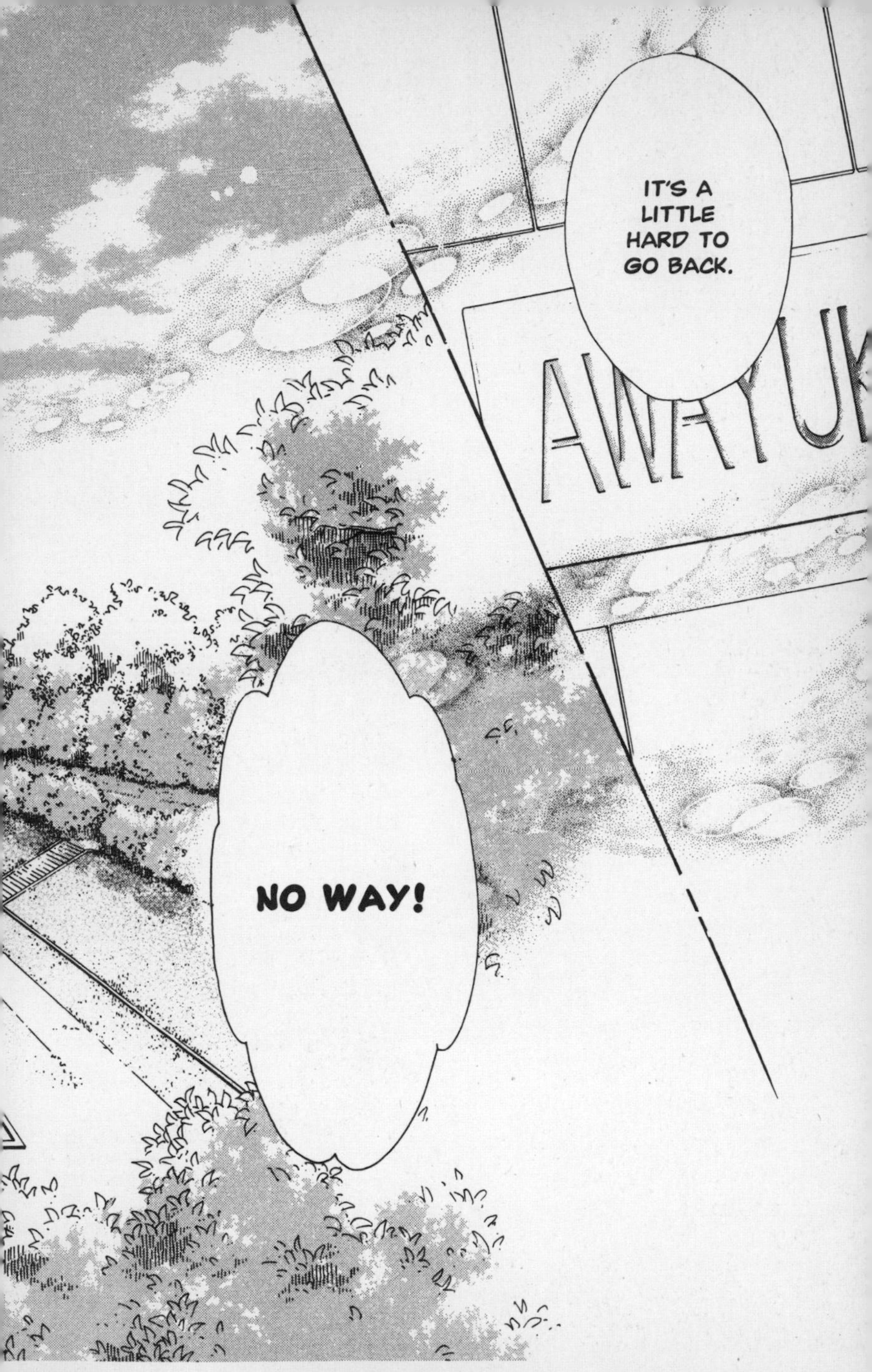
IT'S A LITTLE HARD TO GO BACK.
NO WAY!

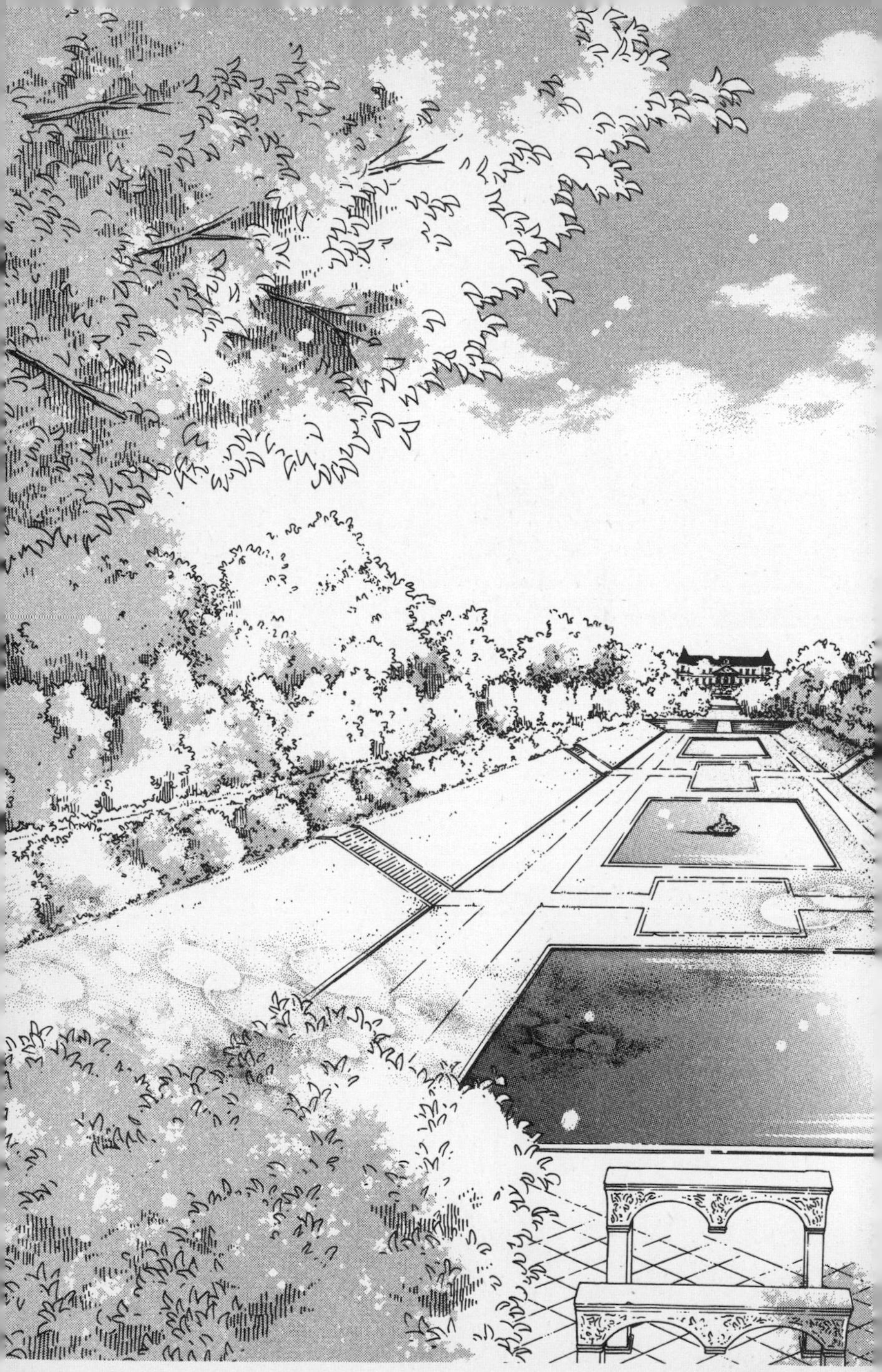

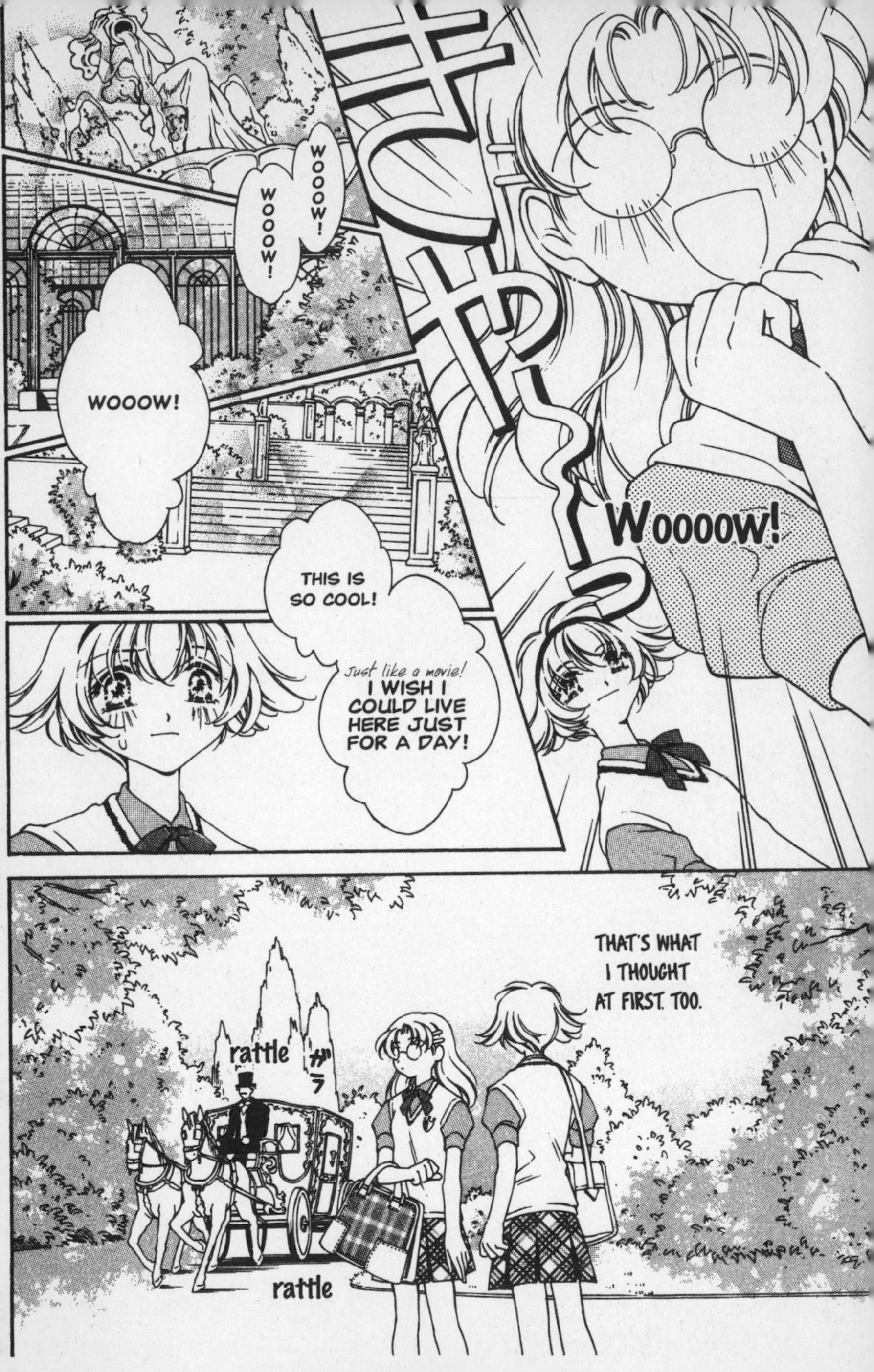
きゃ～っ
Wooooow!
WOOOOW!
WOOOOW!
WOOOW!
THIS IS SO COOL!
Just like a movie!
I WISH I COULD LIVE HERE JUST FOR A DAY!
THAT'S WHAT I THOUGHT AT FIRST, TOO.
rattle
ガラ
rattle

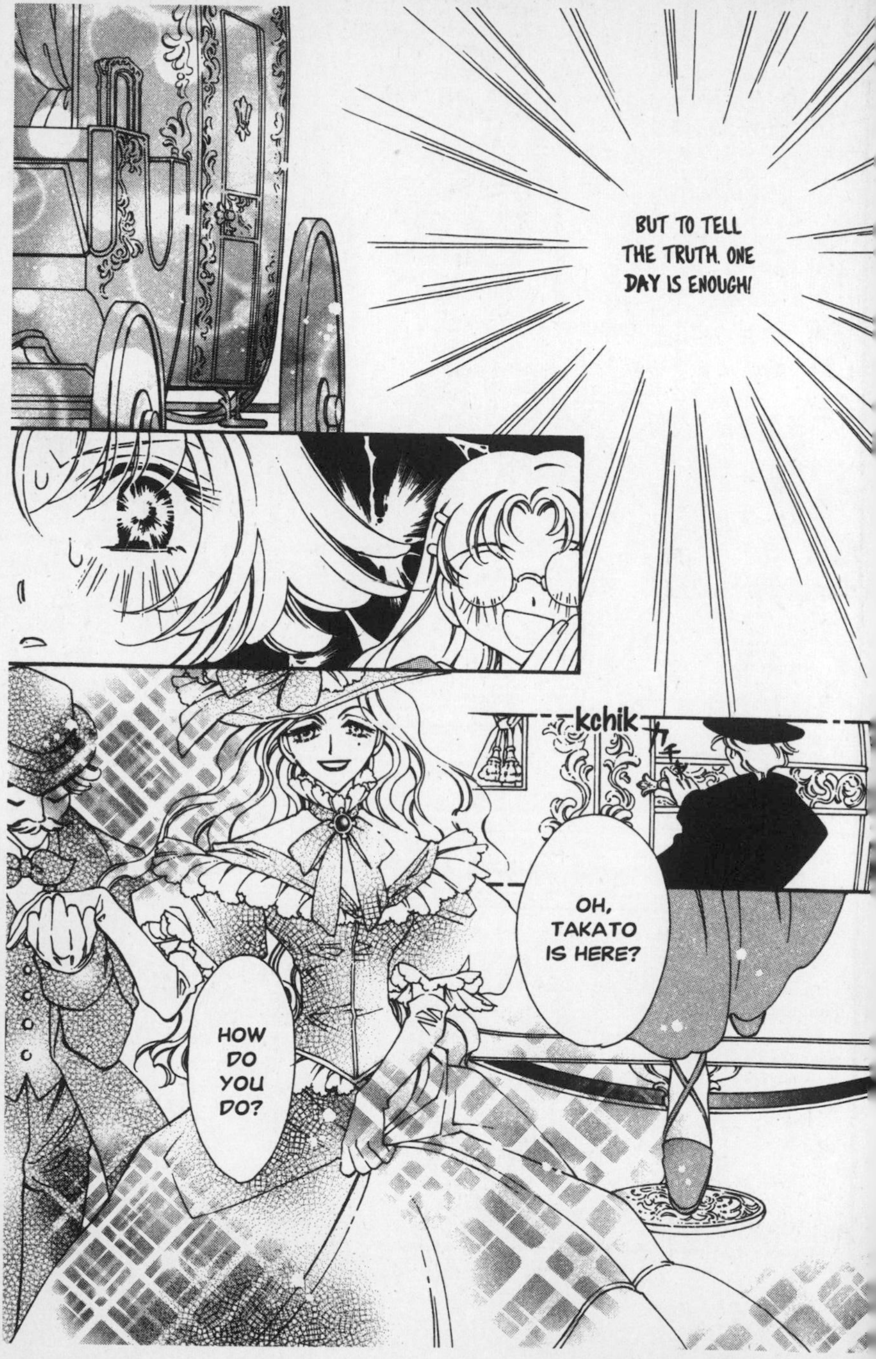
BUT TO TELL THE TRUTH. ONE DAY IS ENOUGH!
kchik
OH, TAKATO IS HERE?
HOW DO YOU DO?

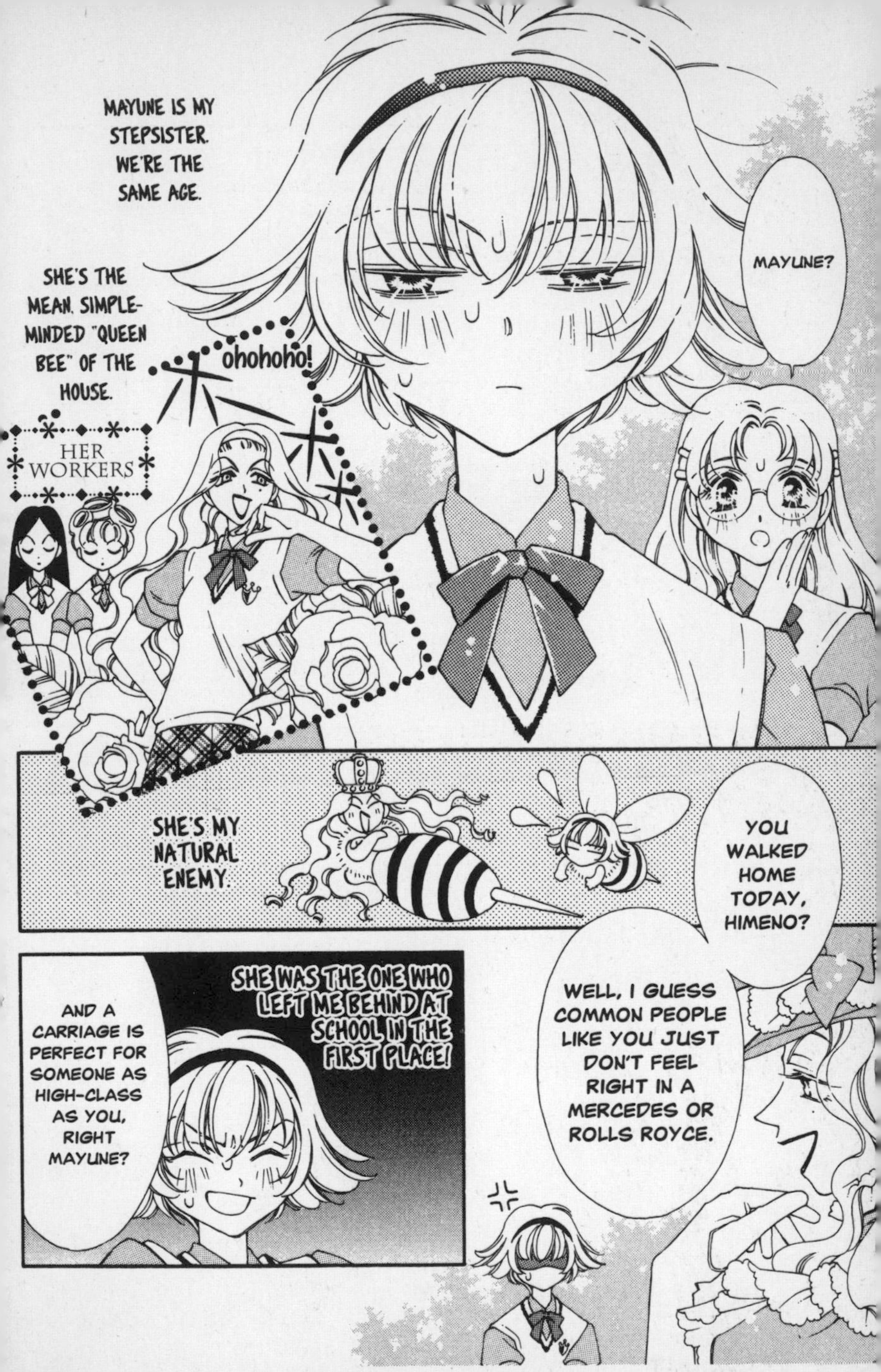
MAYUNE?
MAYUNE IS MY STEPSISTER. WE'RE THE SAME AGE.
SHE'S THE MEAN, SIMPLE-MINDED "QUEEN BEE" OF THE HOUSE.
ohohoho!
HER WORKERS
YOU WALKED HOME TODAY, HIMENO?
SHE'S MY NATURAL ENEMY.
WELL, I GUESS COMMON PEOPLE LIKE YOU JUST DON'T FEEL RIGHT IN A MERCEDES OR ROLLS ROYCE.
SHE WAS THE ONE WHO LEFT ME BEHIND AT SCHOOL IN THE FIRST PLACE!
AND A CARRIAGE IS PERFECT FOR SOMEONE AS HIGH-CLASS AS YOU, RIGHT MAYUNE?

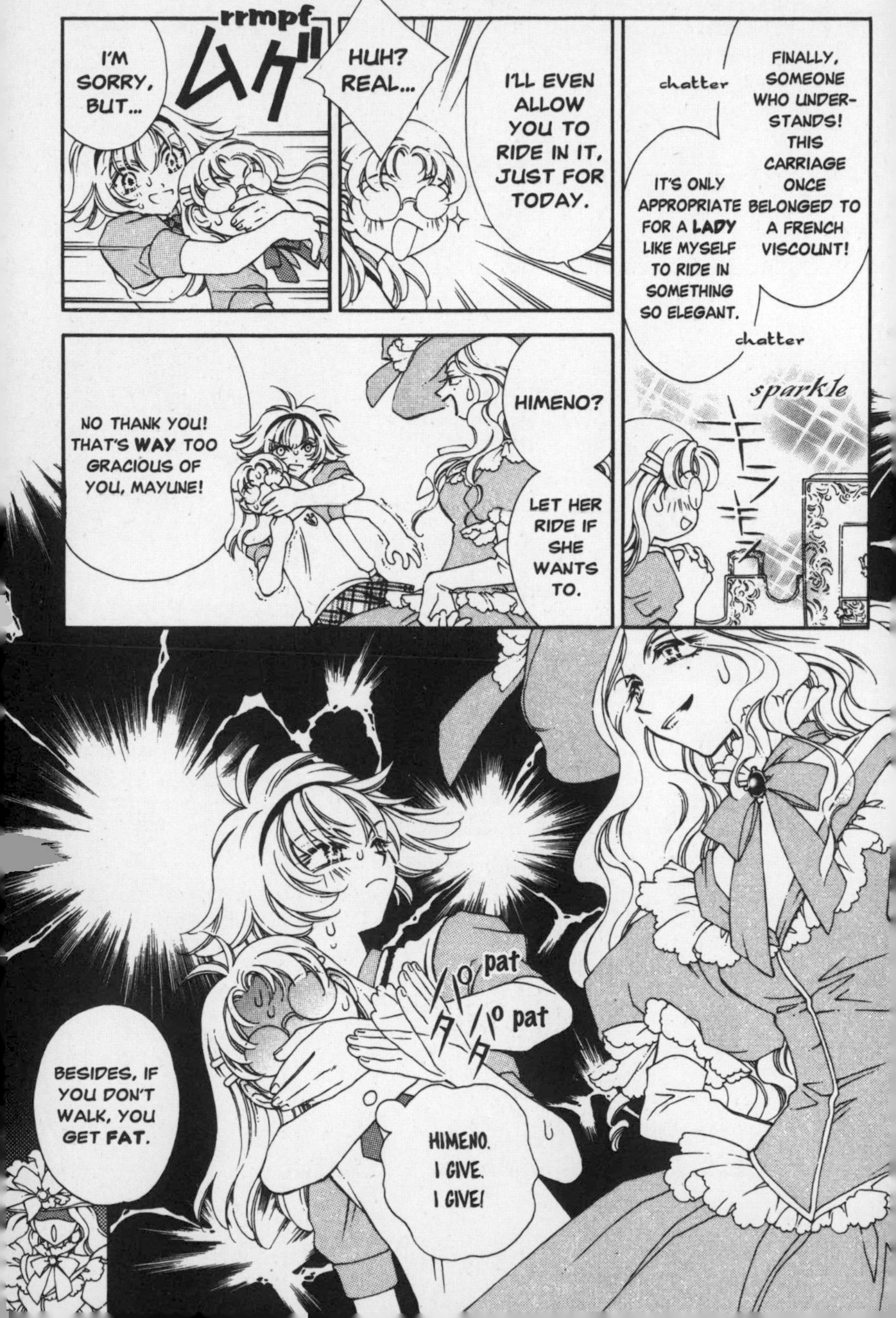
chatter
FINALLY, SOMEONE WHO UNDERSTANDS! THIS CARRIAGE ONCE BELONGED TO A FRENCH VISCOUNT!
IT'S ONLY APPROPRIATE FOR A LADY LIKE MYSELF TO RIDE IN SOMETHING SO ELEGANT.
chatter
sparkle
I'LL EVEN ALLOW YOU TO RIDE IN IT, JUST FOR TODAY.
HUH? REAL...
rrmpf
I'M SORRY, BUT...
HIMENO?
LET HER RIDE IF SHE WANTS TO.
NO THANK YOU! THAT'S WAY TOO GRACIOUS OF YOU, MAYUNE!
pat
pat
HIMENO. I GIVE. I GIVE!
BESIDES, IF YOU DON'T WALK, YOU GET FAT.

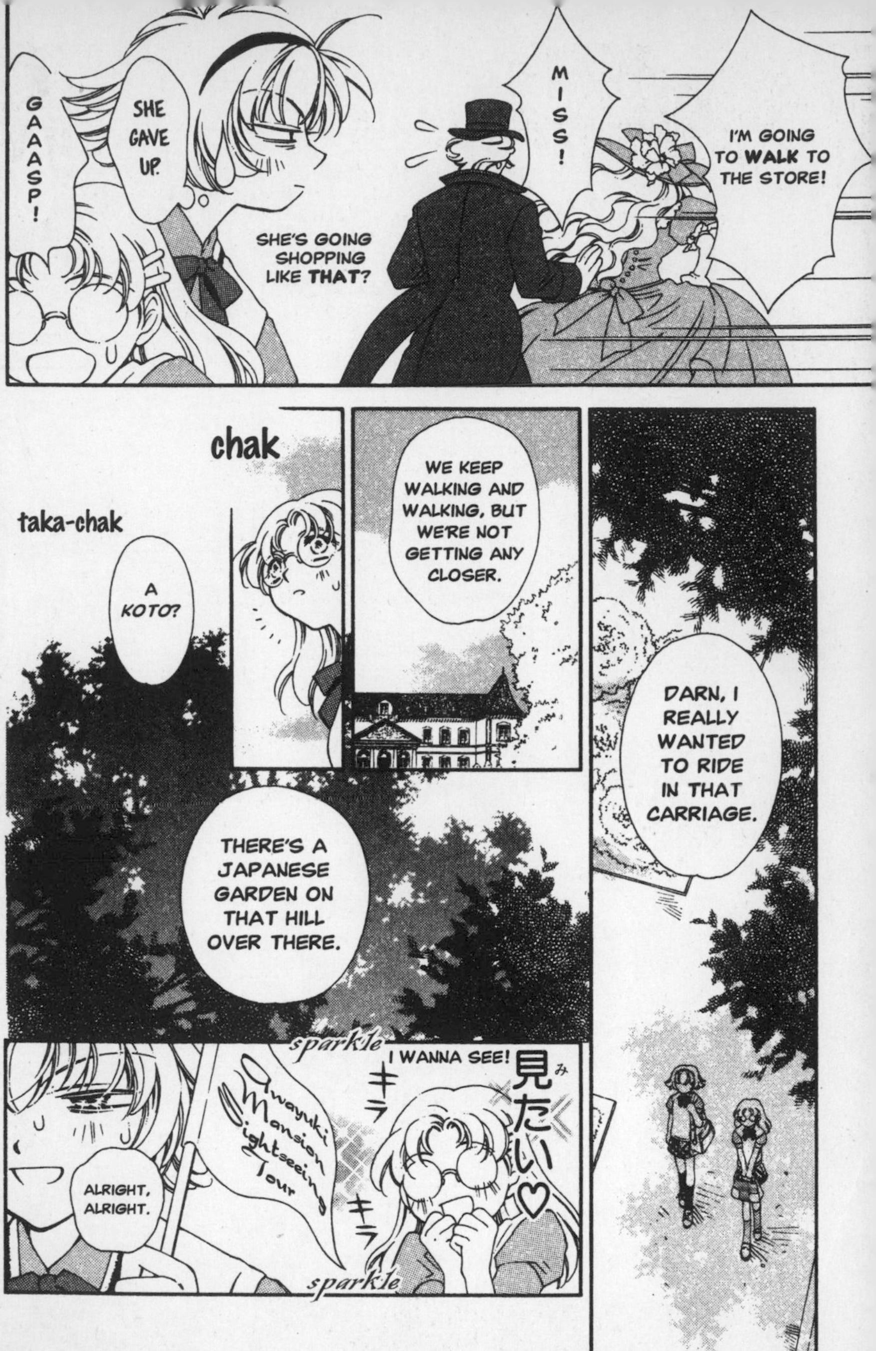
I'M GOING TO WALK TO THE STORE!
MISS!
SHE'S GOING SHOPPING LIKE THAT?
SHE GAVE UP.
GAAASP!
DARN, I REALLY WANTED TO RIDE IN THAT CARRIAGE.
WE KEEP WALKING AND WALKING, BUT WE'RE NOT GETTING ANY CLOSER.
chak
taka-chak
A KOTO?
THERE'S A JAPANESE GARDEN ON THAT HILL OVER THERE.
I WANNA SEE!
見たい♡
sparkle
キラ
キラ
sparkle
Awayuki Mansion Sightseeing Tour
ALRIGHT, ALRIGHT.

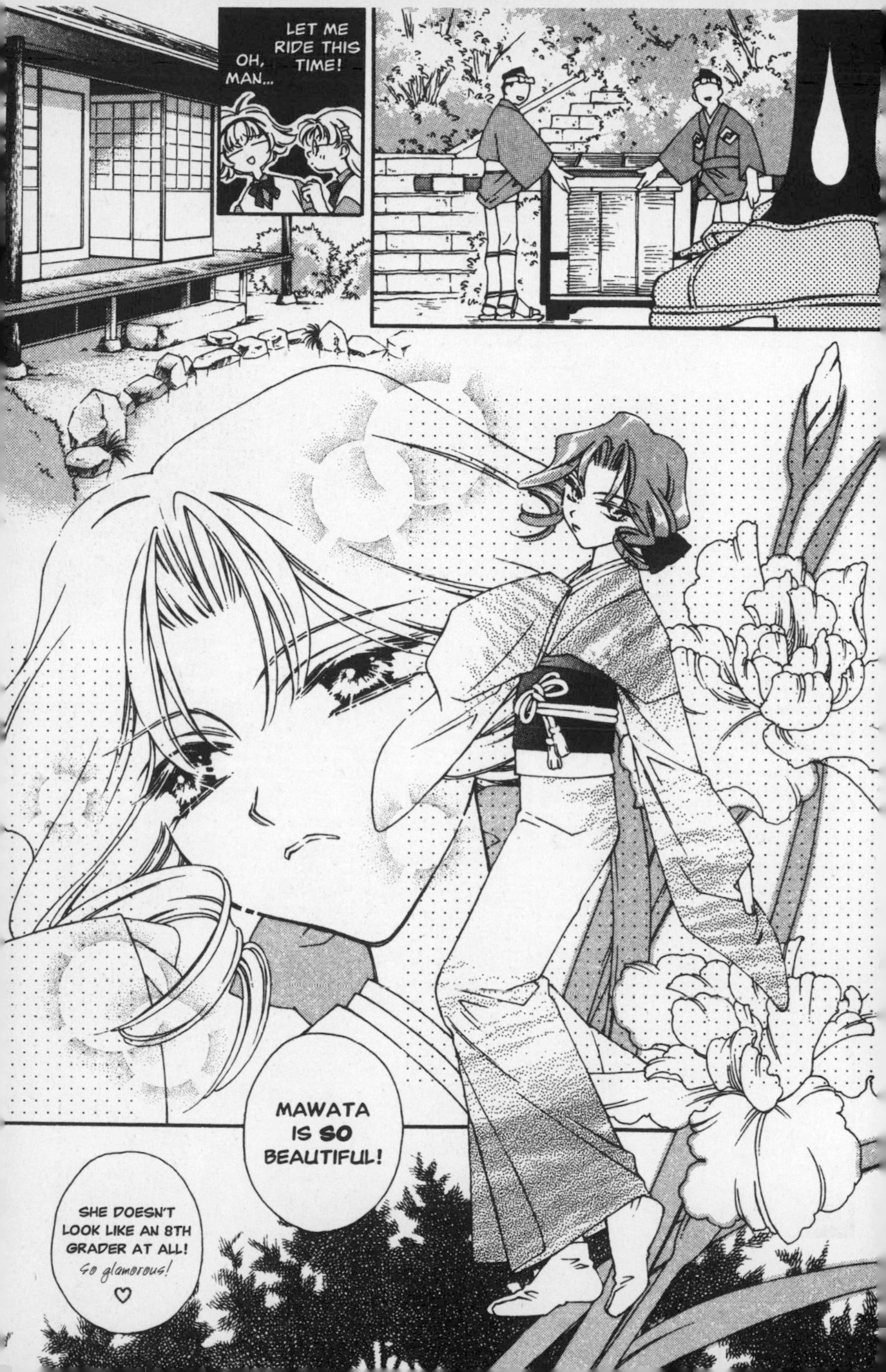
LET ME RIDE THIS TIME!
OH, MAN...
MAWATA IS SO BEAUTIFUL!
SHE DOESN'T LOOK LIKE AN 8TH GRADER AT ALL! So glamorous! ♡

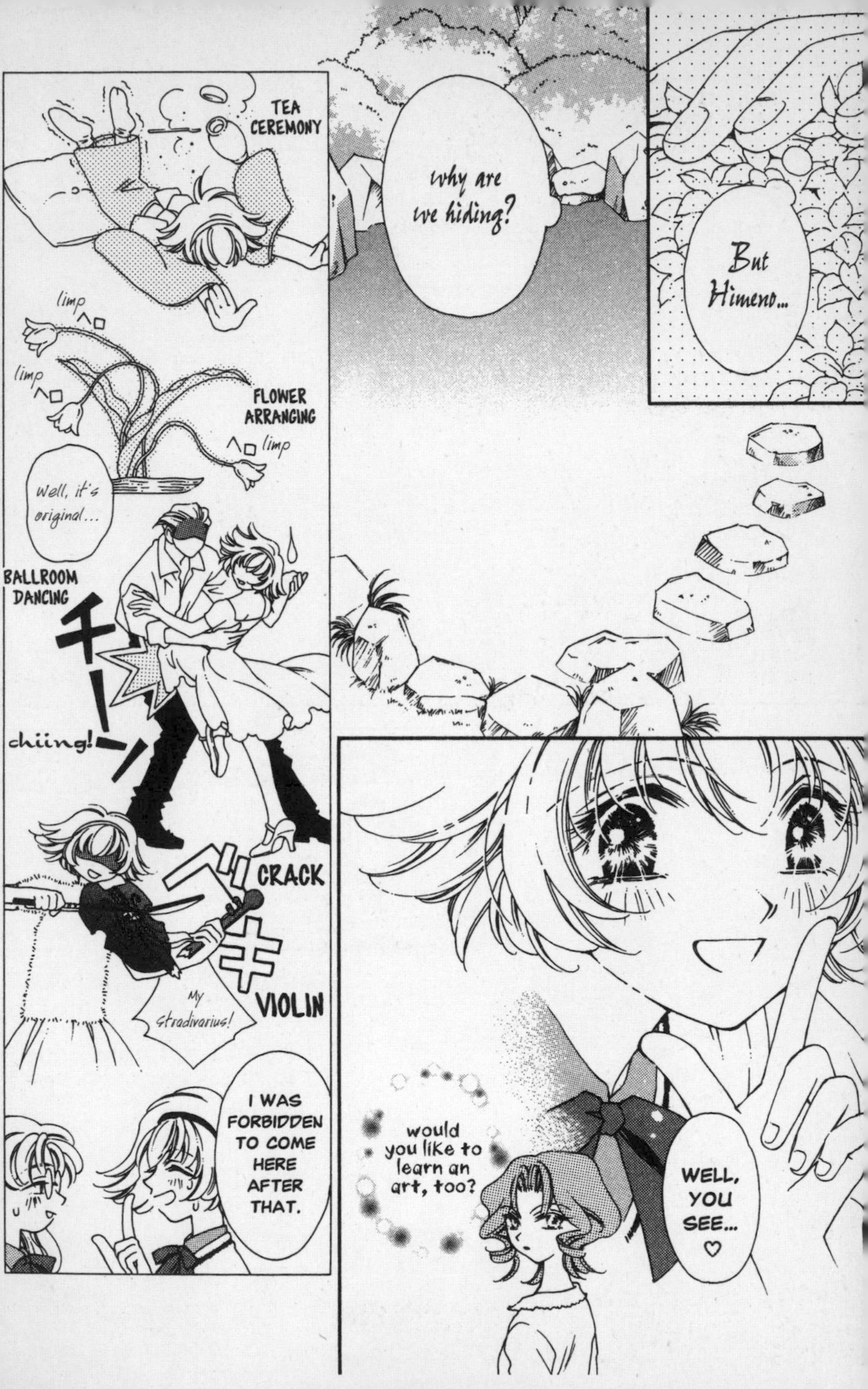

But Himeno...
why are we hiding?
WELL, YOU SEE... ♡
would you like to learn an art, too?
TEA CEREMONY
limp
limp
FLOWER ARRANGING
limp
Well, it's original...
BALLROOM DANCING
chiing!
CRACK
VIOLIN
My Stradivarius!
I WAS FORBIDDEN TO COME HERE AFTER THAT.

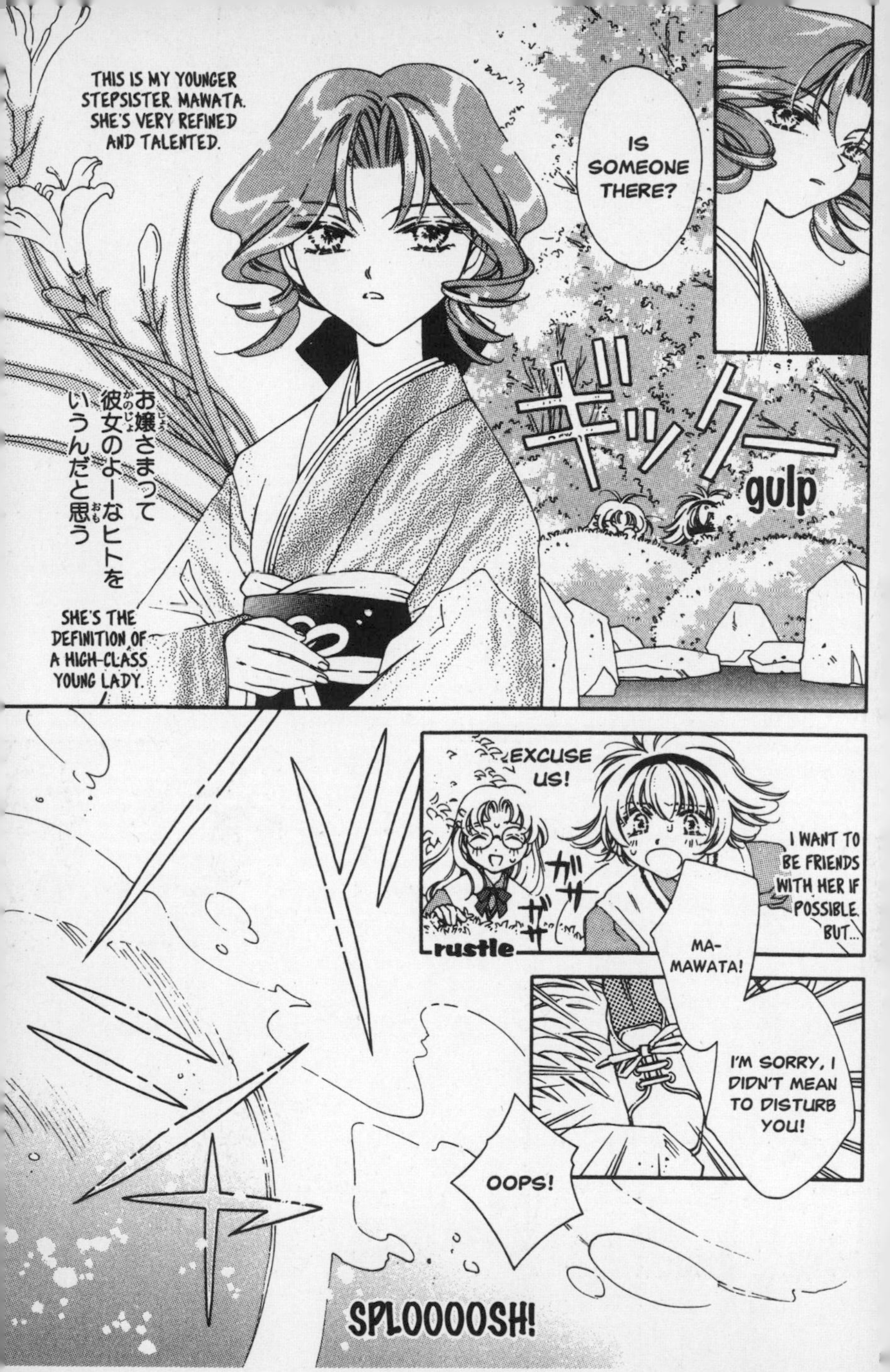

THIS IS MY YOUNGER STEPSISTER. MAWATA. SHE'S VERY REFINED AND TALENTED.
IS SOMEONE THERE?
ギックー
gulp
お嬢さまって彼女のよーなヒトをいうんだと思う
SHE'S THE DEFINITION OF A HIGH-CLASS YOUNG LADY.
EXCUSE US!
I WANT TO BE FRIENDS WITH HER IF POSSIBLE. BUT...
ガサガサ
rustle
MA-MAWATA!
I'M SORRY, I DIDN'T MEAN TO DISTURB YOU!
OOPS!
SPLOOOOSH!

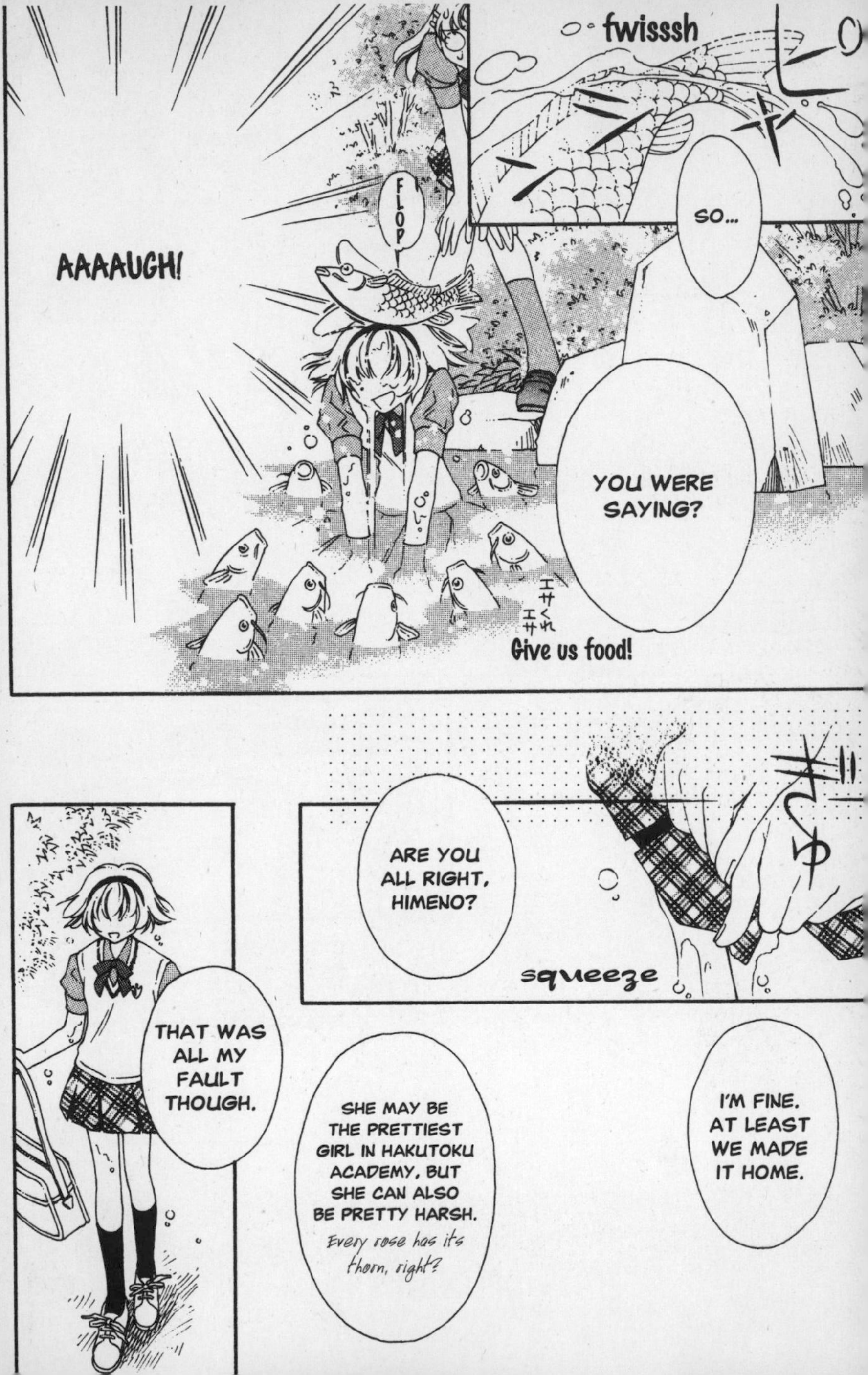
fwisssh
SO...
YOU WERE SAYING?
FLOP
AAAAUGH!
Give us food!
ARE YOU ALL RIGHT, HIMENO?
squeeze
I'M FINE. AT LEAST WE MADE IT HOME.
SHE MAY BE THE PRETTIEST GIRL IN HAKUTOKU ACADEMY, BUT SHE CAN ALSO BE PRETTY HARSH.
Every rose has its thorn, right?
THAT WAS ALL MY FAULT THOUGH.

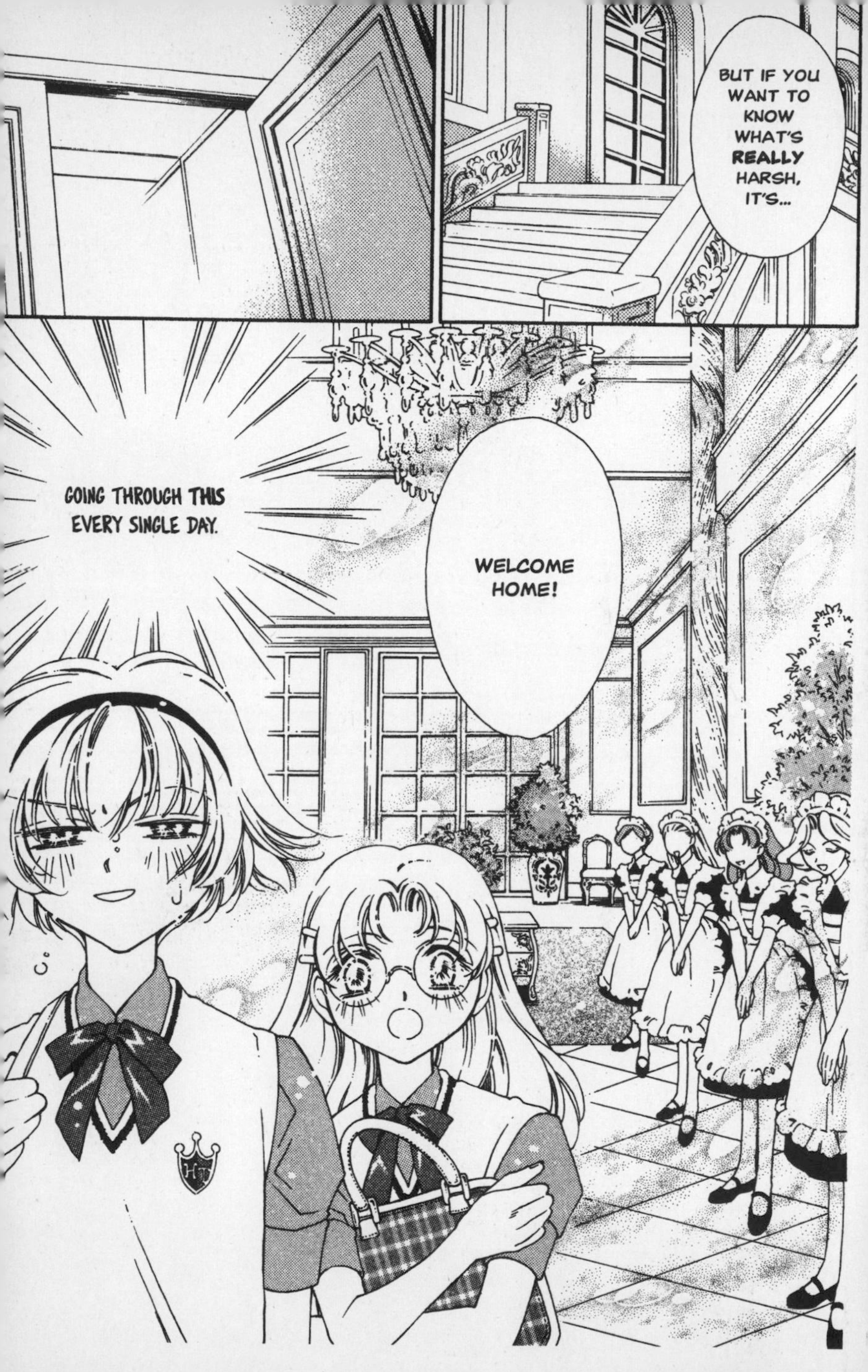
BUT IF YOU WANT TO KNOW WHAT'S **REALLY** HARSH, IT'S...
WELCOME HOME!
GOING THROUGH THIS EVERY SINGLE DAY.

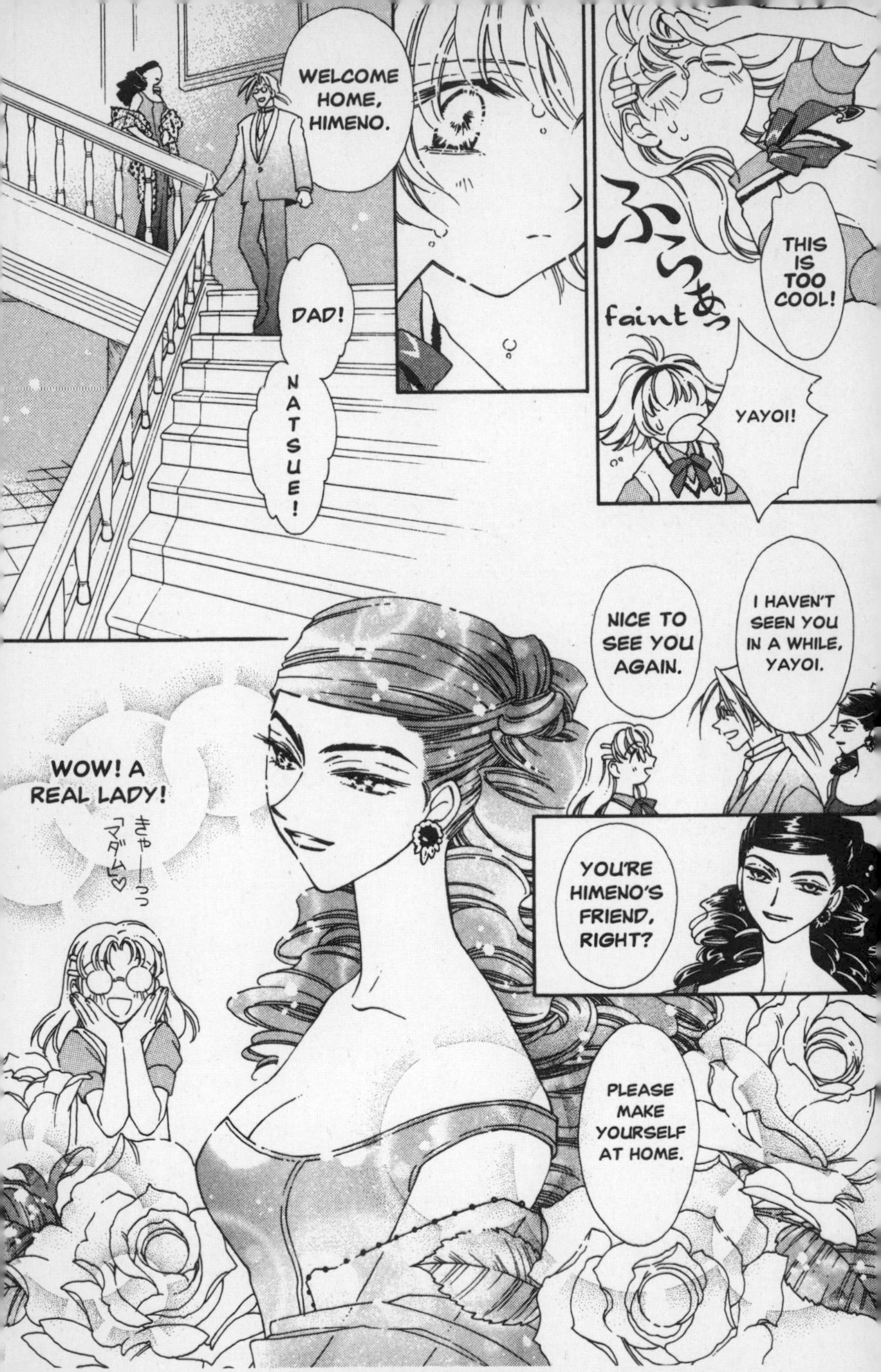
THIS IS TOO COOL!
ふらあっ
faint
YAYOI!
WELCOME HOME, HIMENO.
DAD!
NATSUE!
I HAVEN'T SEEN YOU IN A WHILE, YAYOI.
NICE TO SEE YOU AGAIN.
YOU'RE HIMENO'S FRIEND, RIGHT?
PLEASE MAKE YOURSELF AT HOME.
WOW! A REAL LADY!
きゃーっっ「マダム」♡

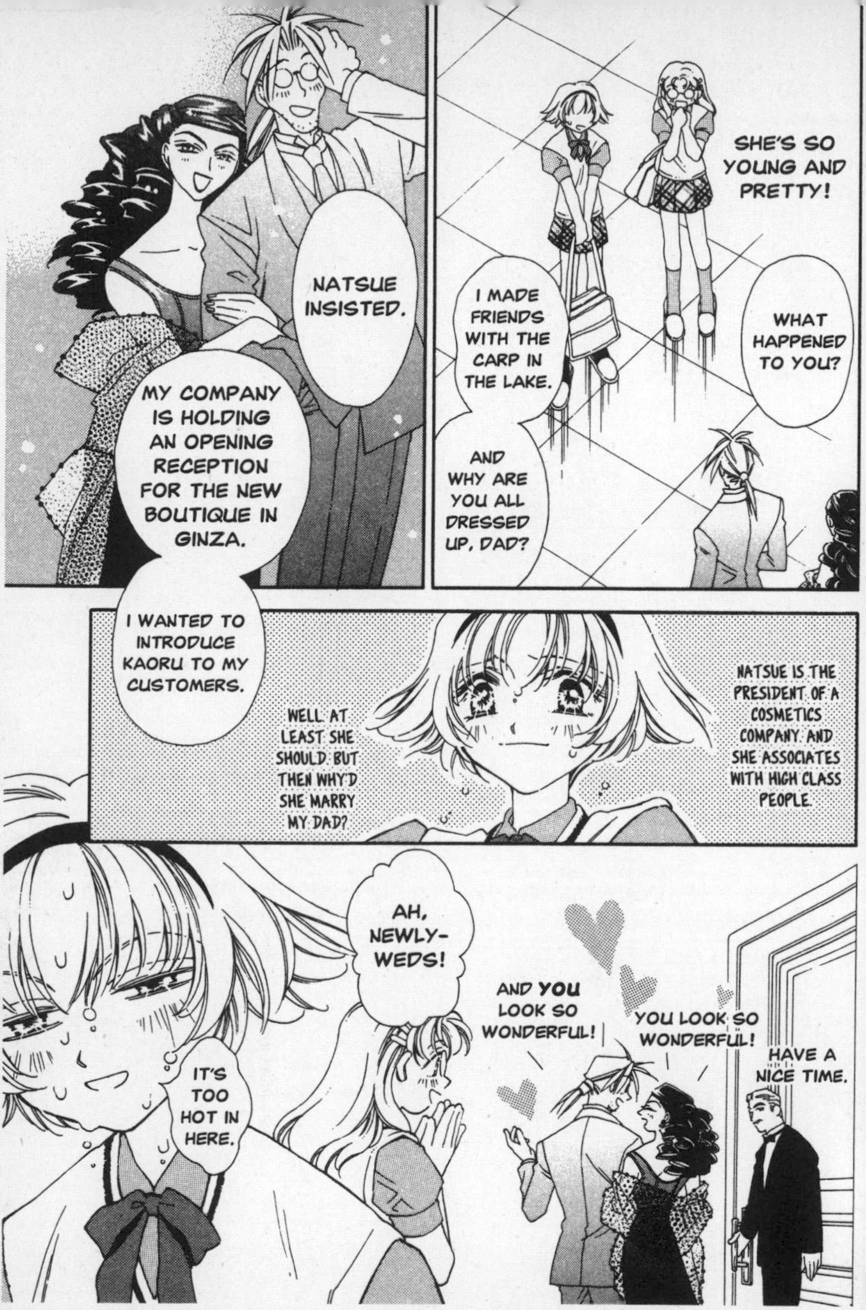
SHE'S SO YOUNG AND PRETTY!
WHAT HAPPENED TO YOU?
I MADE FRIENDS WITH THE CARP IN THE LAKE.
AND WHY ARE YOU ALL DRESSED UP, DAD?
NATSUE INSISTED.
MY COMPANY IS HOLDING AN OPENING RECEPTION FOR THE NEW BOUTIQUE IN GINZA.
I WANTED TO INTRODUCE KAORU TO MY CUSTOMERS.
NATSUE IS THE PRESIDENT OF A COSMETICS COMPANY AND SHE ASSOCIATES WITH HIGH CLASS PEOPLE.
WELL AT LEAST SHE SHOULD BUT THEN WHY'D SHE MARRY MY DAD?
HAVE A NICE TIME.
YOU LOOK SO WONDERFUL!
AND YOU LOOK SO WONDERFUL!
AH, NEWLY-WEDS!
IT'S TOO HOT IN HERE.

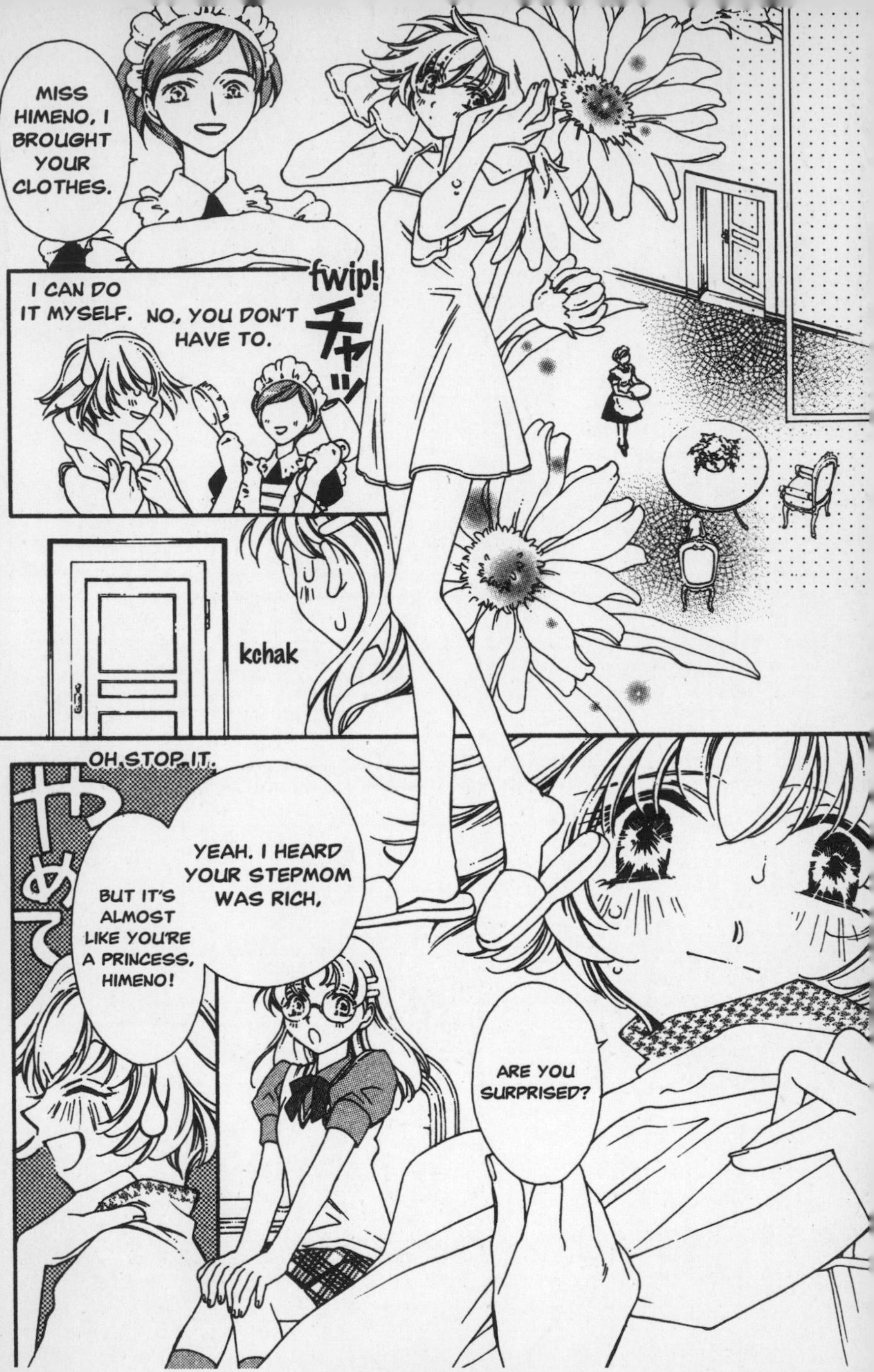
MISS HIMENO, I BROUGHT YOUR CLOTHES.
fwip!
チャッ
NO, YOU DON'T HAVE TO.
I CAN DO IT MYSELF.
kchak
YEAH. I HEARD YOUR STEPMOM WAS RICH,
BUT IT'S ALMOST LIKE YOU'RE A PRINCESS, HIMENO!
ARE YOU SURPRISED?
OH, STOP IT.
やめて

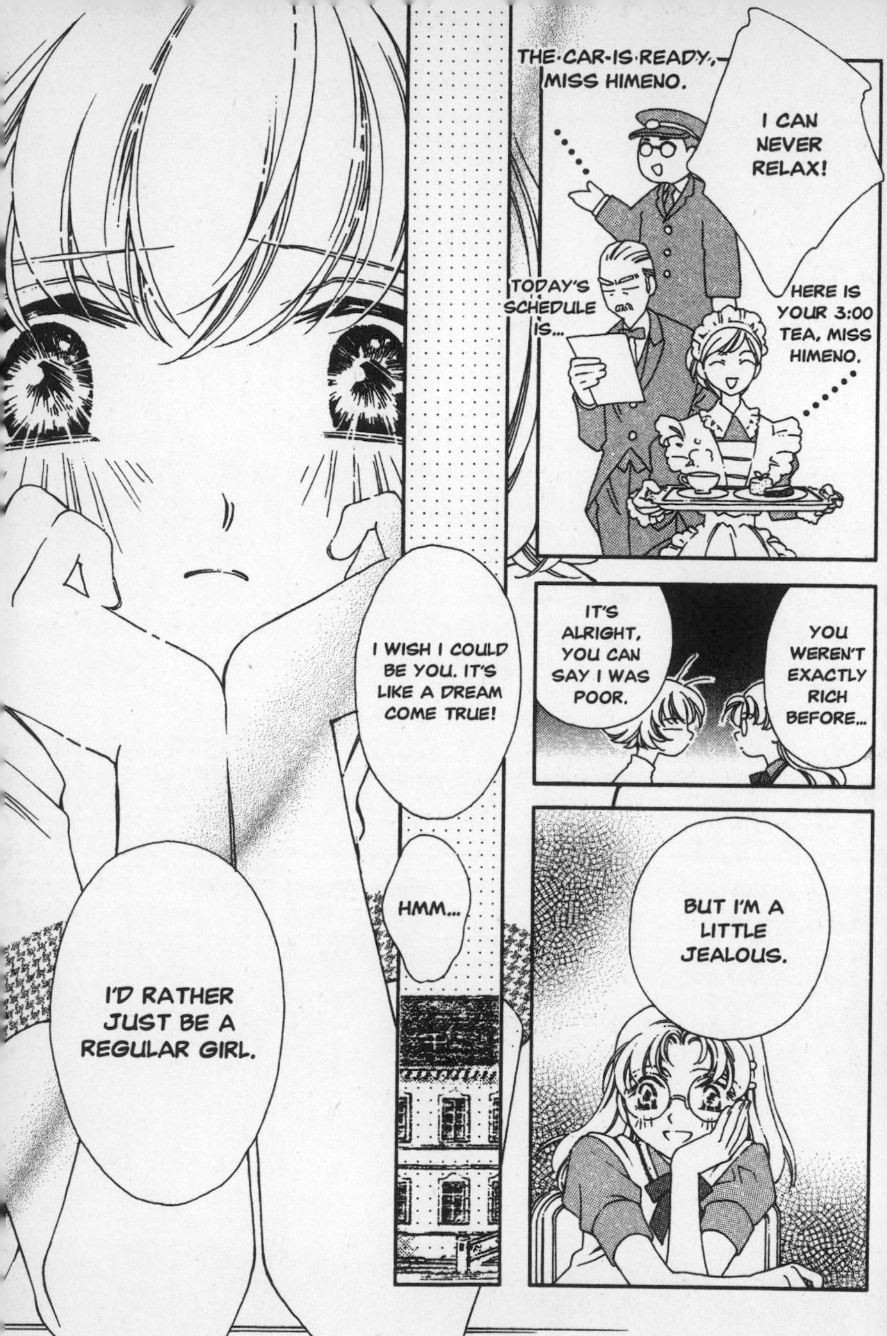
THE·CAR·IS·READY, MISS HIMENO.
I CAN NEVER RELAX!
HERE IS YOUR 3:00 TEA, MISS HIMENO.
TODAY'S SCHEDULE IS...
YOU WEREN'T EXACTLY RICH BEFORE...
IT'S ALRIGHT, YOU CAN SAY I WAS POOR.
BUT I'M A LITTLE JEALOUS.
I WISH I COULD BE YOU. IT'S LIKE A DREAM COME TRUE!
HMM...
I'D RATHER JUST BE A REGULAR GIRL.

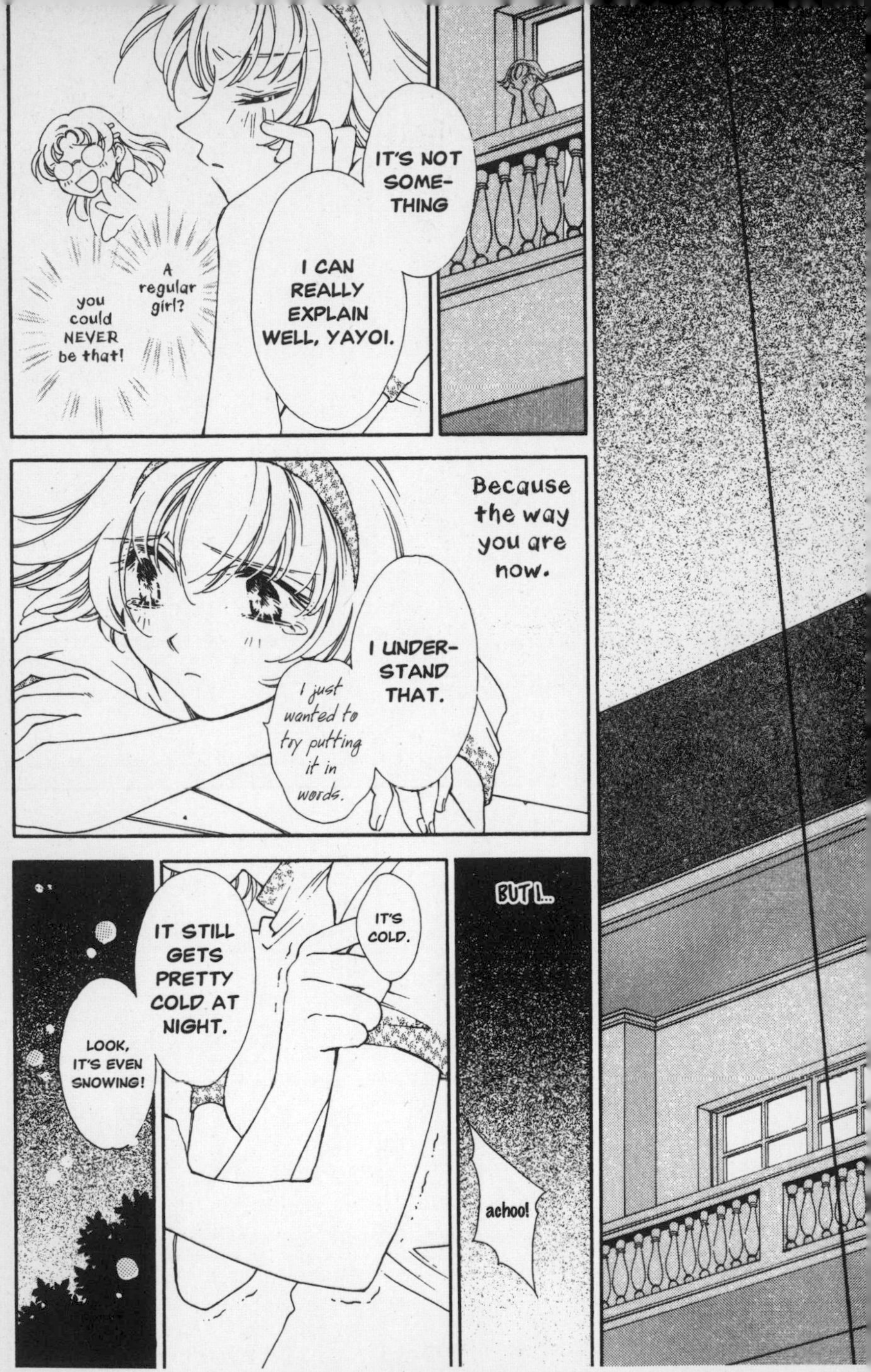

IT'S NOT SOMETHING I CAN REALLY EXPLAIN WELL, YAYOI.
A regular girl?
you could NEVER be that!
Because the way you are now.
I UNDERSTAND THAT.
I just wanted to try putting it in words.
BUT I...
achoo!
IT'S COLD.
IT STILL GETS PRETTY COLD AT NIGHT.
LOOK, IT'S EVEN SNOWING!

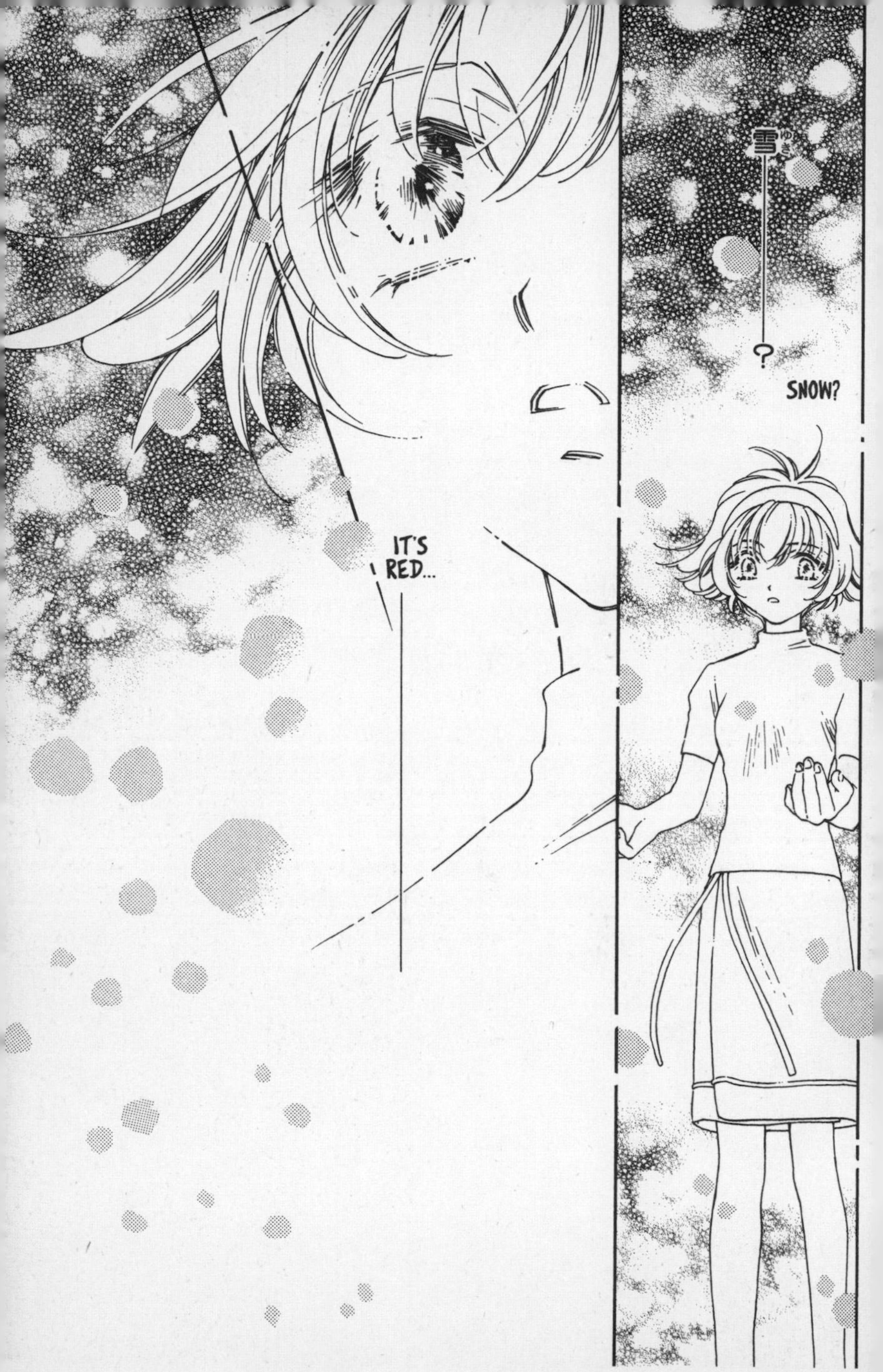
雪？
SNOW?
IT'S RED...

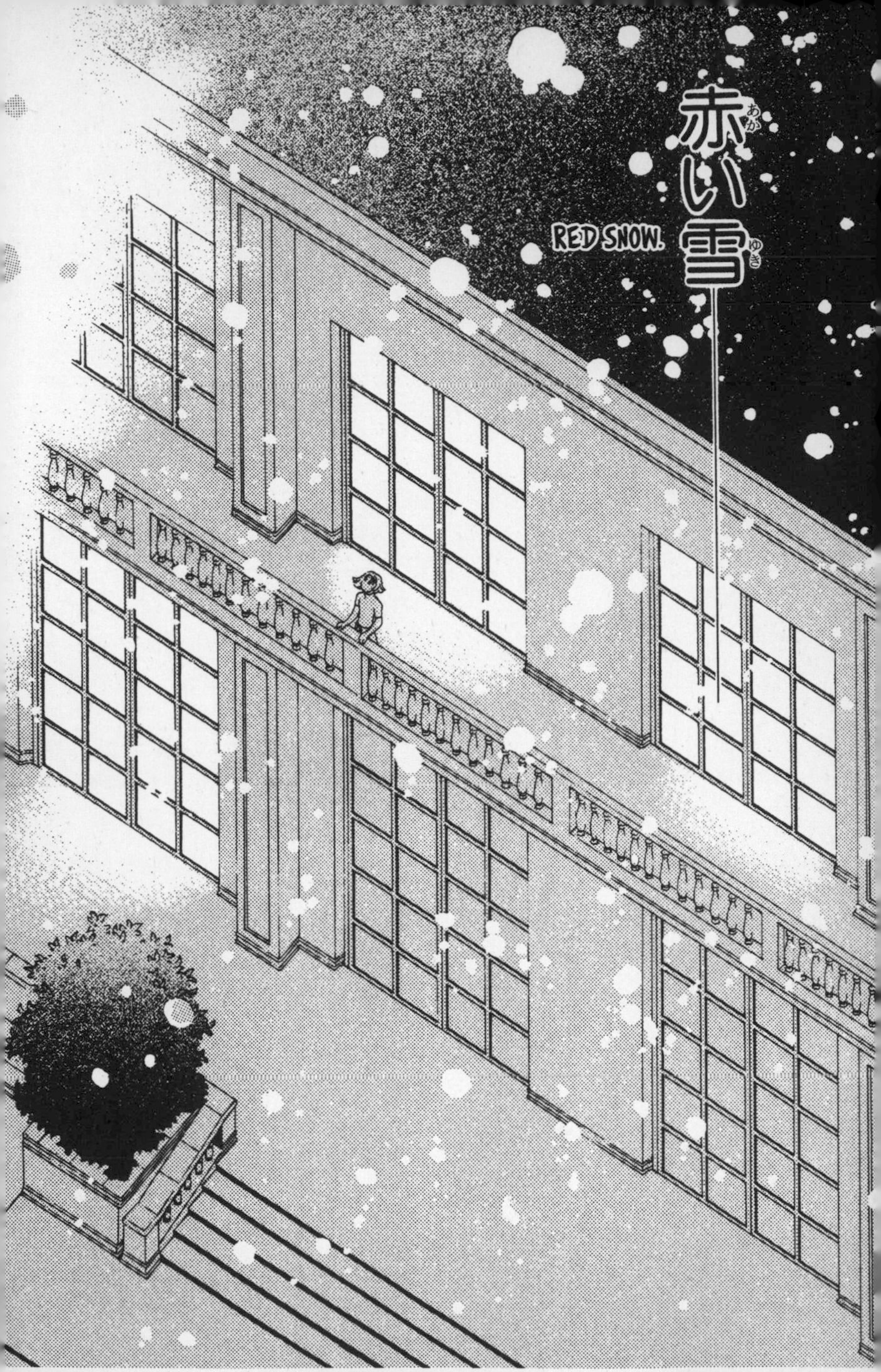
赤い雪
RED SNOW.

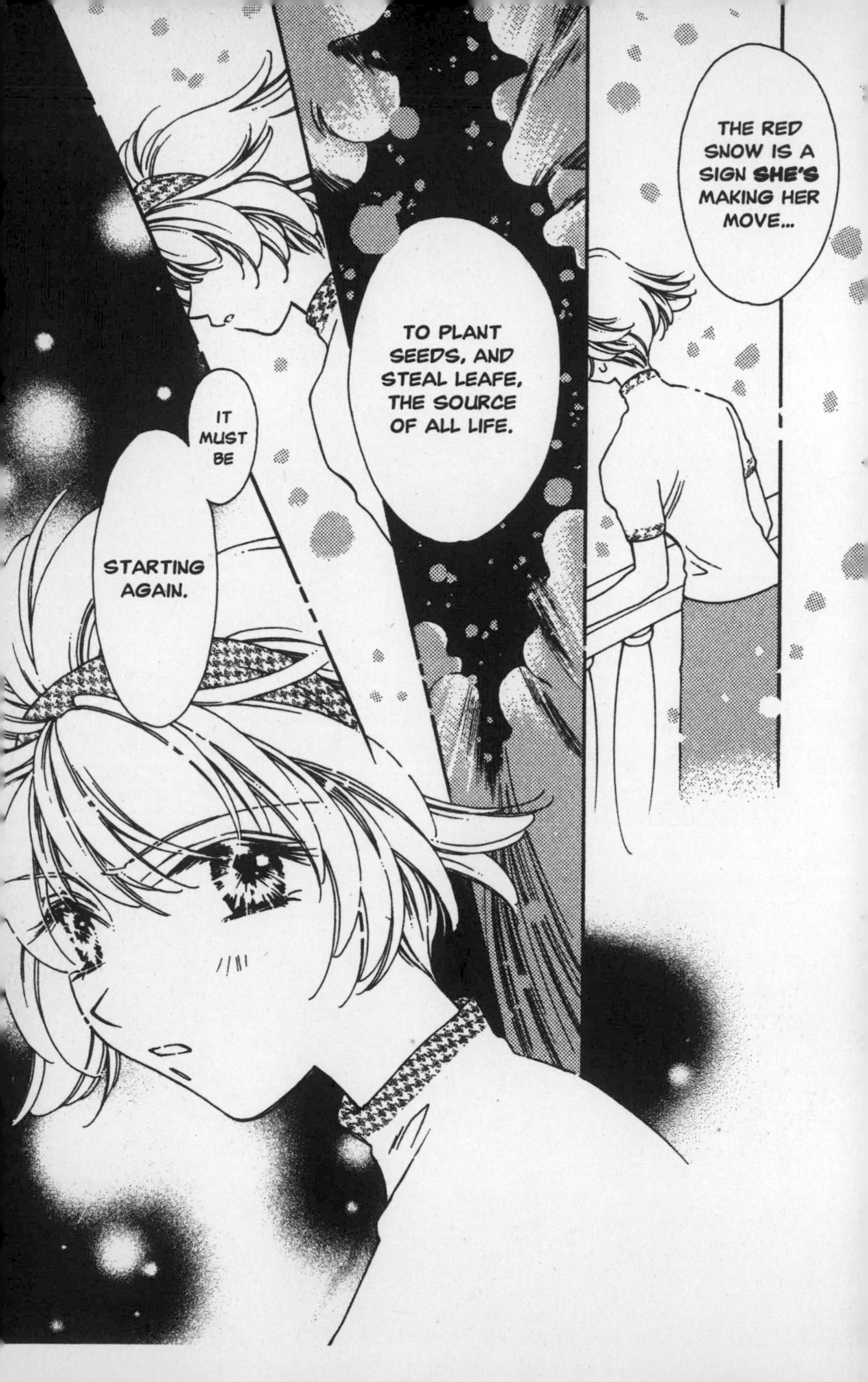
THE RED SNOW IS A SIGN SHE'S MAKING HER MOVE...
TO PLANT SEEDS, AND STEAL LEAFE, THE SOURCE OF ALL LIFE.
IT MUST BE
STARTING AGAIN.

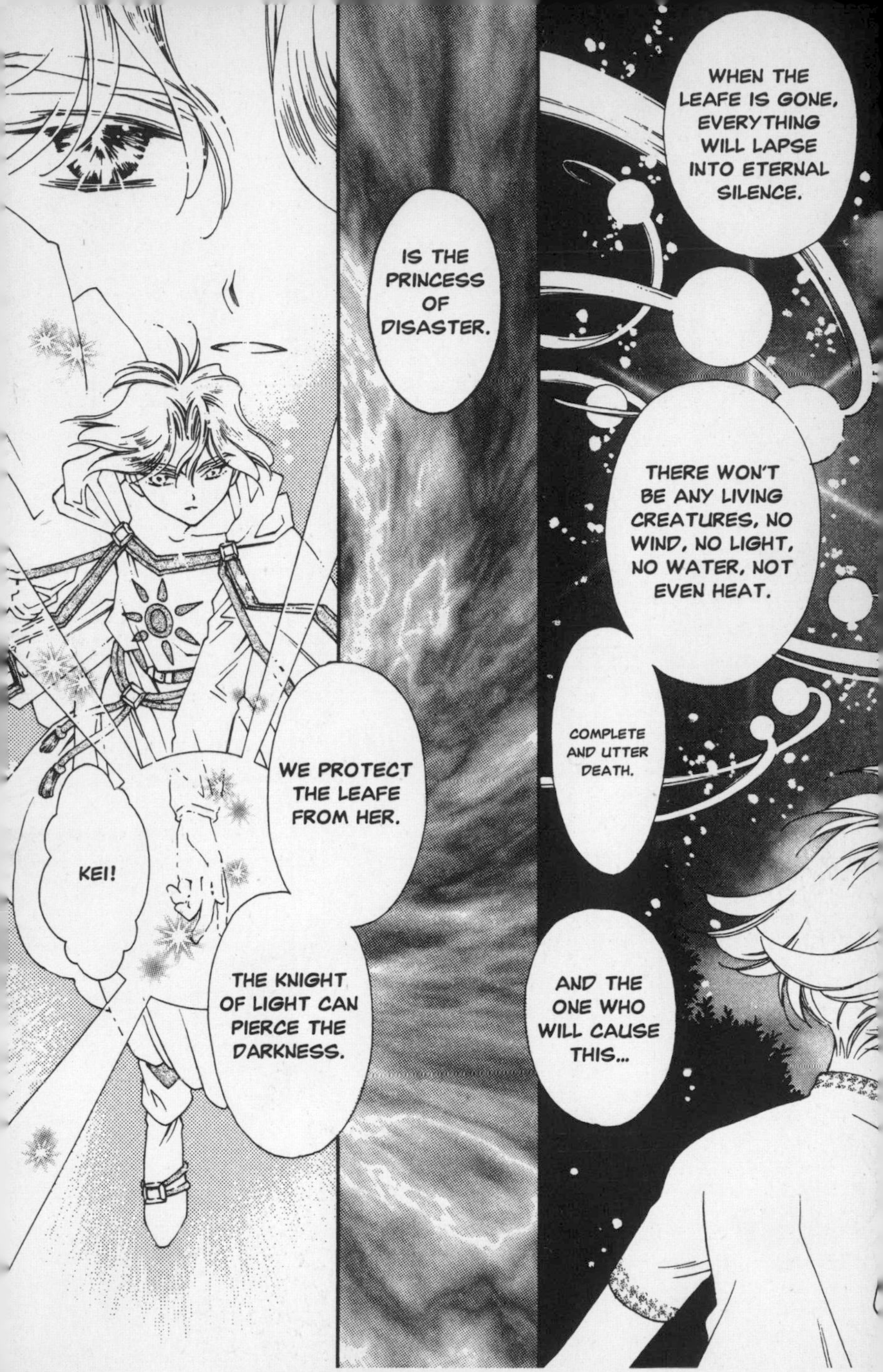
WHEN THE LEAFE IS GONE, EVERYTHING WILL LAPSE INTO ETERNAL SILENCE.
THERE WON'T BE ANY LIVING CREATURES, NO WIND, NO LIGHT, NO WATER, NOT EVEN HEAT.
COMPLETE AND UTTER DEATH.
AND THE ONE WHO WILL CAUSE THIS...
IS THE PRINCESS OF DISASTER.
WE PROTECT THE LEAFE FROM HER.
THE KNIGHT OF LIGHT CAN PIERCE THE DARKNESS.
KEI!

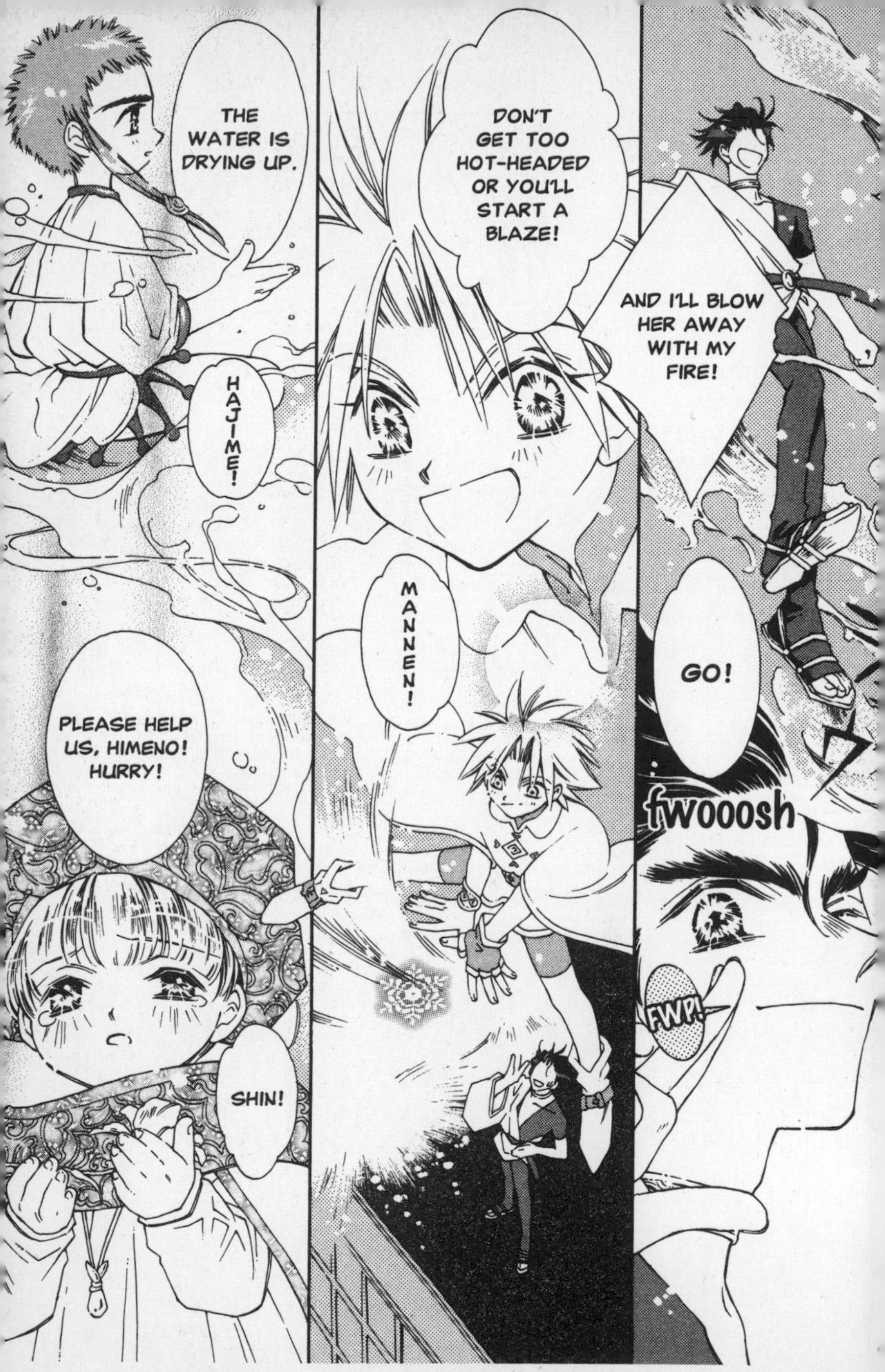
AND I'LL BLOW HER AWAY WITH MY FIRE!
GO!
fwooosh
FWP!
DON'T GET TOO HOT-HEADED OR YOU'LL START A BLAZE!
MANNEN!
THE WATER IS DRYING UP.
HAJIME!
PLEASE HELP US, HIMENO! HURRY!
SHIN!

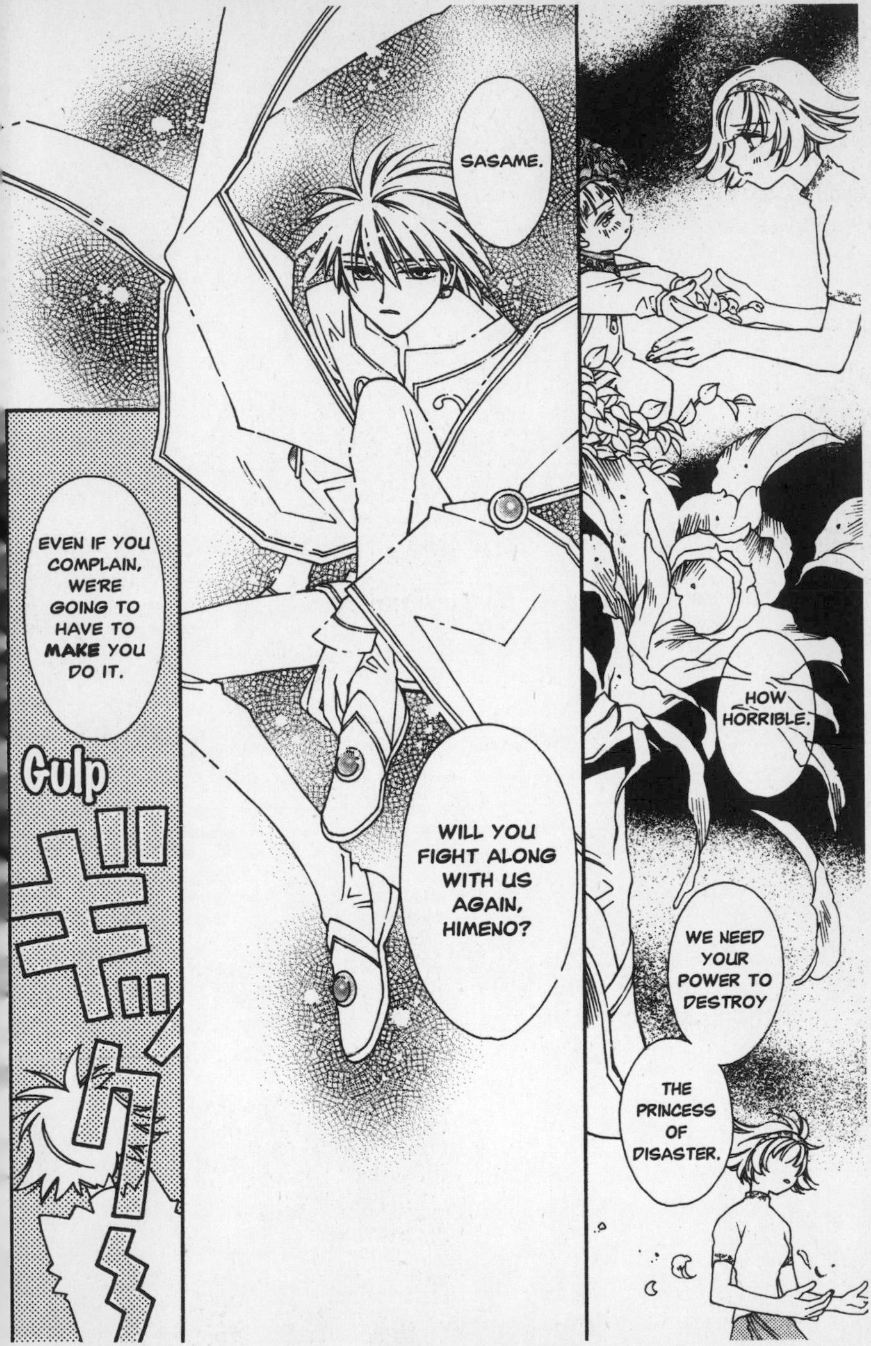
HOW HORRIBLE.
WE NEED YOUR POWER TO DESTROY
THE PRINCESS OF DISASTER.
SASAME.
WILL YOU FIGHT ALONG WITH US AGAIN, HIMENO?
EVEN IF YOU COMPLAIN, WE'RE GOING TO HAVE TO **MAKE** YOU DO IT.
Gulp

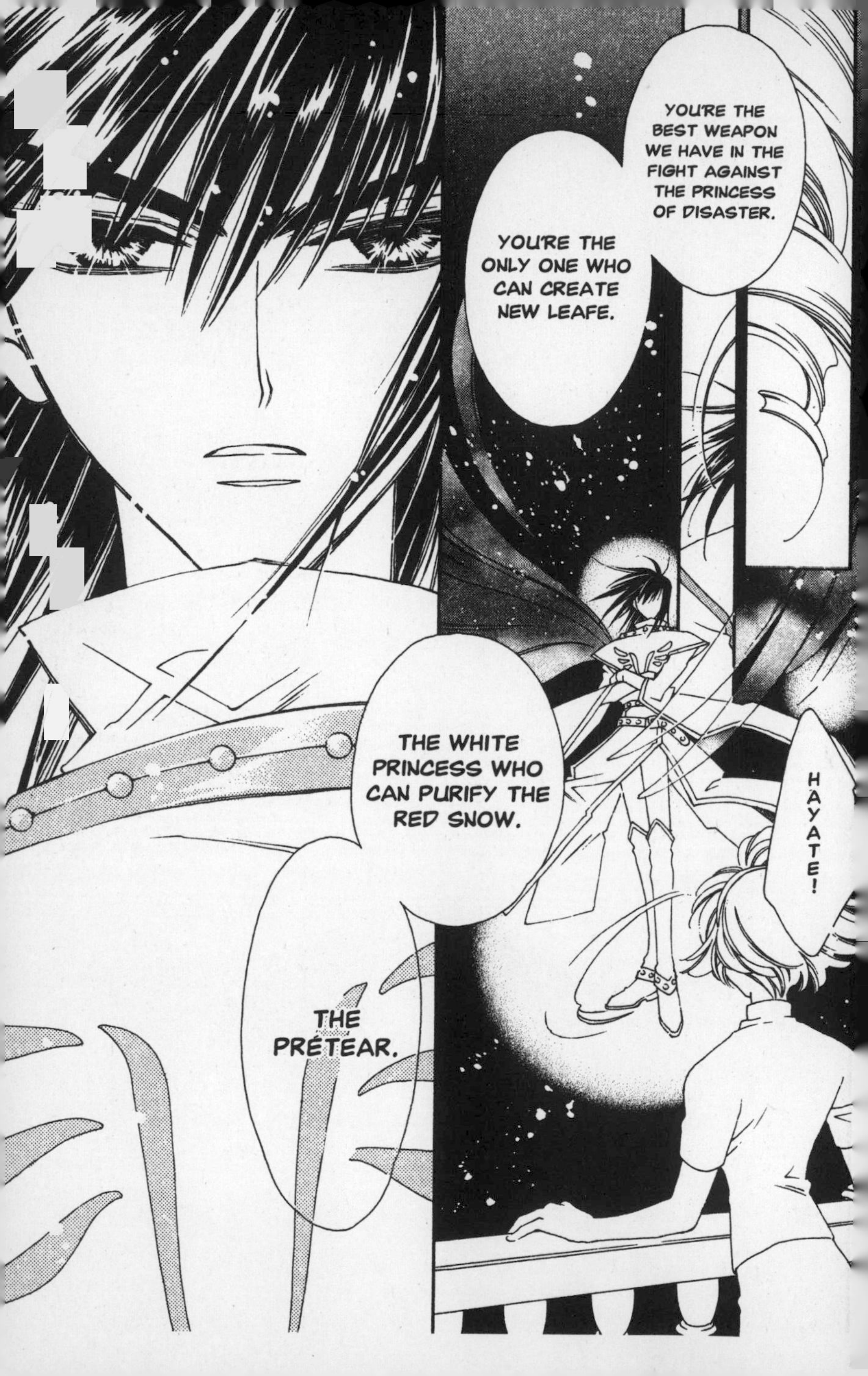
YOU'RE THE BEST WEAPON WE HAVE IN THE FIGHT AGAINST THE PRINCESS OF DISASTER.
YOU'RE THE ONLY ONE WHO CAN CREATE NEW LEAFE.
HAYATE!
THE WHITE PRINCESS WHO CAN PURIFY THE RED SNOW.
THE PRÉTEAR.

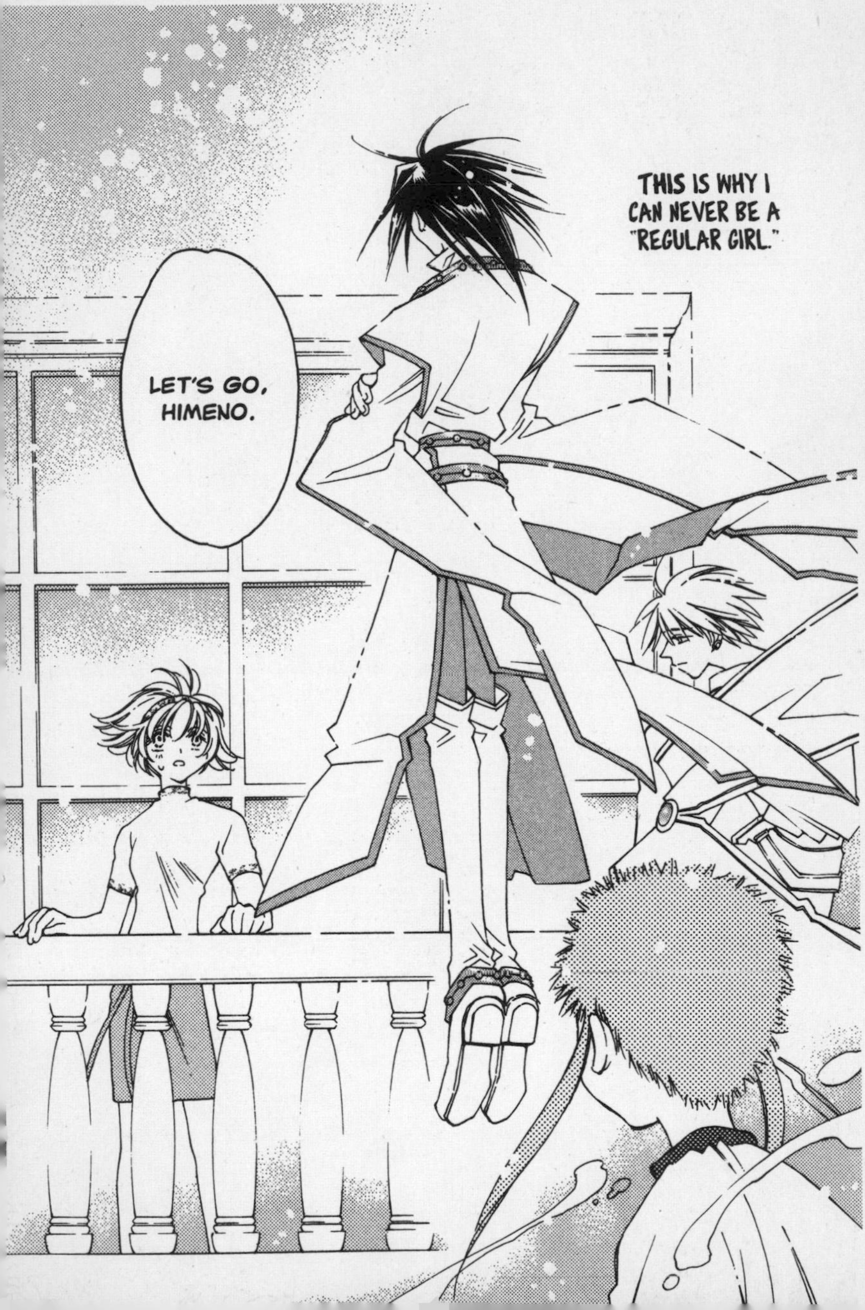
THIS IS WHY I CAN NEVER BE A "REGULAR GIRL."
LET'S GO, HIMENO.

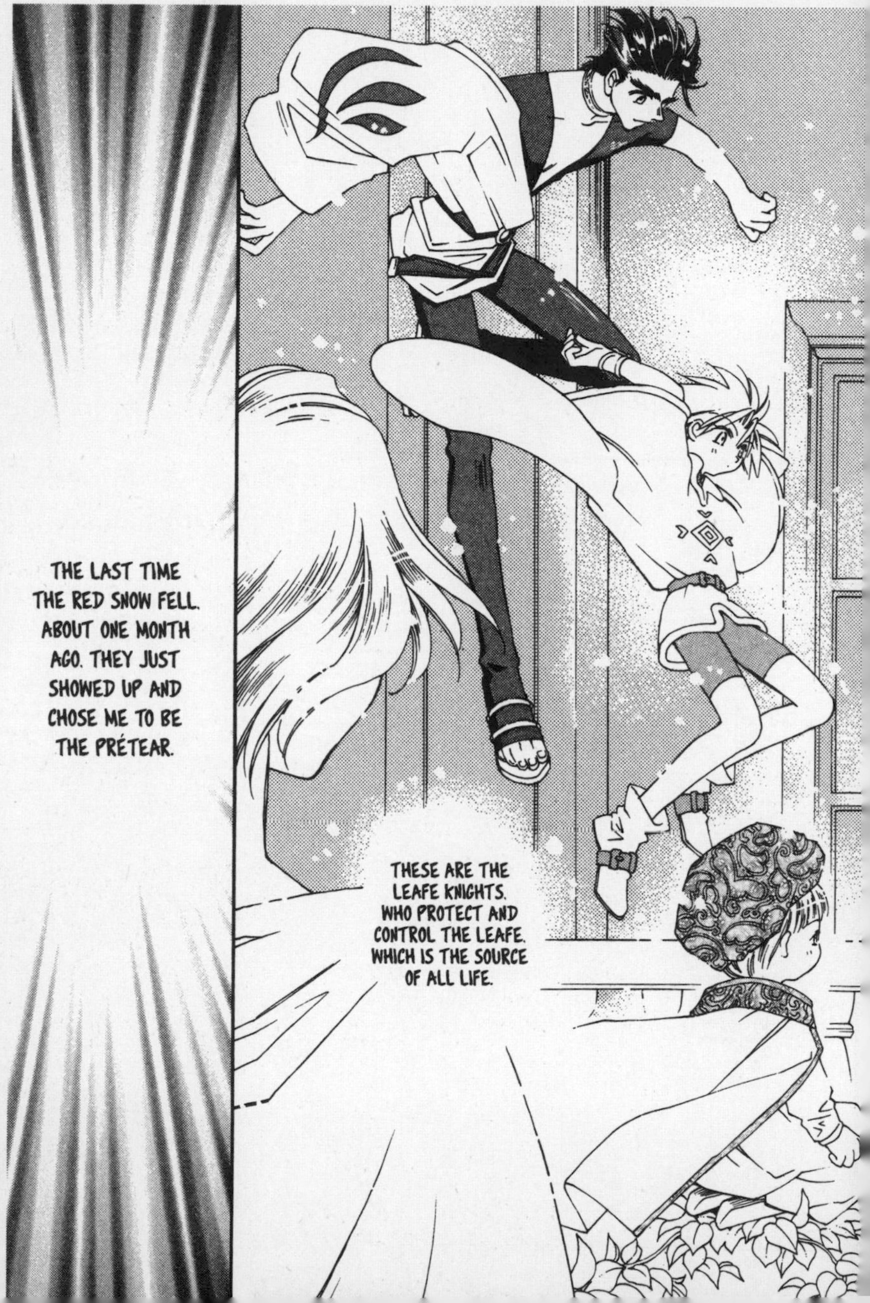
THE LAST TIME THE RED SNOW FELL, ABOUT ONE MONTH AGO, THEY JUST SHOWED UP AND CHOSE ME TO BE THE PRÉTEAR.
THESE ARE THE LEAFE KNIGHTS, WHO PROTECT AND CONTROL THE LEAFE, WHICH IS THE SOURCE OF ALL LIFE.

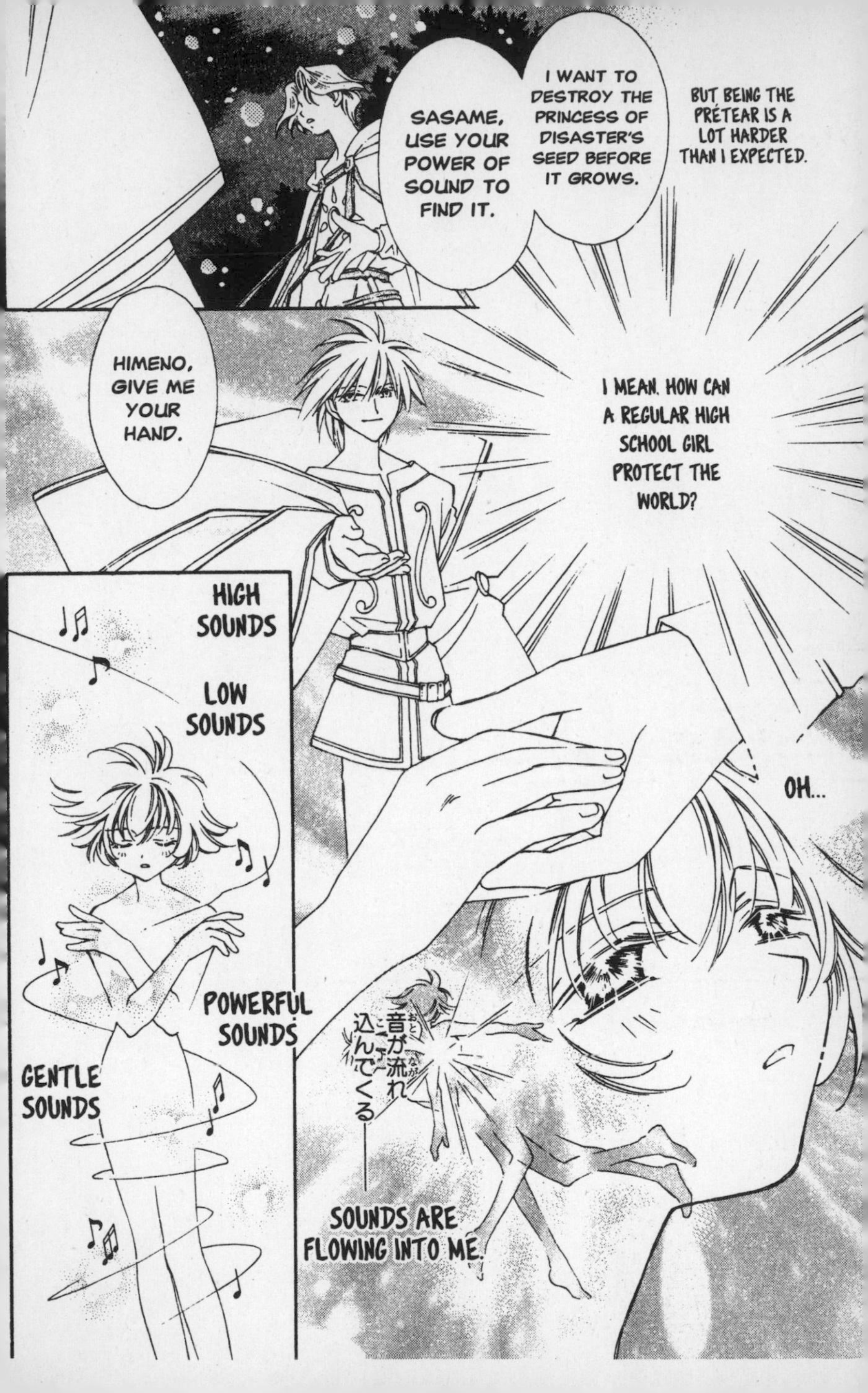

BUT BEING THE PRÉTEAR IS A LOT HARDER THAN I EXPECTED.
I WANT TO DESTROY THE PRINCESS OF DISASTER'S SEED BEFORE IT GROWS.
SASAME, USE YOUR POWER OF SOUND TO FIND IT.
I MEAN. HOW CAN A REGULAR HIGH SCHOOL GIRL PROTECT THE WORLD?
HIMENO, GIVE ME YOUR HAND.
OH...
音が流れ込んでくる——
SOUNDS ARE FLOWING INTO ME.
HIGH SOUNDS
LOW SOUNDS
POWERFUL SOUNDS
GENTLE SOUNDS

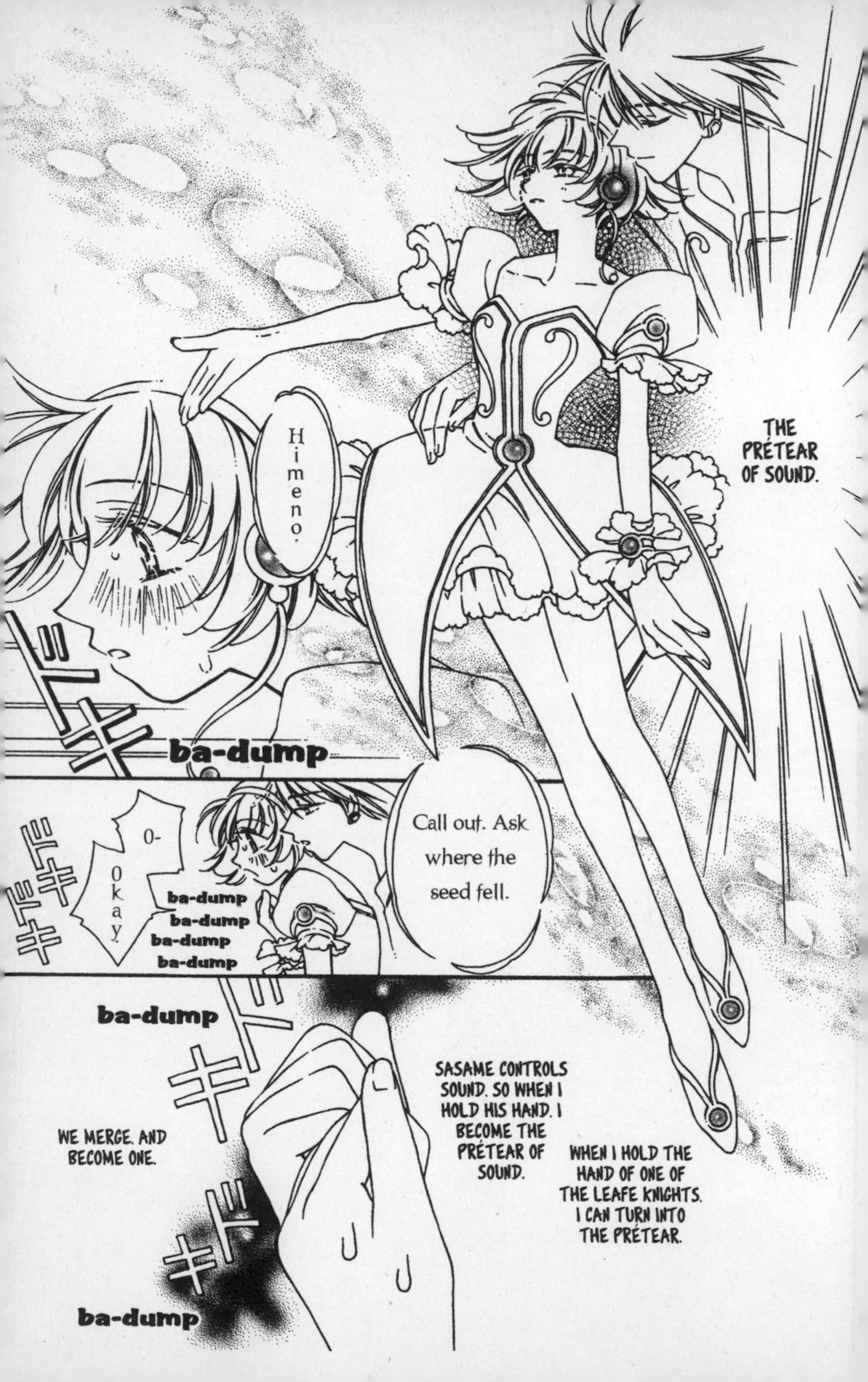
THE PRÉTEAR OF SOUND.
Himeno.
ba-dump
Call out. Ask where the seed fell.
O- Okay.
ba-dump
ba-dump
ba-dump
ba-dump
WHEN I HOLD THE HAND OF ONE OF THE LEAFE KNIGHTS, I CAN TURN INTO THE PRÉTEAR.
SASAME CONTROLS SOUND, SO WHEN I HOLD HIS HAND, I BECOME THE PRÉTEAR OF SOUND.
WE MERGE, AND BECOME ONE.
ba-dump
ba-dump

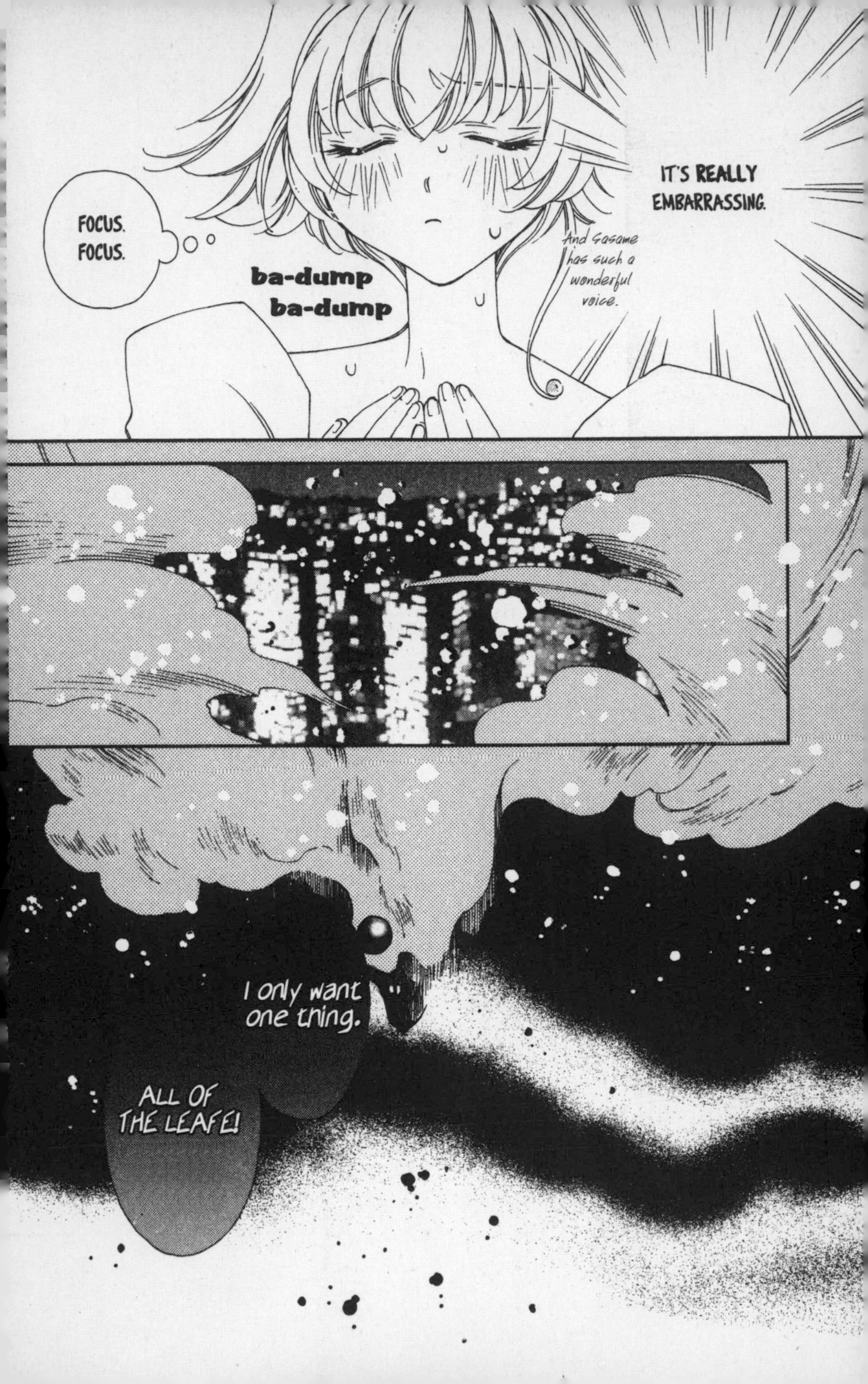
IT'S REALLY EMBARRASSING.
And Sasame has such a wonderful voice.
FOCUS. FOCUS.
ba-dump ba-dump
I only want one thing.
ALL OF THE LEAFE!

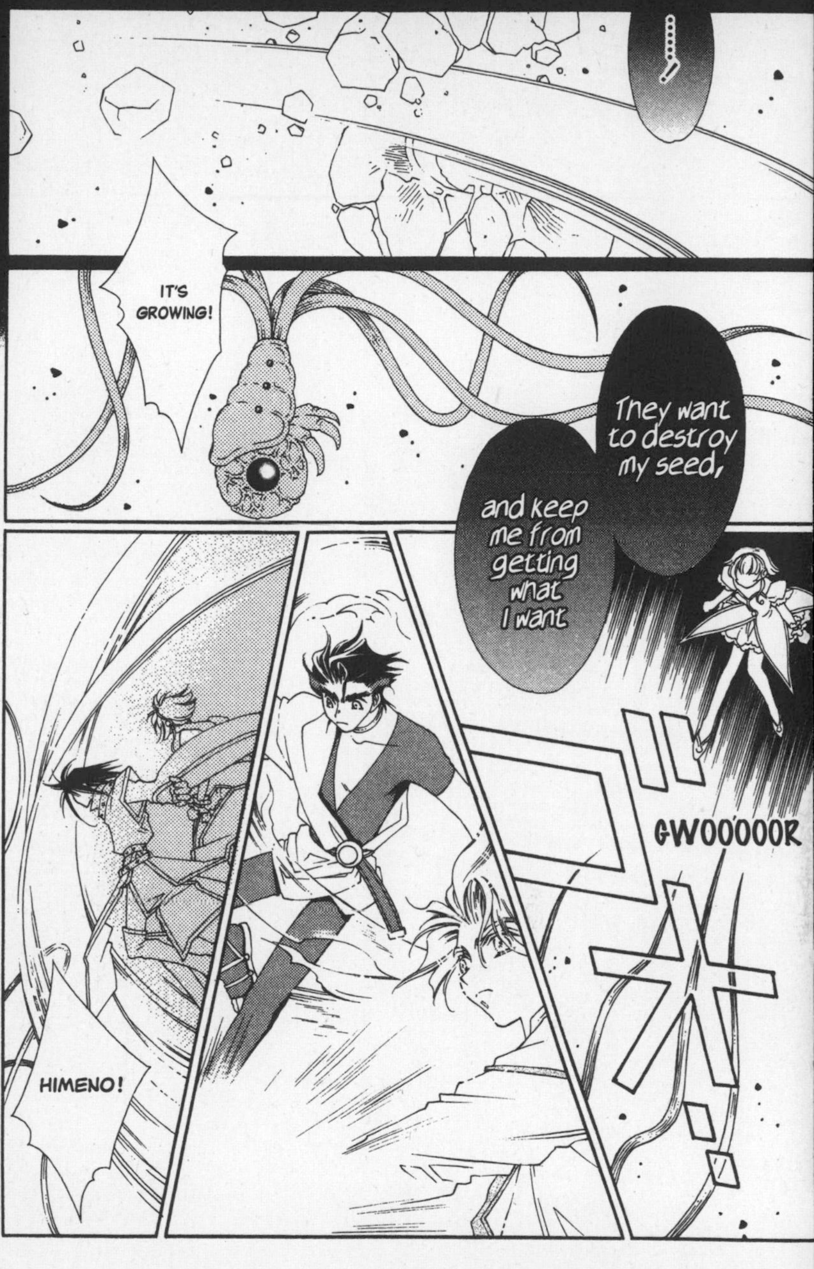
IT'S GROWING!
They want to destroy my seed,
and keep me from getting what I want
GWOOOOOR
HIMENO!

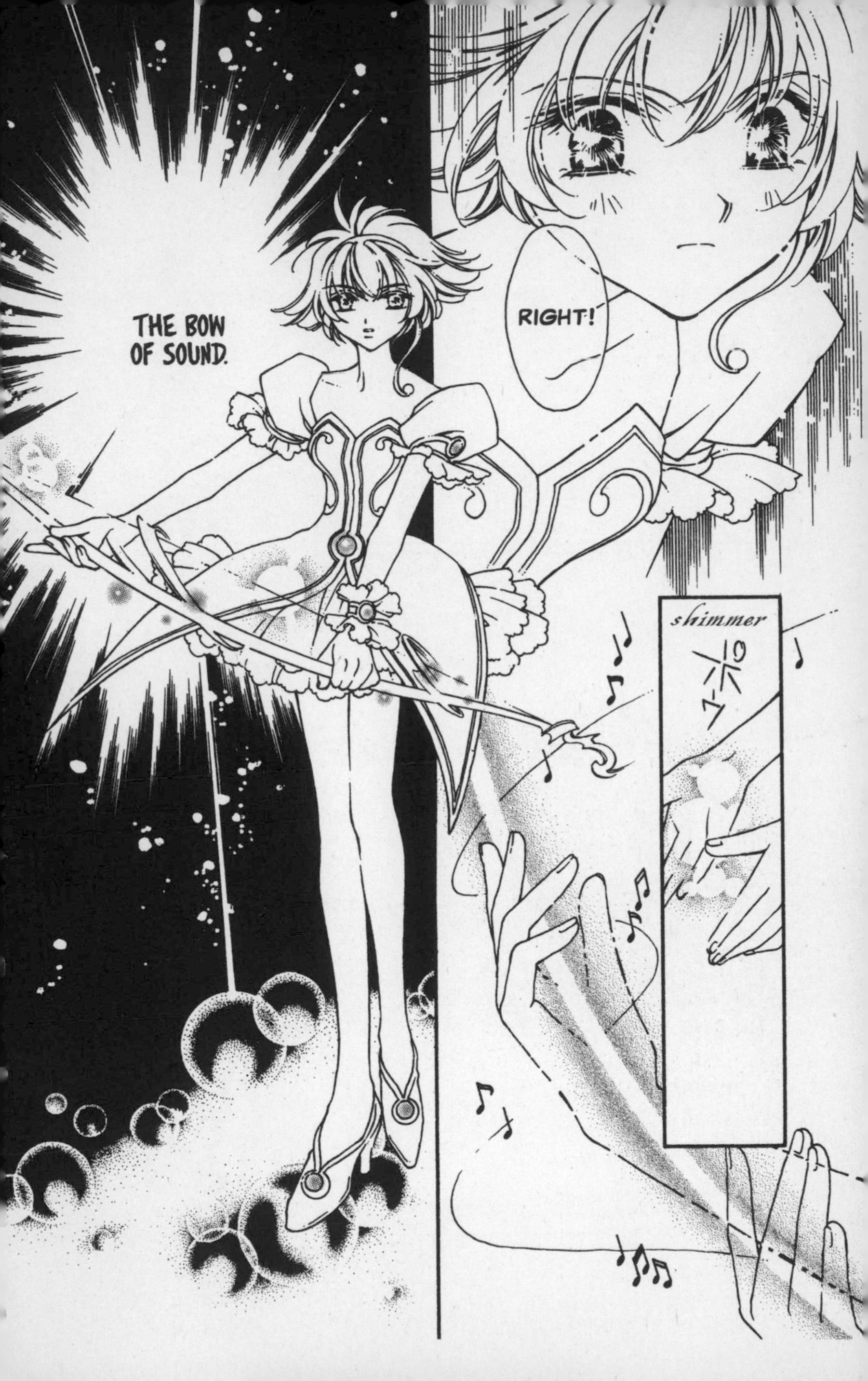
RIGHT!
shimmer
THE BOW OF SOUND.

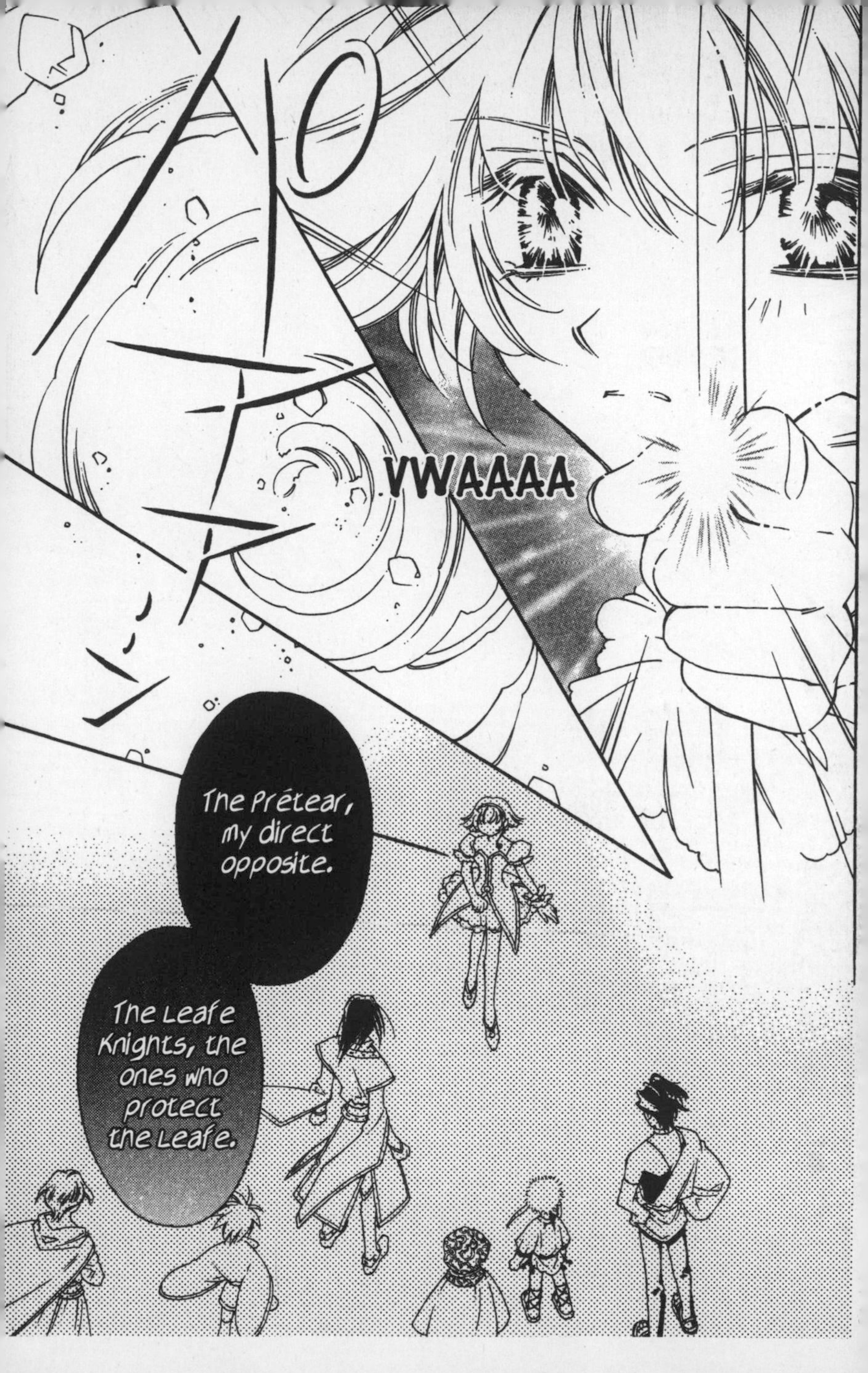
VWAAAA
The Prétear, my direct opposite.
The Leafe Knights, the ones who protect the Leafe.

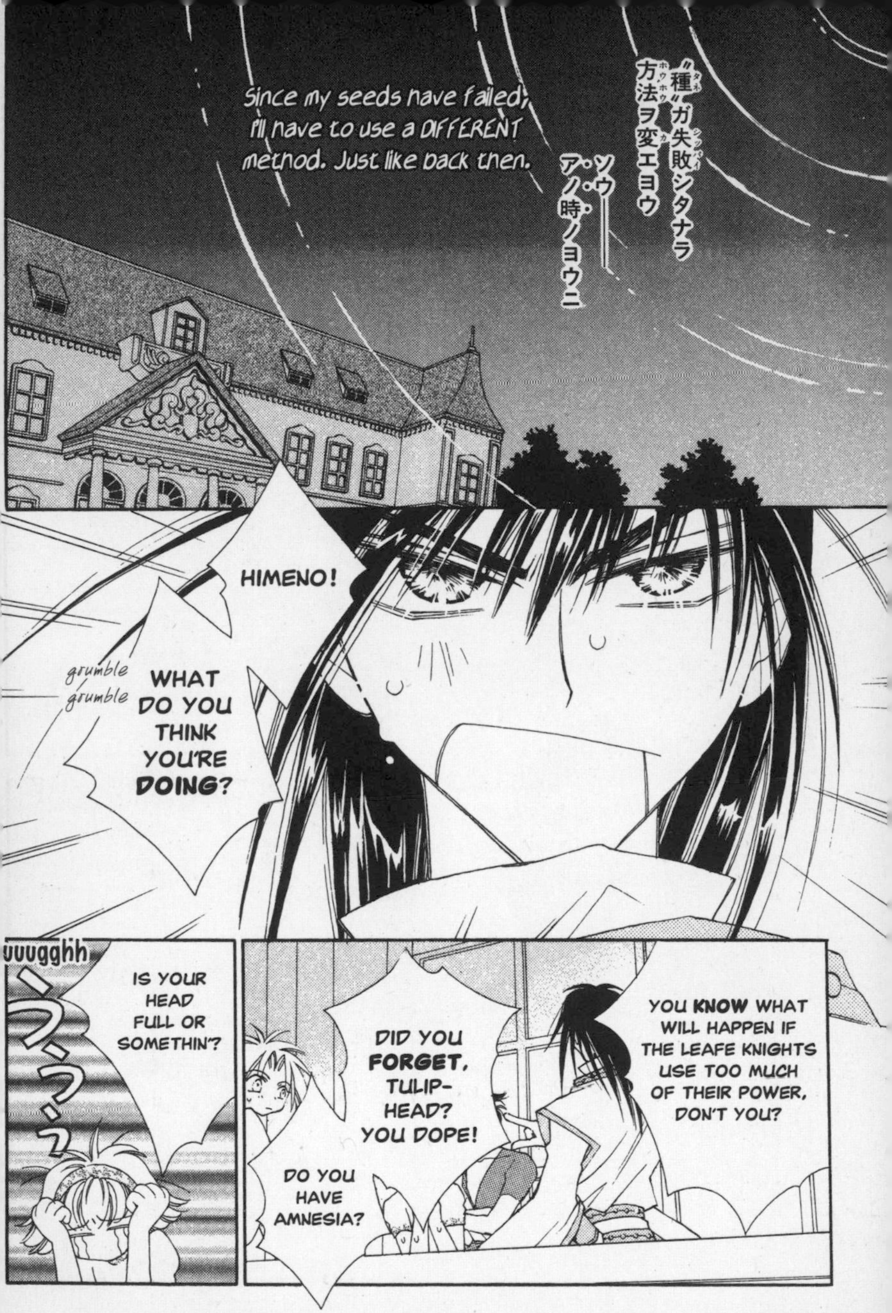
"種"ガ失敗シタナラ
方法ヲ変エヨウ
ソウ──
アノ時ノヨウニ
Since my seeds have failed, I'll have to use a DIFFERENT method. Just like back then.
HIMENO!
WHAT DO YOU THINK YOU'RE **DOING**?
grumble grumble
YOU **KNOW** WHAT WILL HAPPEN IF THE LEAFE KNIGHTS USE TOO MUCH OF THEIR POWER, DON'T YOU?
DID YOU **FORGET**, TULIP-HEAD? YOU DOPE!
DO YOU HAVE AMNESIA?
IS YOUR HEAD FULL OR SOMETHIN'?
uuugghh

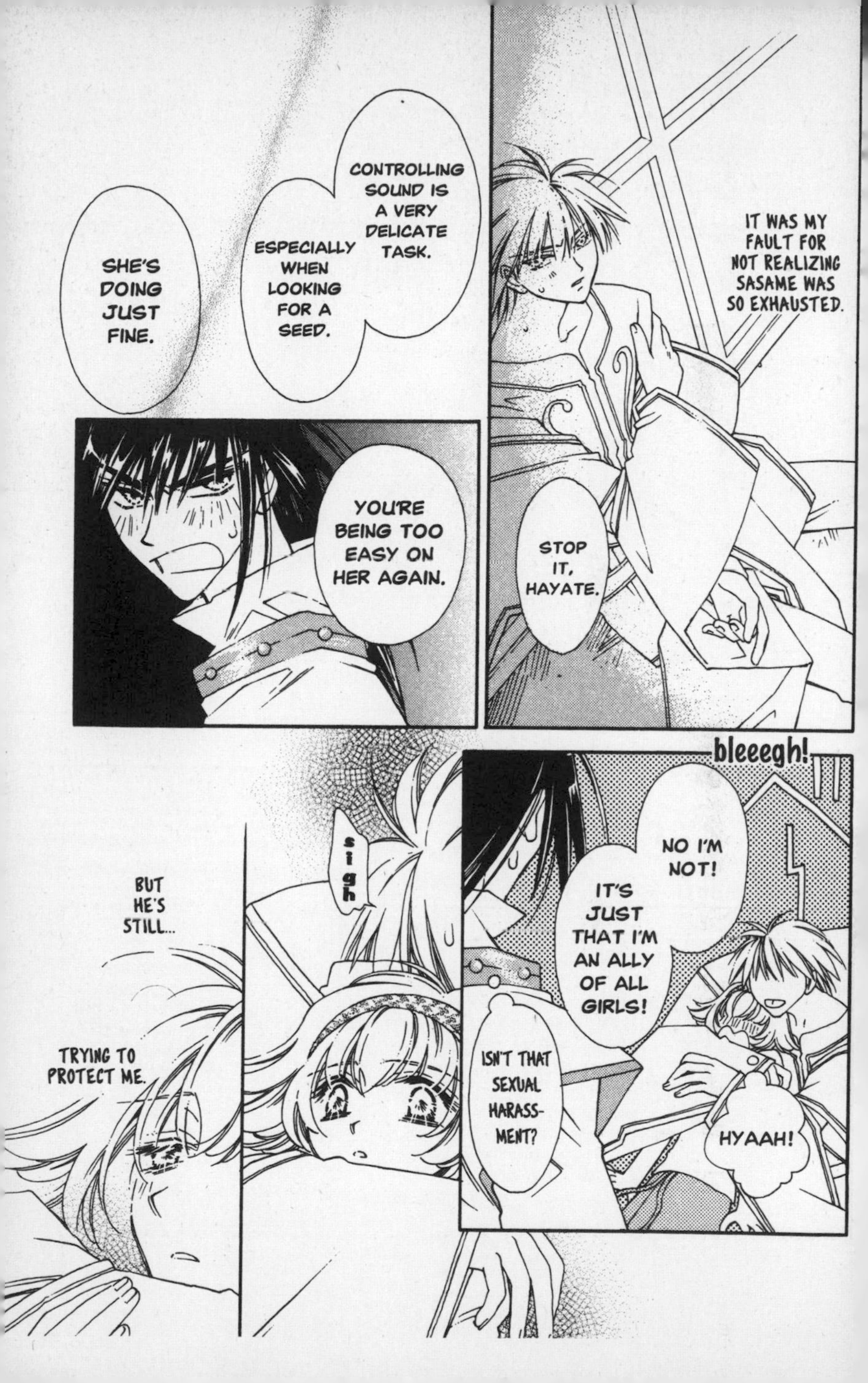
IT WAS MY FAULT FOR NOT REALIZING SASAME WAS SO EXHAUSTED.
CONTROLLING SOUND IS A VERY DELICATE TASK.
ESPECIALLY WHEN LOOKING FOR A SEED.
SHE'S DOING JUST FINE.
STOP IT, HAYATE.
YOU'RE BEING TOO EASY ON HER AGAIN.
bleeegh!
NO I'M NOT!
IT'S JUST THAT I'M AN ALLY OF ALL GIRLS!
HYAAH!
ISN'T THAT SEXUAL HARASS-MENT?
sigh
BUT HE'S STILL...
TRYING TO PROTECT ME.

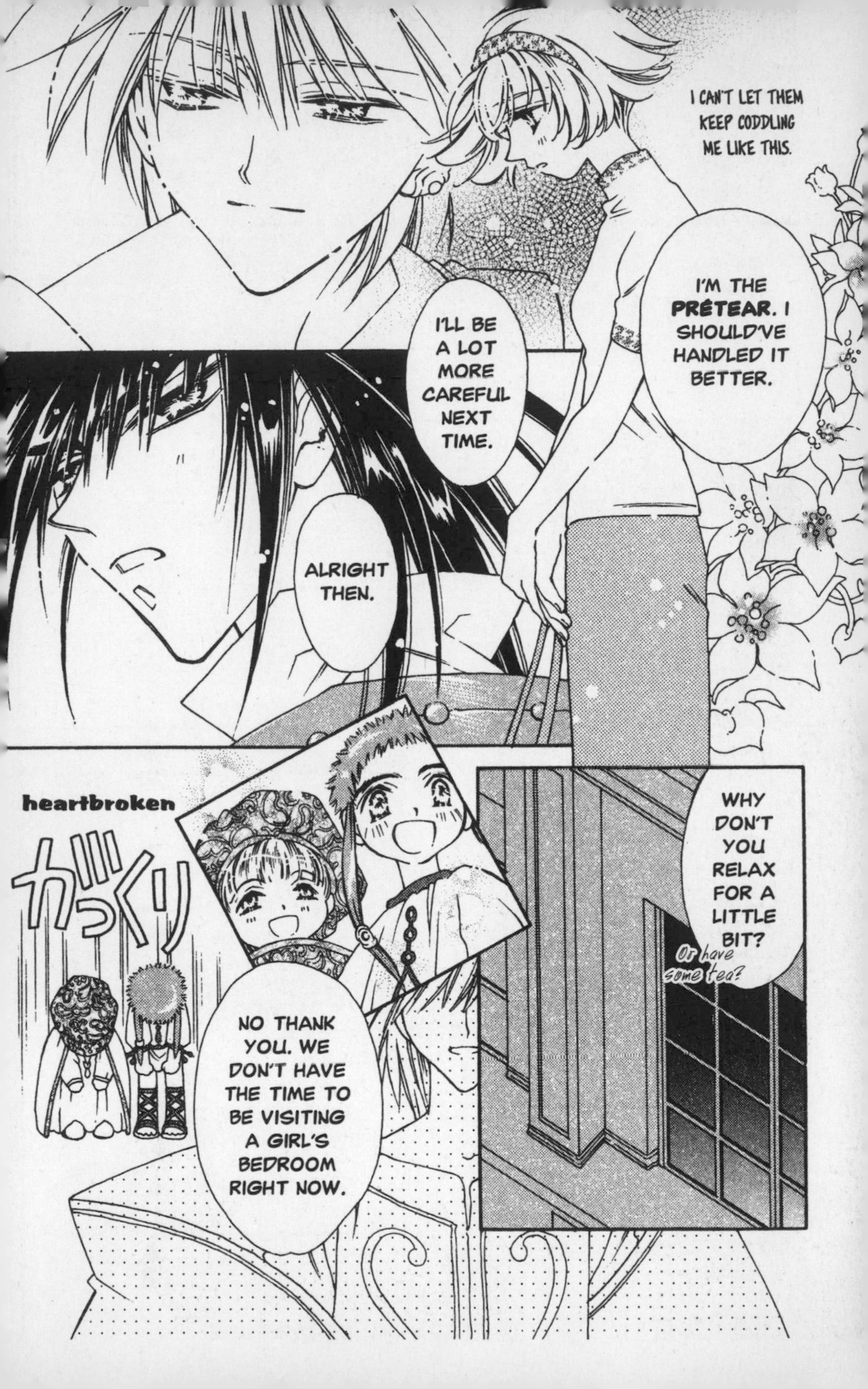

I CAN'T LET THEM KEEP CODDLING ME LIKE THIS.
I'M THE PRÉTEAR. I SHOULD'VE HANDLED IT BETTER.
I'LL BE A LOT MORE CAREFUL NEXT TIME.
ALRIGHT THEN.
WHY DON'T YOU RELAX FOR A LITTLE BIT?
Or have some tea?
NO THANK YOU. WE DON'T HAVE THE TIME TO BE VISITING A GIRL'S BEDROOM RIGHT NOW.
heartbroken
がっくり

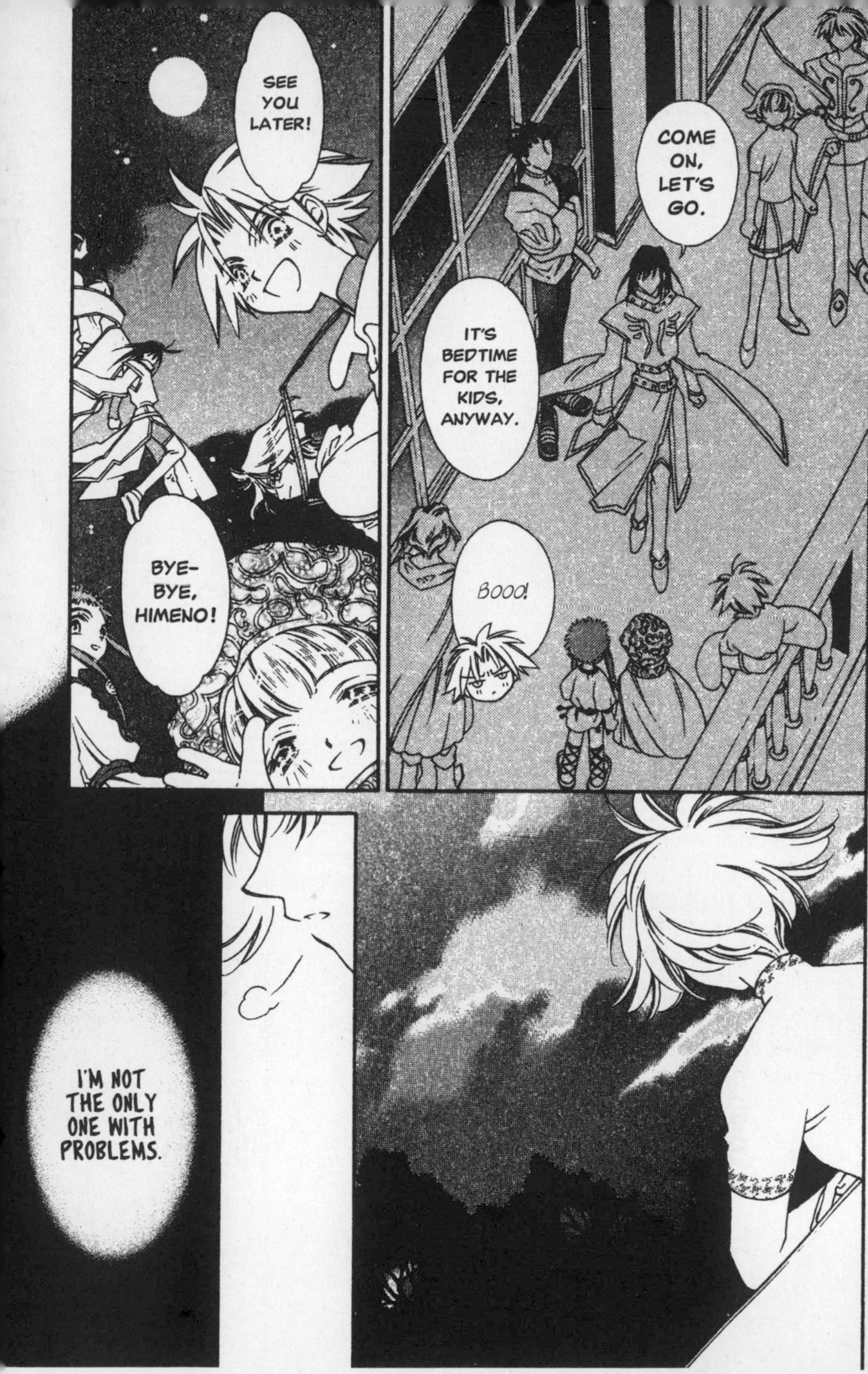
COME ON, LET'S GO.
IT'S BEDTIME FOR THE KIDS, ANYWAY.
Booo!
SEE YOU LATER!
BYE-BYE, HIMENO!
I'M NOT THE ONLY ONE WITH PROBLEMS.

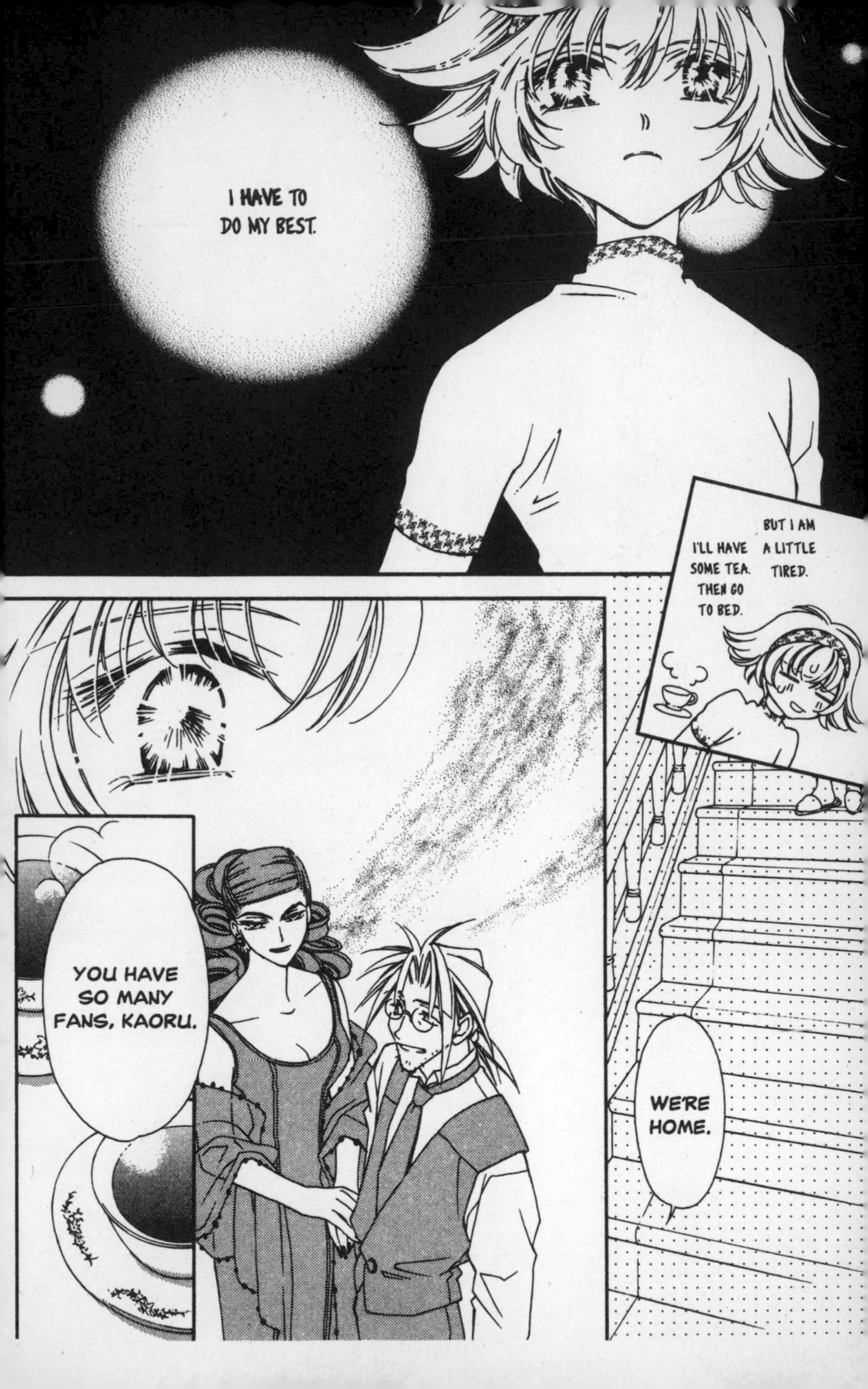
I HAVE TO DO MY BEST.
BUT I AM A LITTLE TIRED.
I'LL HAVE SOME TEA. THEN GO TO BED.
WE'RE HOME.
YOU HAVE SO MANY FANS, KAORU.

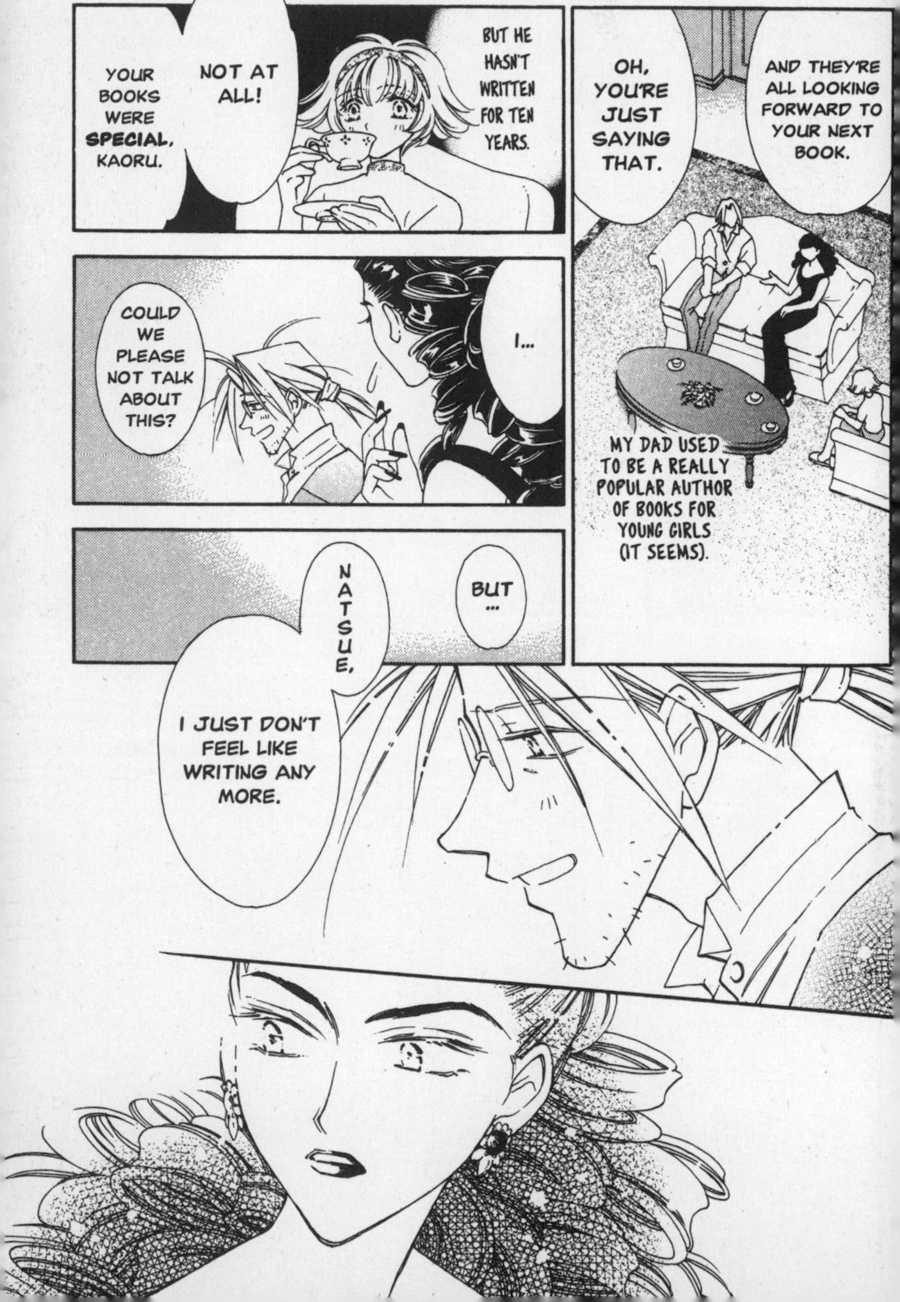
AND THEY'RE ALL LOOKING FORWARD TO YOUR NEXT BOOK.
OH, YOU'RE JUST SAYING THAT.
MY DAD USED TO BE A REALLY POPULAR AUTHOR OF BOOKS FOR YOUNG GIRLS (IT SEEMS).
BUT HE HASN'T WRITTEN FOR TEN YEARS.
NOT AT ALL!
YOUR BOOKS WERE **SPECIAL**, KAORU.
I...
COULD WE PLEASE NOT TALK ABOUT THIS?
BUT...
NATSUE,
I JUST DON'T FEEL LIKE WRITING ANY MORE.

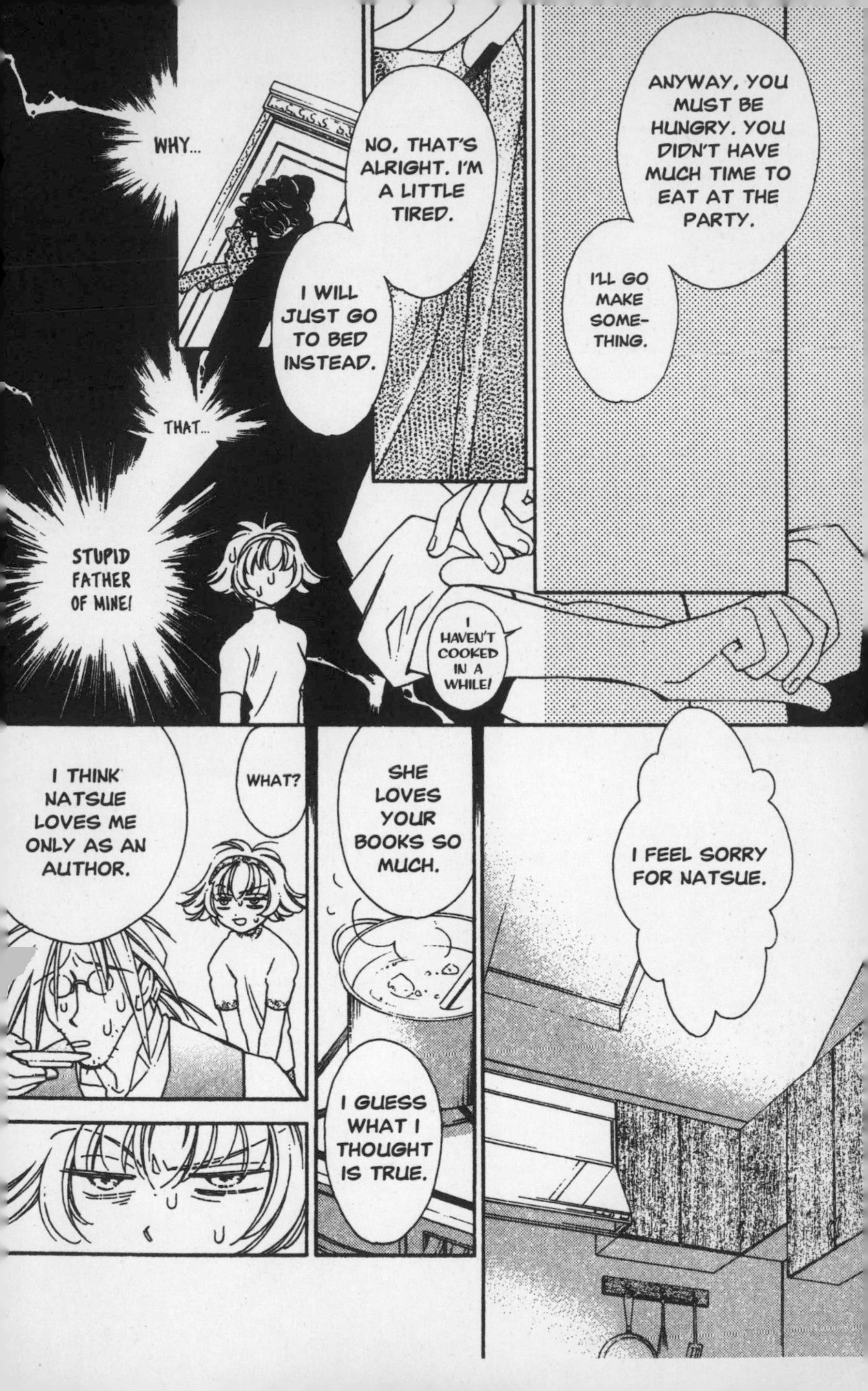
ANYWAY, YOU MUST BE HUNGRY. YOU DIDN'T HAVE MUCH TIME TO EAT AT THE PARTY.
I'LL GO MAKE SOME-THING.
I HAVEN'T COOKED IN A WHILE!
NO, THAT'S ALRIGHT. I'M A LITTLE TIRED.
I WILL JUST GO TO BED INSTEAD.
WHY...
THAT...
STUPID FATHER OF MINE!
I FEEL SORRY FOR NATSUE.
SHE LOVES YOUR BOOKS SO MUCH.
I GUESS WHAT I THOUGHT IS TRUE.
WHAT?
I THINK NATSUE LOVES ME ONLY AS AN AUTHOR.

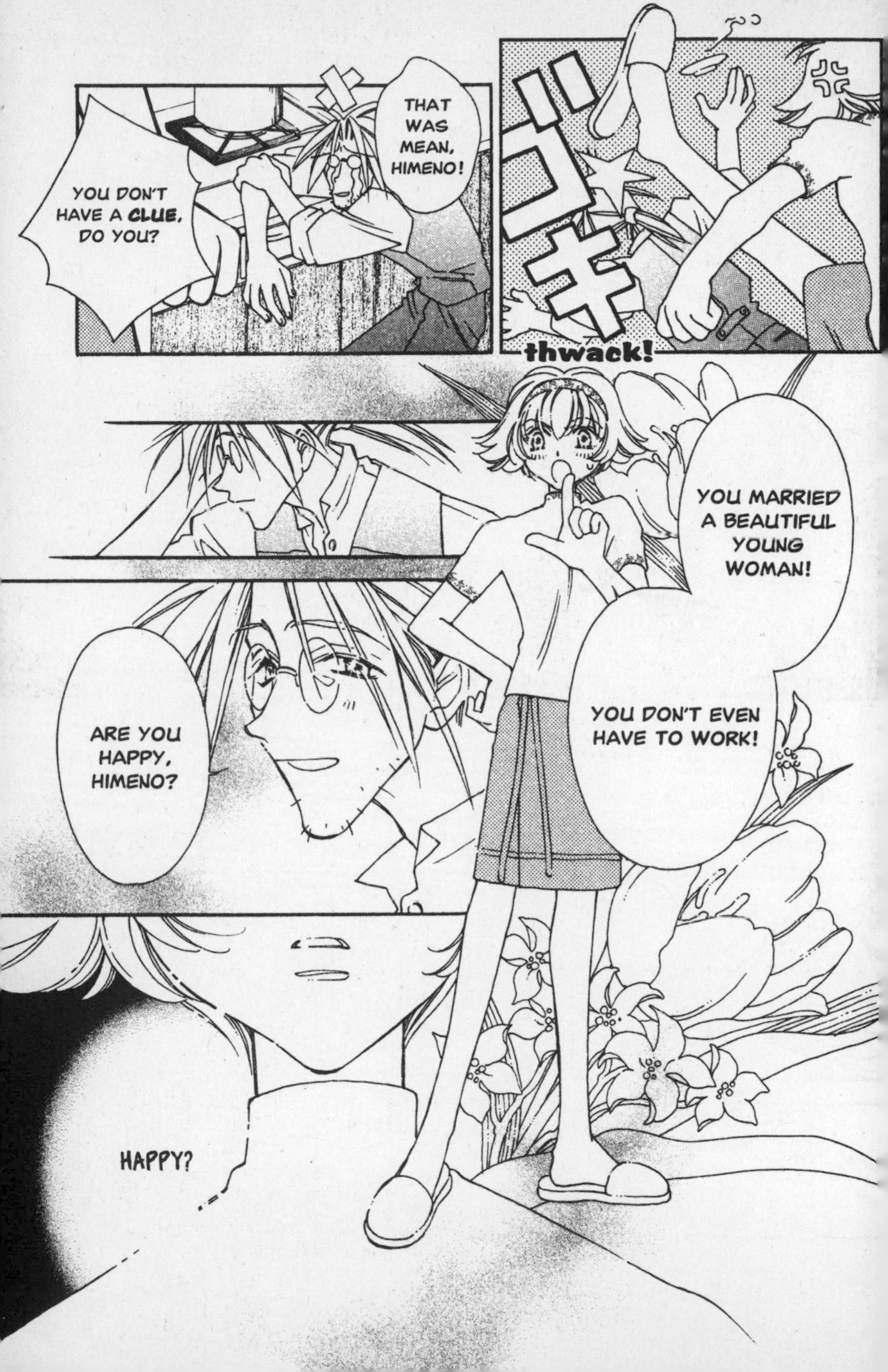
ゴキ
thwack!
THAT WAS MEAN, HIMENO!
YOU DON'T HAVE A **CLUE**, DO YOU?
YOU MARRIED A BEAUTIFUL YOUNG WOMAN!
YOU DON'T EVEN HAVE TO WORK!
ARE YOU HAPPY, HIMENO?
HAPPY?

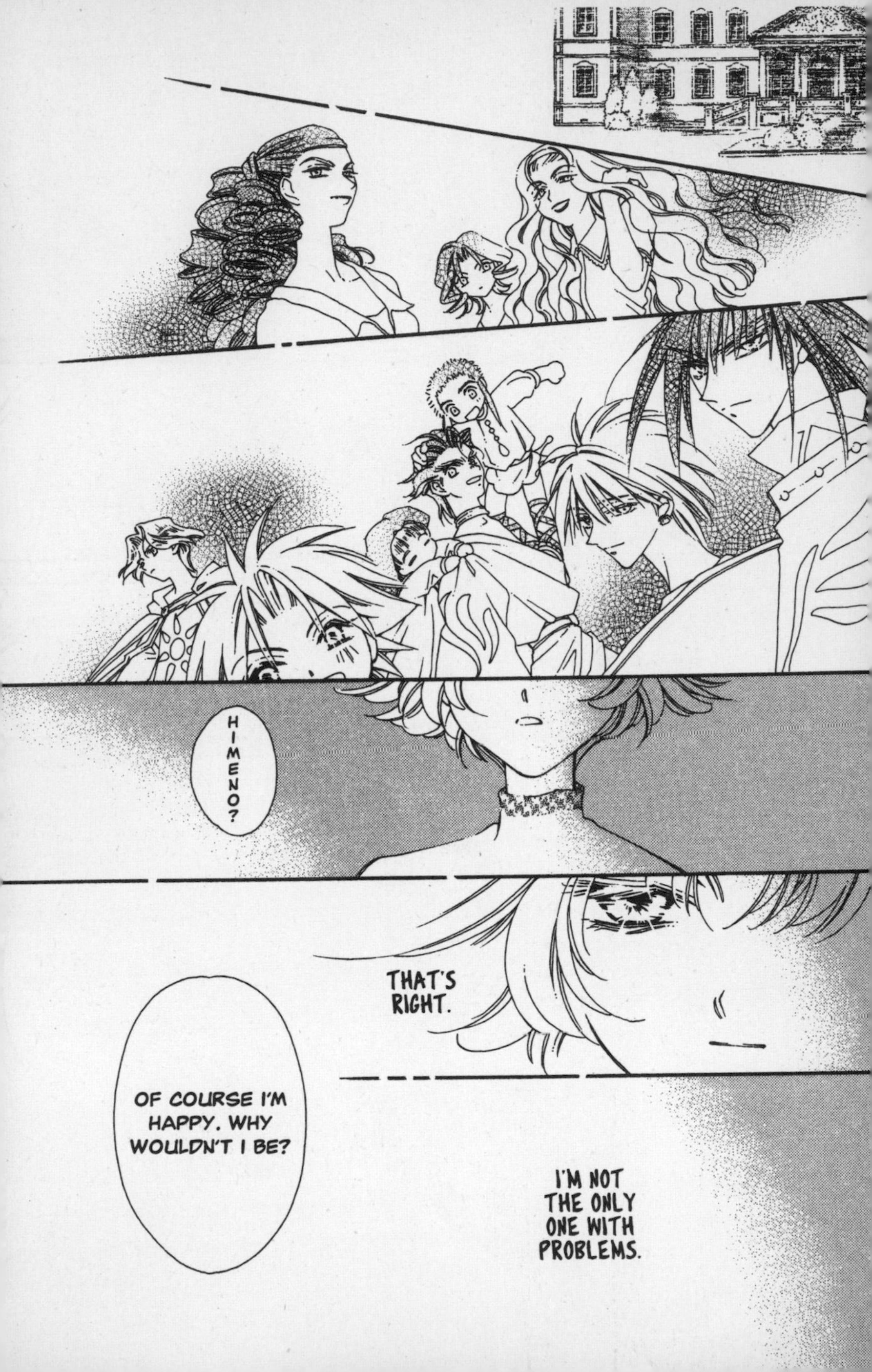
HIMENO?
THAT'S RIGHT.
OF COURSE I'M HAPPY. WHY WOULDN'T I BE?
I'M NOT THE ONLY ONE WITH PROBLEMS.

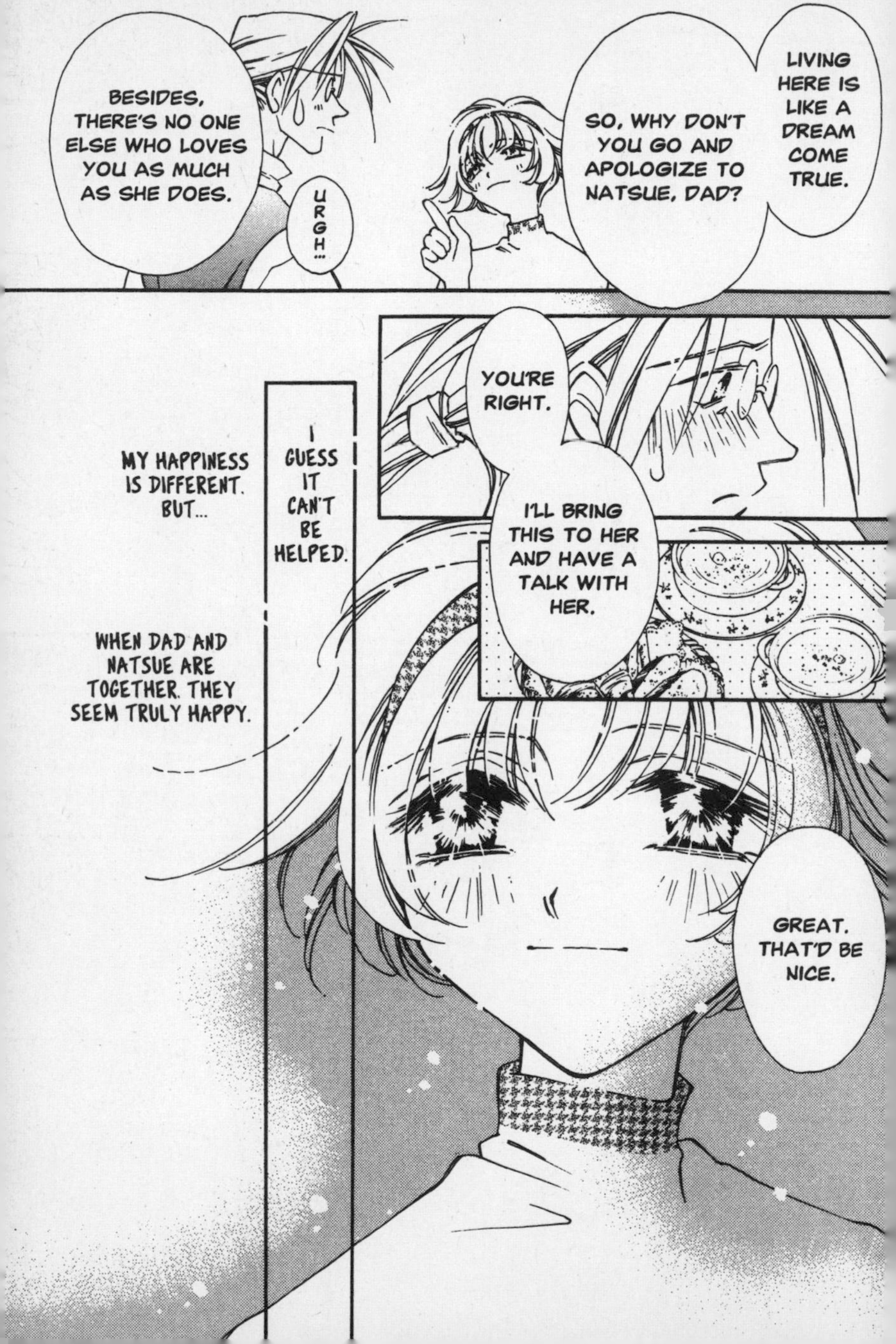
LIVING HERE IS LIKE A DREAM COME TRUE.
SO, WHY DON'T YOU GO AND APOLOGIZE TO NATSUE, DAD?
URGH...
BESIDES, THERE'S NO ONE ELSE WHO LOVES YOU AS MUCH AS SHE DOES.
YOU'RE RIGHT.
I'LL BRING THIS TO HER AND HAVE A TALK WITH HER.
I GUESS IT CAN'T BE HELPED.
MY HAPPINESS IS DIFFERENT. BUT...
WHEN DAD AND NATSUE ARE TOGETHER. THEY SEEM TRULY HAPPY.
GREAT. THAT'D BE NICE.

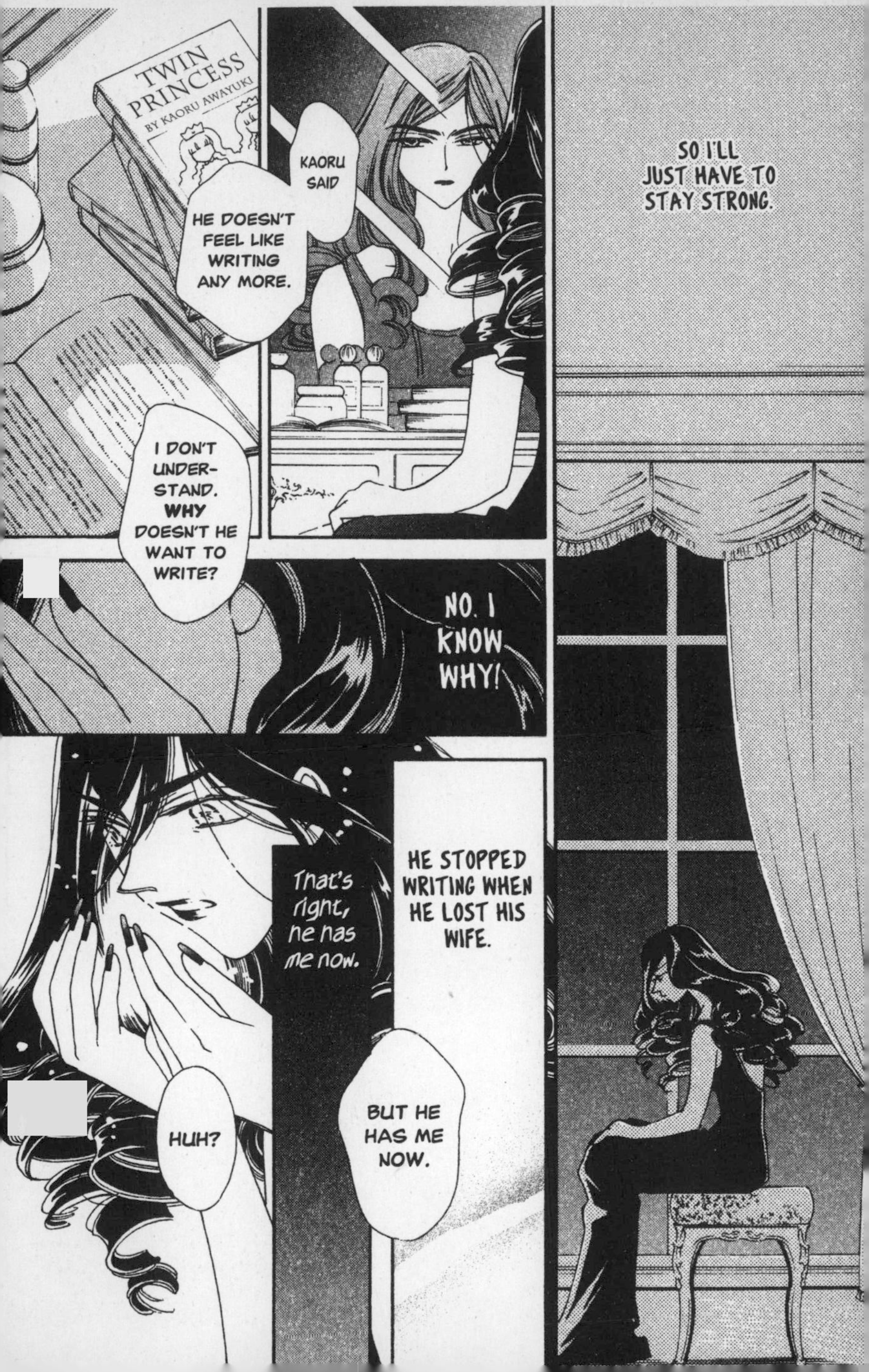
TWIN PRINCESS
BY KAORU AWAYUKI
KAORU SAID
HE DOESN'T FEEL LIKE WRITING ANY MORE.
I DON'T UNDER-STAND. WHY DOESN'T HE WANT TO WRITE?
NO. I KNOW WHY!
HE STOPPED WRITING WHEN HE LOST HIS WIFE.
BUT HE HAS ME NOW.
That's right, he has me now.
HUH?
SO I'LL JUST HAVE TO STAY STRONG.

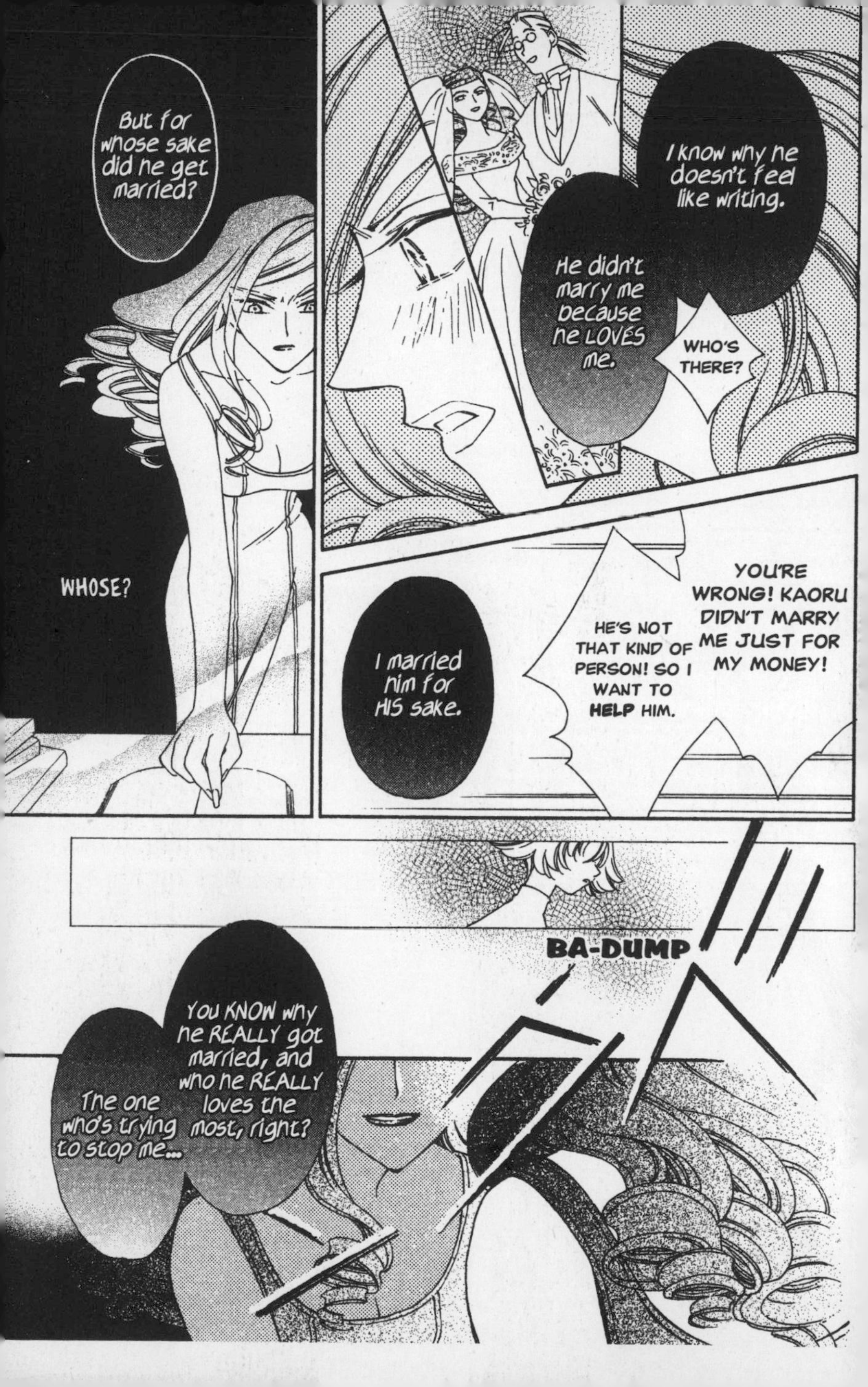

I know why he doesn't feel like writing.
He didn't marry me because he LOVES me.
WHO'S THERE?
YOU'RE WRONG! KAORU DIDN'T MARRY ME JUST FOR MY MONEY!
HE'S NOT THAT KIND OF PERSON! SO I WANT TO HELP HIM.
I married him for HIS sake.
But for whose sake did he get married?
WHOSE?
BA-DUMP
You KNOW why he REALLY got married, and who he REALLY loves the most, right?
The one who's trying to stop me...

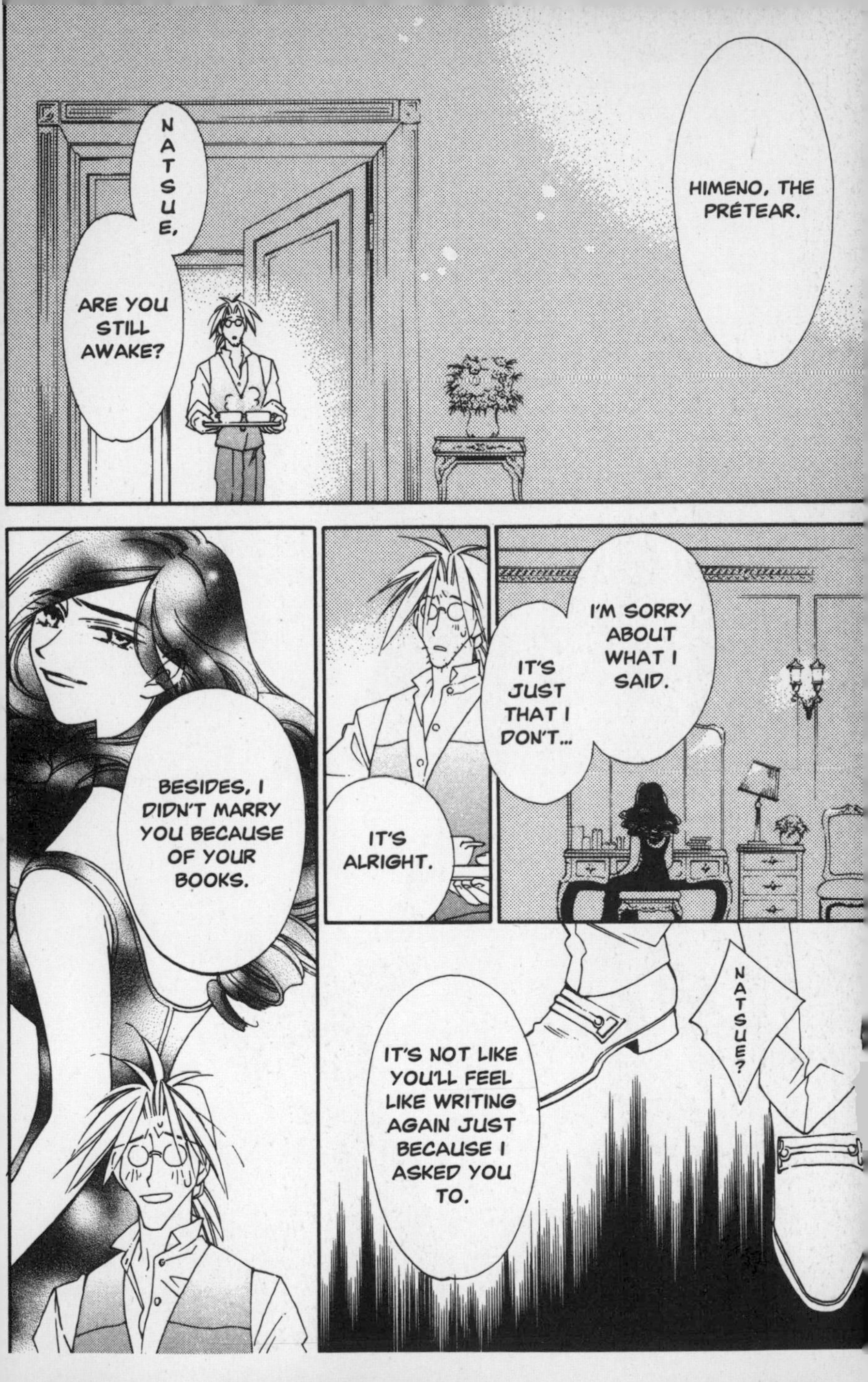
HIMENO, THE PRÉTEAR.
NATSUE, ARE YOU STILL AWAKE?
I'M SORRY ABOUT WHAT I SAID.
IT'S JUST THAT I DON'T...
IT'S ALRIGHT.
NATSUE?
IT'S NOT LIKE YOU'LL FEEL LIKE WRITING AGAIN JUST BECAUSE I ASKED YOU TO.
BESIDES, I DIDN'T MARRY YOU BECAUSE OF YOUR BOOKS.

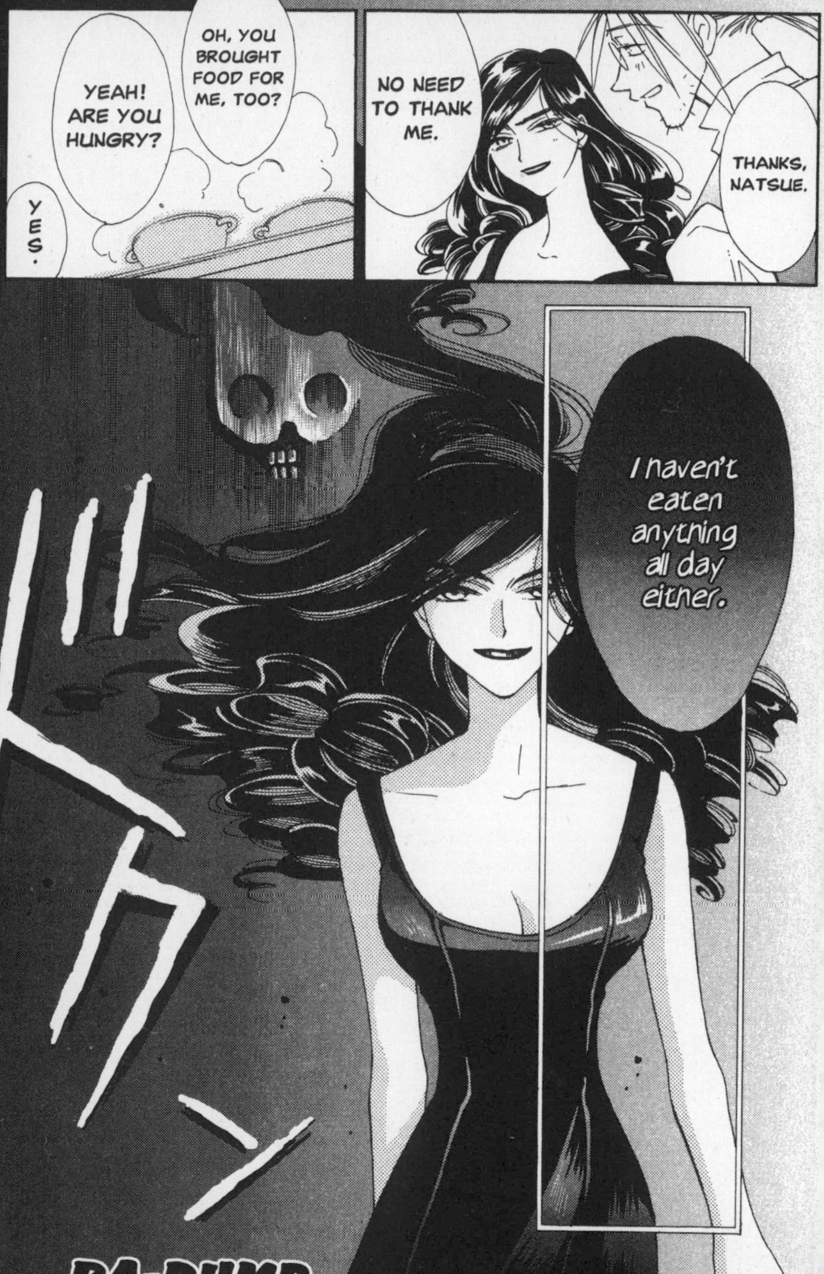
THANKS, NATSUE.
NO NEED TO THANK ME.
OH, YOU BROUGHT FOOD FOR ME, TOO?
YEAH! ARE YOU HUNGRY?
YES.
I haven't eaten anything all day either.
BA-DUMP

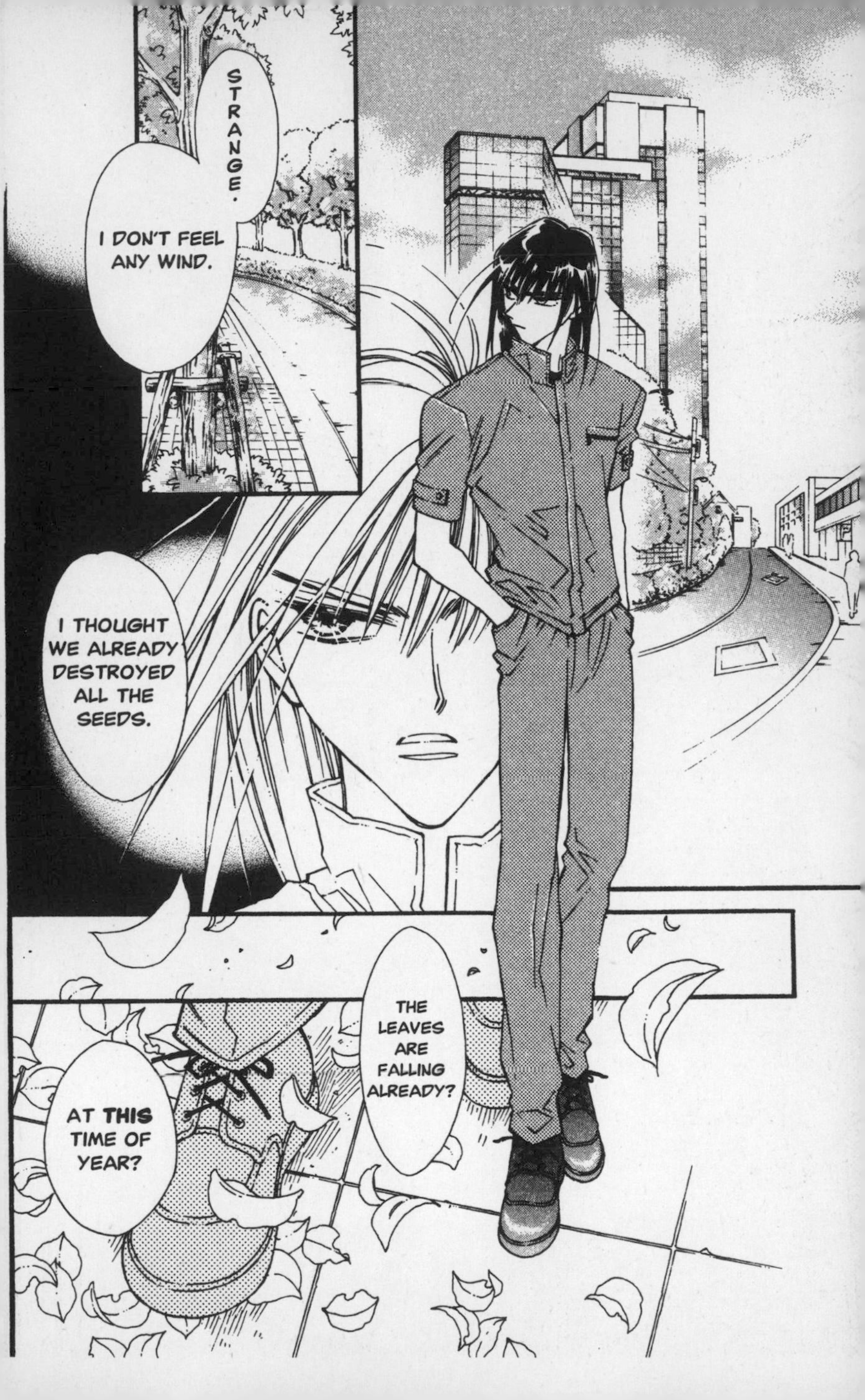
STRANGE.
I DON'T FEEL ANY WIND.
I THOUGHT WE ALREADY DESTROYED ALL THE SEEDS.
THE LEAVES ARE FALLING ALREADY?
AT THIS TIME OF YEAR?

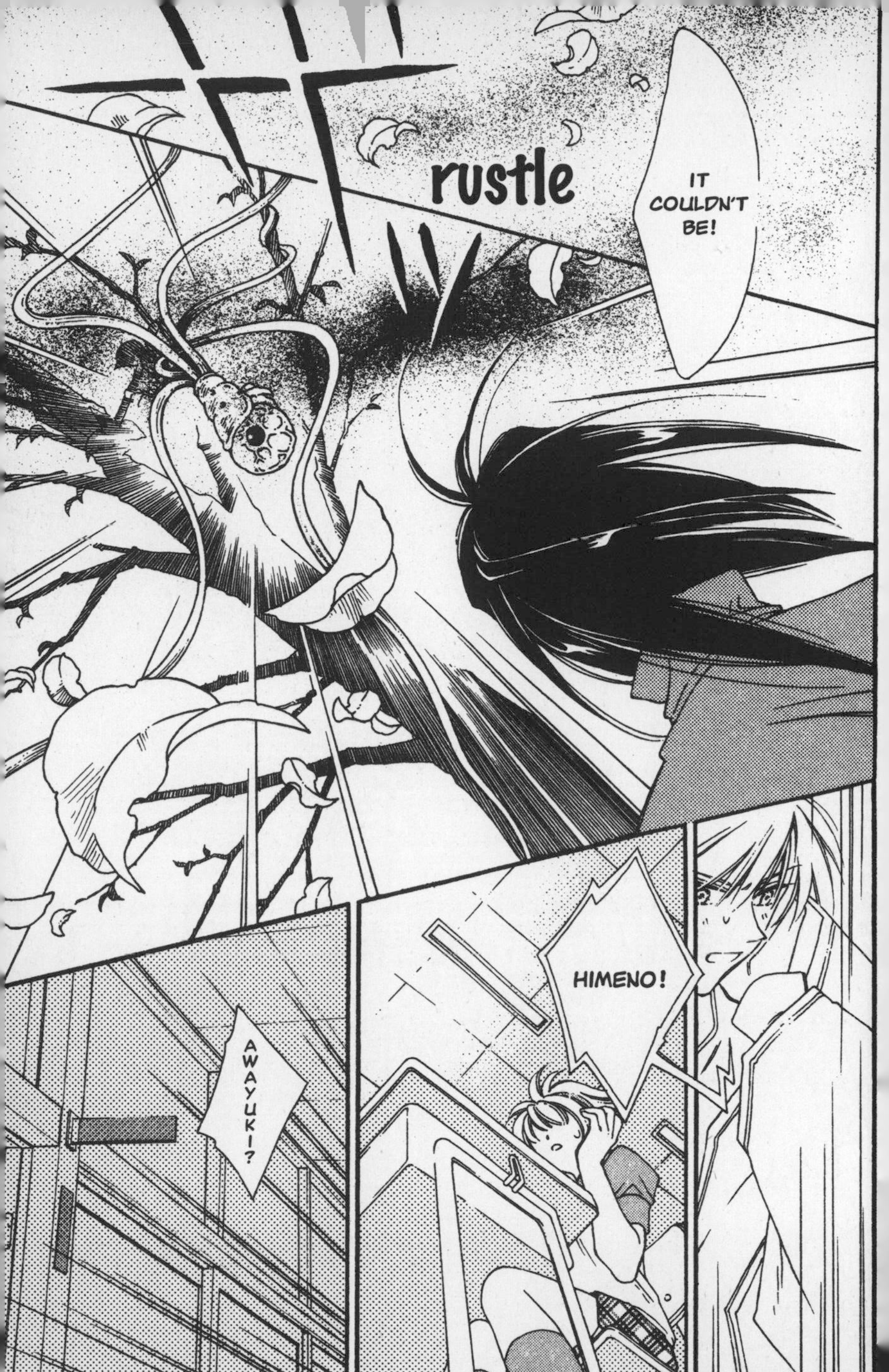
rustle
IT COULDN'T BE!
HIMENO!
AWAYUKI!?

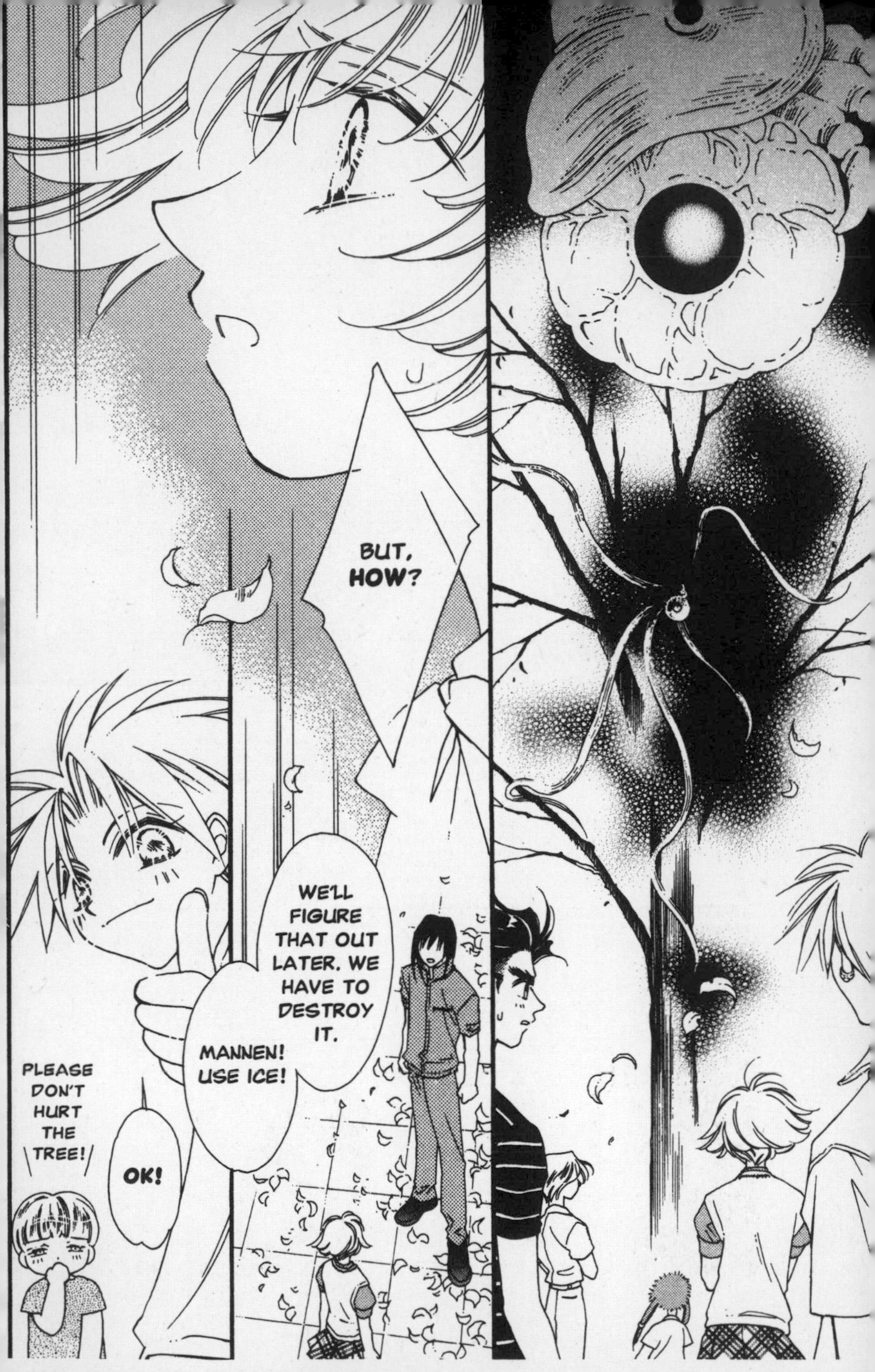
BUT, HOW?
WE'LL FIGURE THAT OUT LATER. WE HAVE TO DESTROY IT.
MANNEN! USE ICE!
OK!
PLEASE DON'T HURT THE TREE!

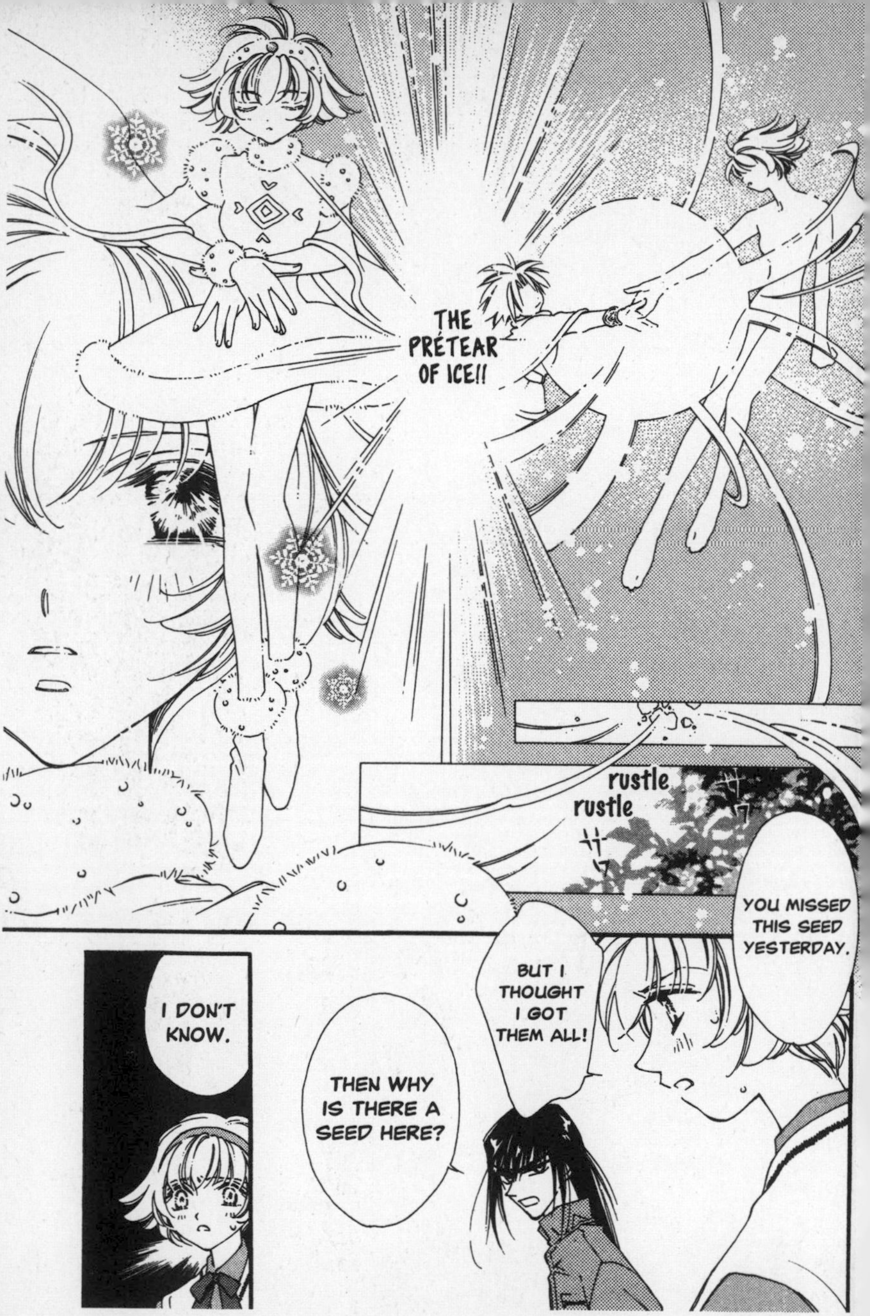
THE PRÉTEAR OF ICE!!
rustle
rustle
YOU MISSED THIS SEED YESTERDAY.
BUT I THOUGHT I GOT THEM ALL!
THEN WHY IS THERE A SEED HERE?
I DON'T KNOW.

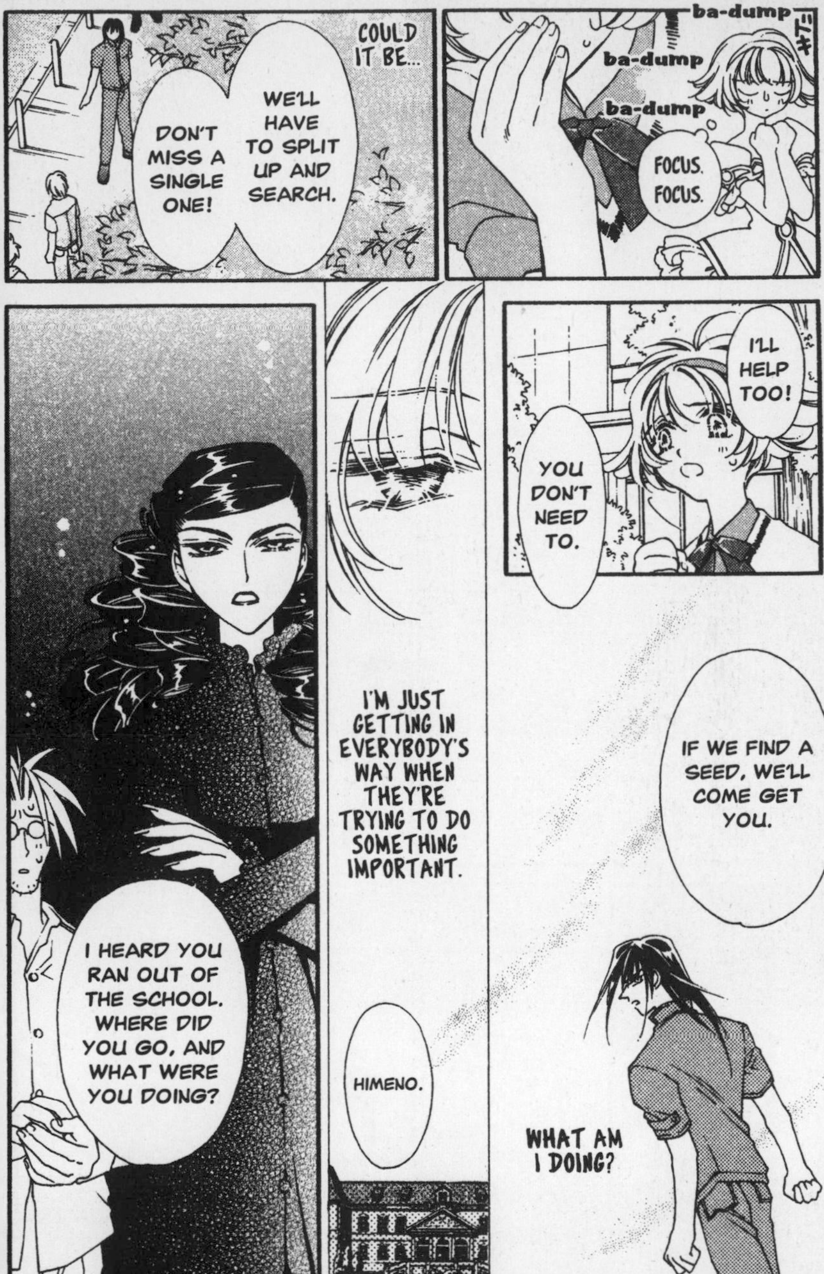
ba-dump
ba-dump
ba-dump
FOCUS. FOCUS.
COULD IT BE...
WE'LL HAVE TO SPLIT UP AND SEARCH.
DON'T MISS A SINGLE ONE!
I'LL HELP TOO!
YOU DON'T NEED TO.
IF WE FIND A SEED, WE'LL COME GET YOU.
WHAT AM I DOING?
I'M JUST GETTING IN EVERYBODY'S WAY WHEN THEY'RE TRYING TO DO SOMETHING IMPORTANT.
HIMENO.
I HEARD YOU RAN OUT OF THE SCHOOL. WHERE DID YOU GO, AND WHAT WERE YOU DOING?

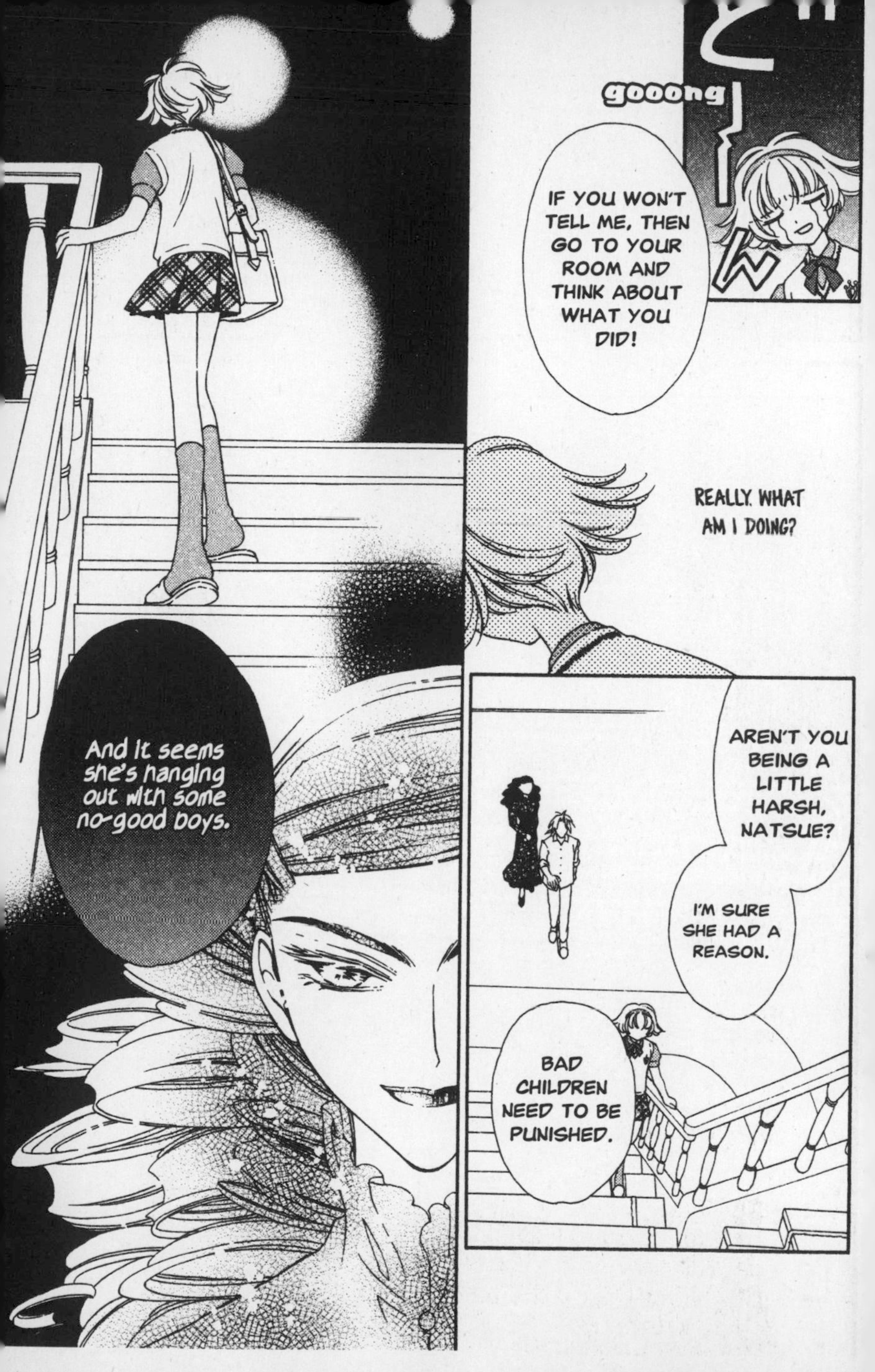
gooong
IF YOU WON'T TELL ME, THEN GO TO YOUR ROOM AND THINK ABOUT WHAT YOU DID!
REALLY. WHAT AM I DOING?
AREN'T YOU BEING A LITTLE HARSH, NATSUE?
I'M SURE SHE HAD A REASON.
BAD CHILDREN NEED TO BE PUNISHED.
And it seems she's hanging out with some no-good boys.

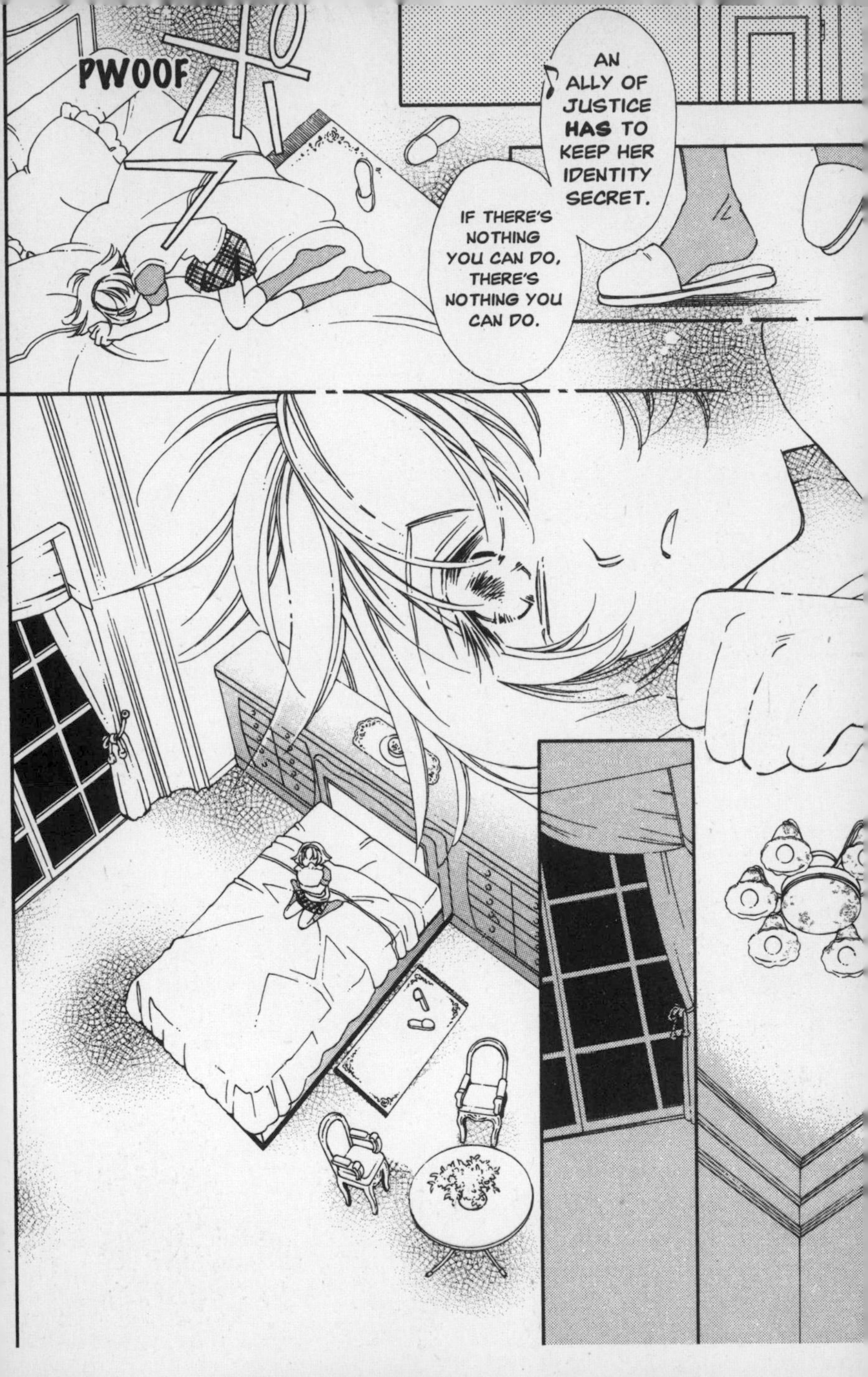
AN ALLY OF JUSTICE HAS TO KEEP HER IDENTITY SECRET.
IF THERE'S NOTHING YOU CAN DO, THERE'S NOTHING YOU CAN DO.
PWOOF

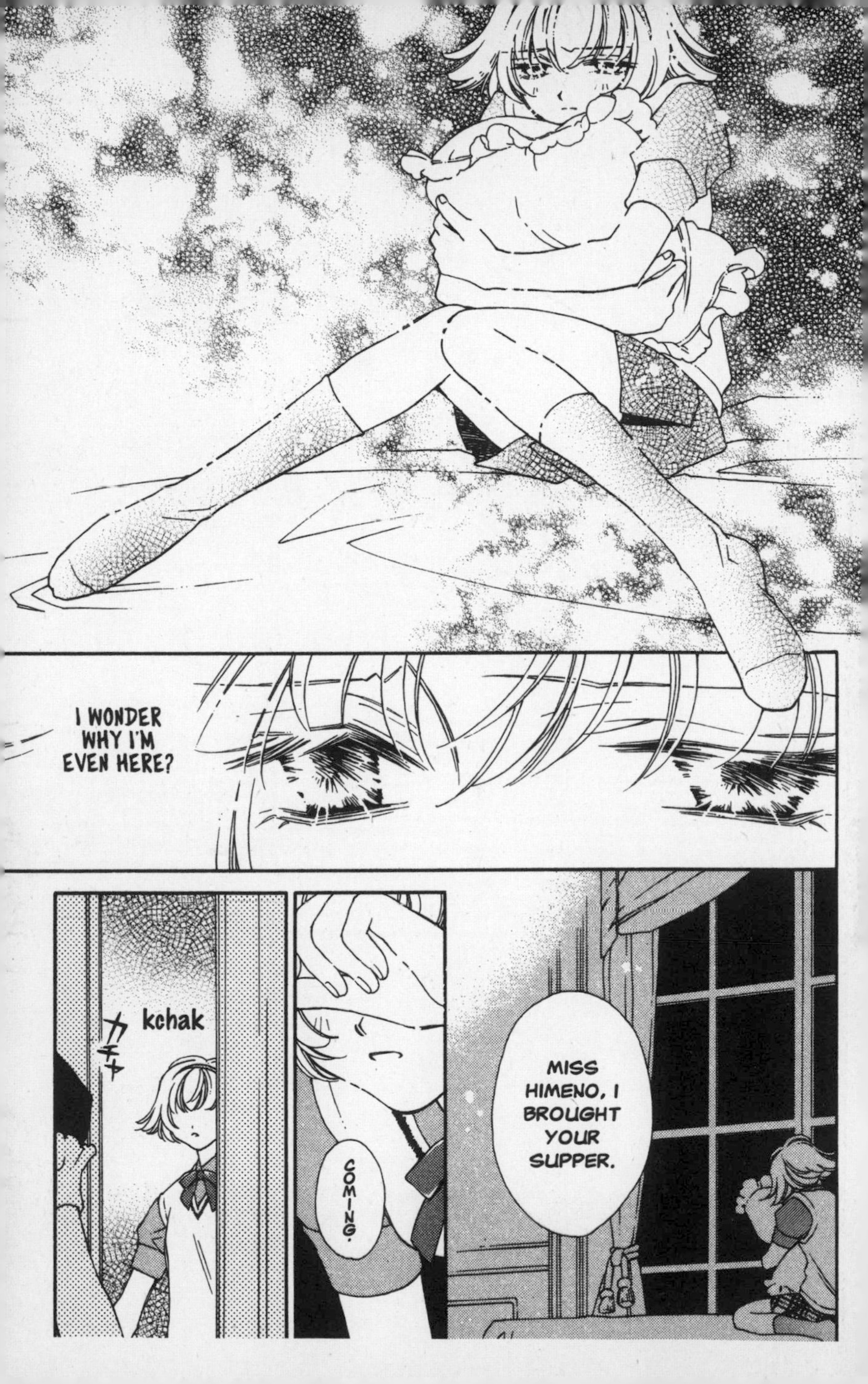
I WONDER WHY I'M EVEN HERE?
MISS HIMENO, I BROUGHT YOUR SUPPER.
COMING.
kchak

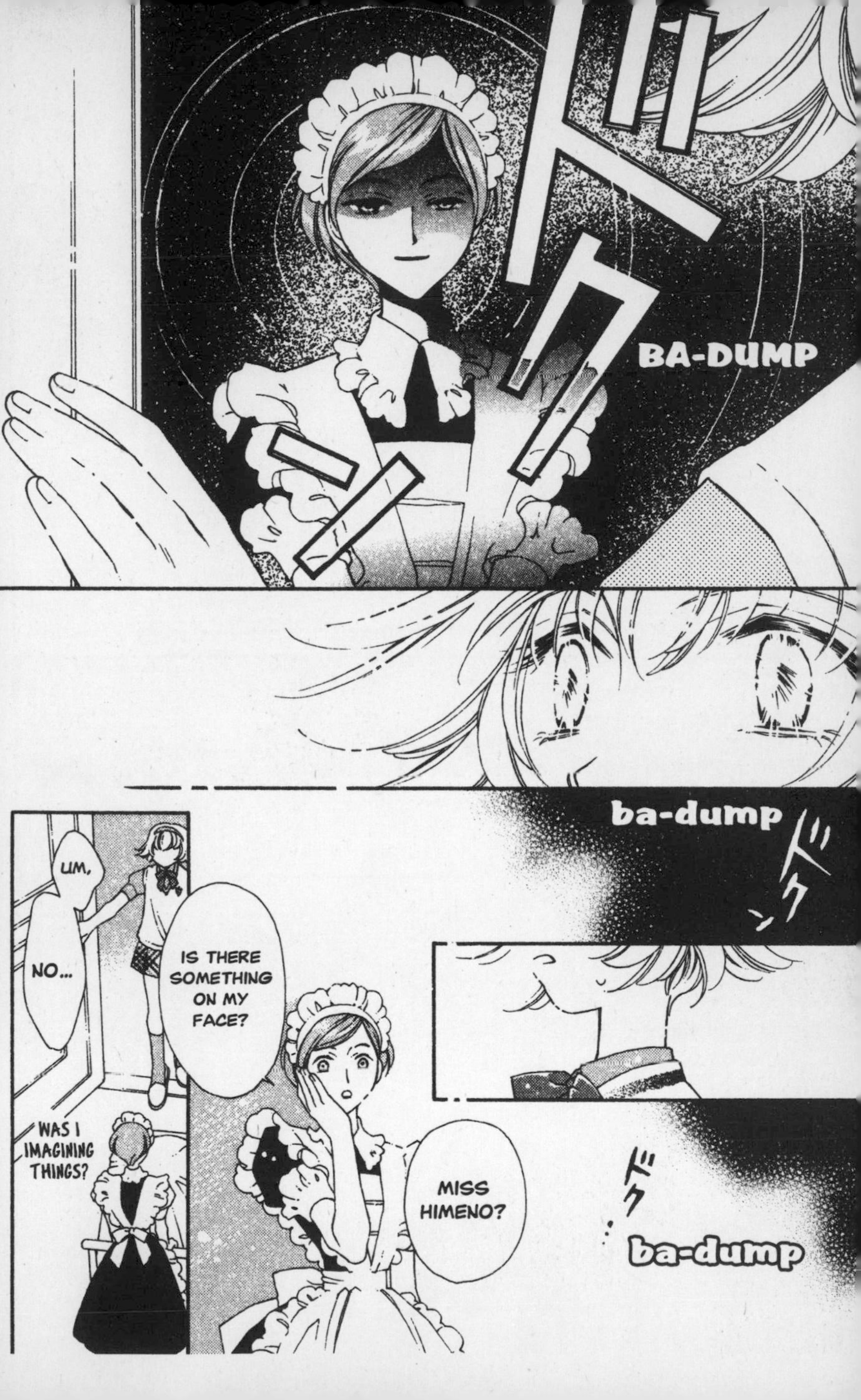

BA-DUMP
ba-dump
UM,
NO...
IS THERE SOMETHING ON MY FACE?
ba-dump
MISS HIMENO?
WAS I IMAGINING THINGS?

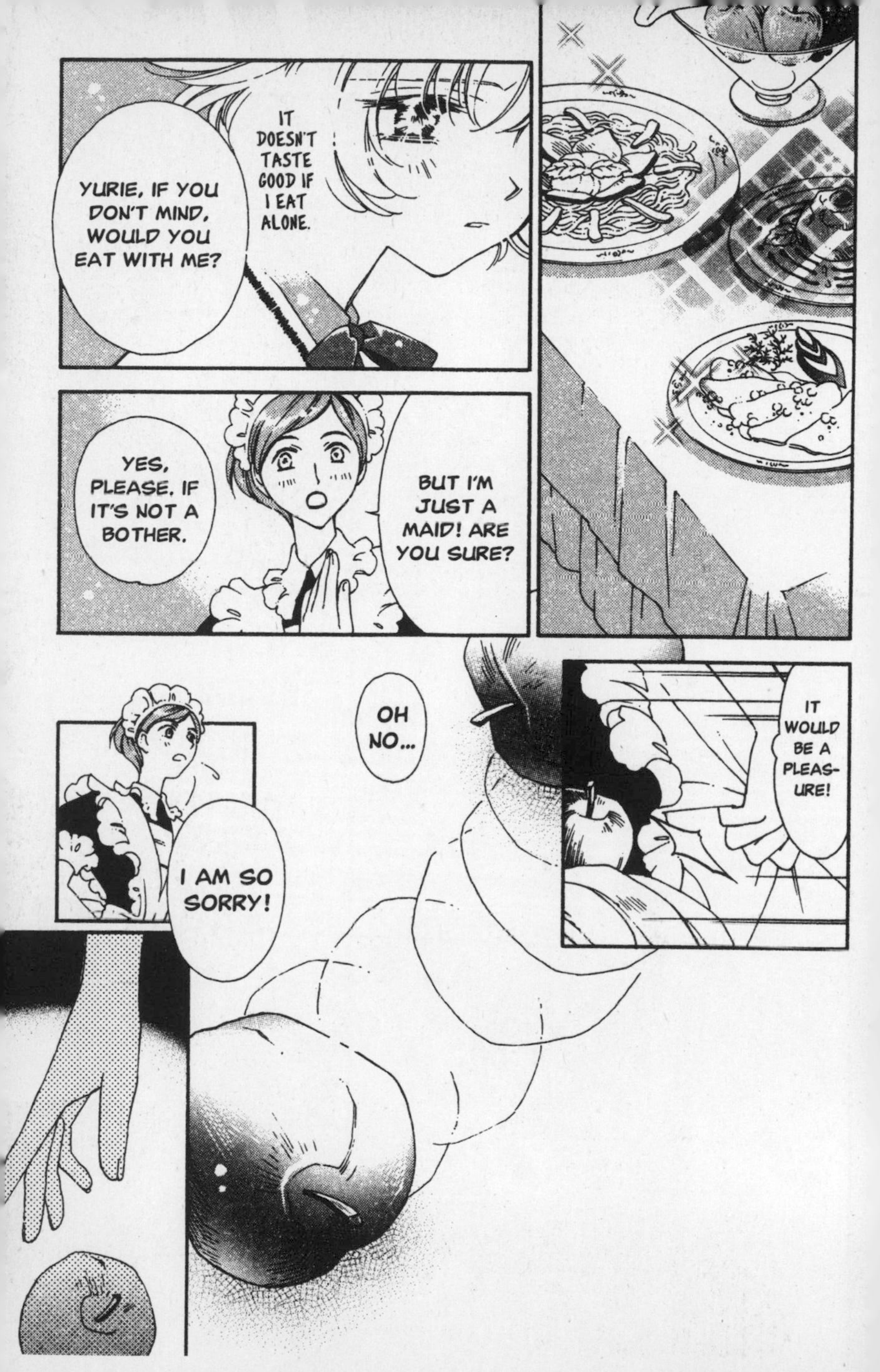
YURIE, IF YOU DON'T MIND, WOULD YOU EAT WITH ME?
IT DOESN'T TASTE GOOD IF I EAT ALONE.
BUT I'M JUST A MAID! ARE YOU SURE?
YES, PLEASE. IF IT'S NOT A BOTHER.
IT WOULD BE A PLEAS-URE!
OH NO...
I AM SO SORRY!

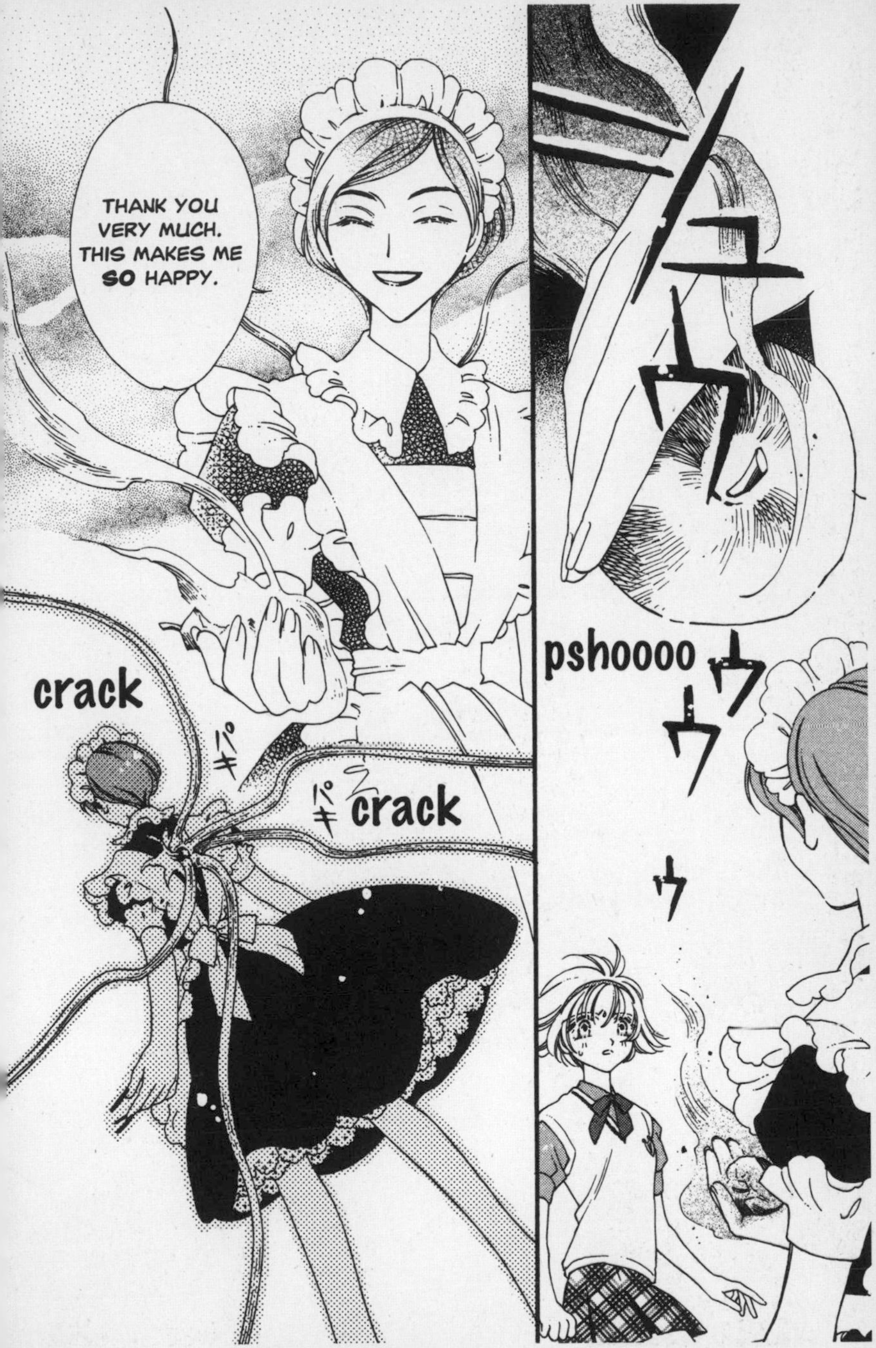
pshoooo
THANK YOU VERY MUCH. THIS MAKES ME SO HAPPY.
crack
crack

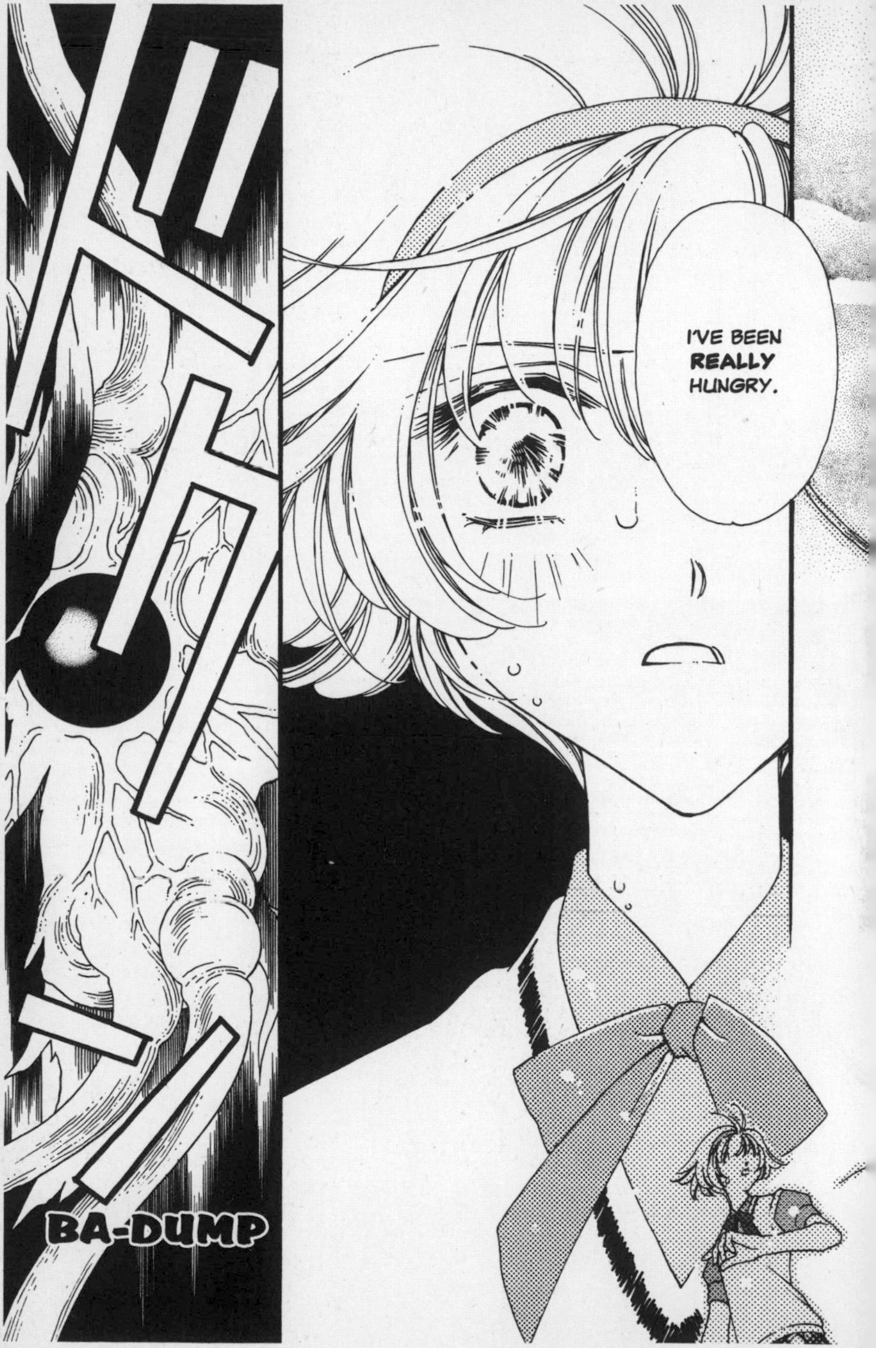

I'VE BEEN REALLY HUNGRY.
BA-DUMP

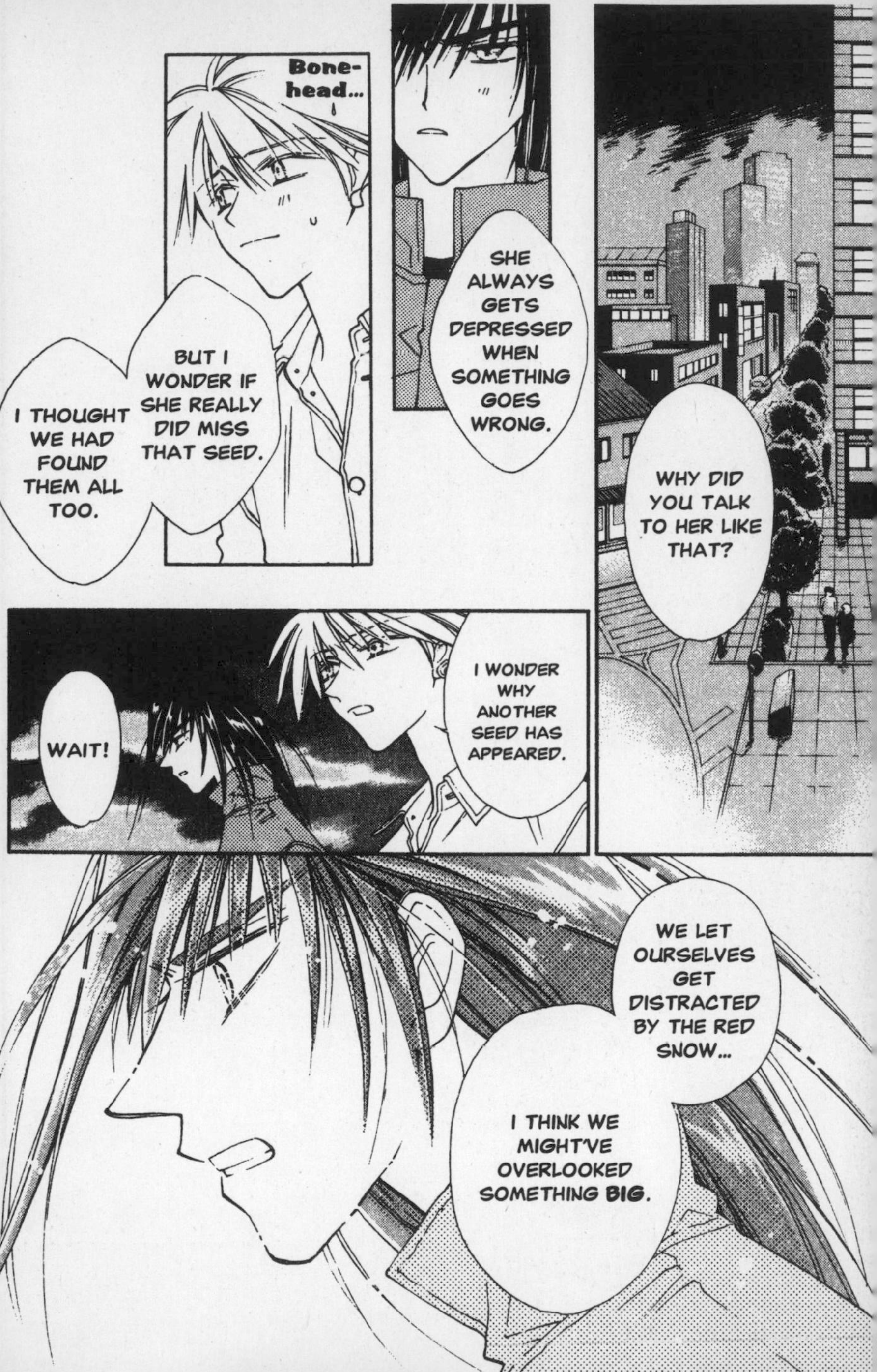
WHY DID YOU TALK TO HER LIKE THAT?
SHE ALWAYS GETS DEPRESSED WHEN SOMETHING GOES WRONG.
Bone-head...
BUT I WONDER IF SHE REALLY DID MISS THAT SEED.
I THOUGHT WE HAD FOUND THEM ALL TOO.
I WONDER WHY ANOTHER SEED HAS APPEARED.
WAIT!
WE LET OURSELVES GET DISTRACTED BY THE RED SNOW...
I THINK WE MIGHT'VE OVERLOOKED SOMETHING BIG.

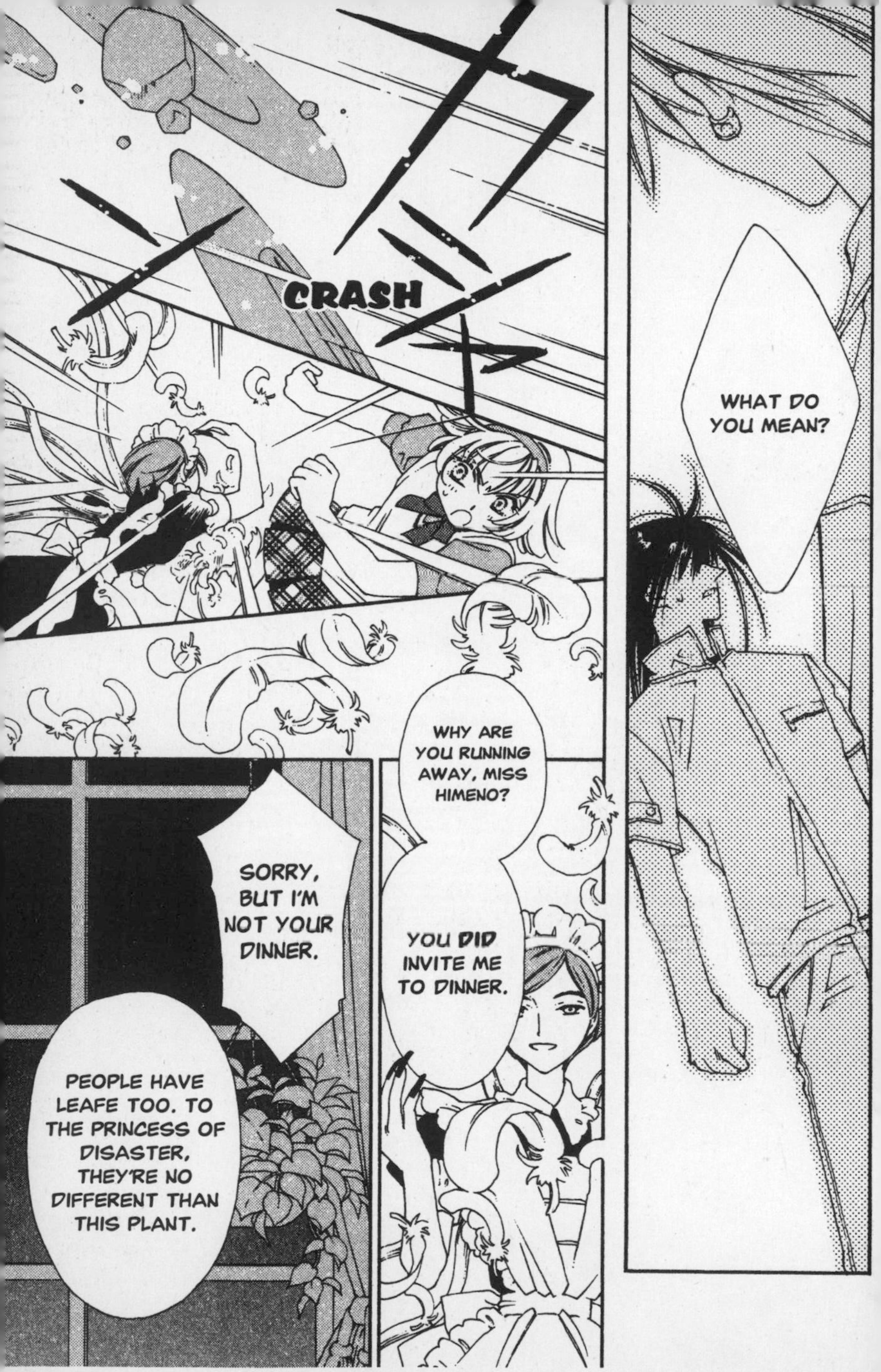
WHAT DO YOU MEAN?
CRASH
WHY ARE YOU RUNNING AWAY, MISS HIMENO?
YOU **DID** INVITE ME TO DINNER.
SORRY, BUT I'M NOT YOUR DINNER.
PEOPLE HAVE LEAFE TOO. TO THE PRINCESS OF DISASTER, THEY'RE NO DIFFERENT THAN THIS PLANT.

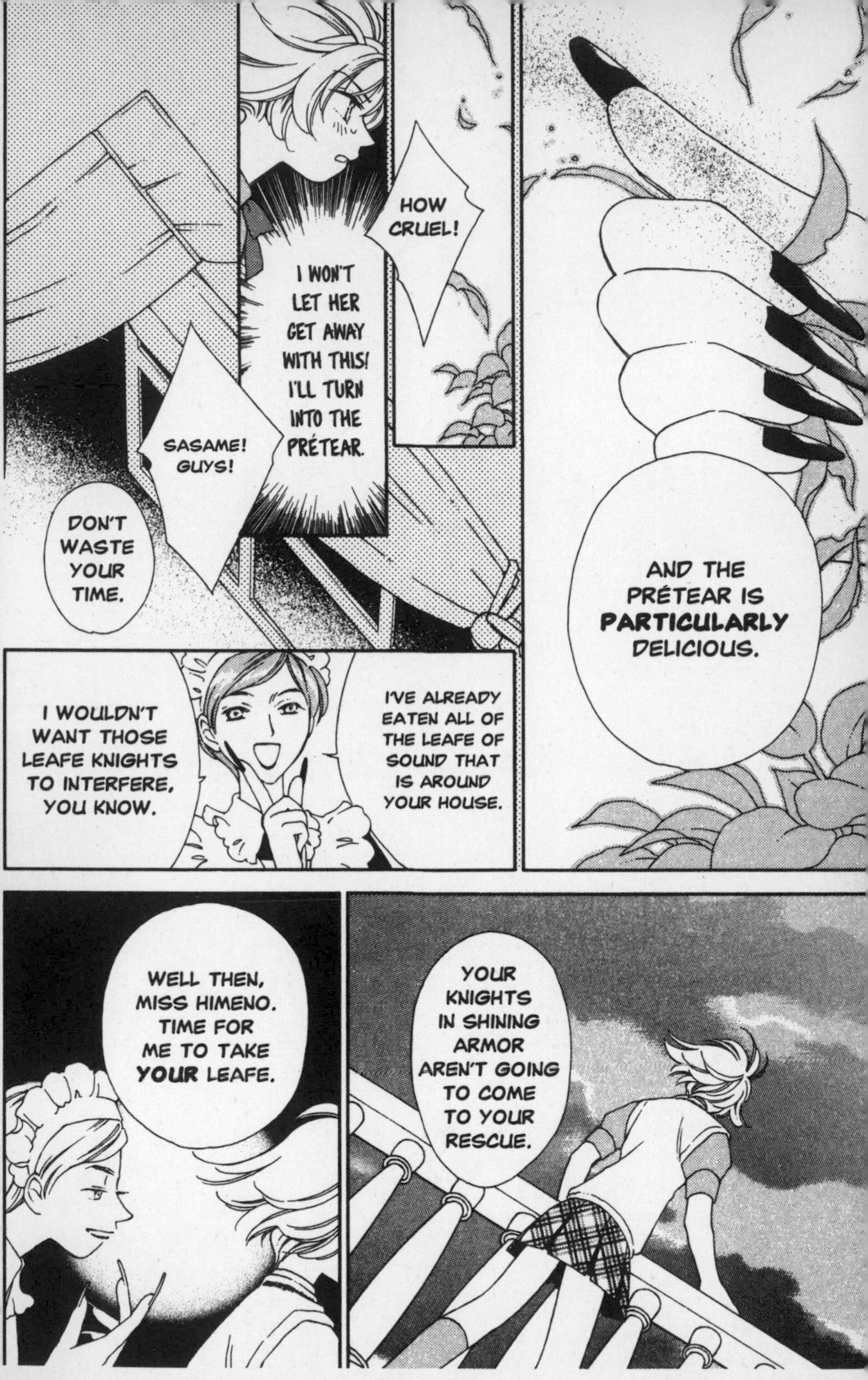

HOW CRUEL!
I WON'T LET HER GET AWAY WITH THIS! I'LL TURN INTO THE PRÉTEAR.
SASAME! GUYS!
DON'T WASTE YOUR TIME.
I'VE ALREADY EATEN ALL OF THE LEAFE OF SOUND THAT IS AROUND YOUR HOUSE.
I WOULDN'T WANT THOSE LEAFE KNIGHTS TO INTERFERE, YOU KNOW.
AND THE PRÉTEAR IS PARTICULARLY DELICIOUS.
YOUR KNIGHTS IN SHINING ARMOR AREN'T GOING TO COME TO YOUR RESCUE.
WELL THEN, MISS HIMENO. TIME FOR ME TO TAKE YOUR LEAFE.

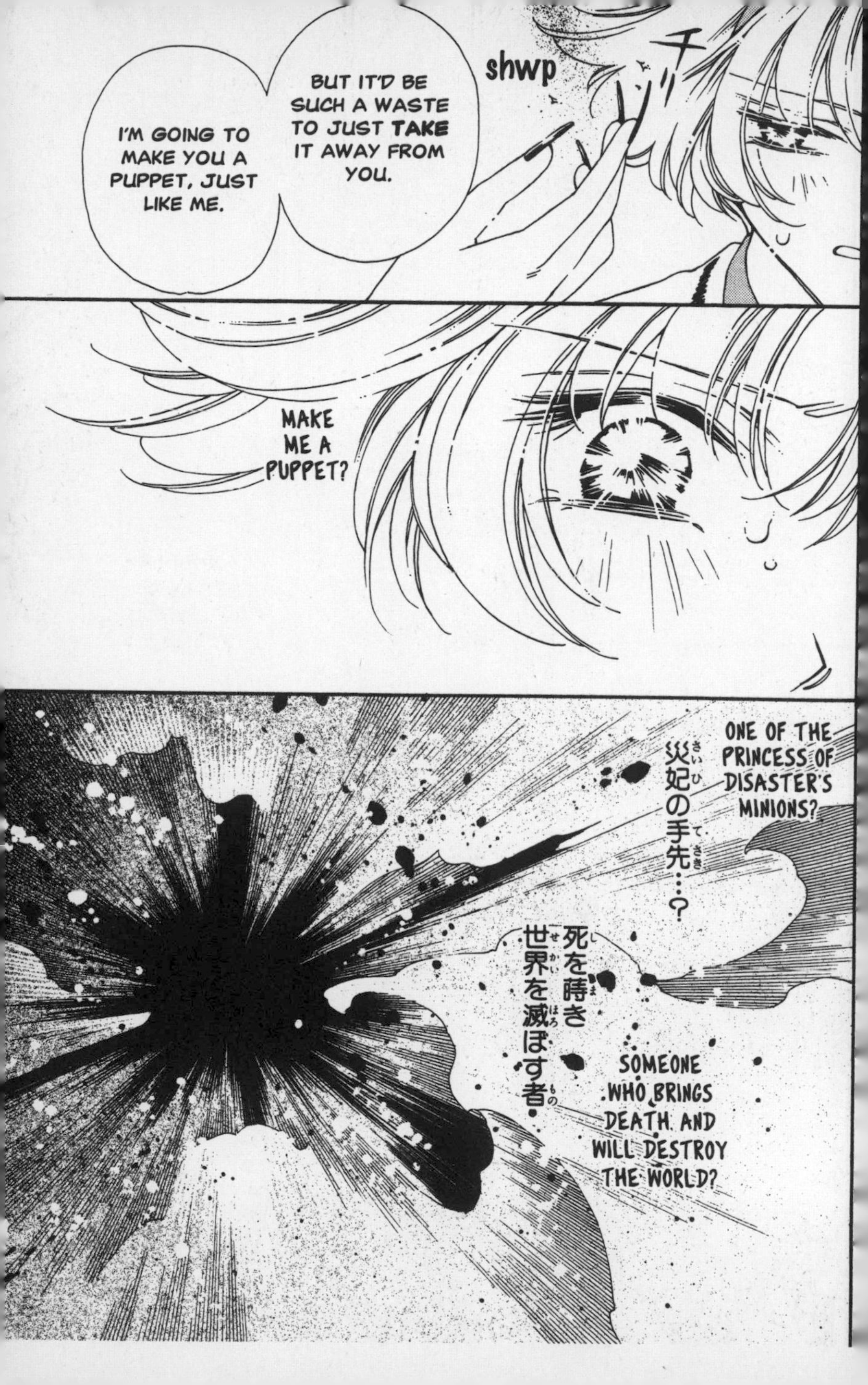
shwp
BUT IT'D BE SUCH A WASTE TO JUST TAKE IT AWAY FROM YOU.
I'M GOING TO MAKE YOU A PUPPET, JUST LIKE ME.
MAKE ME A PUPPET?
災妃の手先…？
ONE OF THE PRINCESS OF DISASTER'S MINIONS?
死を蒔き世界を滅ぼす者
SOMEONE WHO BRINGS DEATH AND WILL DESTROY THE WORLD?

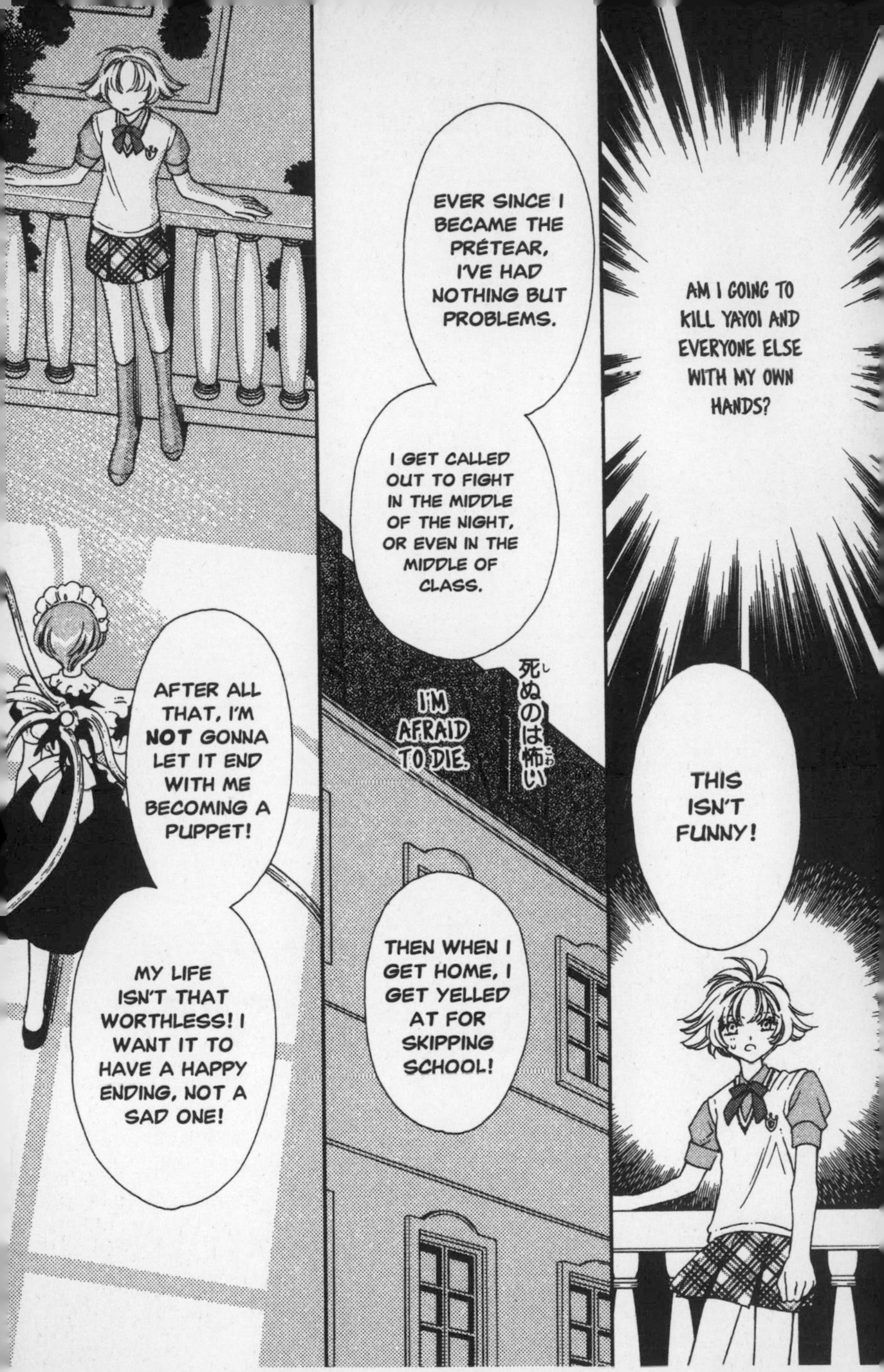
AM I GOING TO KILL YAYOI AND EVERYONE ELSE WITH MY OWN HANDS?
THIS ISN'T FUNNY!
EVER SINCE I BECAME THE PRÉTEAR, I'VE HAD NOTHING BUT PROBLEMS.
I GET CALLED OUT TO FIGHT IN THE MIDDLE OF THE NIGHT, OR EVEN IN THE MIDDLE OF CLASS.
死ぬのは怖い
I'M AFRAID TO DIE.
THEN WHEN I GET HOME, I GET YELLED AT FOR SKIPPING SCHOOL!
AFTER ALL THAT, I'M **NOT** GONNA LET IT END WITH ME BECOMING A PUPPET!
MY LIFE ISN'T THAT WORTHLESS! I WANT IT TO HAVE A HAPPY ENDING, NOT A SAD ONE!

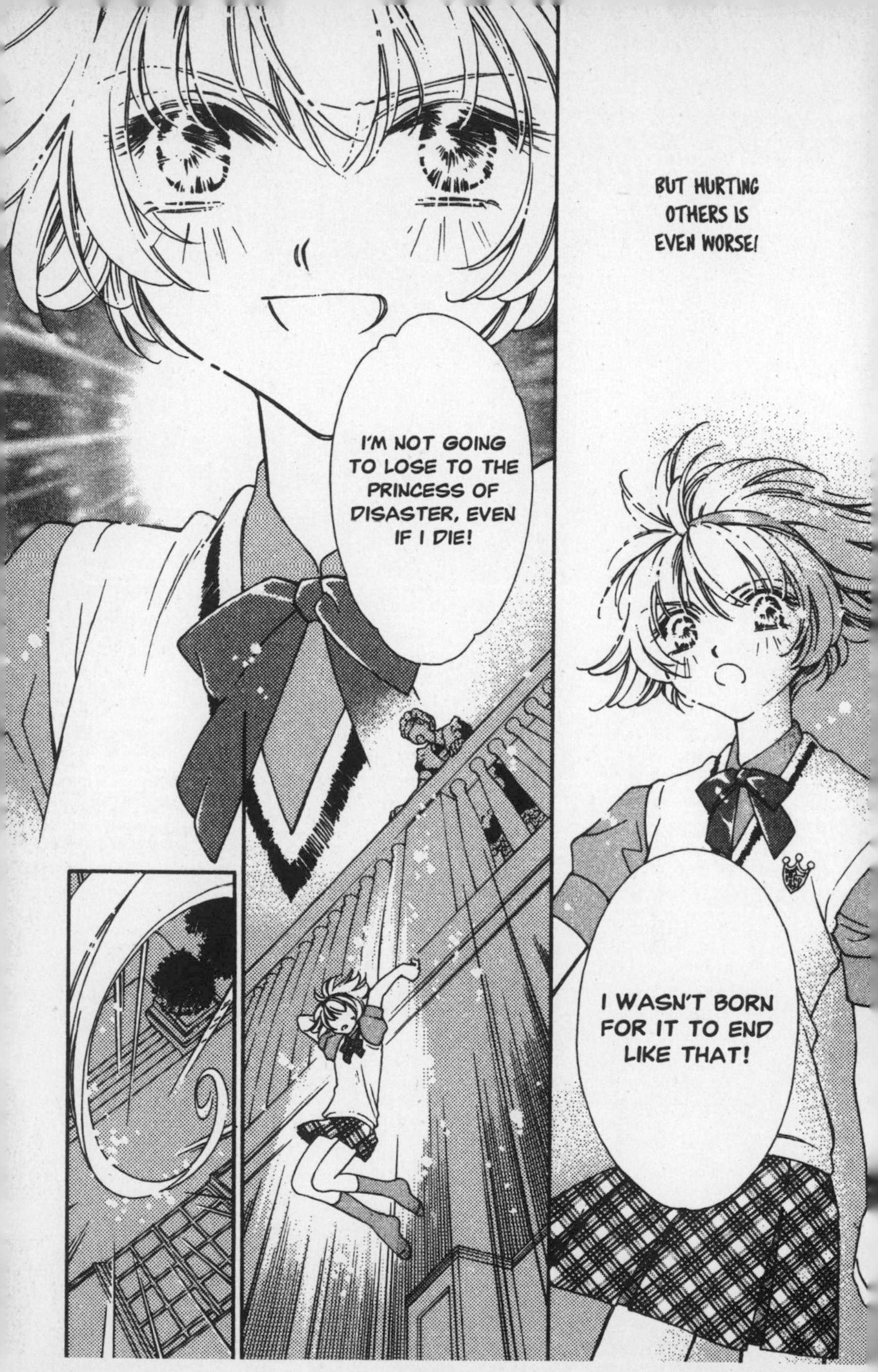
BUT HURTING OTHERS IS EVEN WORSE!
I WASN'T BORN FOR IT TO END LIKE THAT!
I'M NOT GOING TO LOSE TO THE PRINCESS OF DISASTER, EVEN IF I DIE!

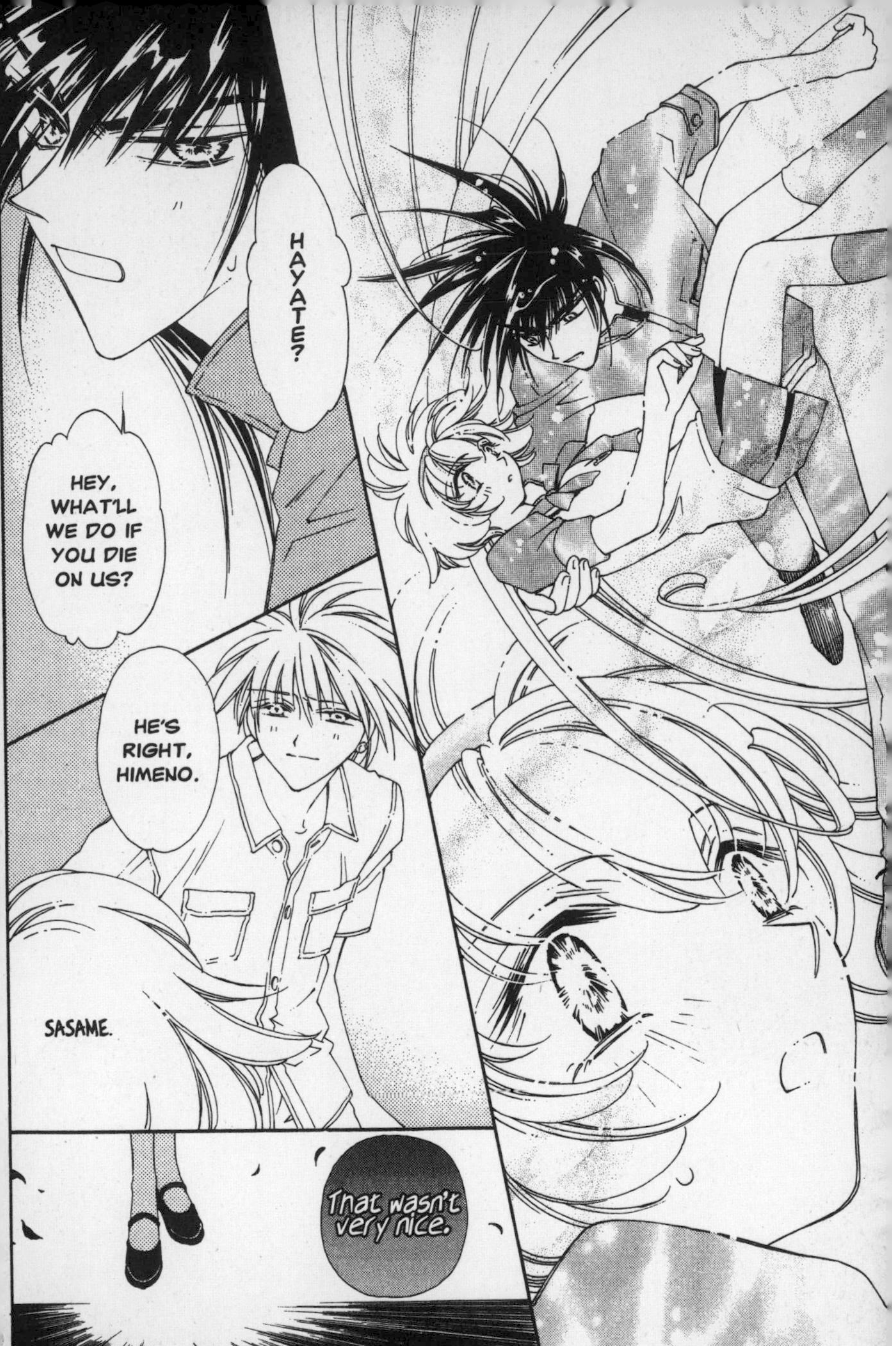
HAYATE?
HEY, WHAT'LL WE DO IF YOU DIE ON US?
HE'S RIGHT, HIMENO.
SASAME.
That wasn't very nice.

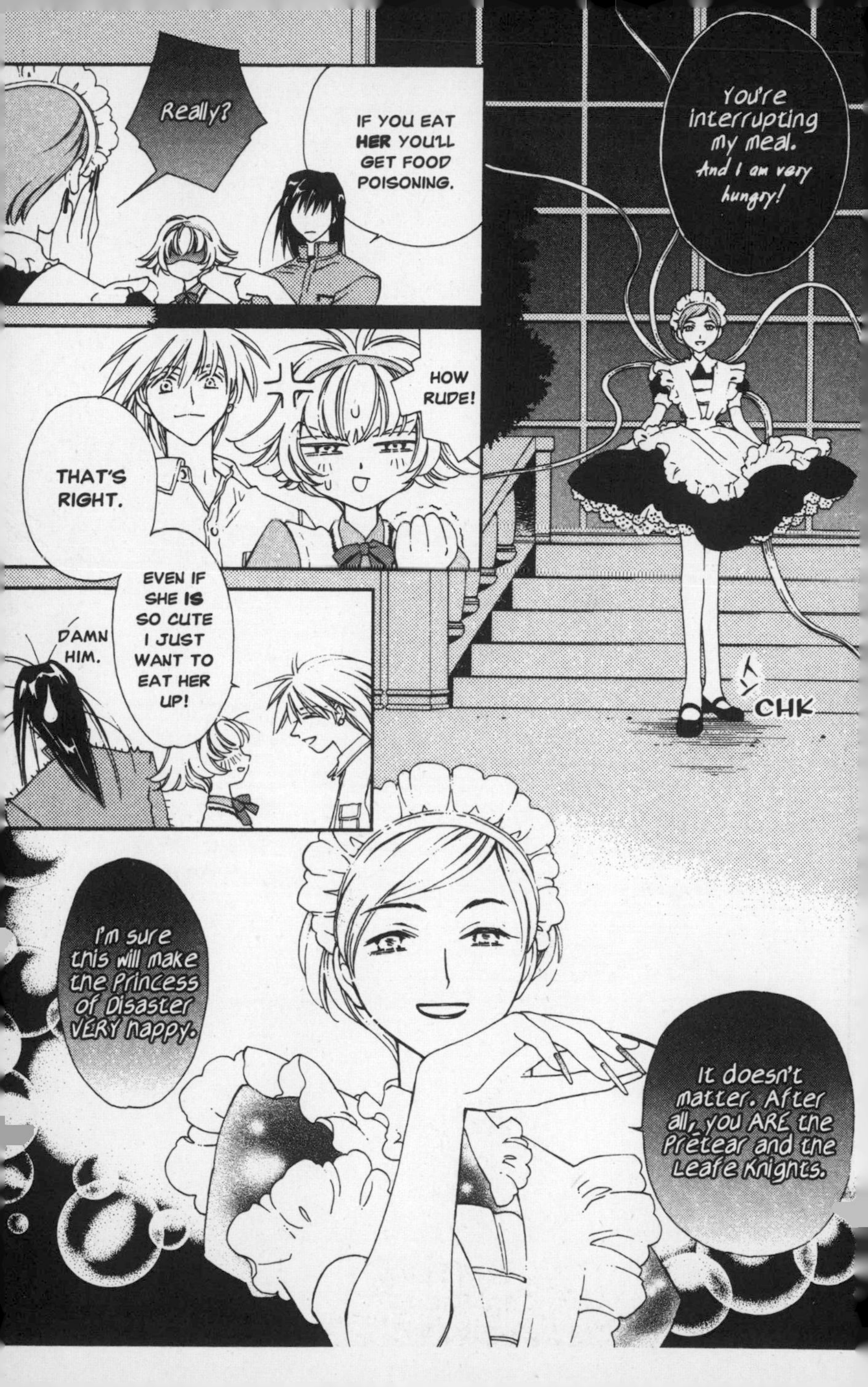
You're interrupting my meal. And I am very hungry!
IF YOU EAT HER YOU'LL GET FOOD POISONING.
Really?
HOW RUDE!
THAT'S RIGHT.
EVEN IF SHE IS SO CUTE I JUST WANT TO EAT HER UP!
DAMN HIM.
CHK
It doesn't matter. After all, you ARE the Pretear and the Leafe Knights.
I'm sure this will make the Princess of Disaster VERY happy.

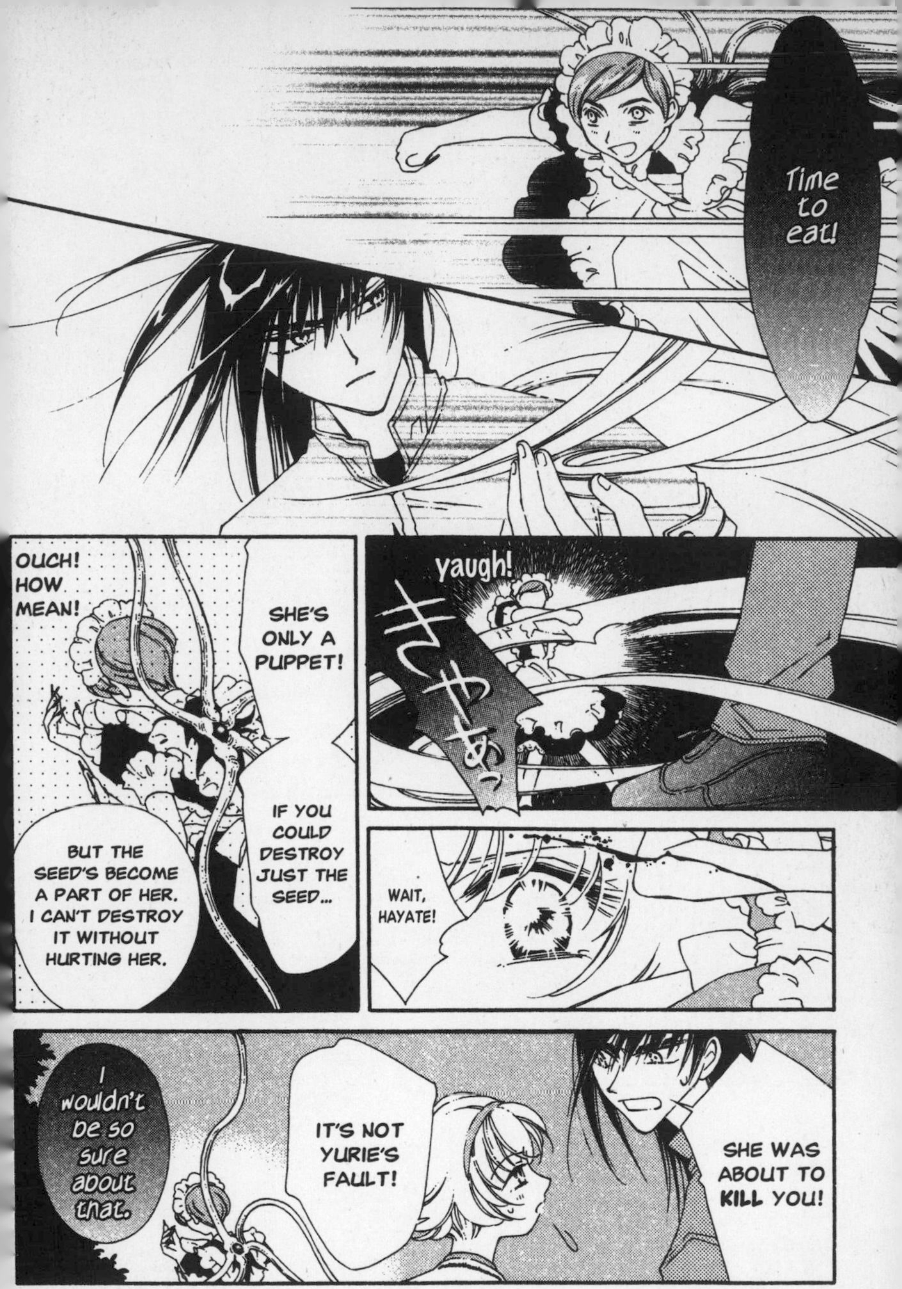
Time to eat!
yaugh!
きゃあっ
WAIT, HAYATE!
SHE'S ONLY A PUPPET!
IF YOU COULD DESTROY JUST THE SEED...
OUCH! HOW MEAN!
BUT THE SEED'S BECOME A PART OF HER. I CAN'T DESTROY IT WITHOUT HURTING HER.
SHE WAS ABOUT TO **KILL** YOU!
IT'S NOT YURIE'S FAULT!
I wouldn't be so sure about that.

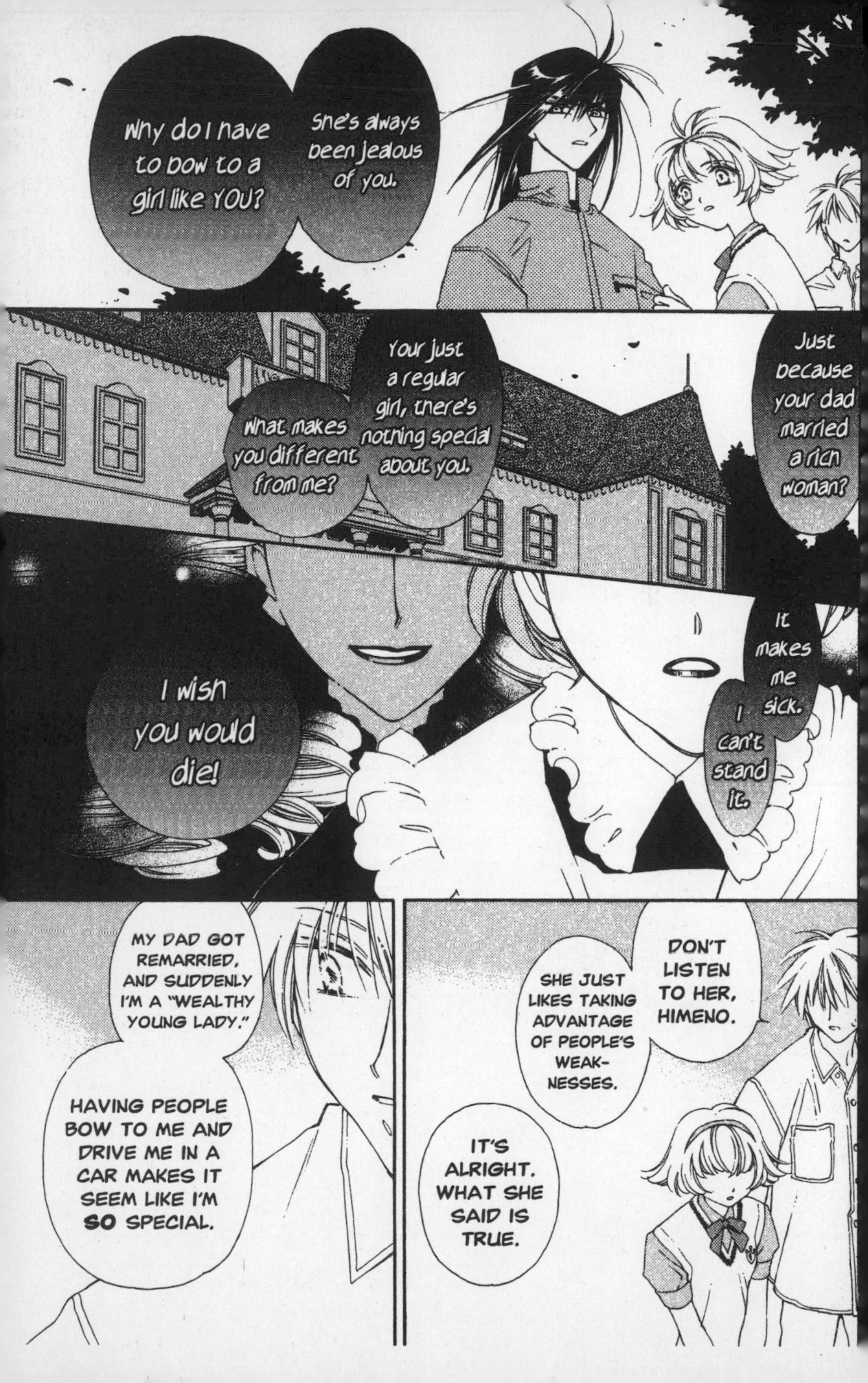
She's always been jealous of you.
Why do I have to bow to a girl like YOU?
Just because your dad married a rich woman?
Your just a regular girl, there's nothing special about you.
What makes you different from me?
It makes me sick.
I can't stand it.
I wish you would die!
DON'T LISTEN TO HER, HIMENO.
SHE JUST LIKES TAKING ADVANTAGE OF PEOPLE'S WEAK-NESSES.
IT'S ALRIGHT. WHAT SHE SAID IS TRUE.
MY DAD GOT REMARRIED, AND SUDDENLY I'M A "WEALTHY YOUNG LADY."
HAVING PEOPLE BOW TO ME AND DRIVE ME IN A CAR MAKES IT SEEM LIKE I'M SO SPECIAL.

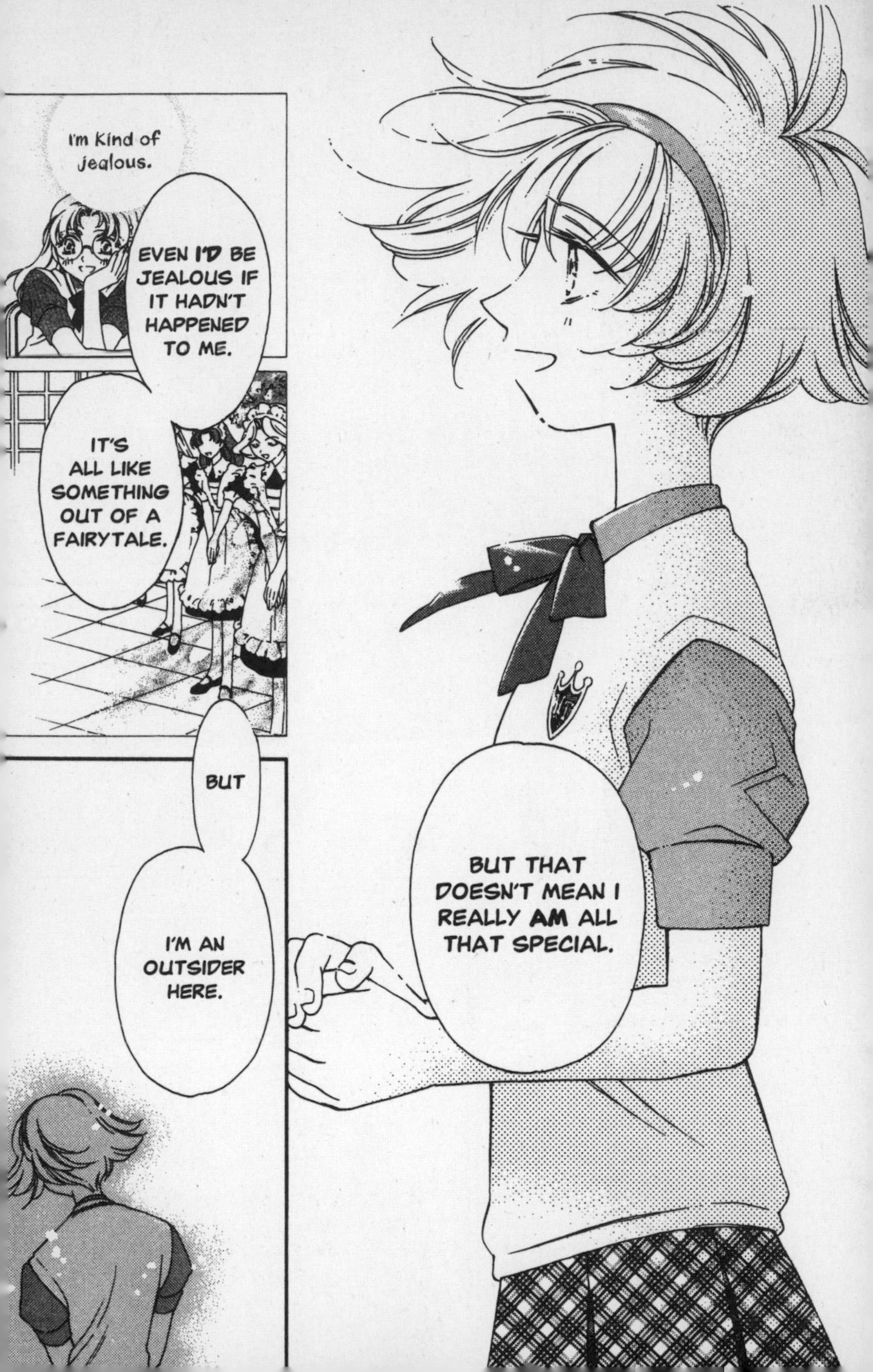
I'm Kind of jealous.
EVEN I'D BE JEALOUS IF IT HADN'T HAPPENED TO ME.
IT'S ALL LIKE SOMETHING OUT OF A FAIRYTALE.
BUT THAT DOESN'T MEAN I REALLY AM ALL THAT SPECIAL.
BUT
I'M AN OUTSIDER HERE.

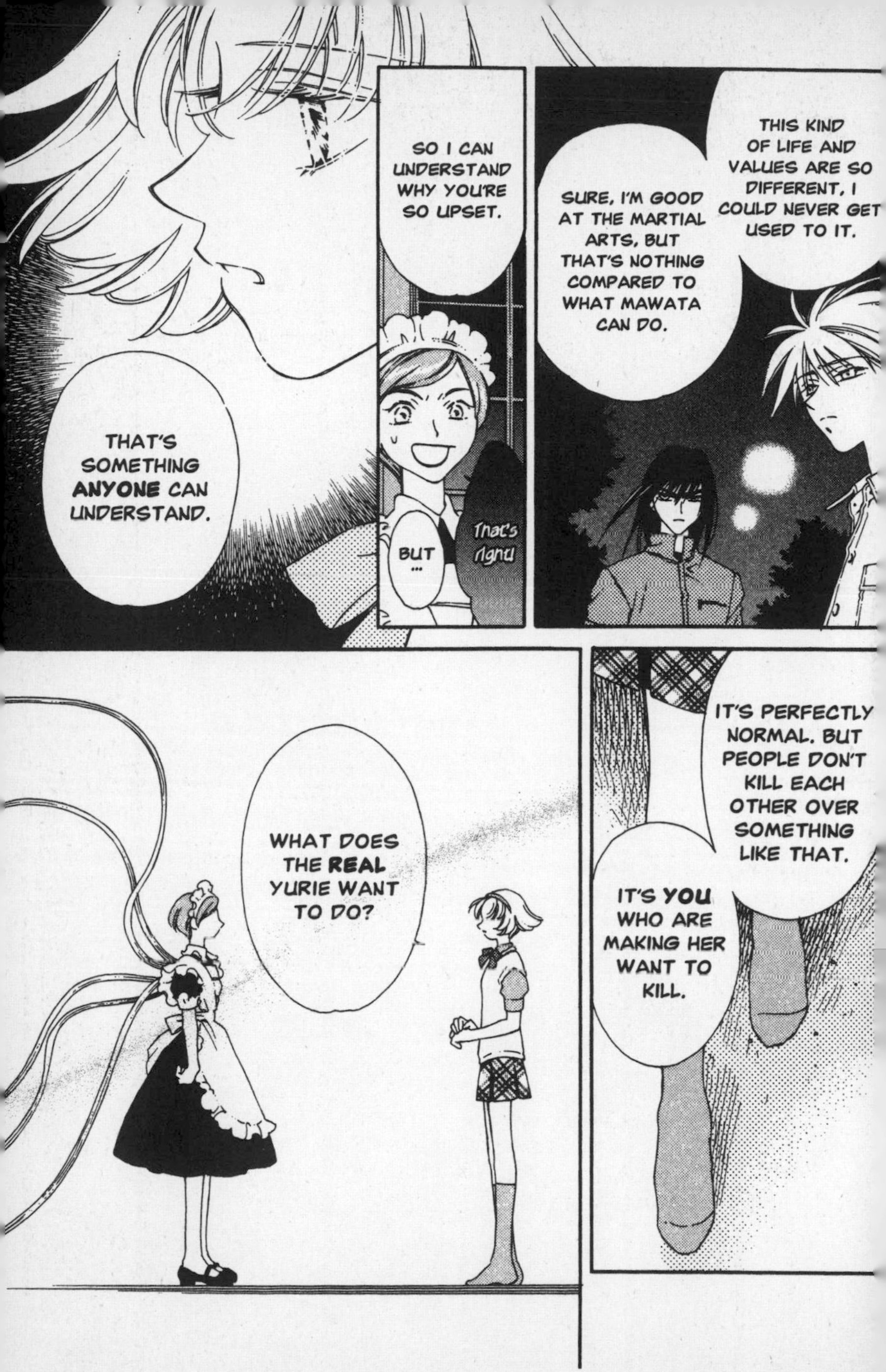
THIS KIND OF LIFE AND VALUES ARE SO DIFFERENT, I COULD NEVER GET USED TO IT.
SURE, I'M GOOD AT THE MARTIAL ARTS, BUT THAT'S NOTHING COMPARED TO WHAT MAWATA CAN DO.
SO I CAN UNDERSTAND WHY YOU'RE SO UPSET.
That's right!
BUT ...
THAT'S SOMETHING **ANYONE** CAN UNDERSTAND.
IT'S PERFECTLY NORMAL. BUT PEOPLE DON'T KILL EACH OTHER OVER SOMETHING LIKE THAT.
IT'S **YOU** WHO ARE MAKING HER WANT TO KILL.
WHAT DOES THE **REAL** YURIE WANT TO DO?

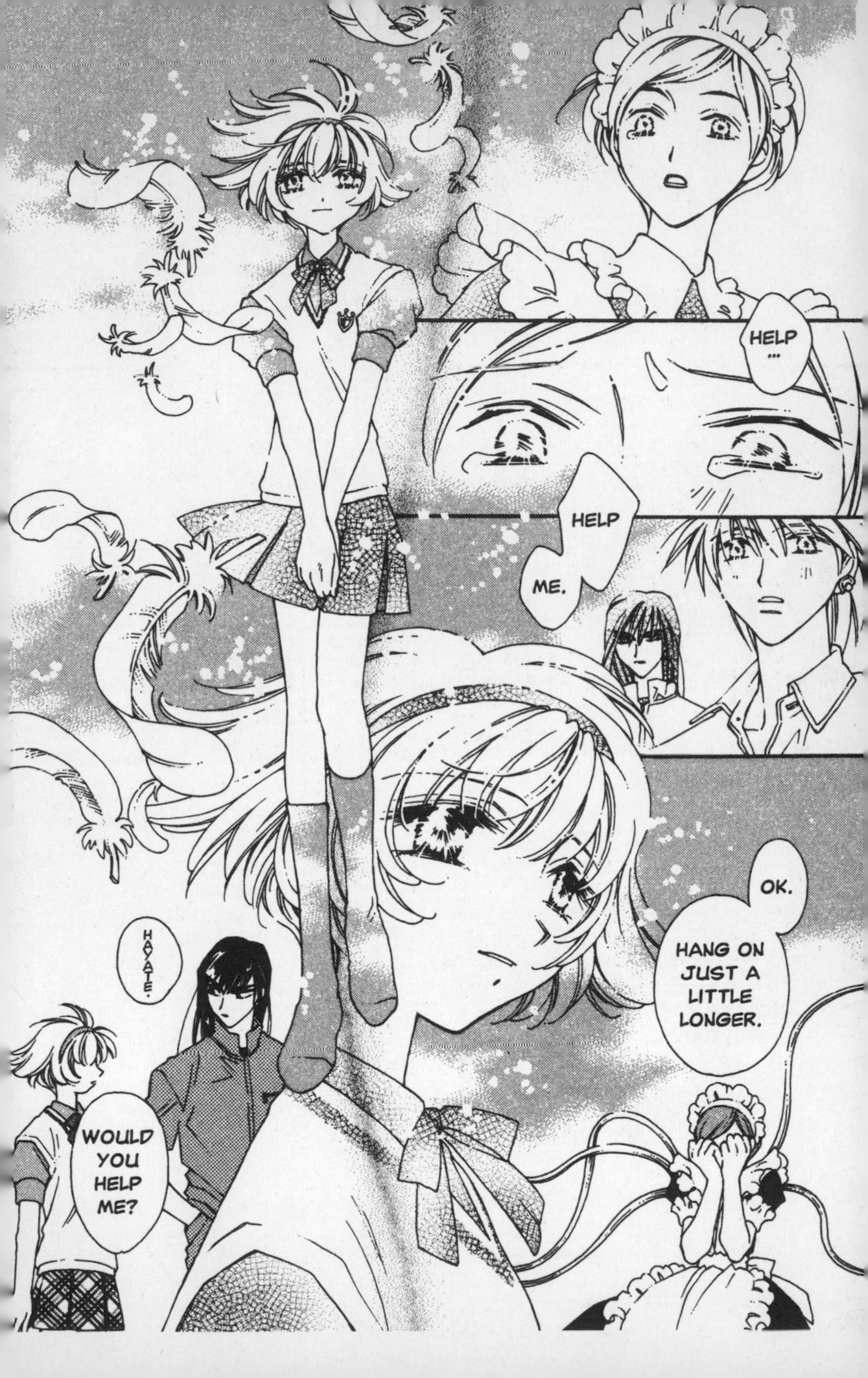
HELP ...
HELP
ME.
OK.
HANG ON JUST A LITTLE LONGER.
HAYATE.
WOULD YOU HELP ME?

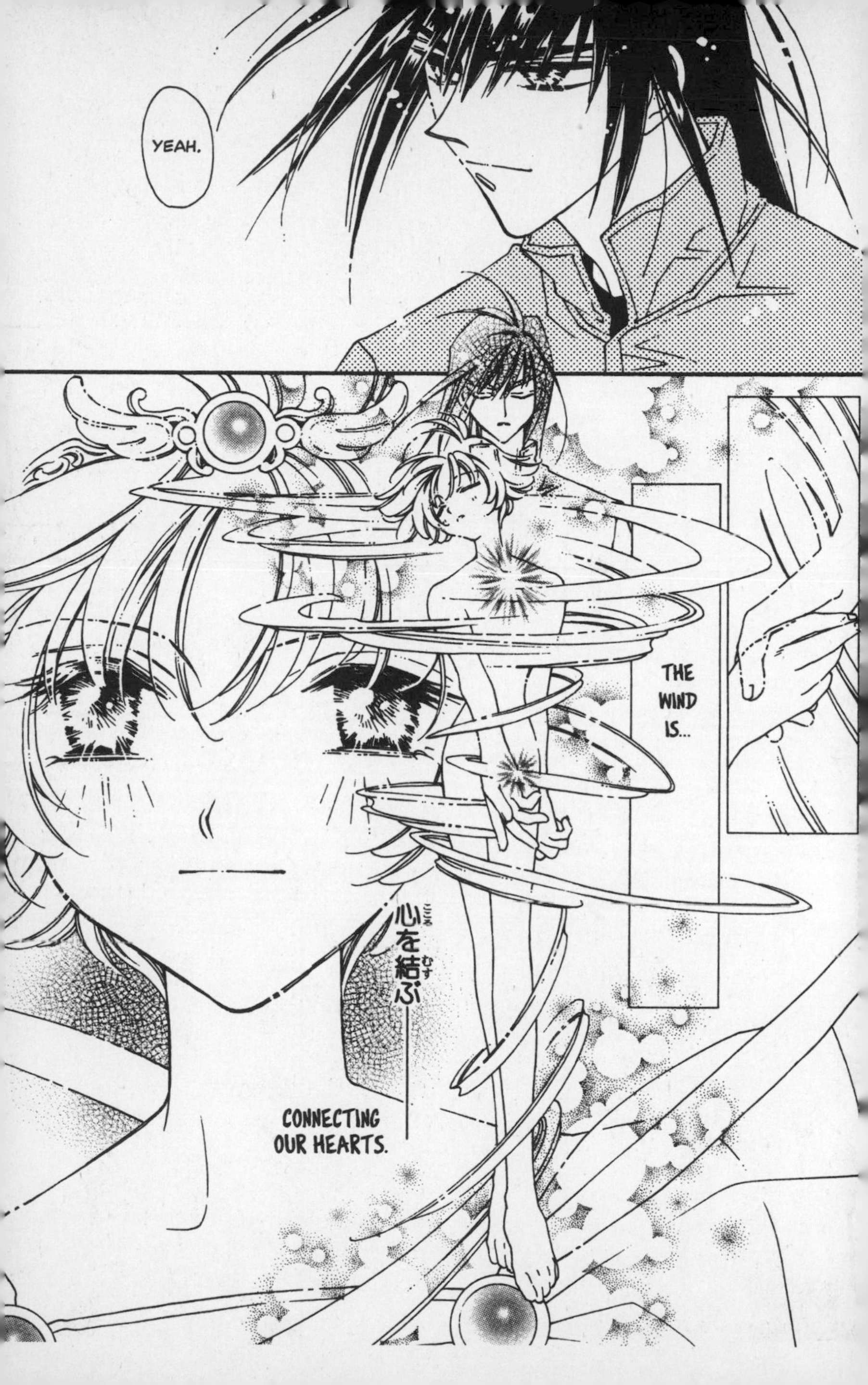
YEAH.
THE WIND IS...
心を結ぶ
CONNECTING OUR HEARTS.

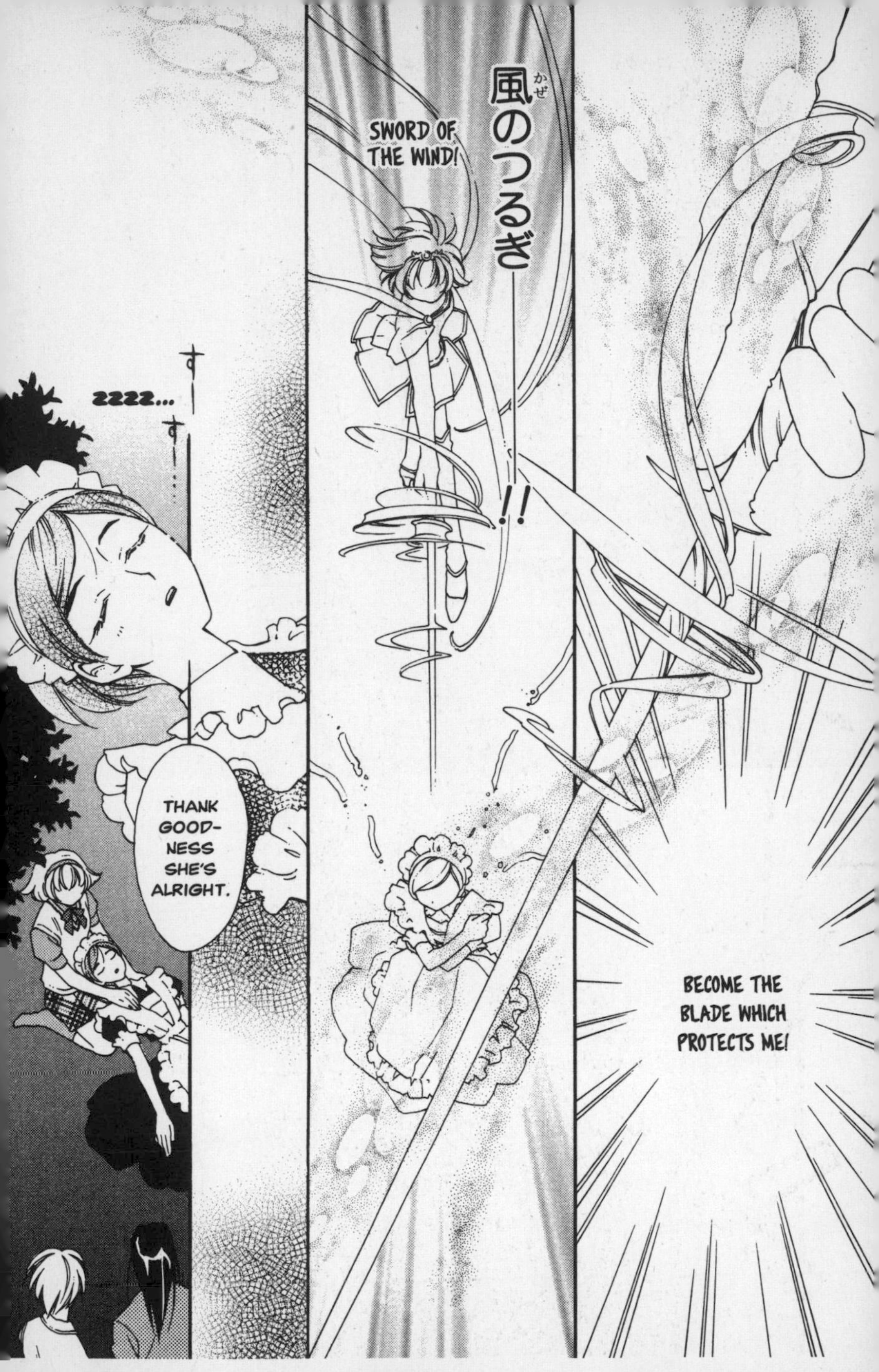
BECOME THE BLADE WHICH PROTECTS ME!
風のつるぎ──
SWORD OF THE WIND!
!!
すー すー…
ZZZZ...
THANK GOOD-NESS SHE'S ALRIGHT.

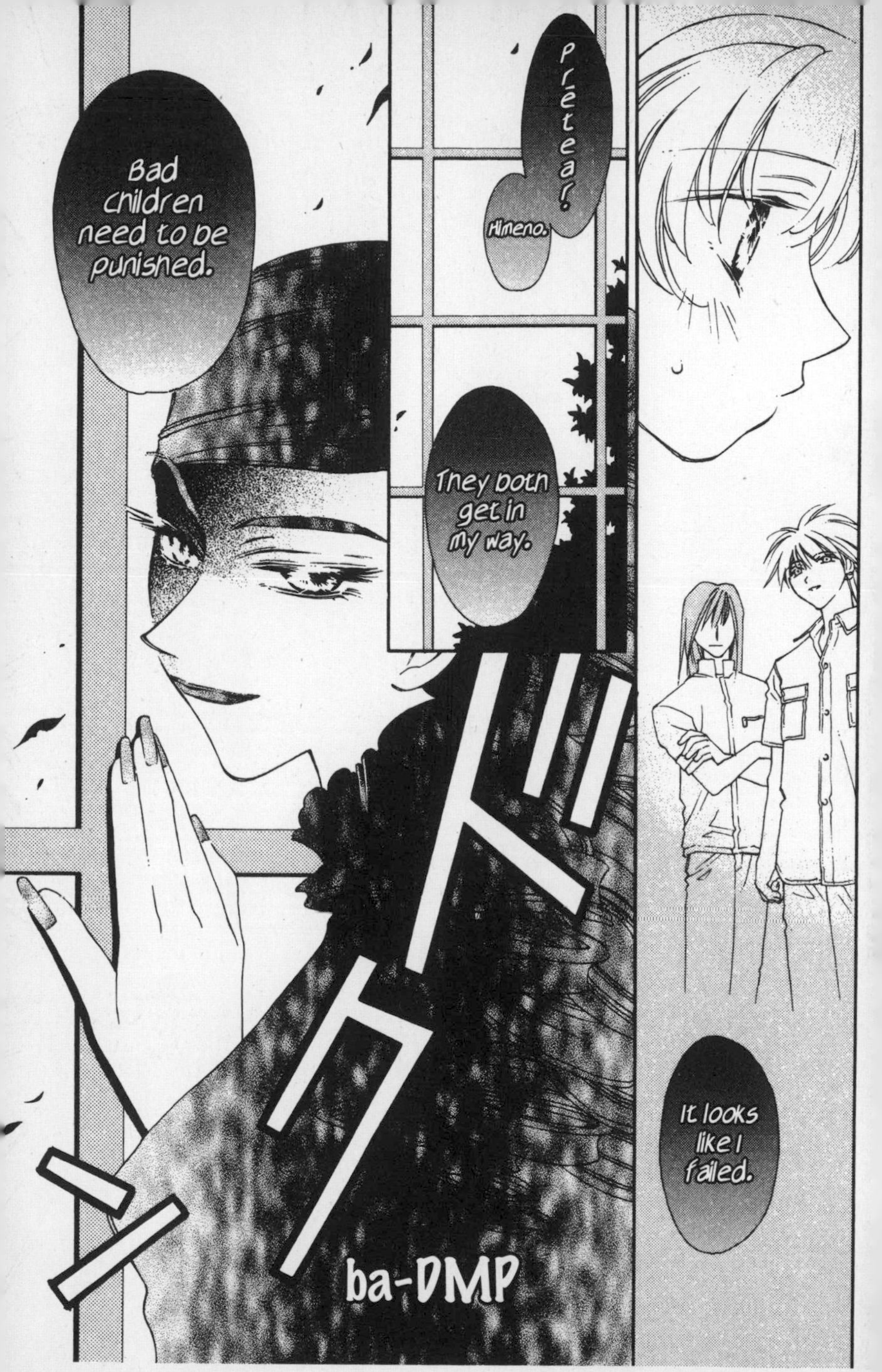
Pretear!
Himeno.
It looks like I failed.
They both get in my way.
Bad children need to be punished.
ba-DMP

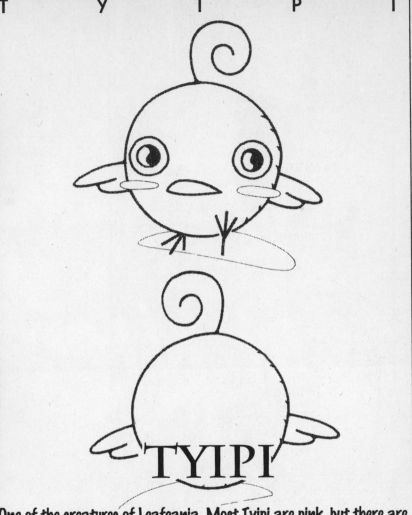

TYIPI

One of the creatures of Leafeania. Most Tyipi are pink, but there are many other color variations, like red, blue and yellow. The rainbow color, gold and white Tyipi are rare. They love black tea, and it has the same effect on them as catnip does on cats.

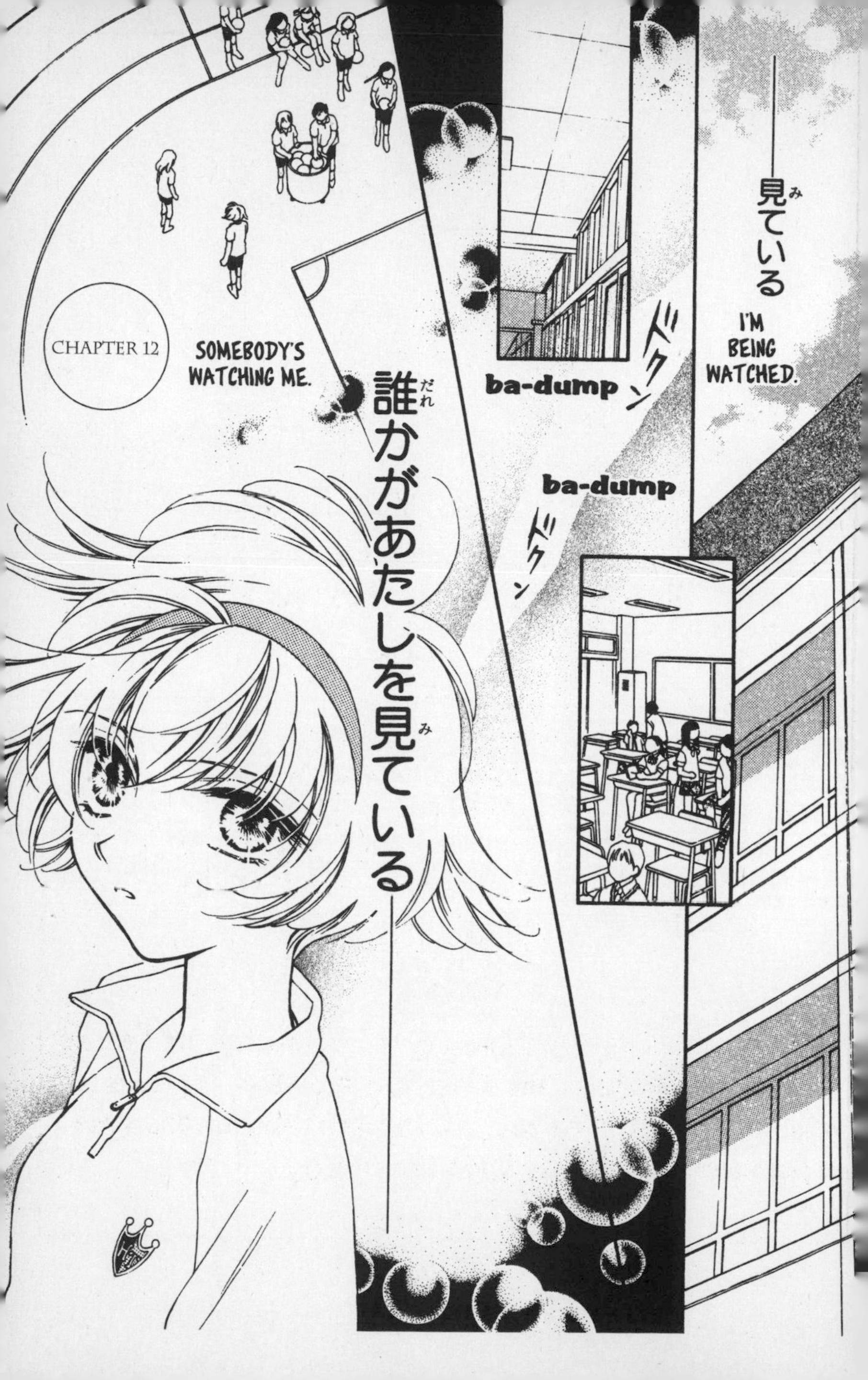
見ている
I'M BEING WATCHED.
ドクン
ba-dump
ドクン
ba-dump
誰かがあたしを見ている
SOMEBODY'S WATCHING ME.
CHAPTER 12

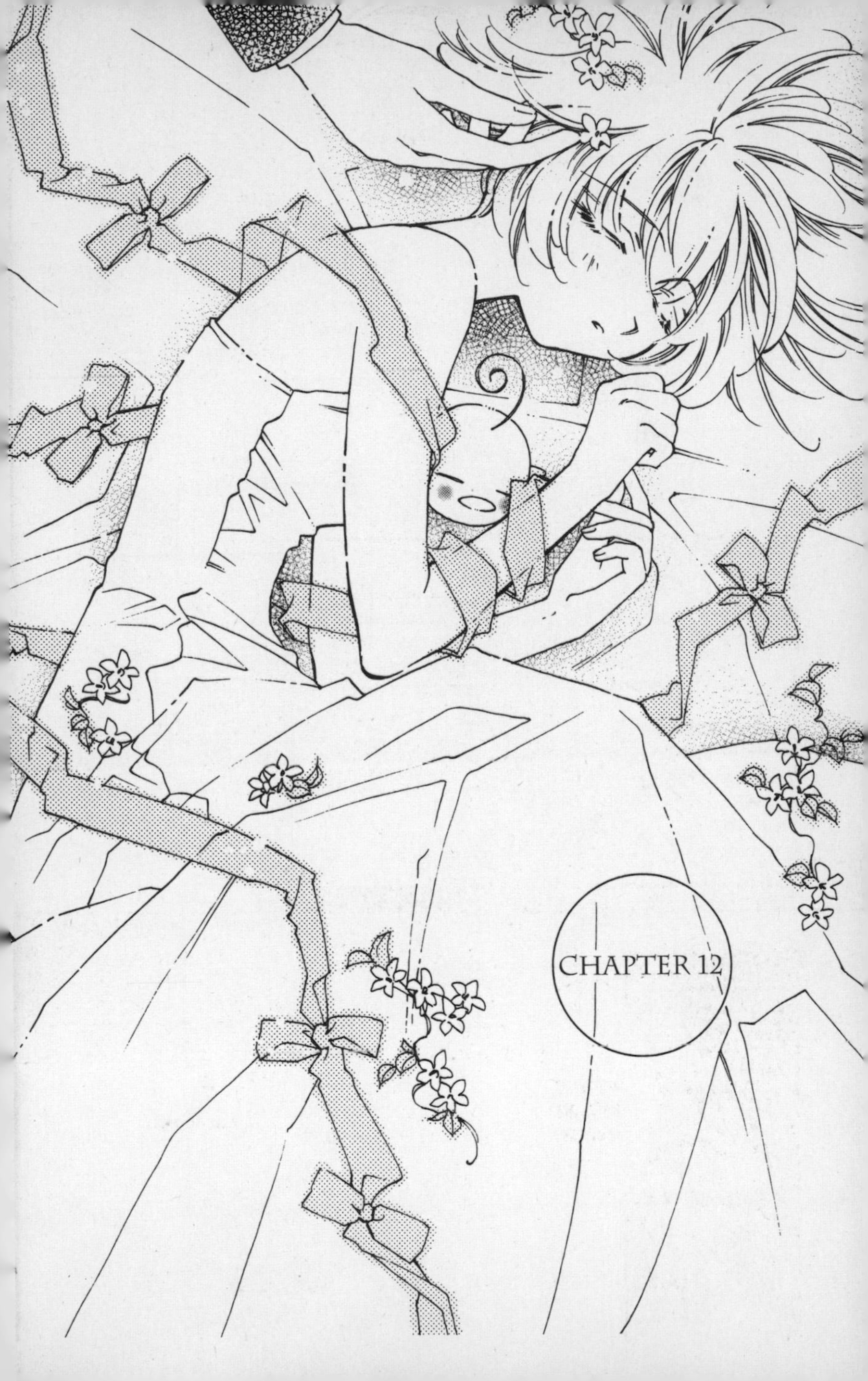
CHAPTER 12

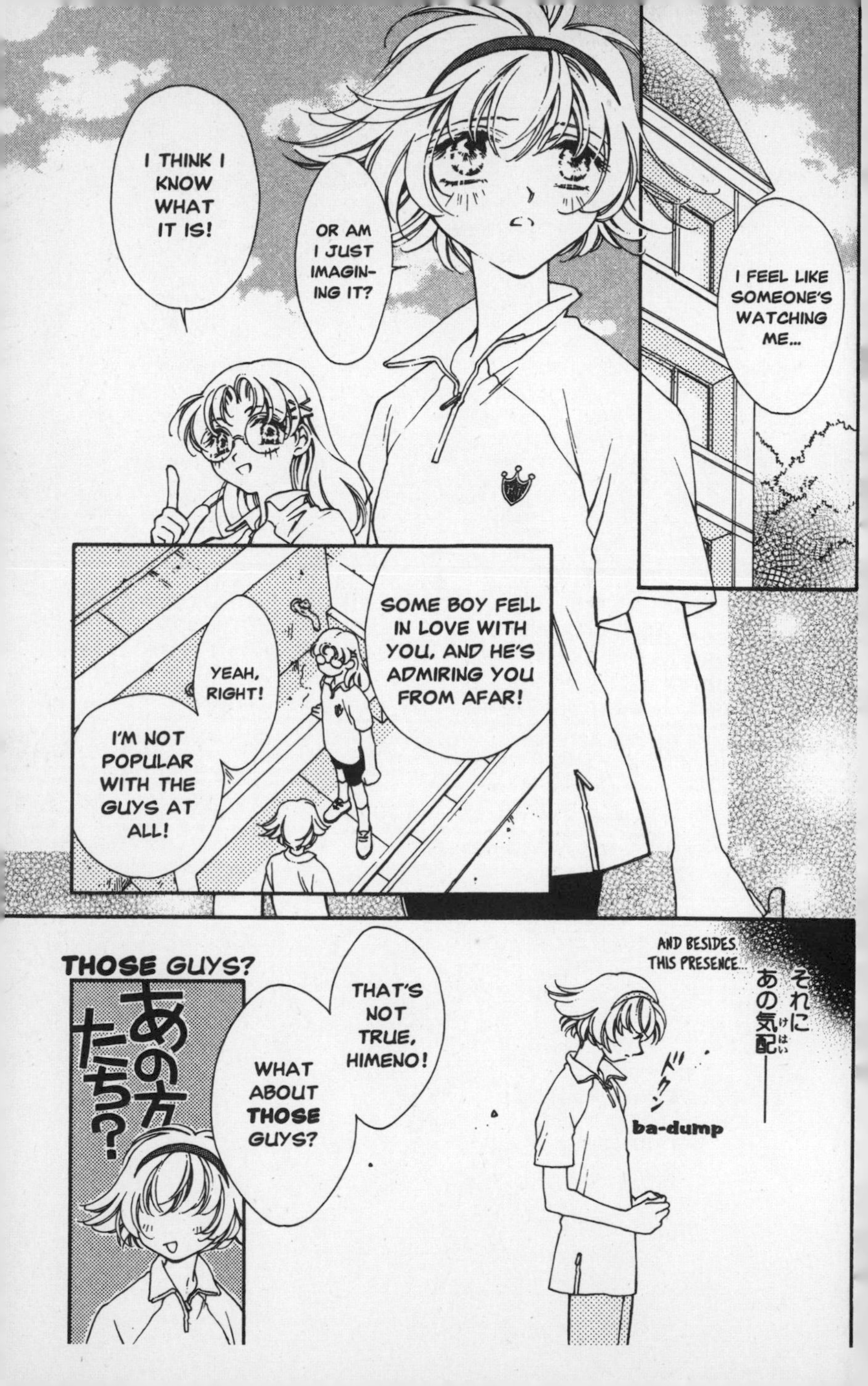

I FEEL LIKE SOMEONE'S WATCHING ME...
OR AM I JUST IMAGINING IT?
I THINK I KNOW WHAT IT IS!
SOME BOY FELL IN LOVE WITH YOU, AND HE'S ADMIRING YOU FROM AFAR!
YEAH, RIGHT!
I'M NOT POPULAR WITH THE GUYS AT ALL!
AND BESIDES, THIS PRESENCE...
それにあの気配——
ドクン
ba-dump
THAT'S NOT TRUE, HIMENO!
WHAT ABOUT THOSE GUYS?
THOSE GUYS?
あの方たち?

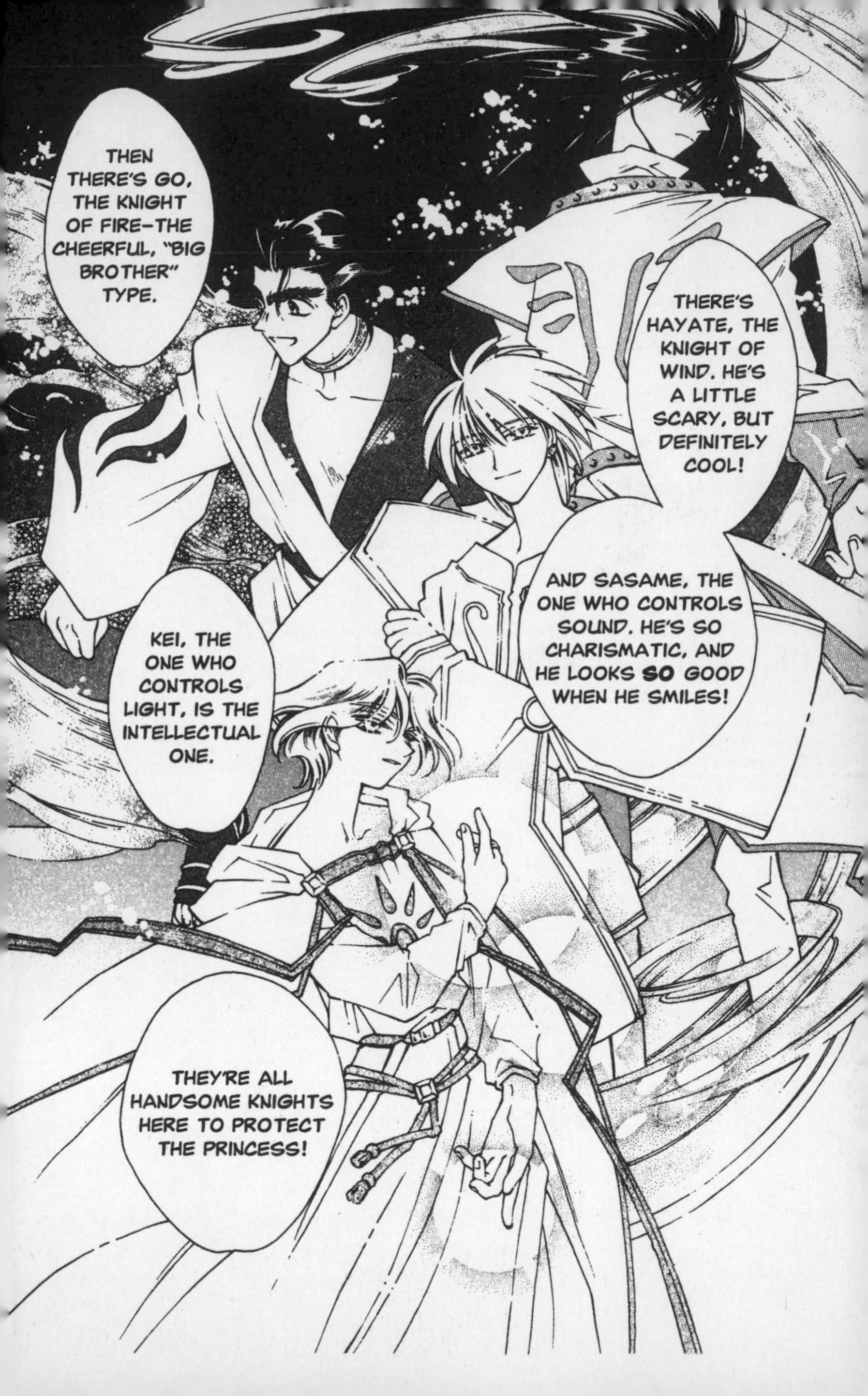
THERE'S HAYATE, THE KNIGHT OF WIND. HE'S A LITTLE SCARY, BUT DEFINITELY COOL!
THEN THERE'S GO, THE KNIGHT OF FIRE–THE CHEERFUL, "BIG BROTHER" TYPE.
AND SASAME, THE ONE WHO CONTROLS SOUND. HE'S SO CHARISMATIC, AND HE LOOKS **SO** GOOD WHEN HE SMILES!
KEI, THE ONE WHO CONTROLS LIGHT, IS THE INTELLECTUAL ONE.
THEY'RE ALL HANDSOME KNIGHTS HERE TO PROTECT THE PRINCESS!

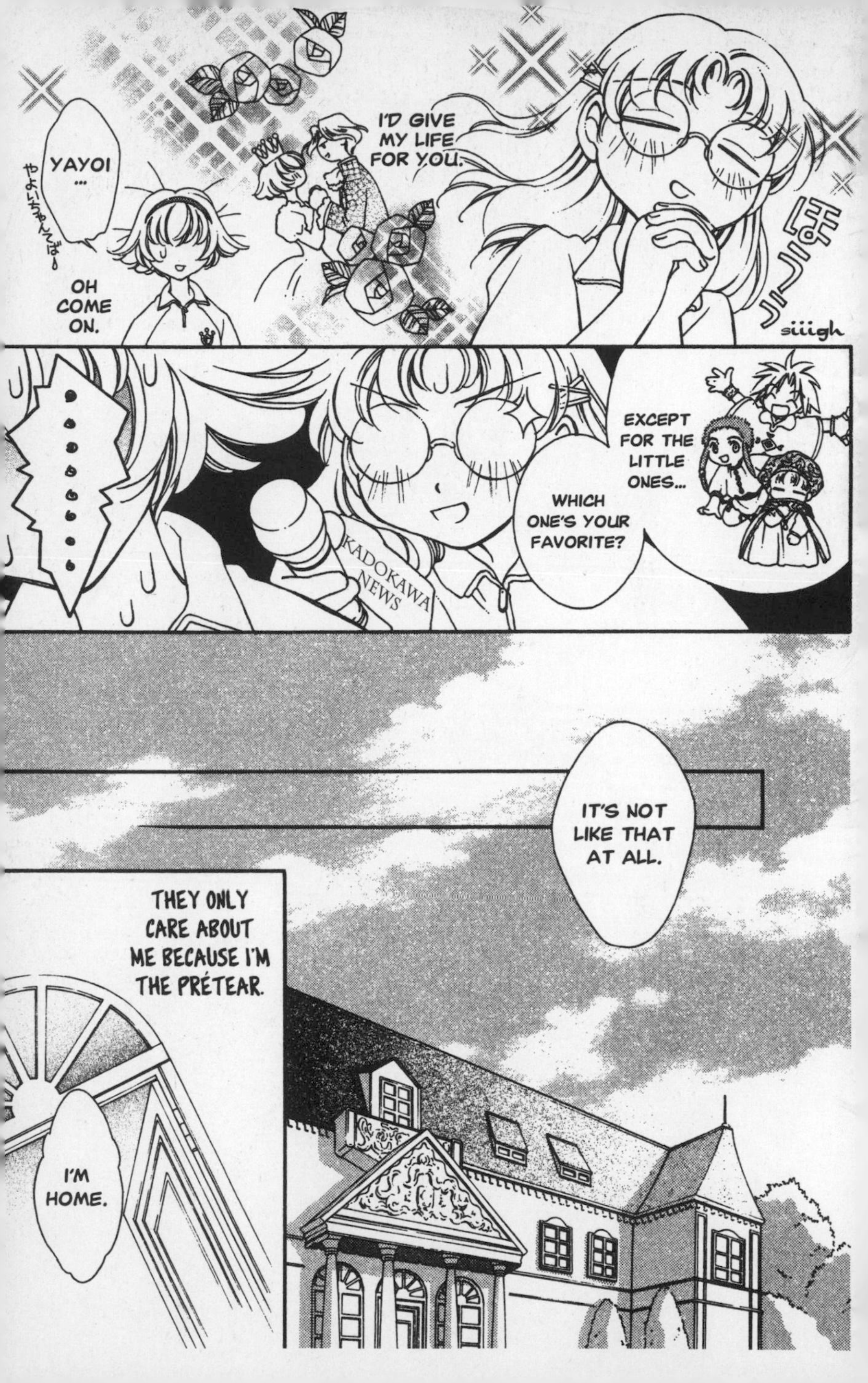
I'D GIVE MY LIFE FOR YOU.
siiigh
YAYOI...
やよいちゃんてば♪
OH COME ON.
EXCEPT FOR THE LITTLE ONES...
WHICH ONE'S YOUR FAVORITE?
KADOKAWA NEWS
....
IT'S NOT LIKE THAT AT ALL.
THEY ONLY CARE ABOUT ME BECAUSE I'M THE PRÉTEAR.
I'M HOME.

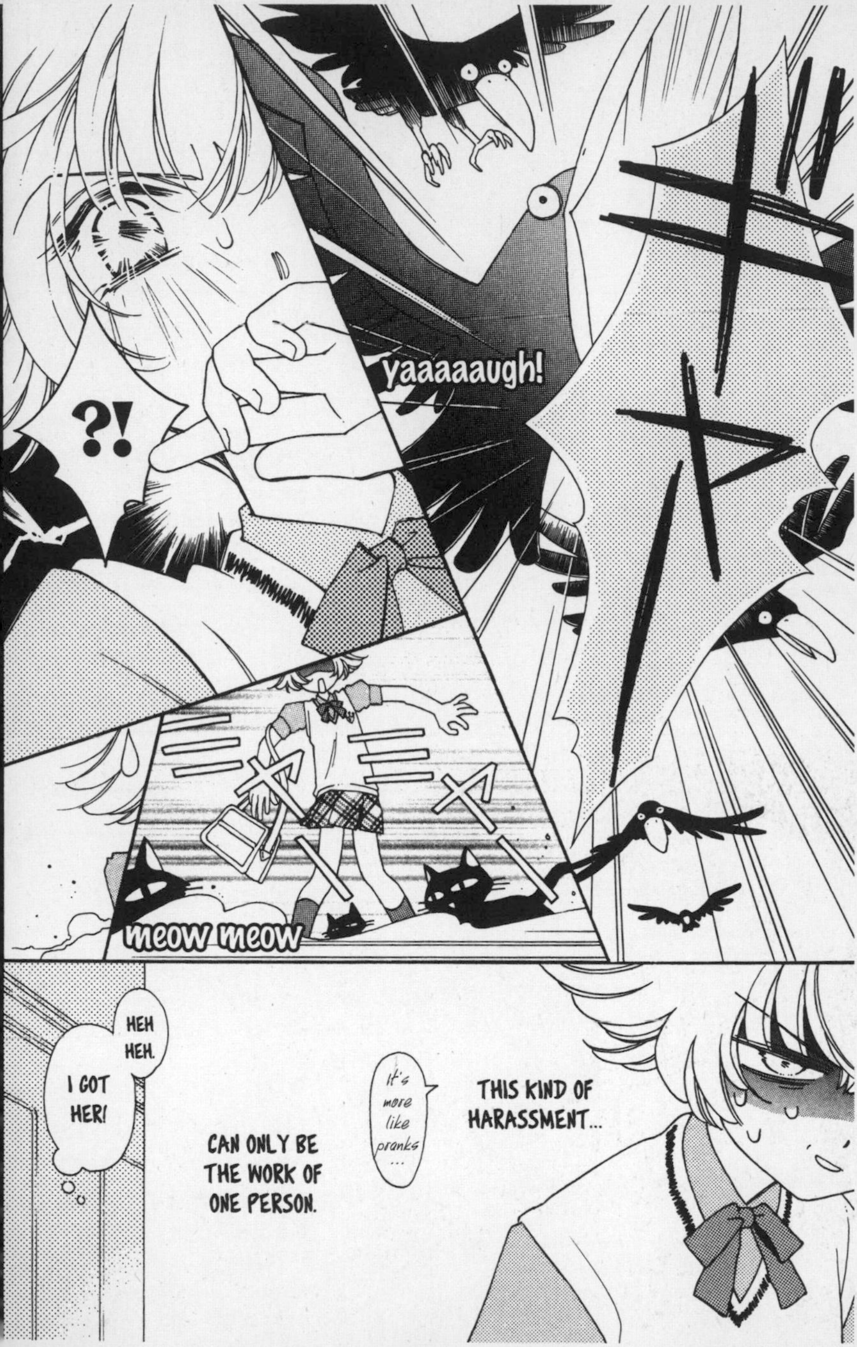
?!
yaaaaaugh!
meow meow
HEH HEH.
I GOT HER!
THIS KIND OF HARASSMENT...
It's more like pranks...
CAN ONLY BE THE WORK OF ONE PERSON.

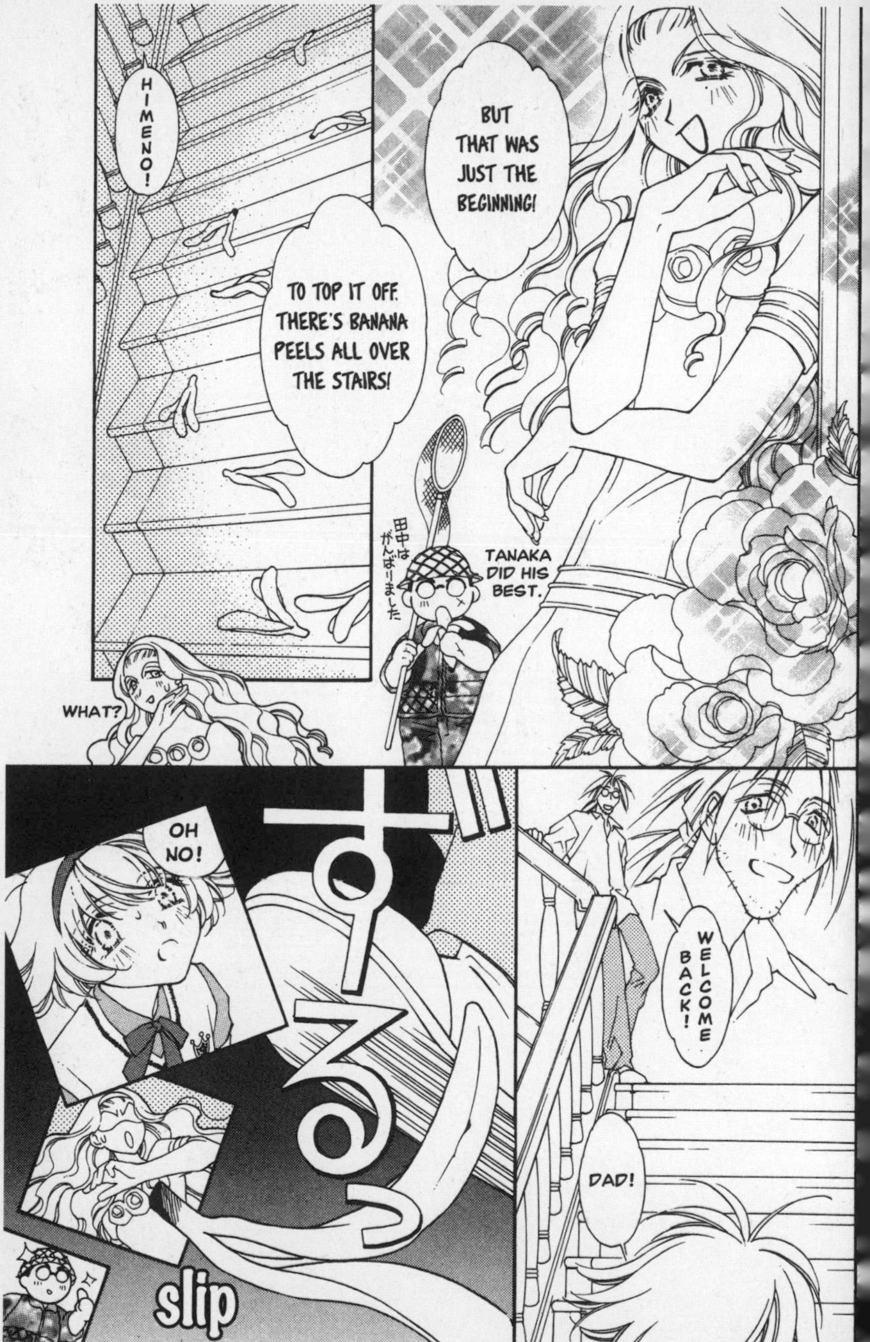
BUT THAT WAS JUST THE BEGINNING!
TO TOP IT OFF. THERE'S BANANA PEELS ALL OVER THE STAIRS!
HIMENO!
田中はがんばりました
TANAKA DID HIS BEST.
WHAT?
WELCOME BACK!
DAD!
OH NO!
するっ
slip

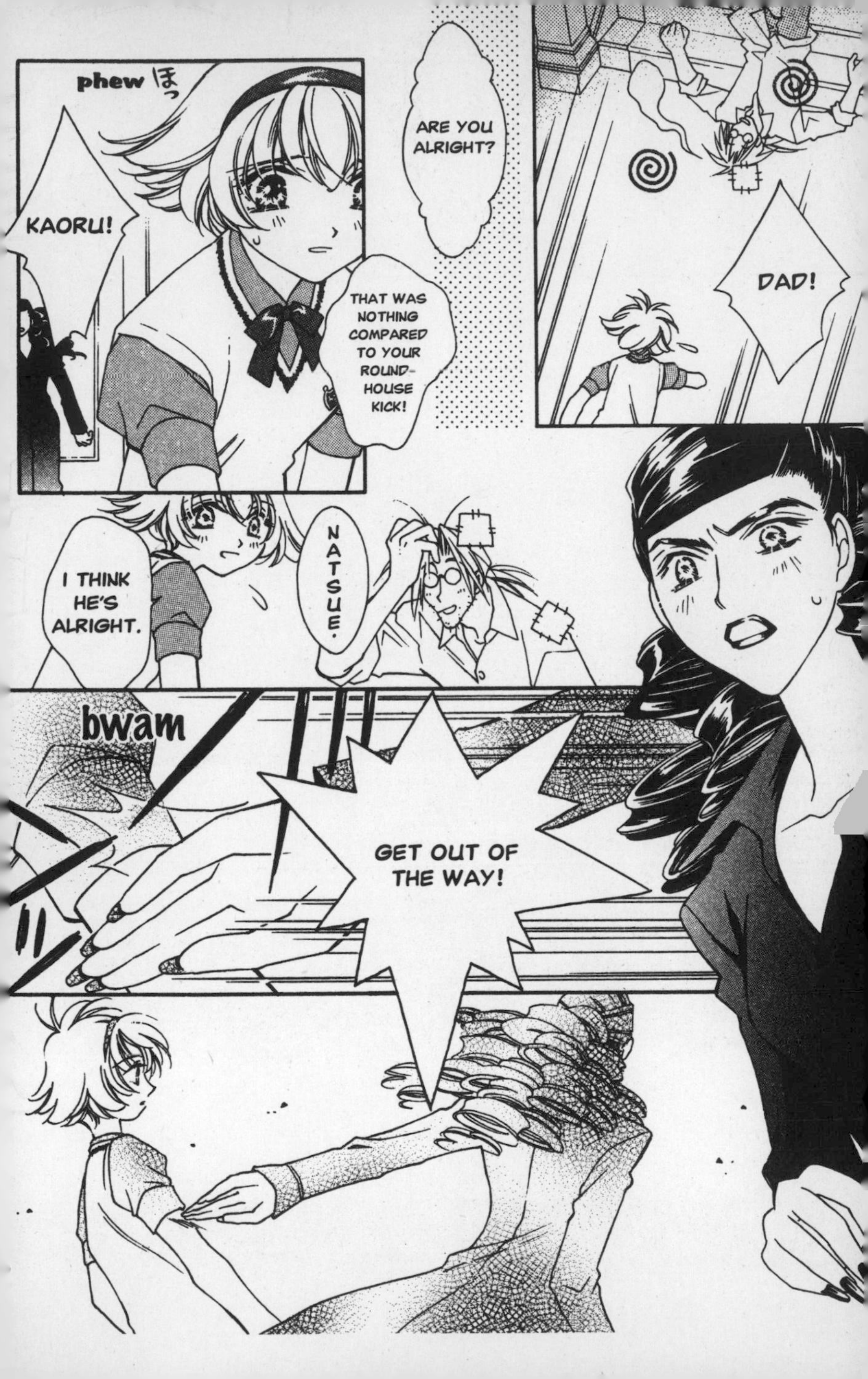
DAD!
ARE YOU ALRIGHT?
THAT WAS NOTHING COMPARED TO YOUR ROUND-HOUSE KICK!
phew ほっ
KAORU!
NATSUE.
I THINK HE'S ALRIGHT.
bwam
GET OUT OF THE WAY!

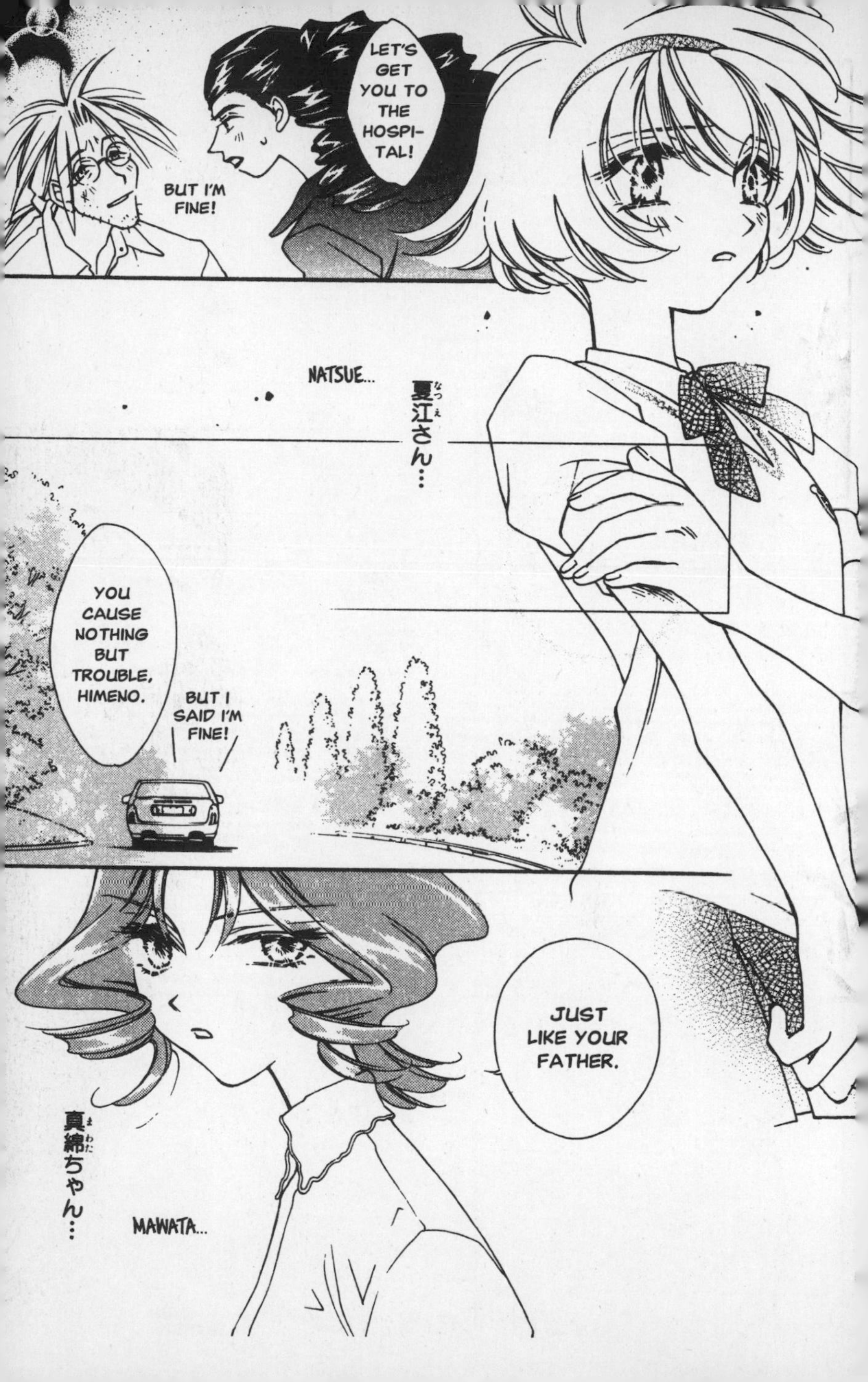
LET'S GET YOU TO THE HOSPI-TAL!
BUT I'M FINE!
NATSUE...
夏江さん…
YOU CAUSE NOTHING BUT TROUBLE, HIMENO.
BUT I SAID I'M FINE!
JUST LIKE YOUR FATHER.
真綿ちゃん…
MAWATA...

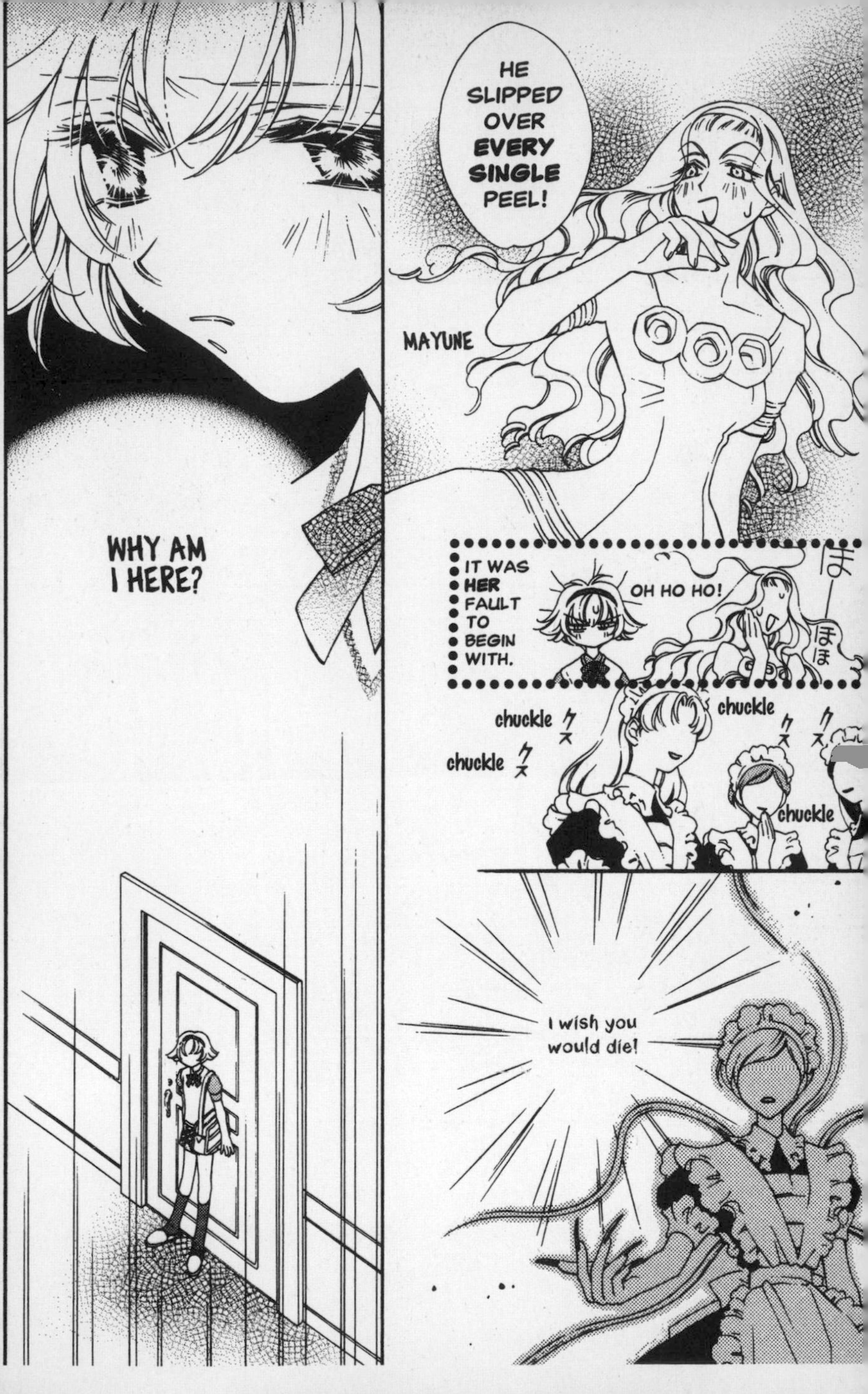
HE SLIPPED OVER EVERY SINGLE PEEL!
MAYUNE
IT WAS HER FAULT TO BEGIN WITH.
OH HO HO!
ほーほほ
chuckle クス
chuckle クス
chuckle クス
chuckle クス
I wish you would die!
WHY AM I HERE?

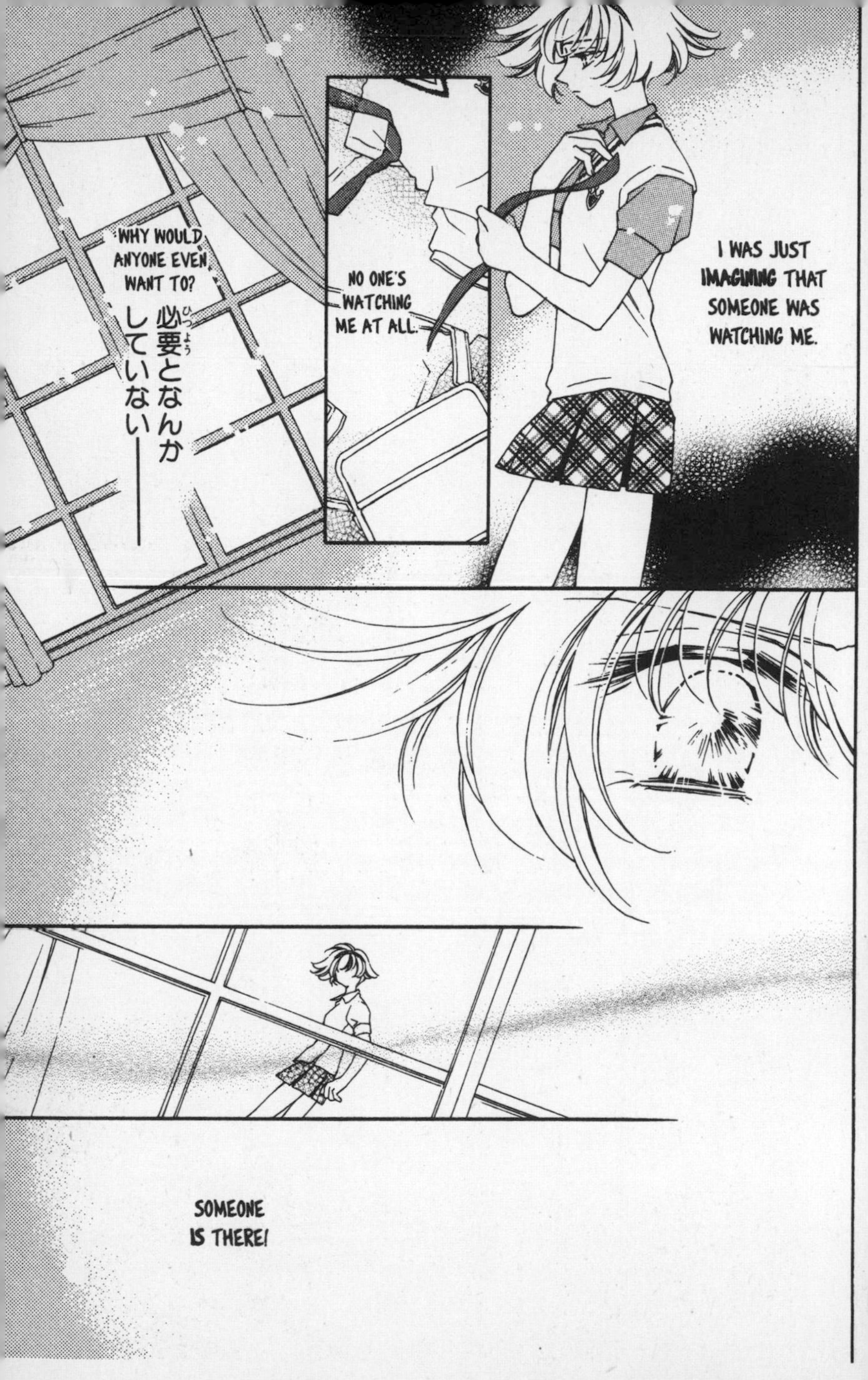
I WAS JUST IMAGINING THAT SOMEONE WAS WATCHING ME.
NO ONE'S WATCHING ME AT ALL.
WHY WOULD ANYONE EVEN WANT TO?
必要となんかしていない——
SOMEONE IS THERE!

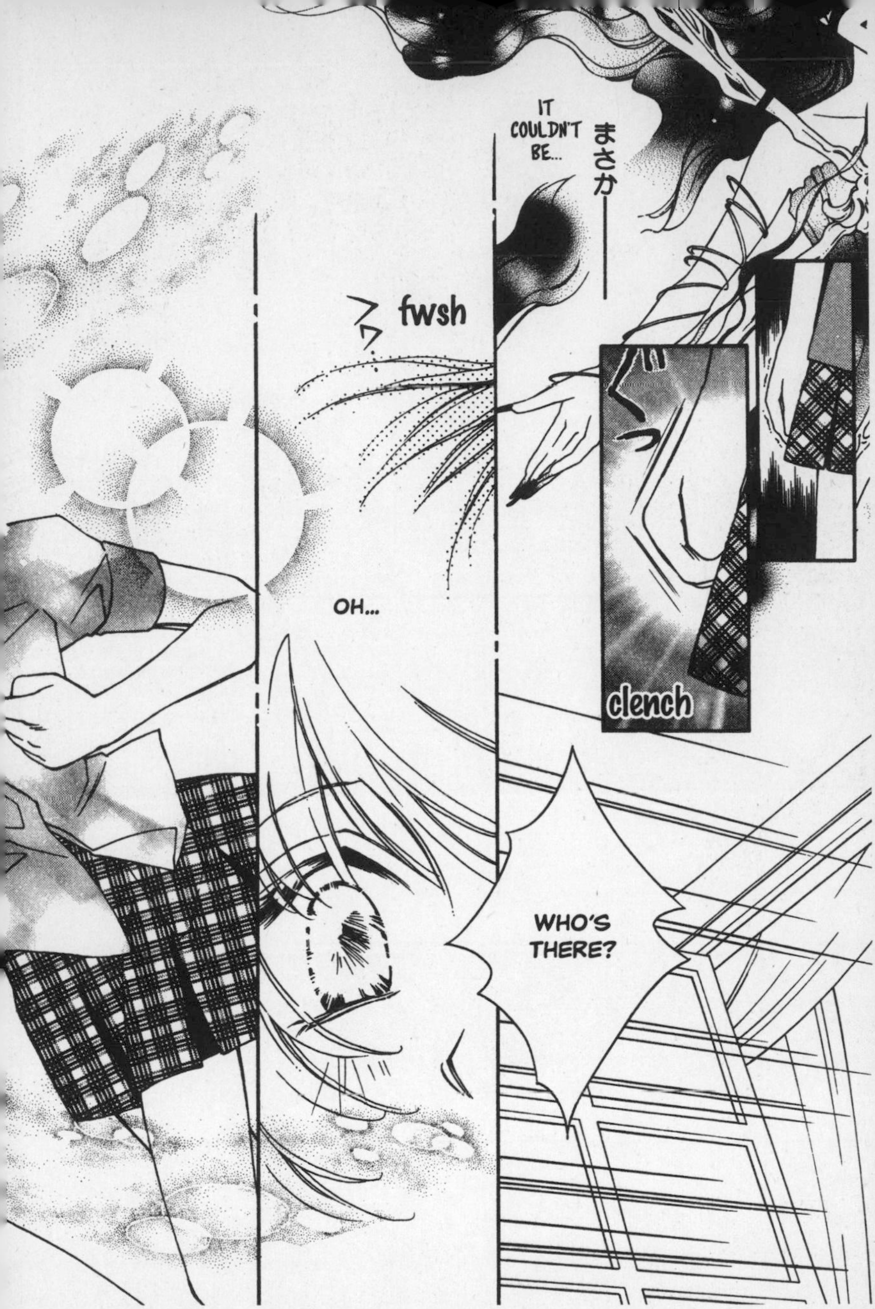
IT COULDN'T BE...
まさか——
clench
fwsh
OH...
WHO'S THERE?

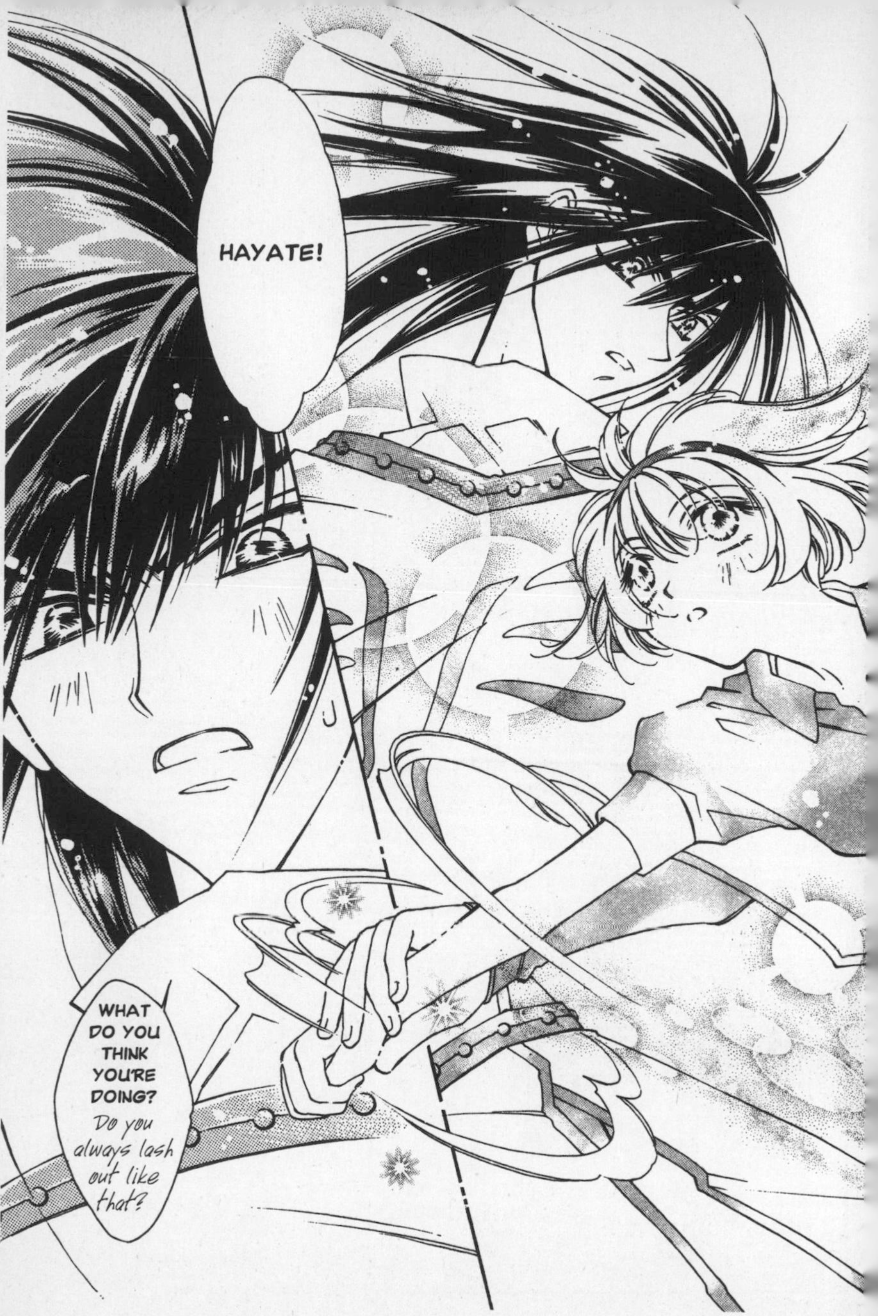
HAYATE!
WHAT DO YOU THINK YOU'RE DOING?
Do you always lash out like that?

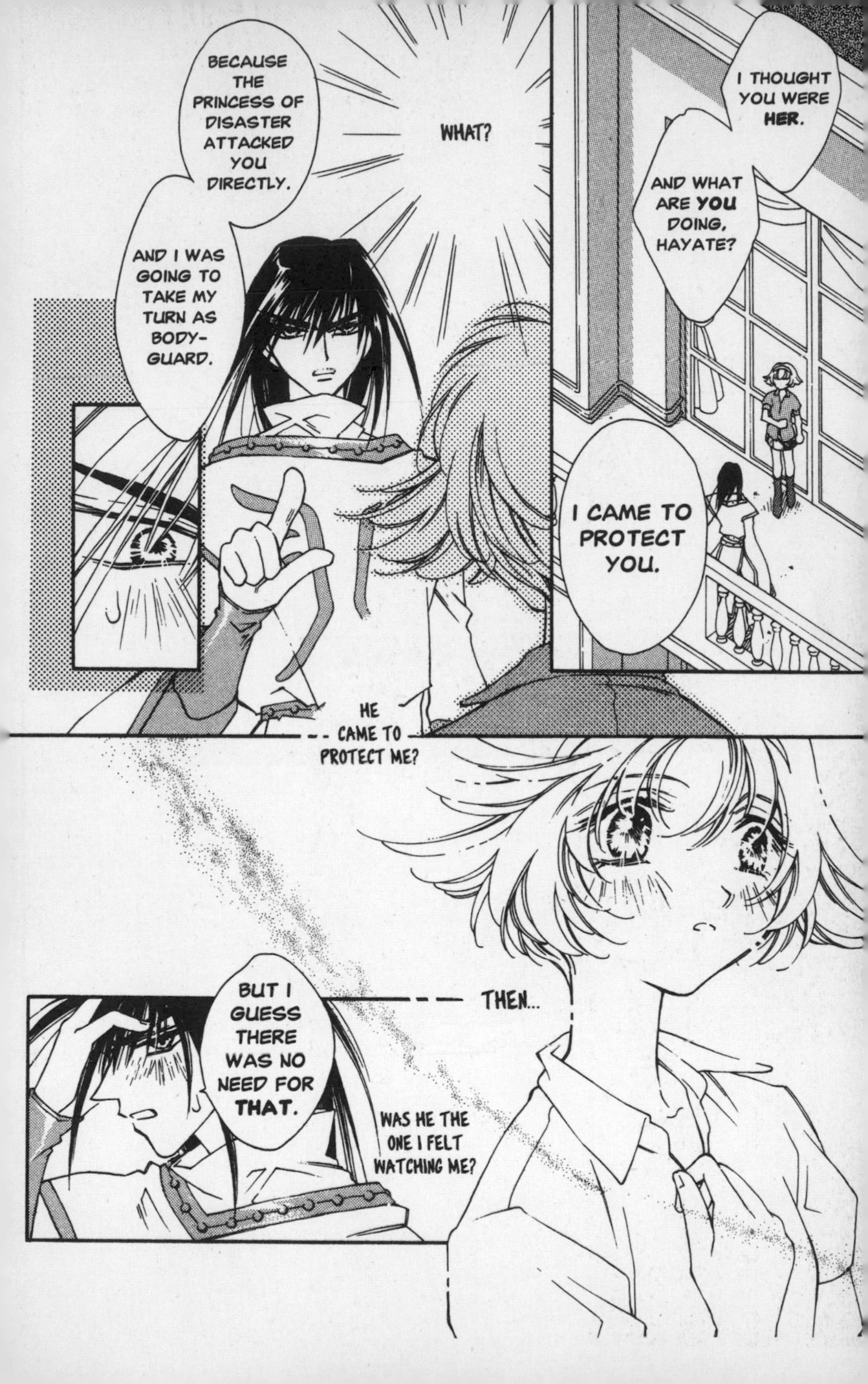

I THOUGHT YOU WERE HER.
AND WHAT ARE YOU DOING, HAYATE?
I CAME TO PROTECT YOU.
WHAT?
BECAUSE THE PRINCESS OF DISASTER ATTACKED YOU DIRECTLY.
AND I WAS GOING TO TAKE MY TURN AS BODY-GUARD.
HE CAME TO PROTECT ME?
BUT I GUESS THERE WAS NO NEED FOR THAT.
THEN...
WAS HE THE ONE I FELT WATCHING ME?

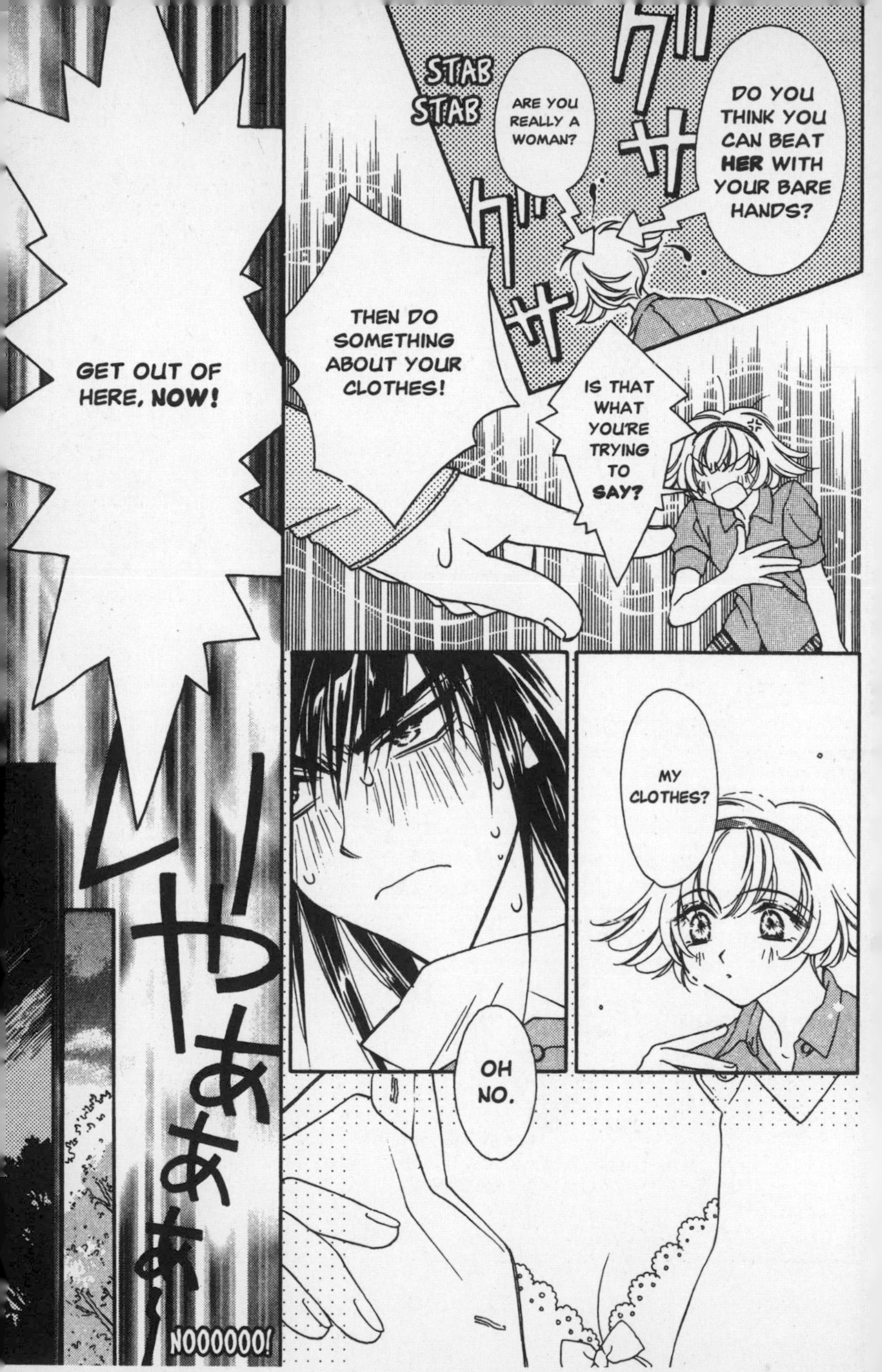
DO YOU THINK YOU CAN BEAT **HER** WITH YOUR BARE HANDS?
ARE YOU REALLY A WOMAN?
STAB STAB
IS THAT WHAT YOU'RE TRYING TO **SAY?**
THEN DO SOMETHING ABOUT YOUR CLOTHES!
MY CLOTHES?
OH NO.
GET OUT OF HERE, **NOW!**
NOOOOOO!

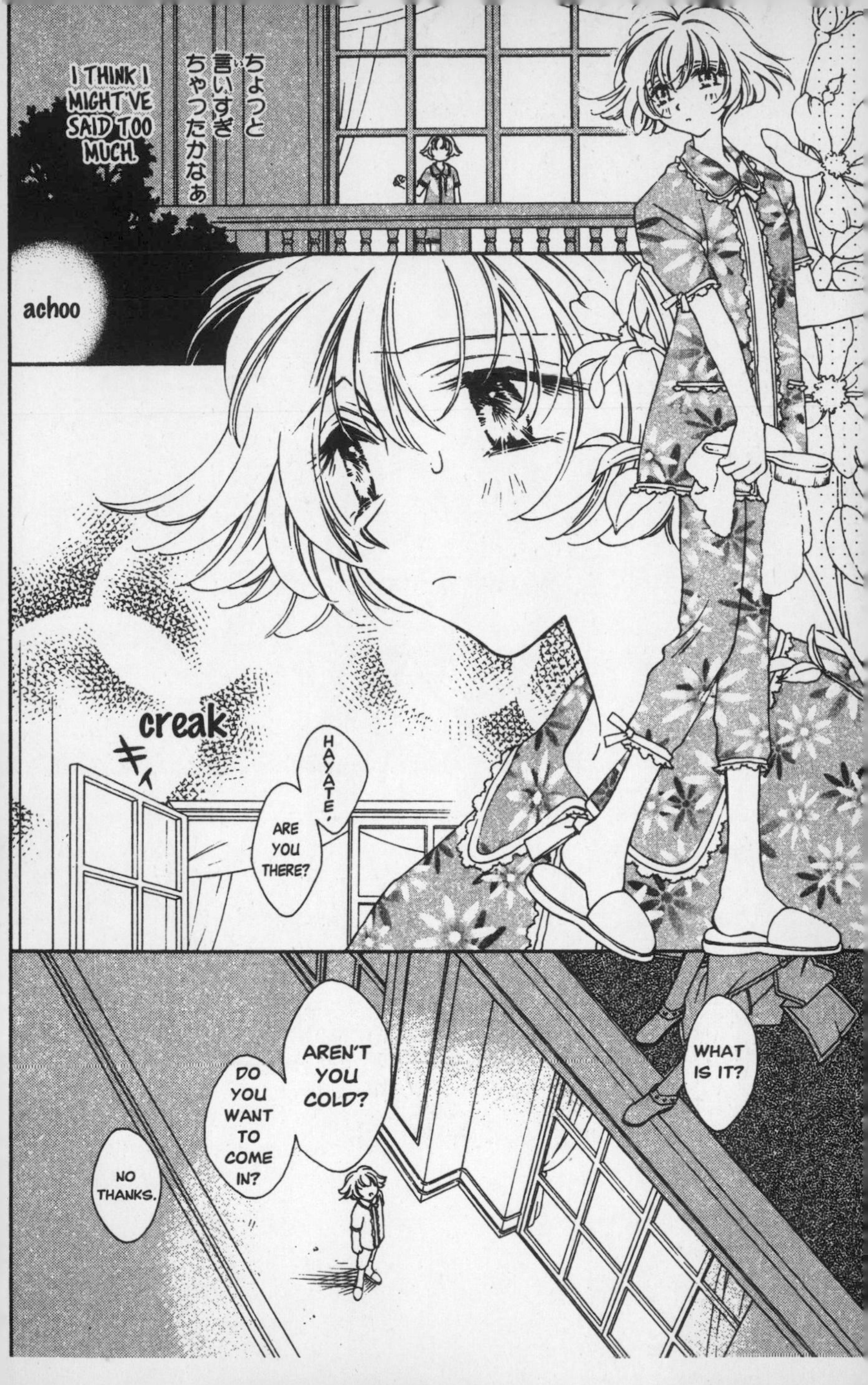
ちょっと言いすぎちゃったかなぁ
I THINK I MIGHT'VE SAID TOO MUCH.
achoo
creak
キィ
HAYATE, ARE YOU THERE?
WHAT IS IT?
AREN'T YOU COLD?
DO YOU WANT TO COME IN?
NO THANKS.

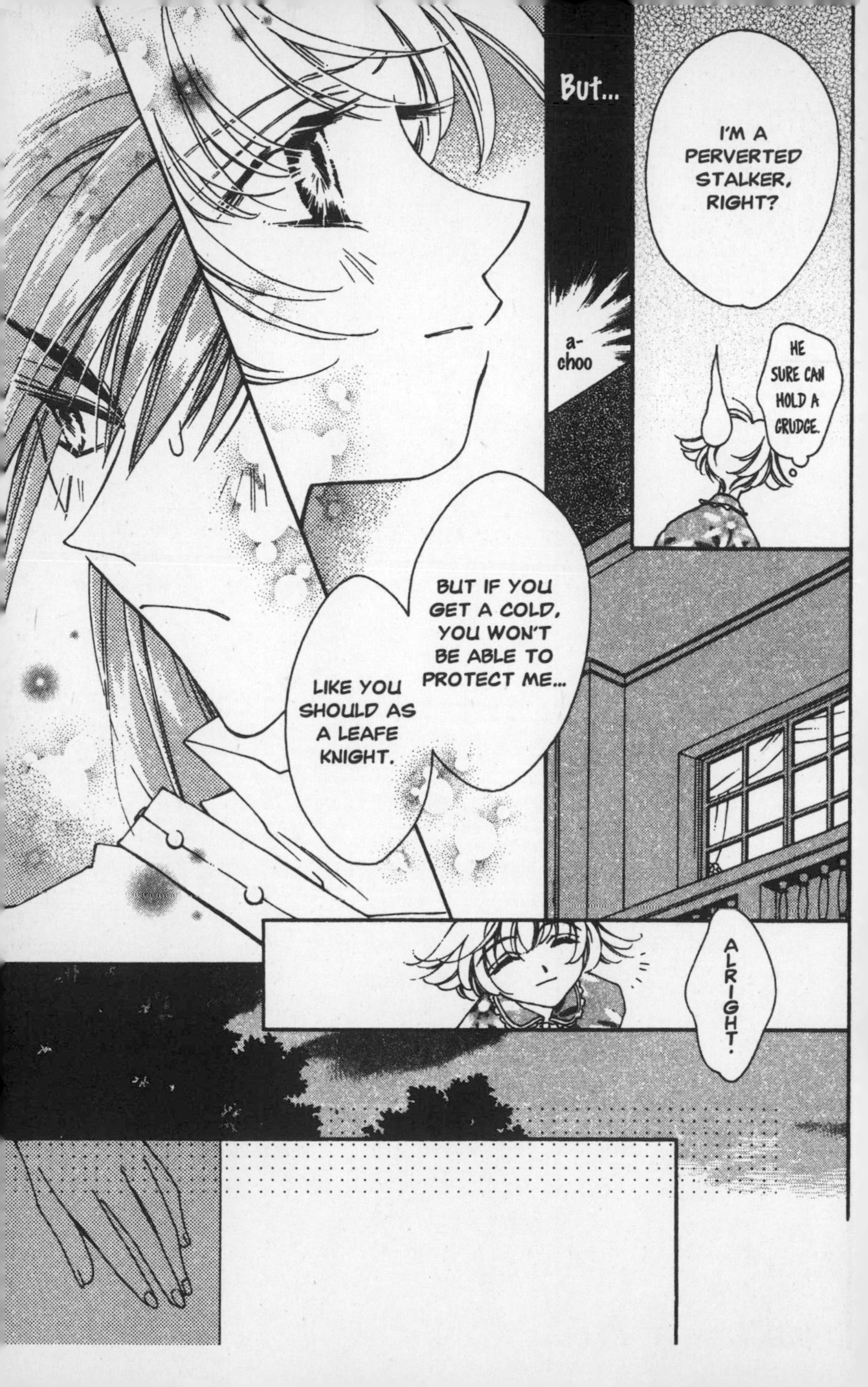
I'M A PERVERTED STALKER, RIGHT?
But...
a-choo
HE SURE CAN HOLD A GRUDGE.
BUT IF YOU GET A COLD, YOU WON'T BE ABLE TO PROTECT ME...
LIKE YOU SHOULD AS A LEAFE KNIGHT.
ALRIGHT.

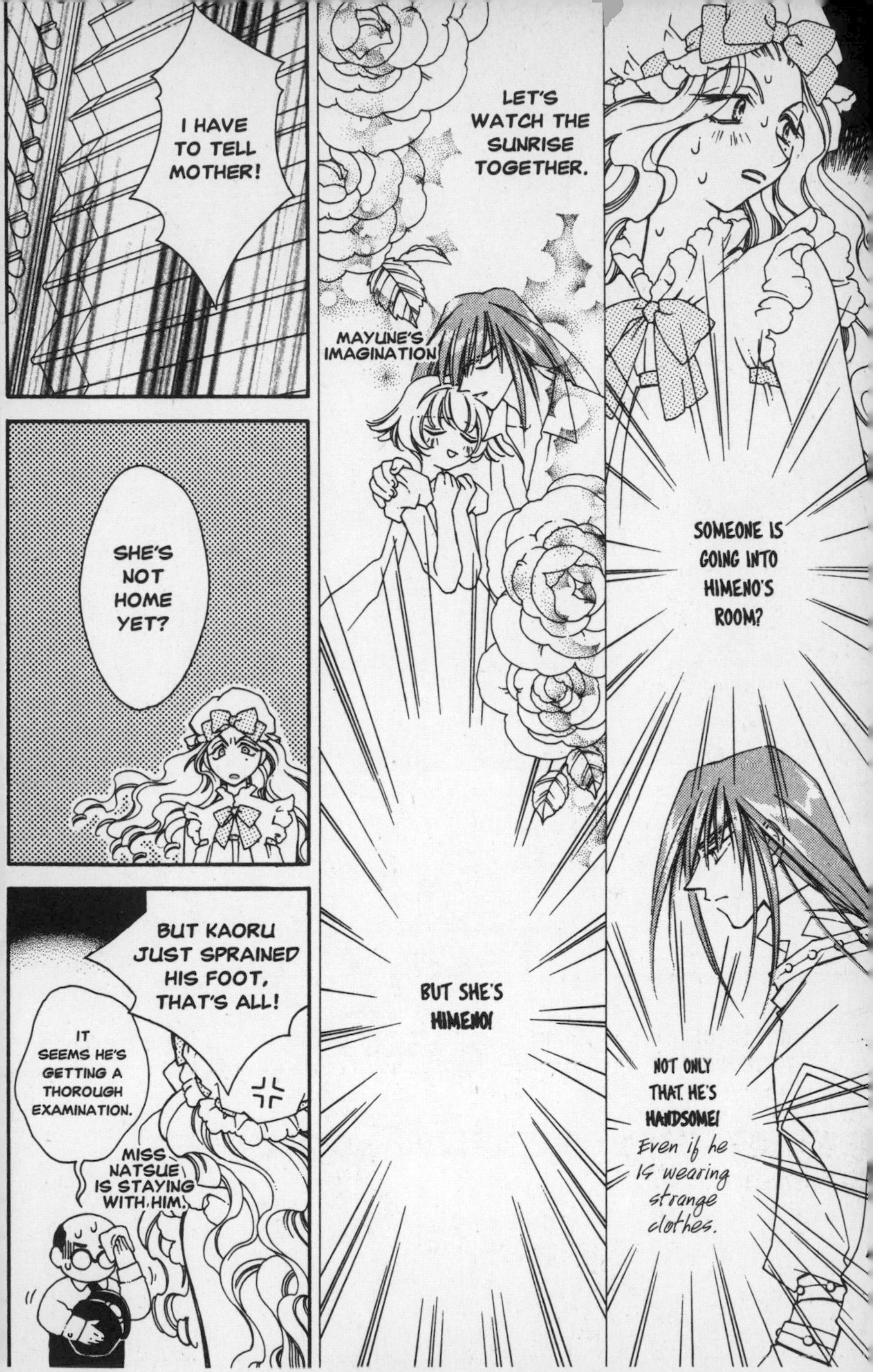
I HAVE TO TELL MOTHER!
SHE'S NOT HOME YET?
BUT KAORU JUST SPRAINED HIS FOOT, THAT'S ALL!
IT SEEMS HE'S GETTING A THOROUGH EXAMINATION.
MISS NATSUE IS STAYING WITH HIM.
LET'S WATCH THE SUNRISE TOGETHER.
MAYUNE'S IMAGINATION
BUT SHE'S HIMENO!
SOMEONE IS GOING INTO HIMENO'S ROOM?
NOT ONLY THAT. HE'S HANDSOME!
Even if he IS wearing strange clothes.

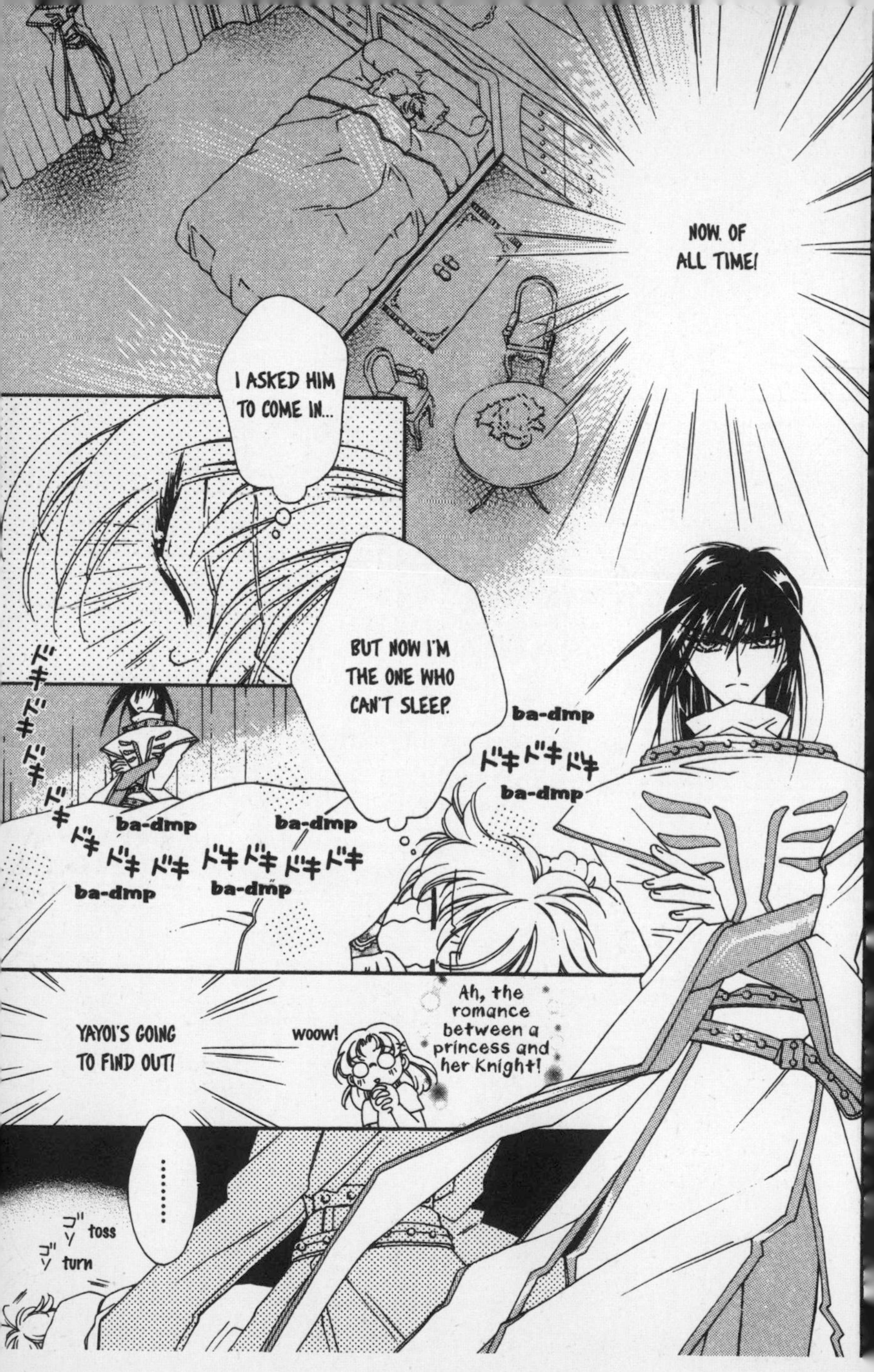
NOW, OF ALL TIME!
I ASKED HIM TO COME IN...
BUT NOW I'M THE ONE WHO CAN'T SLEEP.
ドキドキドキ
ba-dmp
ba-dmp
ドキドキドキドキ
ba-dmp
ドキドキドキドキドキドキ
ba-dmp
ba-dmp
ba-dmp
YAYOI'S GOING TO FIND OUT!
woow!
Ah, the romance between a princess and her knight!
......
ゴソ toss
ゴソ turn

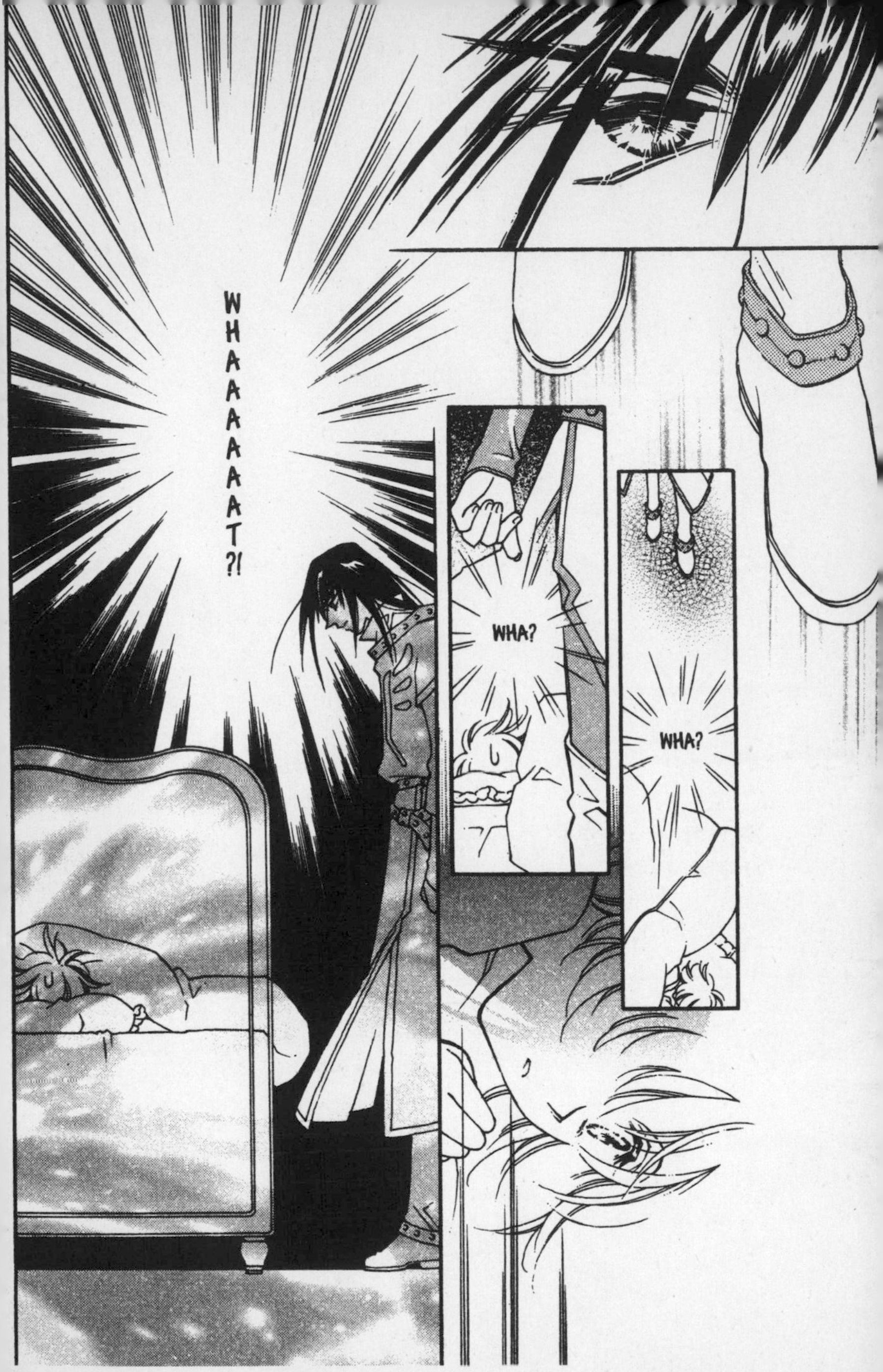
WHAAAAAAAAT?!
WHA?
WHA?

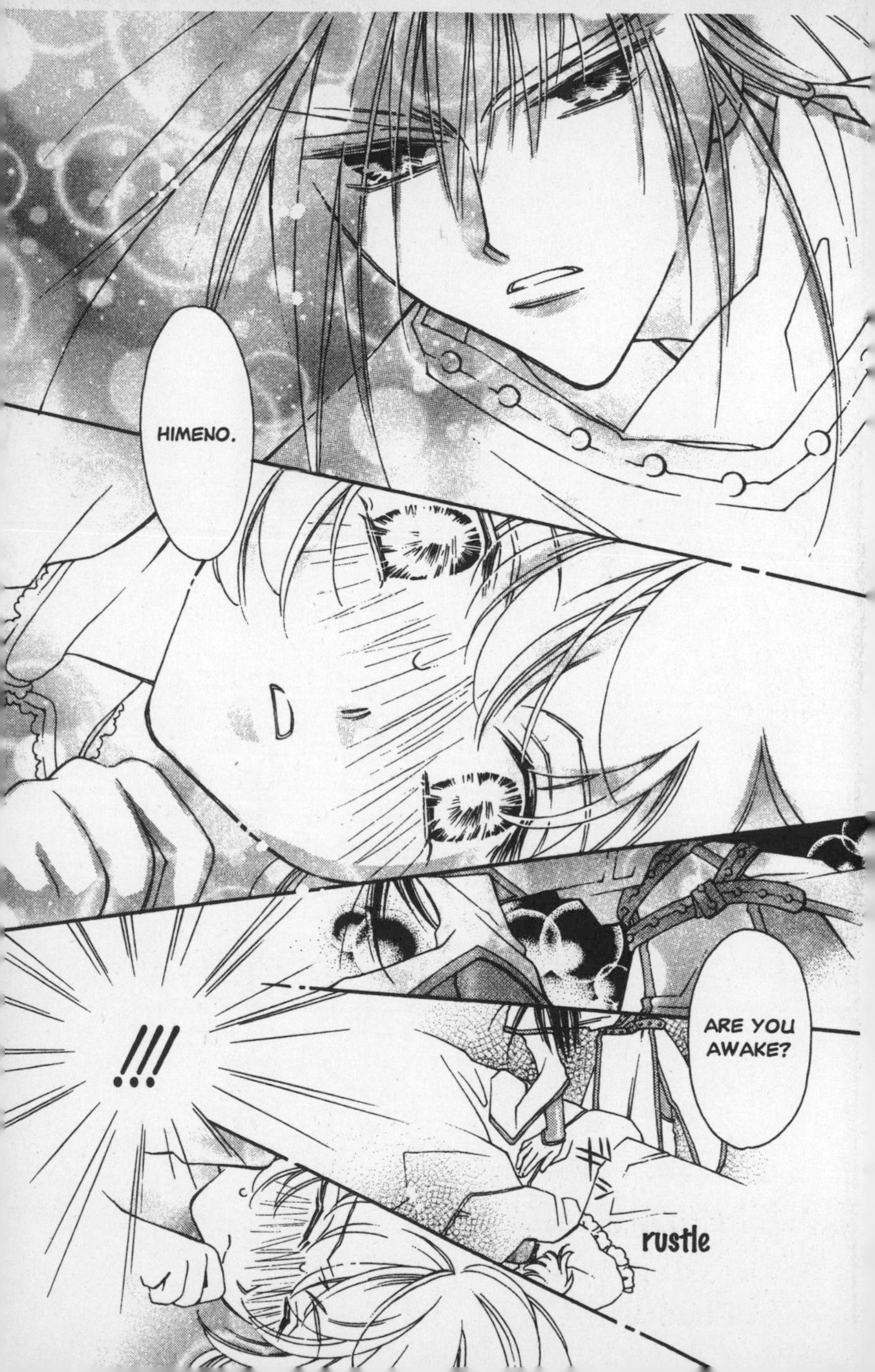
HIMENO.
ARE YOU AWAKE?
!!!
rustle

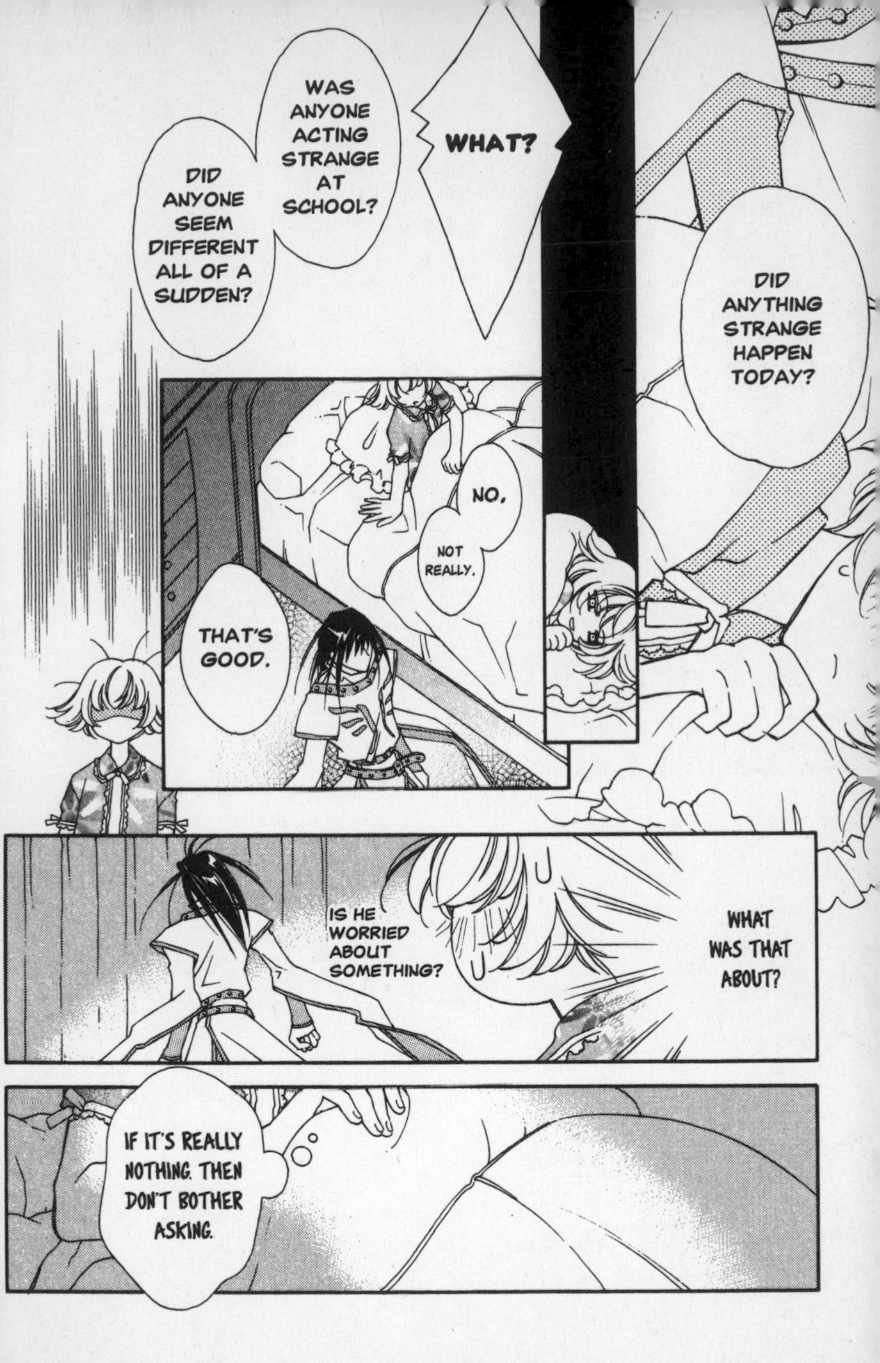
DID ANYTHING STRANGE HAPPEN TODAY?
WHAT?
WAS ANYONE ACTING STRANGE AT SCHOOL?
DID ANYONE SEEM DIFFERENT ALL OF A SUDDEN?
NO,
NOT REALLY.
THAT'S GOOD.
WHAT WAS THAT ABOUT?
IS HE WORRIED ABOUT SOMETHING?
IF IT'S REALLY NOTHING, THEN DON'T BOTHER ASKING.

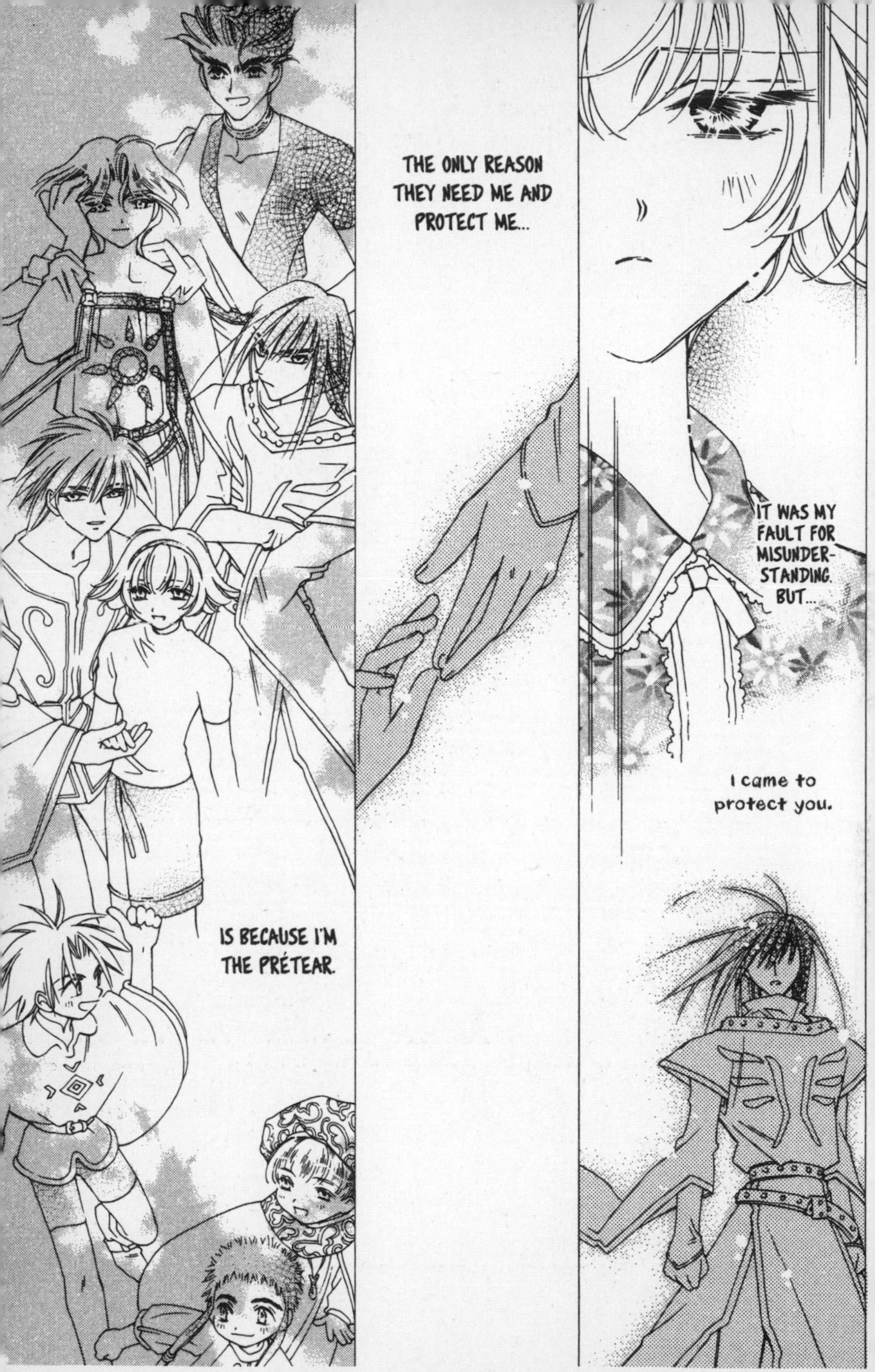
IT WAS MY FAULT FOR MISUNDER-STANDING. BUT...
I came to protect you.
THE ONLY REASON THEY NEED ME AND PROTECT ME...
IS BECAUSE I'M THE PRÉTEAR.

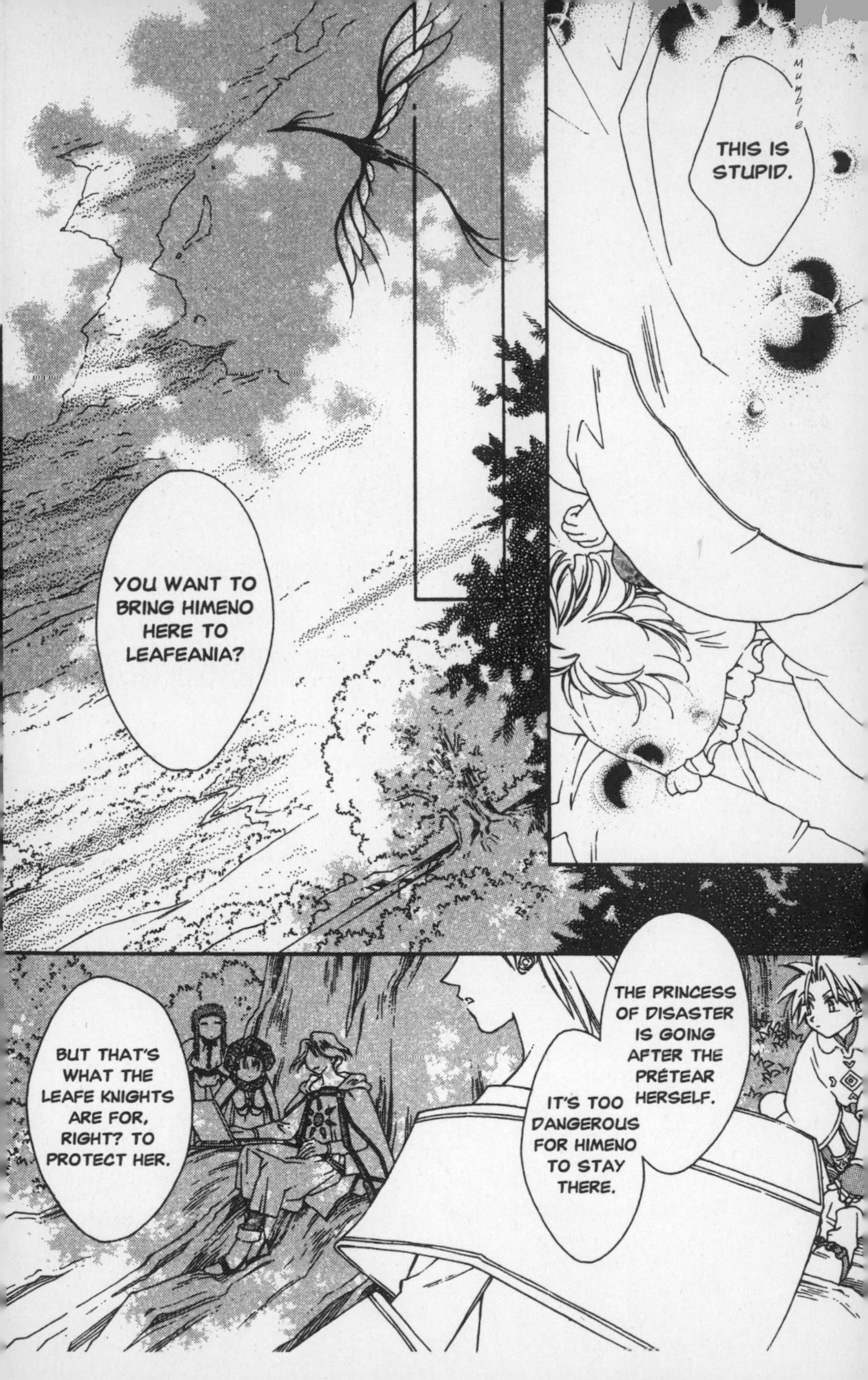

Mumble
THIS IS STUPID.
YOU WANT TO BRING HIMENO HERE TO LEAFEANIA?
THE PRINCESS OF DISASTER IS GOING AFTER THE PRÉTEAR HERSELF.
IT'S TOO DANGEROUS FOR HIMENO TO STAY THERE.
BUT THAT'S WHAT THE LEAFE KNIGHTS ARE FOR, RIGHT? TO PROTECT HER.

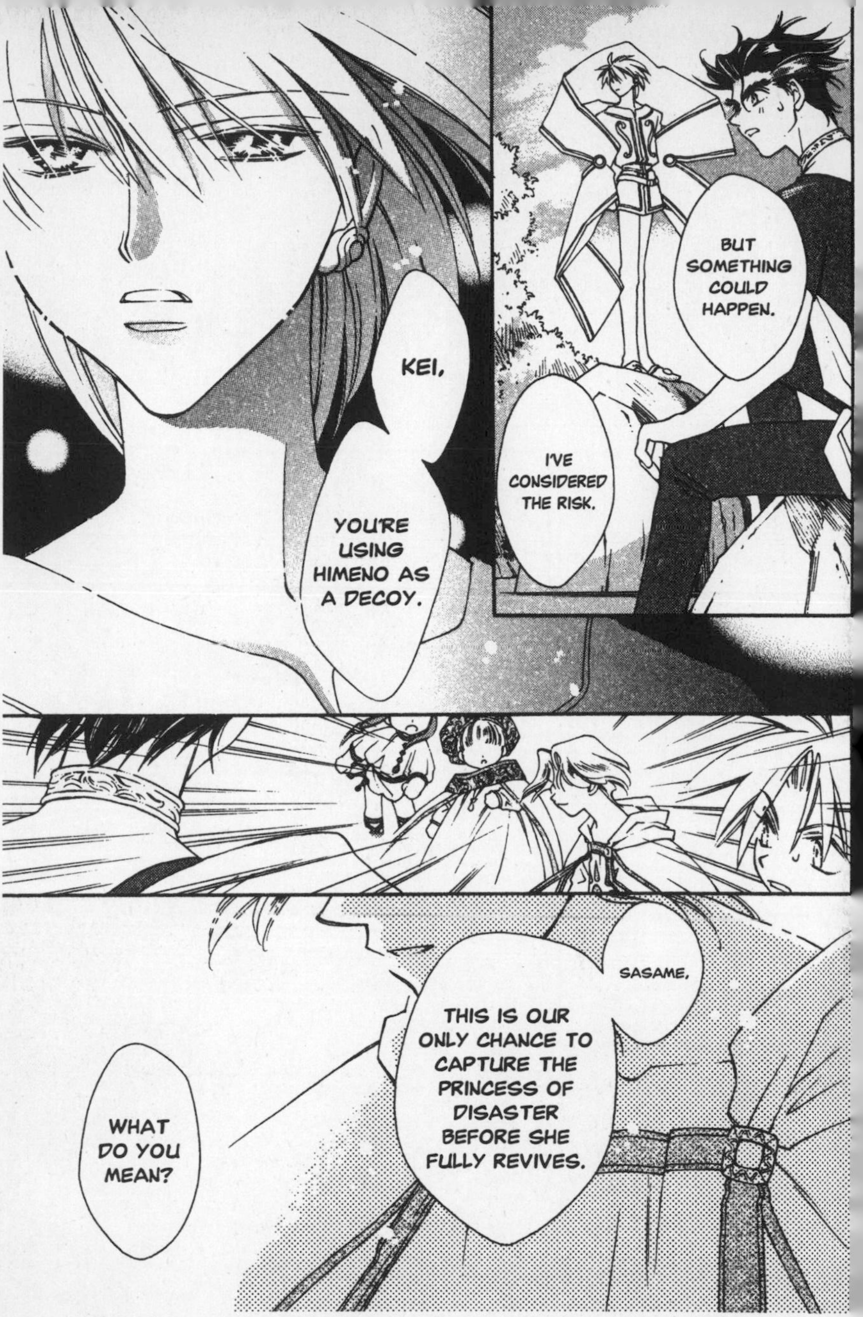
KEI,
YOU'RE USING HIMENO AS A DECOY.
BUT SOMETHING COULD HAPPEN.
I'VE CONSIDERED THE RISK.
SASAME,
THIS IS OUR ONLY CHANCE TO CAPTURE THE PRINCESS OF DISASTER BEFORE SHE FULLY REVIVES.
WHAT DO YOU MEAN?

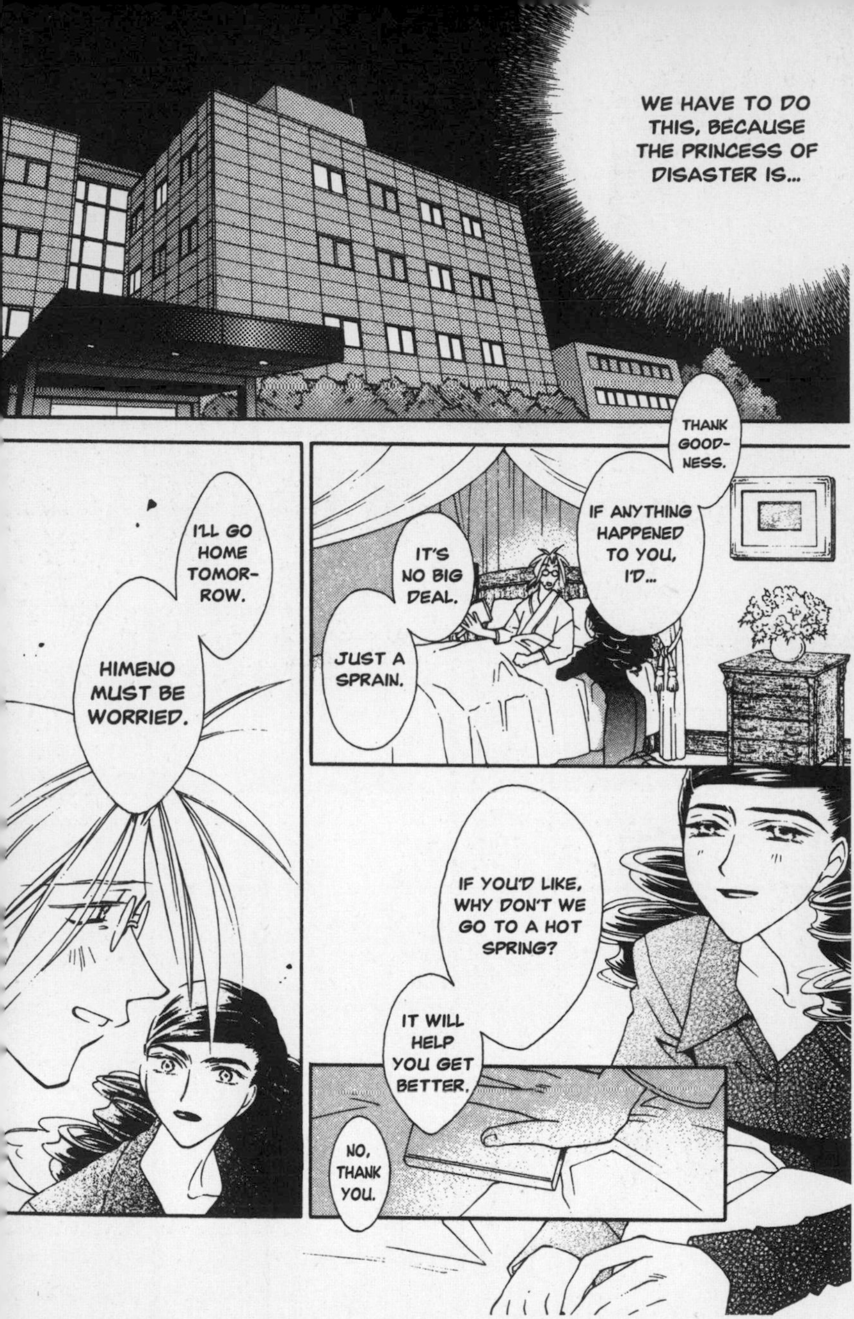
WE HAVE TO DO THIS, BECAUSE THE PRINCESS OF DISASTER IS...
THANK GOODNESS.
IF ANYTHING HAPPENED TO YOU, I'D...
IT'S NO BIG DEAL.
JUST A SPRAIN.
I'LL GO HOME TOMORROW.
HIMENO MUST BE WORRIED.
IF YOU'D LIKE, WHY DON'T WE GO TO A HOT SPRING?
IT WILL HELP YOU GET BETTER.
NO, THANK YOU.

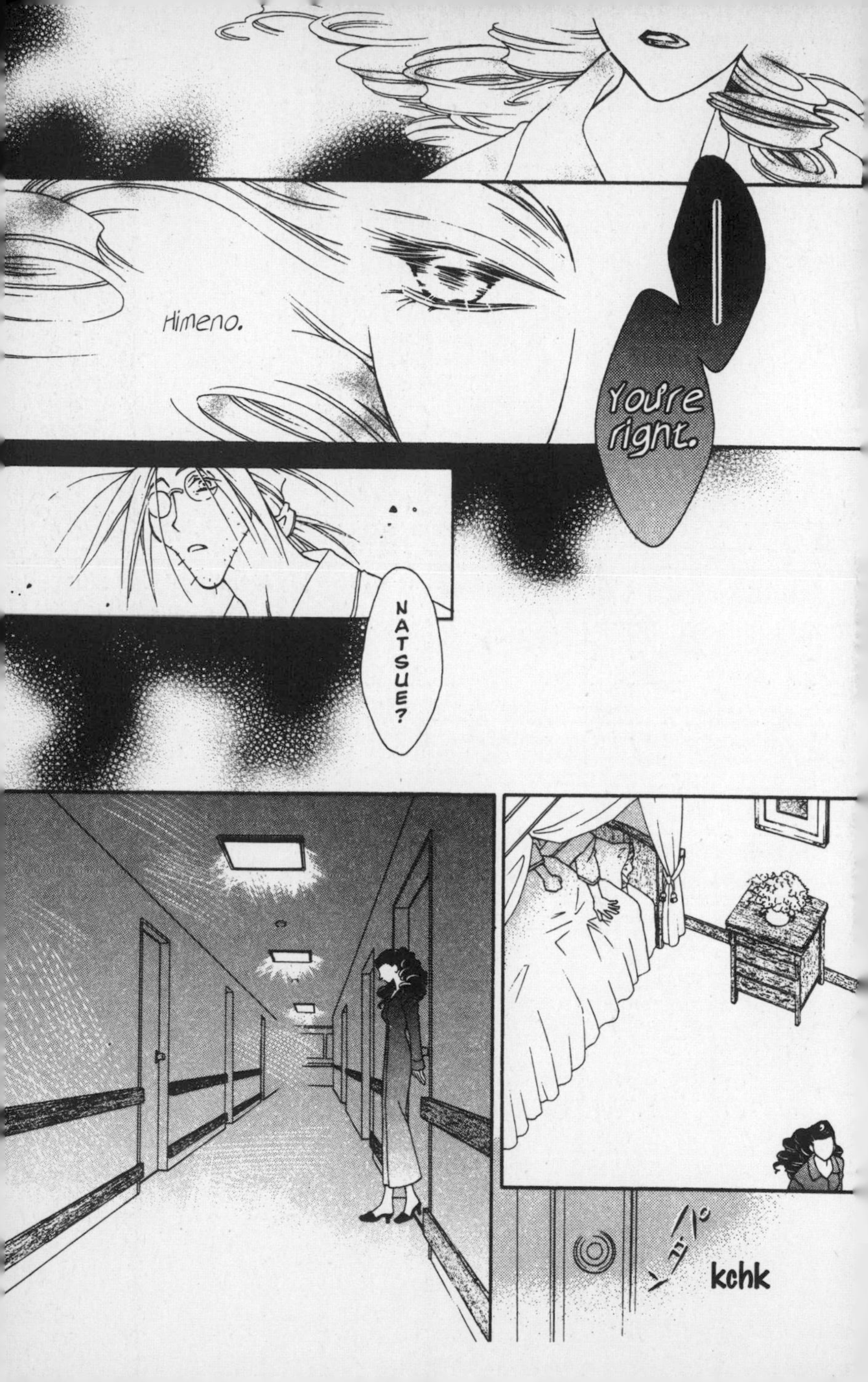
You're right.
Himeno.
NATSUE?
kchk

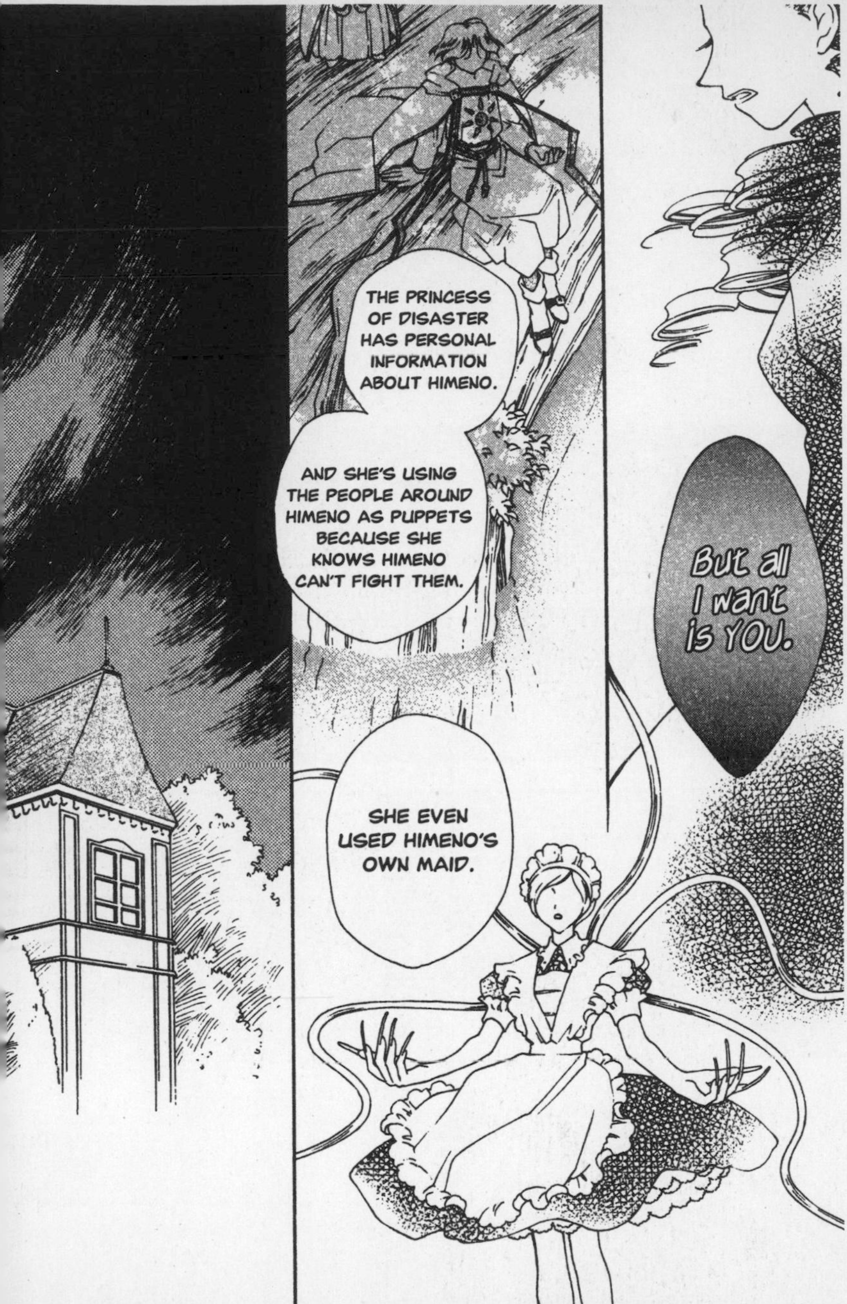

But all I want is YOU.
THE PRINCESS OF DISASTER HAS PERSONAL INFORMATION ABOUT HIMENO.
AND SHE'S USING THE PEOPLE AROUND HIMENO AS PUPPETS BECAUSE SHE KNOWS HIMENO CAN'T FIGHT THEM.
SHE EVEN USED HIMENO'S OWN MAID.

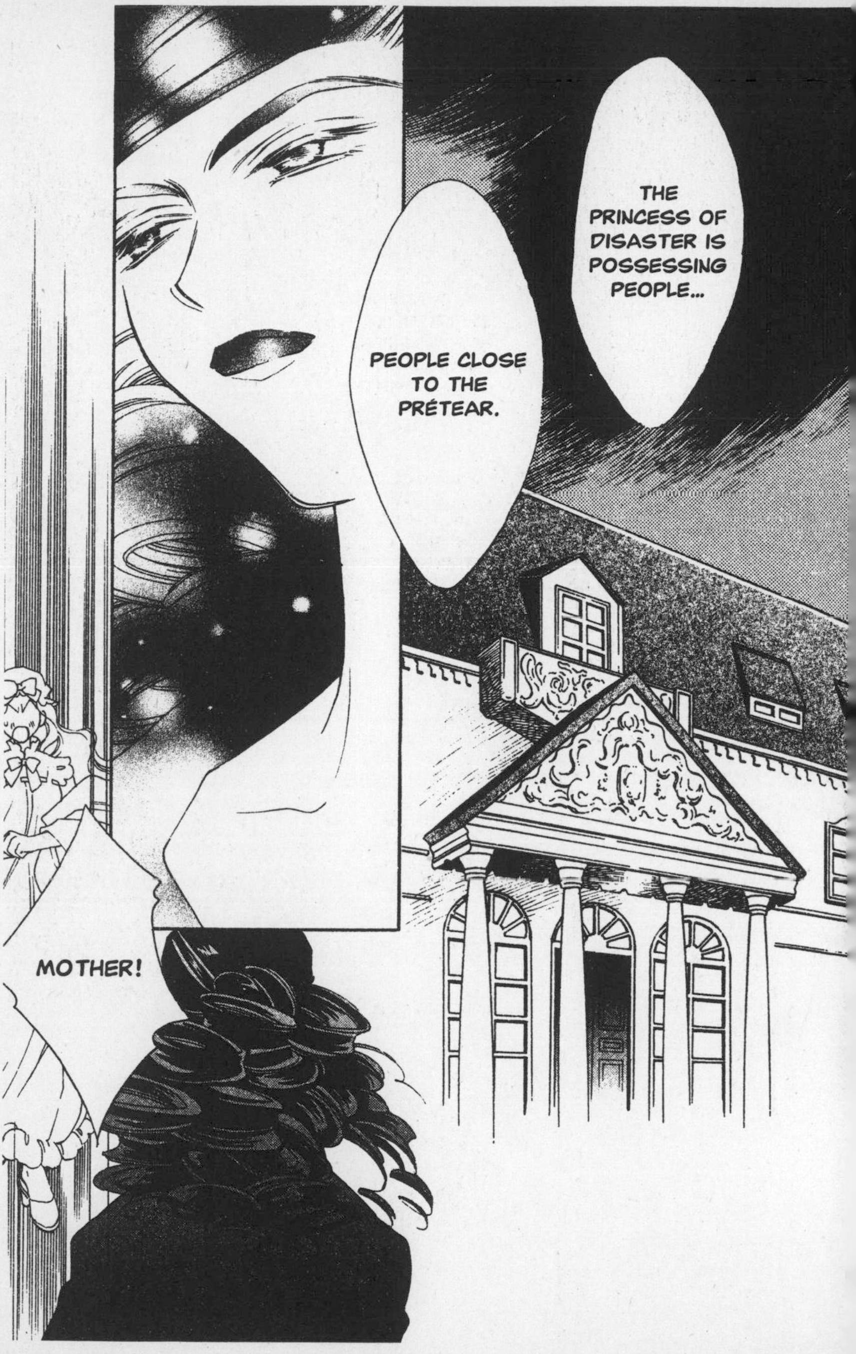
THE PRINCESS OF DISASTER IS POSSESSING PEOPLE...
PEOPLE CLOSE TO THE PRÉTEAR.
MOTHER!

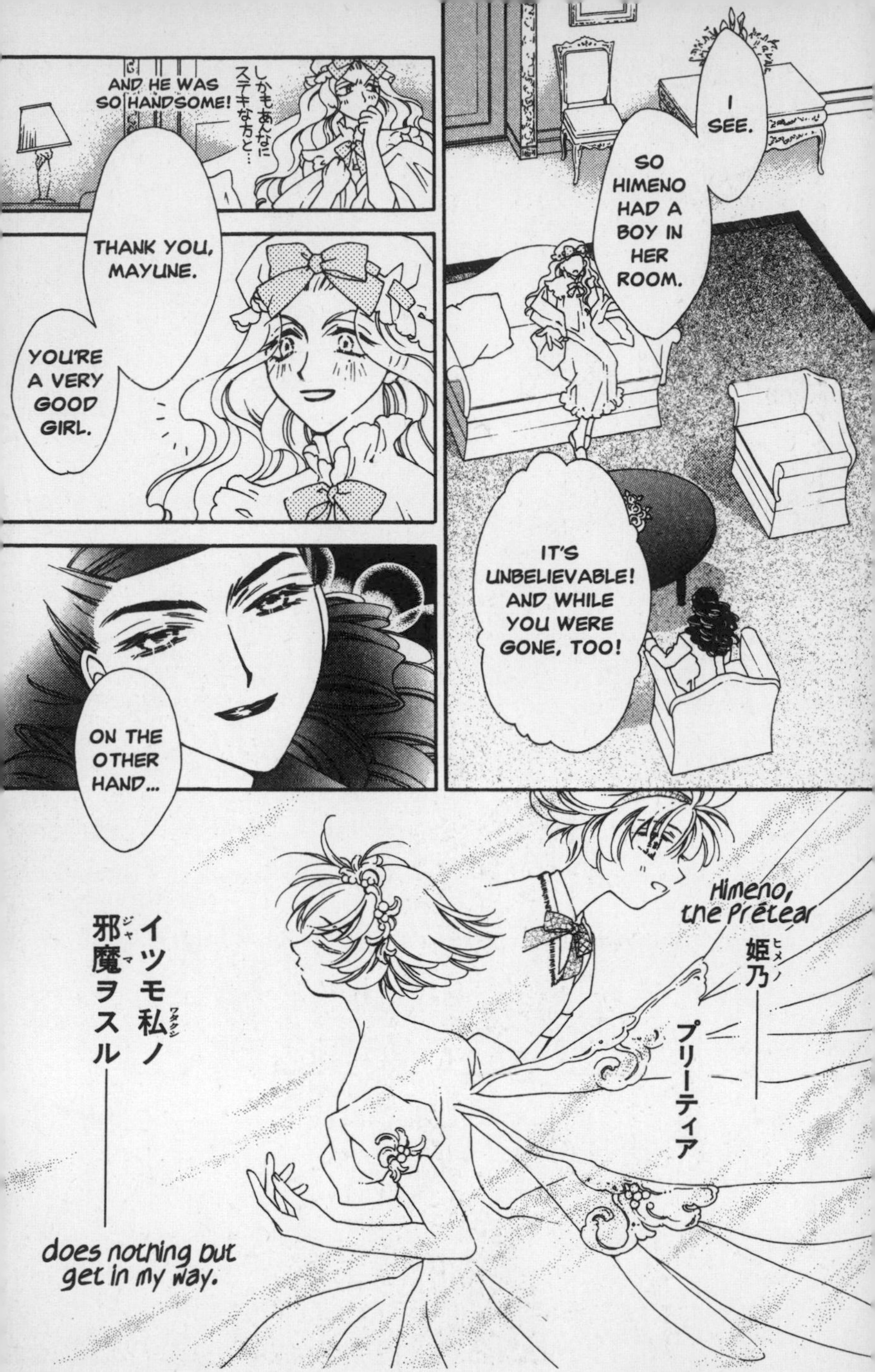
I SEE.
SO HIMENO HAD A BOY IN HER ROOM.
IT'S UNBELIEVABLE! AND WHILE YOU WERE GONE, TOO!
しかもあんなにステキな方と…
AND HE WAS SO HANDSOME!
THANK YOU, MAYUNE.
YOU'RE A VERY GOOD GIRL.
ON THE OTHER HAND...
姫乃プリーティア——
Himeno, the Pretear
イツモ私ノ邪魔ヲスル——
does nothing but get in my way.

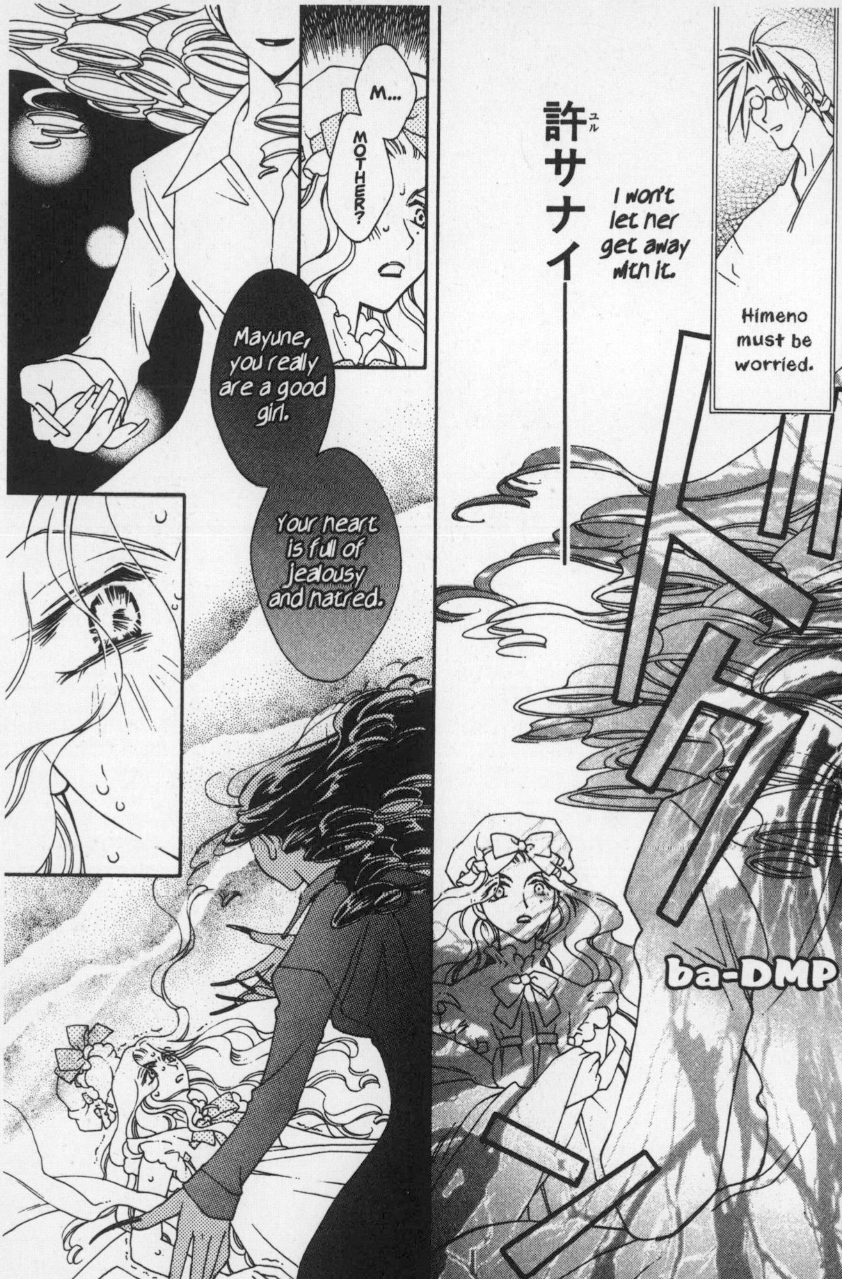
Himeno must be worried.
許サナイ
I won't let her get away with it.
ba-DMP
M... MOTHER?
Mayune, you really are a good girl.
Your heart is full of jealousy and hatred.

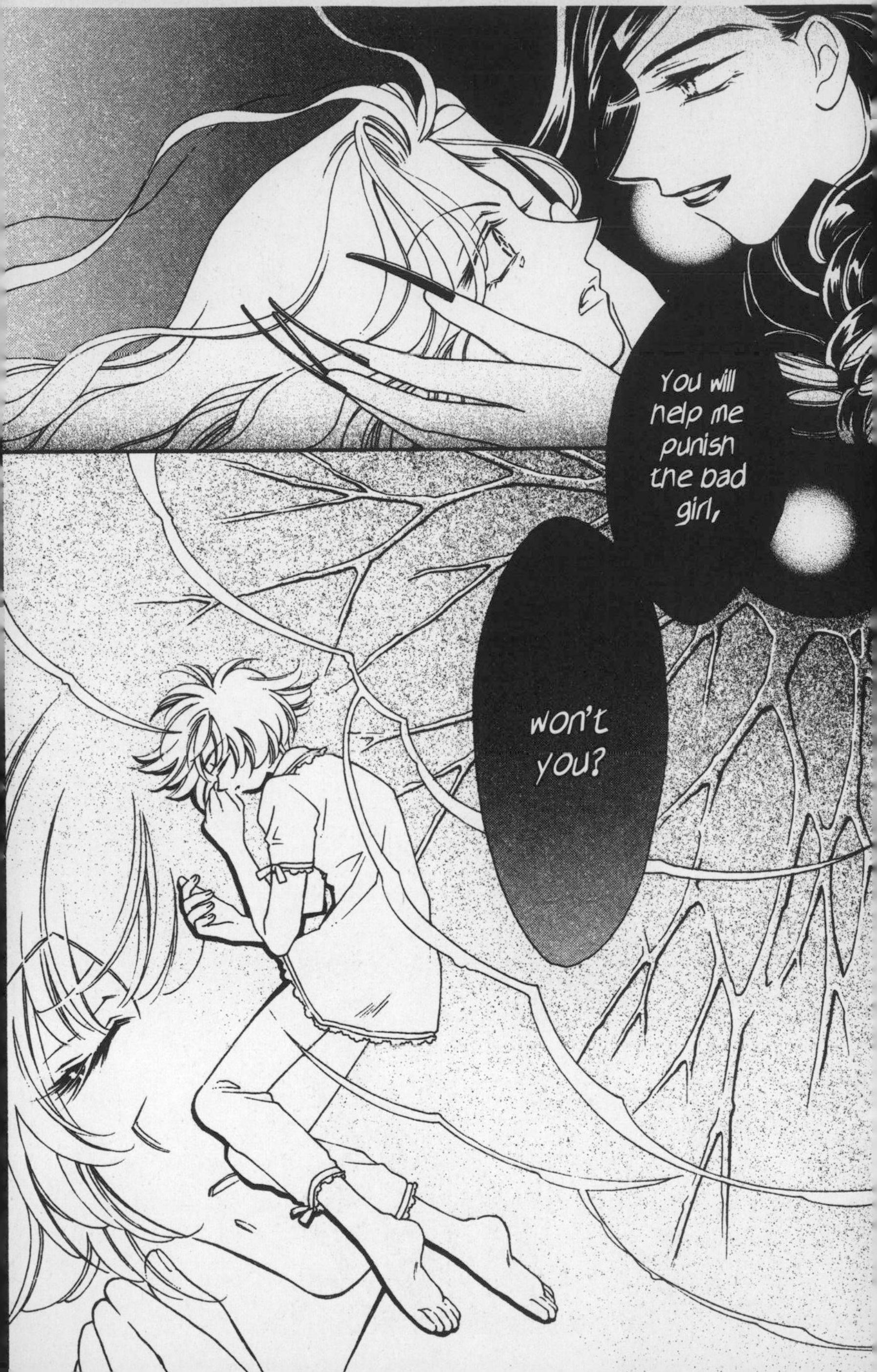
You will help me punish the bad girl,
won't you?

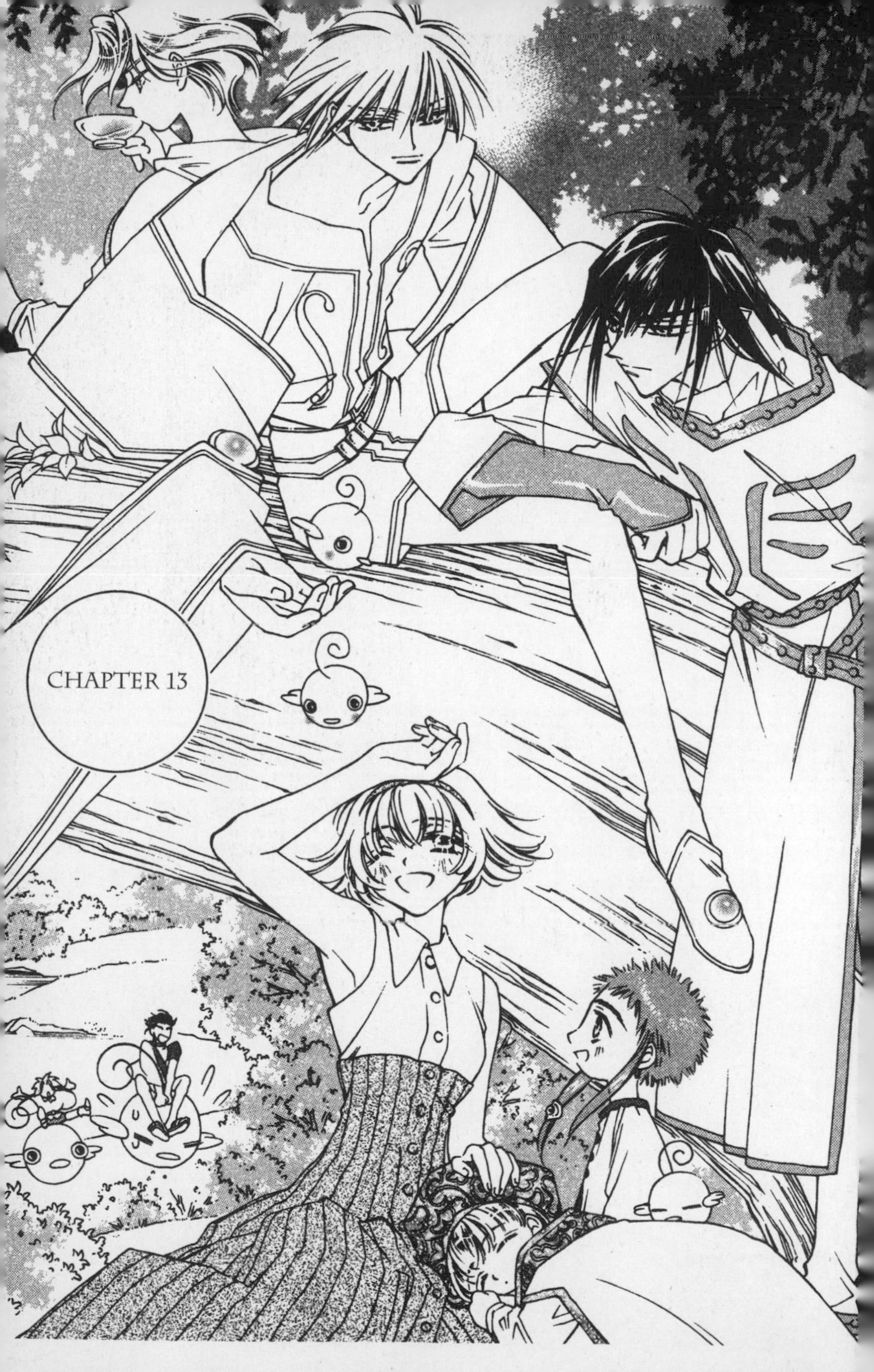
CHAPTER 13

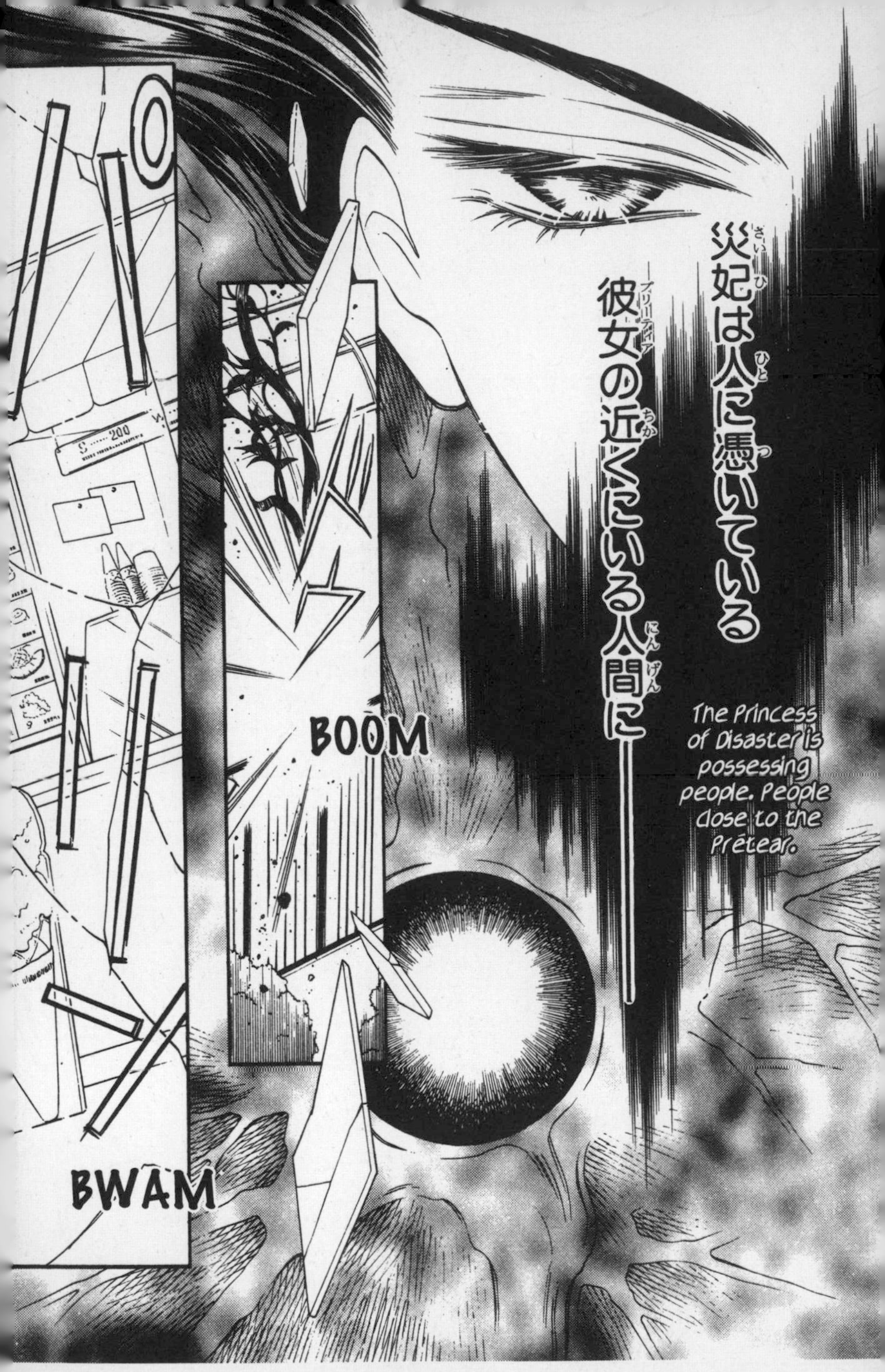
災妃(さいひ)は人(ひと)に憑(つ)いている
彼女(プリーティア)の近(ちか)くにいる人間(にんげん)に――
The Princess of Disaster is possessing people. People close to the Pretear.
BOOM
BWAM

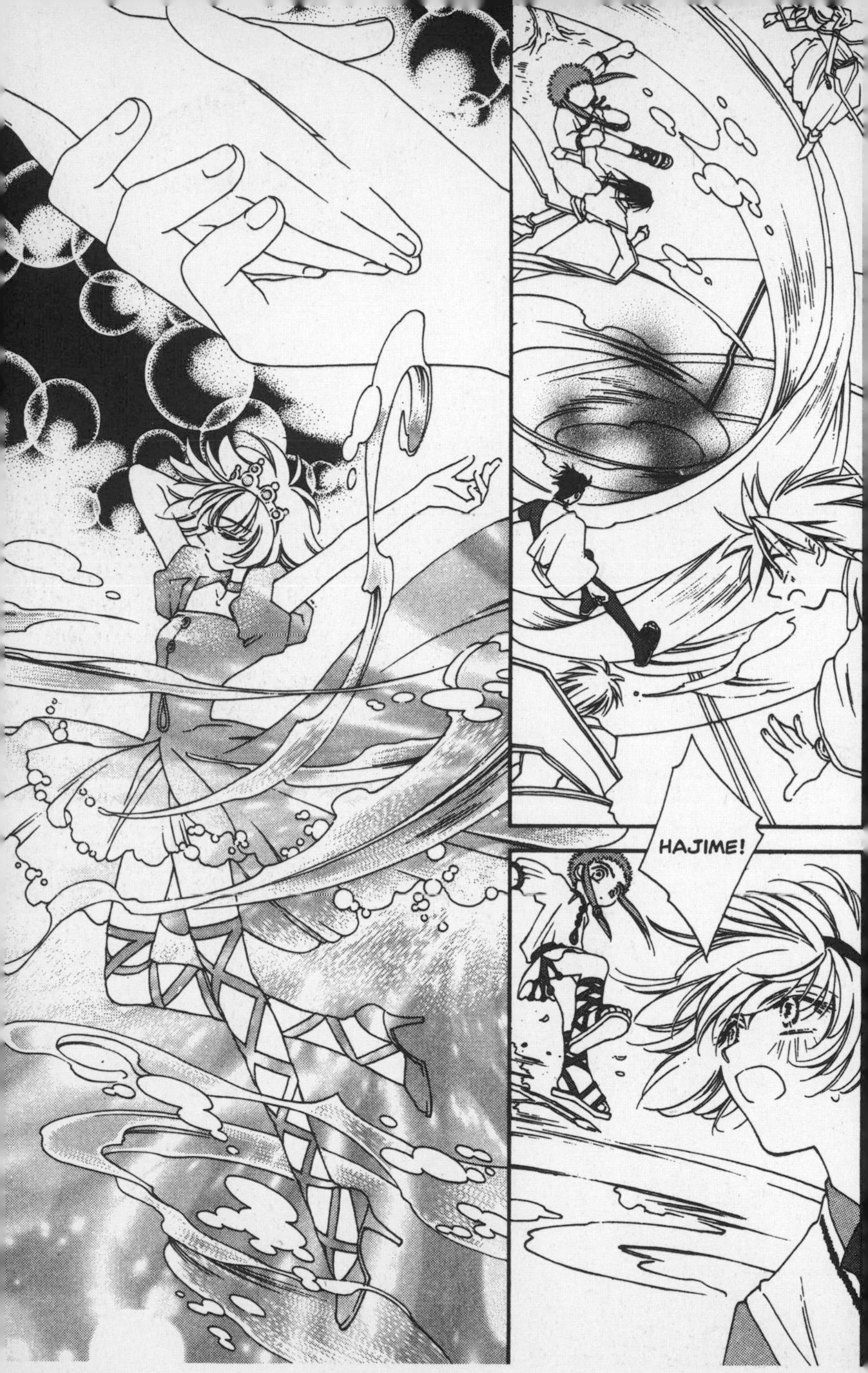
HAJIME!

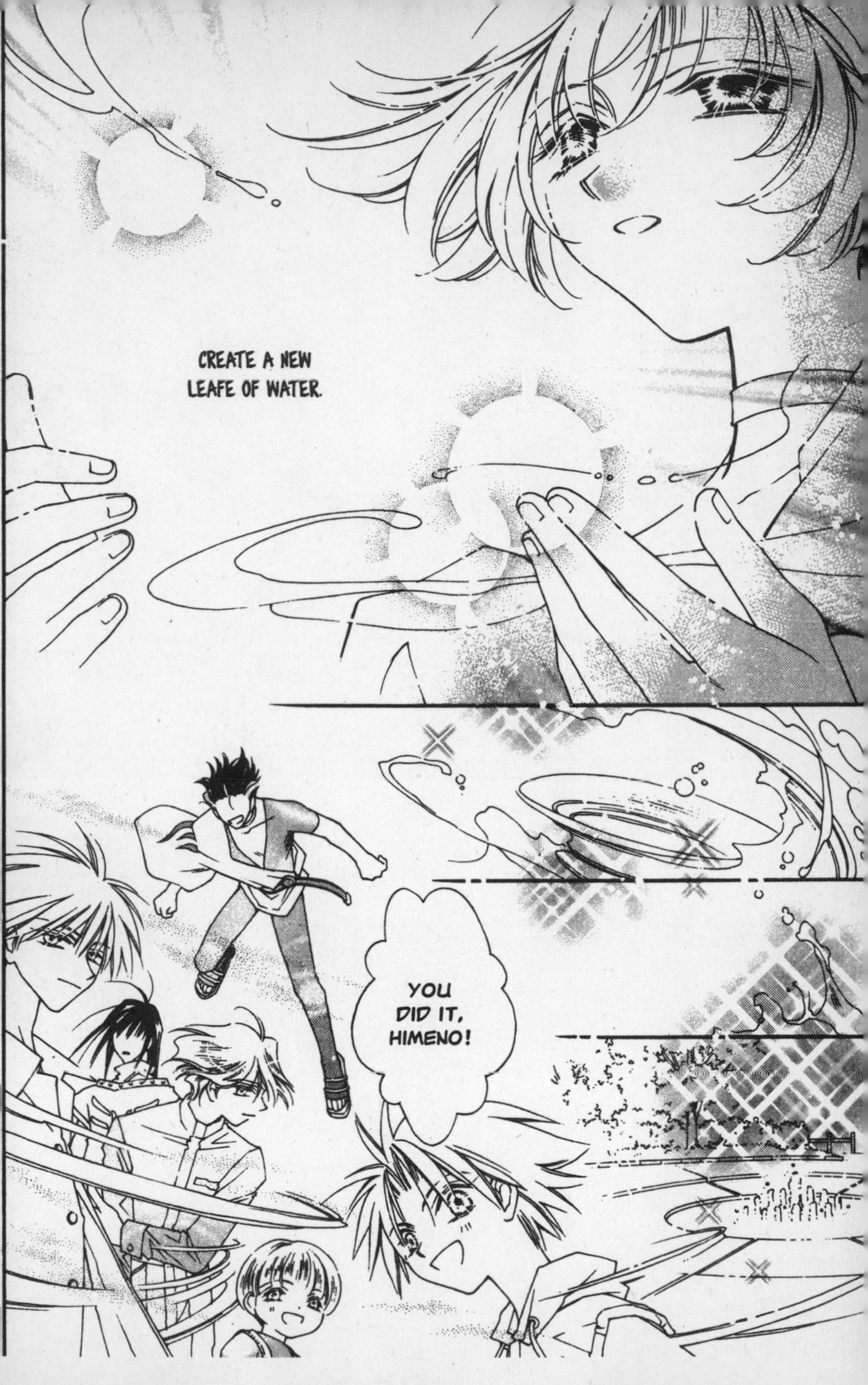
CREATE A NEW LEAFE OF WATER.
YOU DID IT, HIMENO!

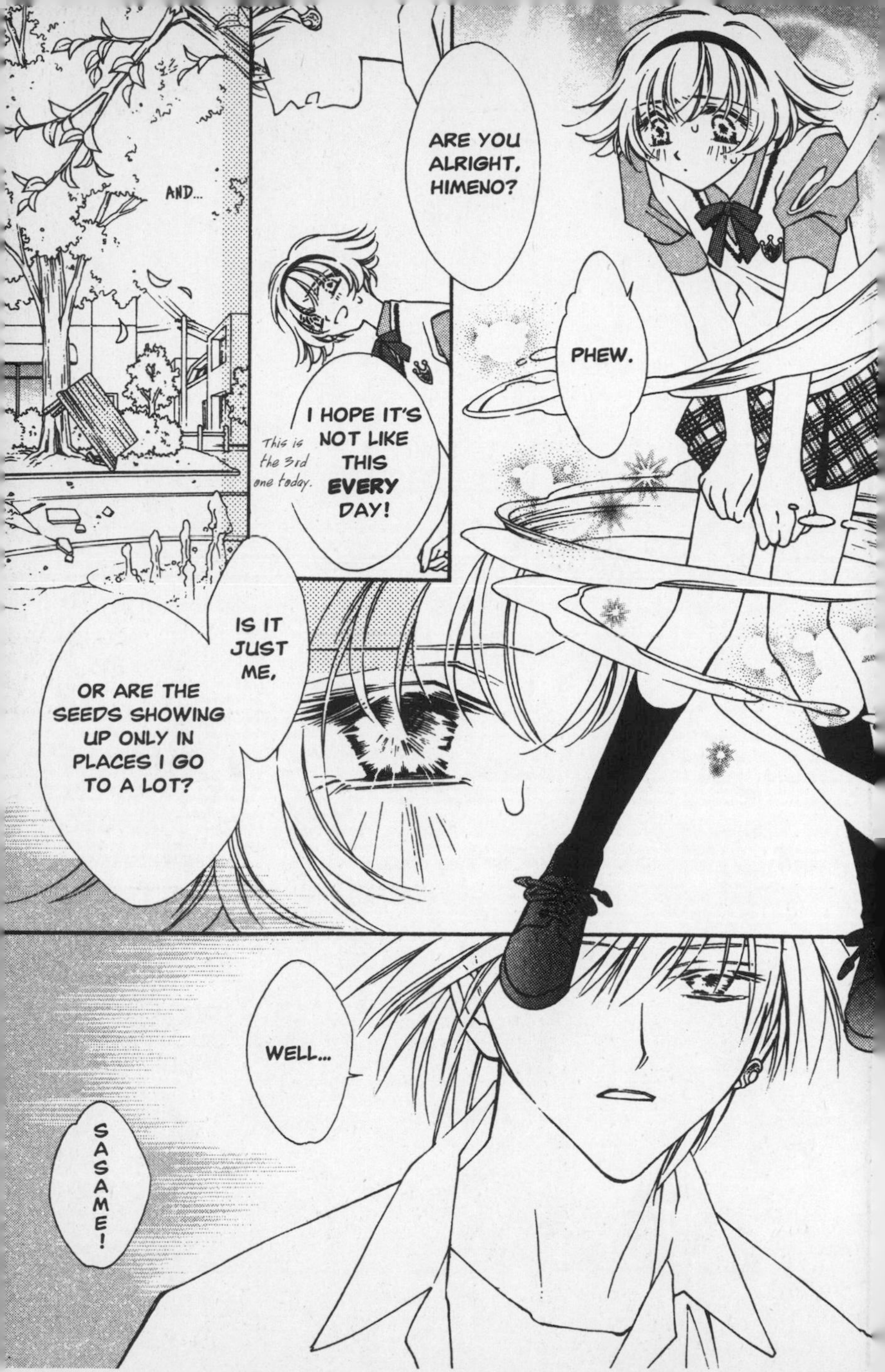

ARE YOU ALRIGHT, HIMENO?
PHEW.
I HOPE IT'S NOT LIKE THIS EVERY DAY!
This is the 3rd one today.
AND...
IS IT JUST ME,
OR ARE THE SEEDS SHOWING UP ONLY IN PLACES I GO TO A LOT?
WELL...
SASAME!

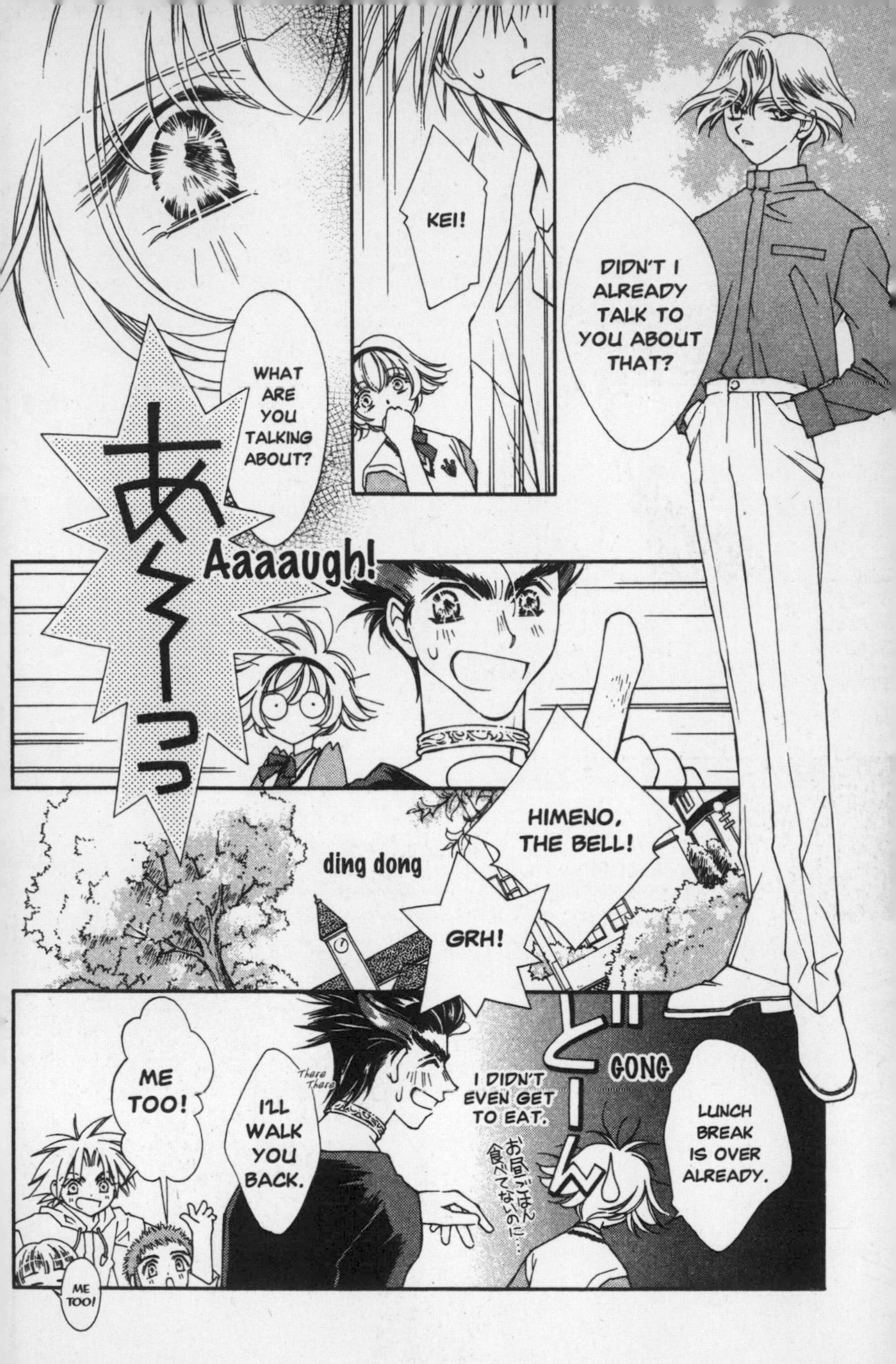
DIDN'T I ALREADY TALK TO YOU ABOUT THAT?
KEI!
WHAT ARE YOU TALKING ABOUT?
あ〜〜っ
Aaaaugh!
HIMENO, THE BELL!
ding dong
GRH!
LUNCH BREAK IS OVER ALREADY.
どーん
GONG
I DIDN'T EVEN GET TO EAT.
お昼ごはん食べてないのに…
There There
I'LL WALK YOU BACK.
ME TOO!
ME TOO!

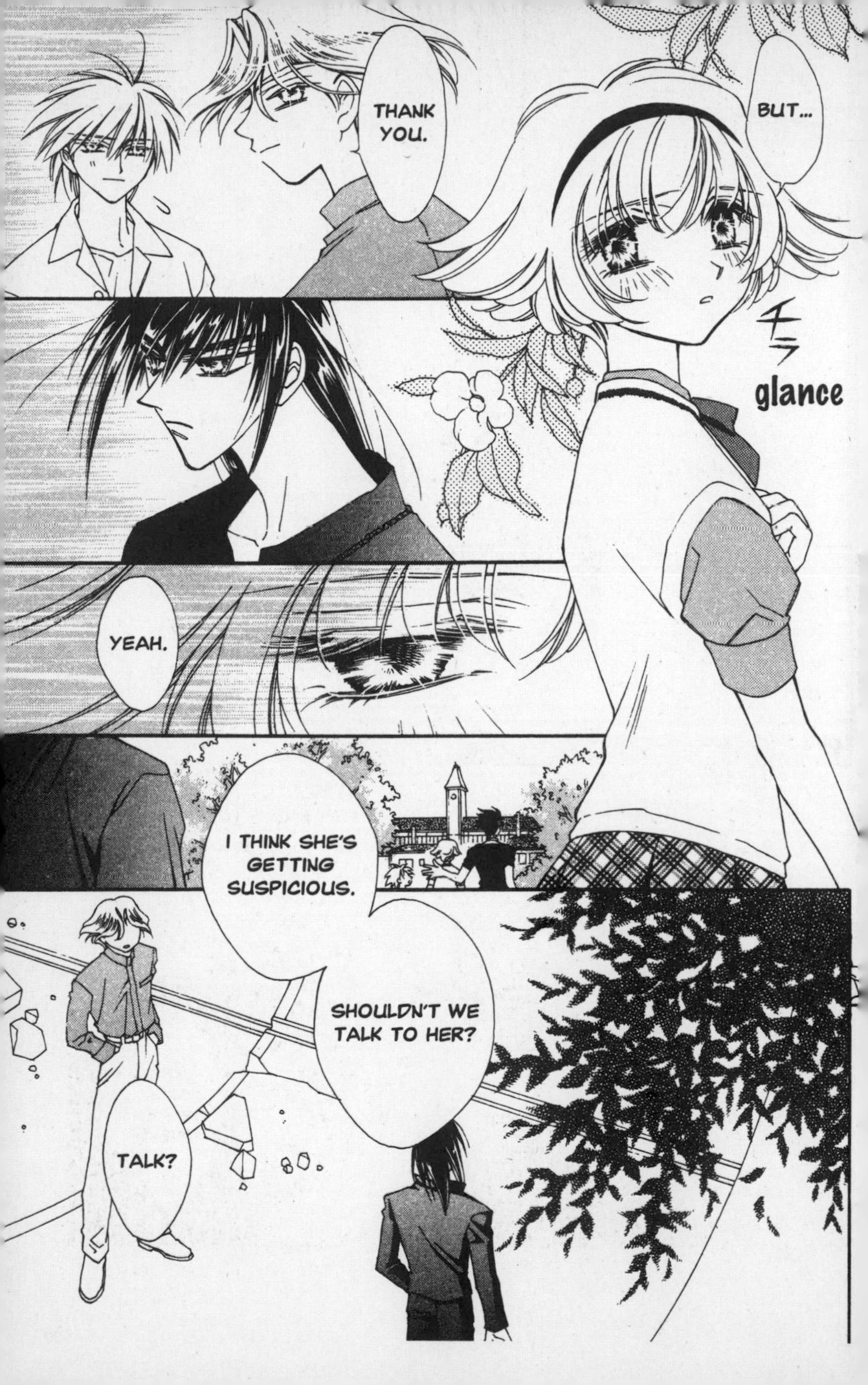
BUT...
THANK YOU.
glance
YEAH.
I THINK SHE'S GETTING SUSPICIOUS.
SHOULDN'T WE TALK TO HER?
TALK?

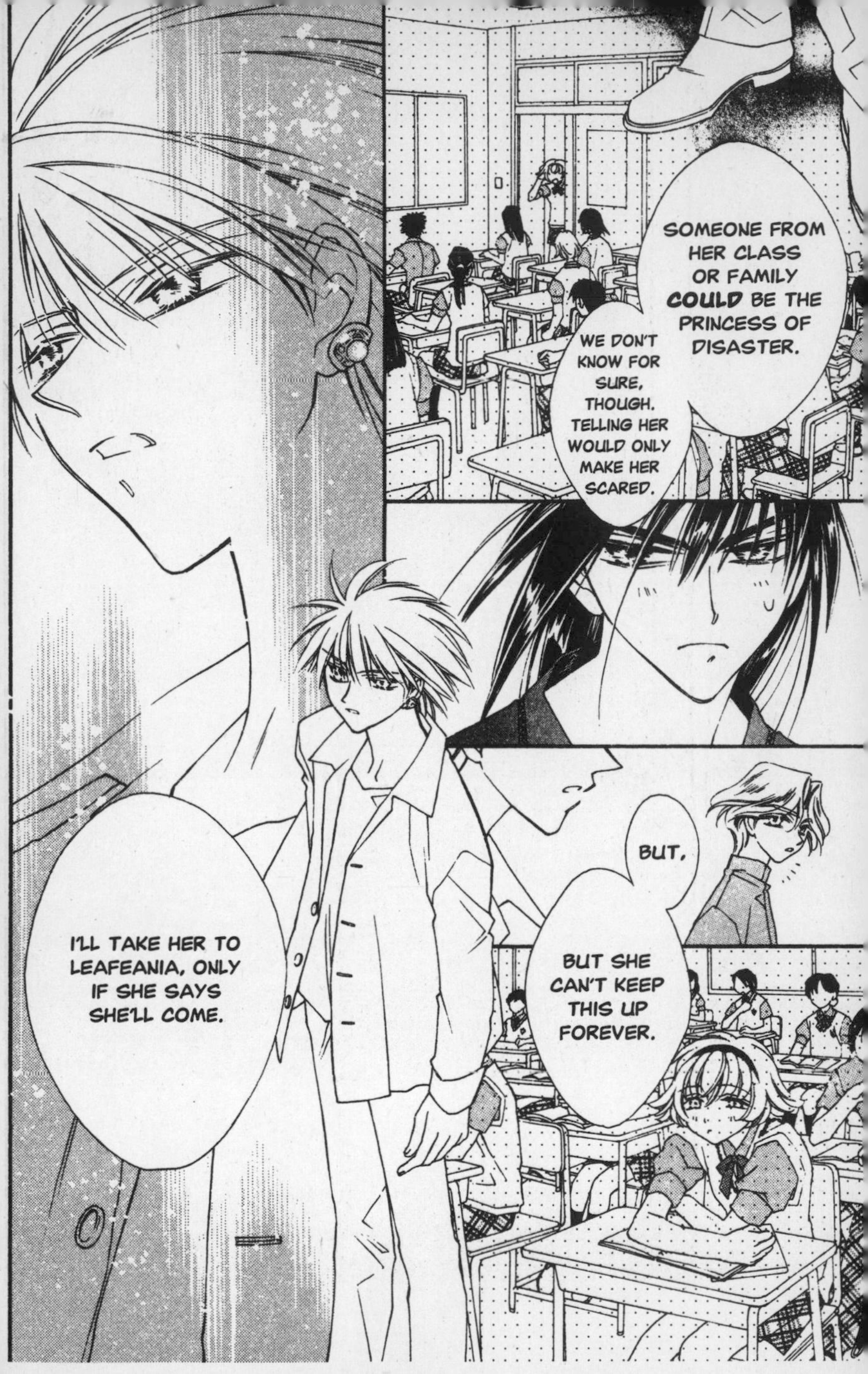
SOMEONE FROM HER CLASS OR FAMILY **COULD** BE THE PRINCESS OF DISASTER.
WE DON'T KNOW FOR SURE, THOUGH. TELLING HER WOULD ONLY MAKE HER SCARED.
BUT,
BUT SHE CAN'T KEEP THIS UP FOREVER.
I'LL TAKE HER TO LEAFEANIA, ONLY IF SHE SAYS SHE'LL COME.

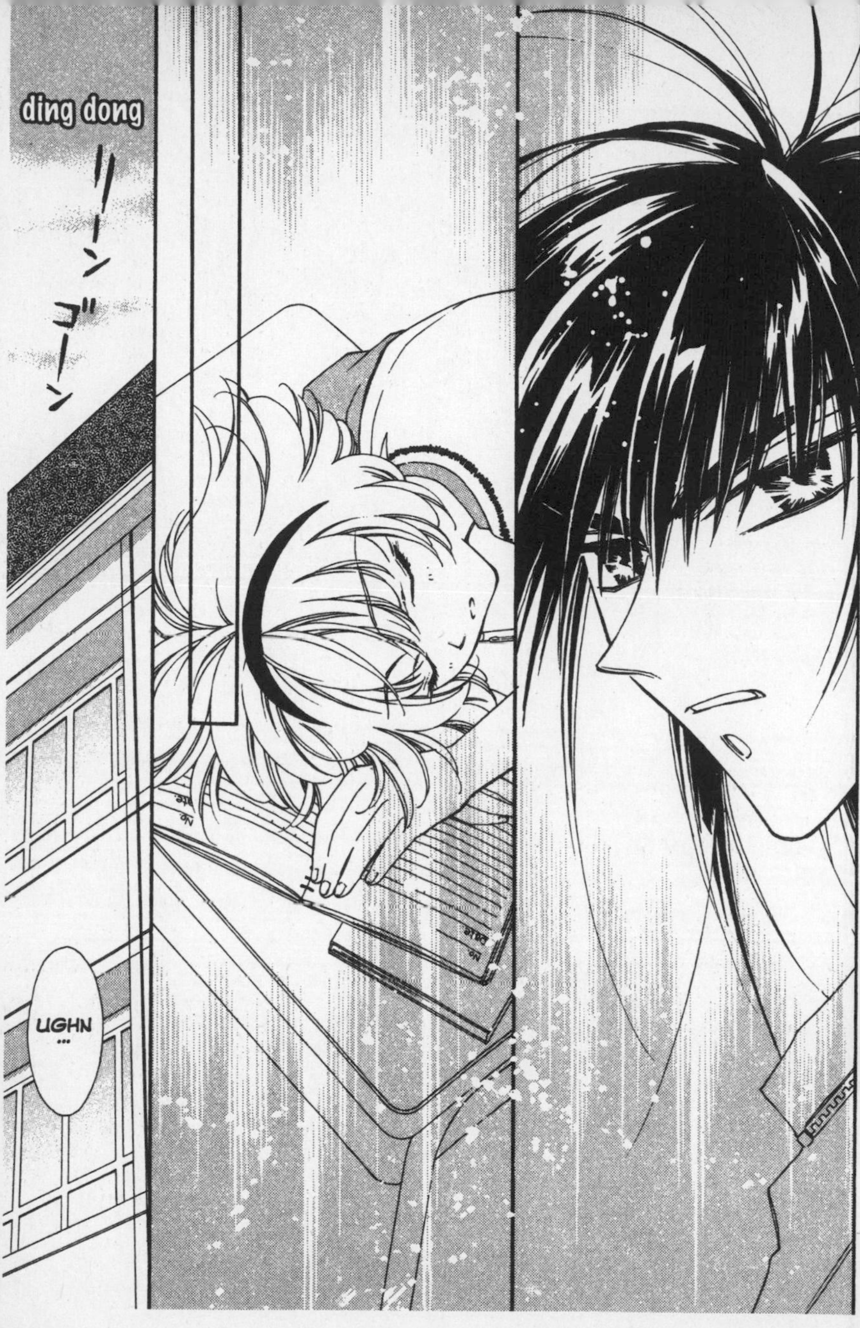
ding dong
リーンゴーン
UGHN ...

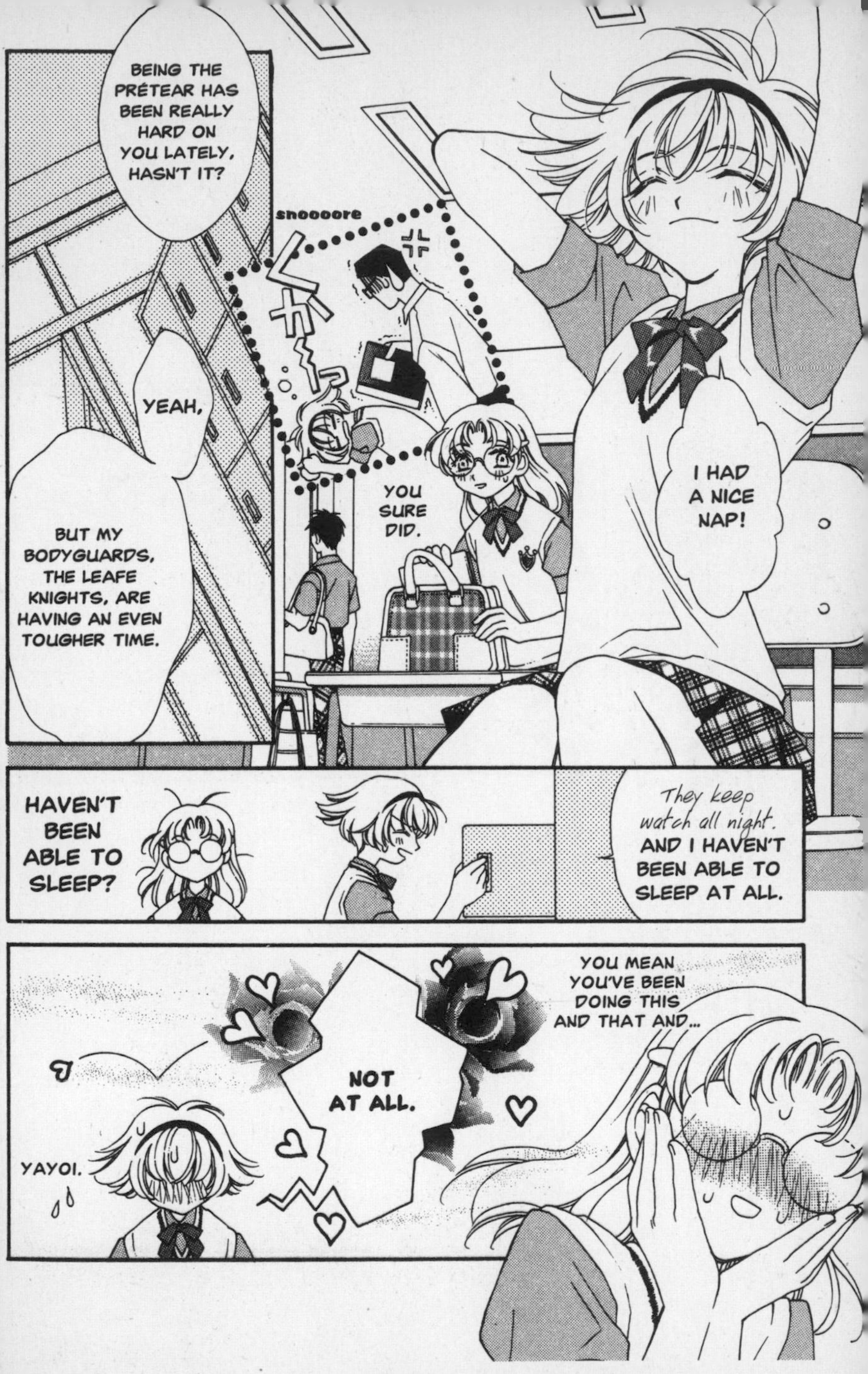
I HAD A NICE NAP!
YOU SURE DID.
snoooore
BEING THE PRÉTEAR HAS BEEN REALLY HARD ON YOU LATELY, HASN'T IT?
YEAH,
BUT MY BODYGUARDS, THE LEAFE KNIGHTS, ARE HAVING AN EVEN TOUGHER TIME.
They keep watch all night.
AND I HAVEN'T BEEN ABLE TO SLEEP AT ALL.
HAVEN'T BEEN ABLE TO SLEEP?
YOU MEAN YOU'VE BEEN DOING THIS AND THAT AND...
NOT AT ALL.
YAYOI.

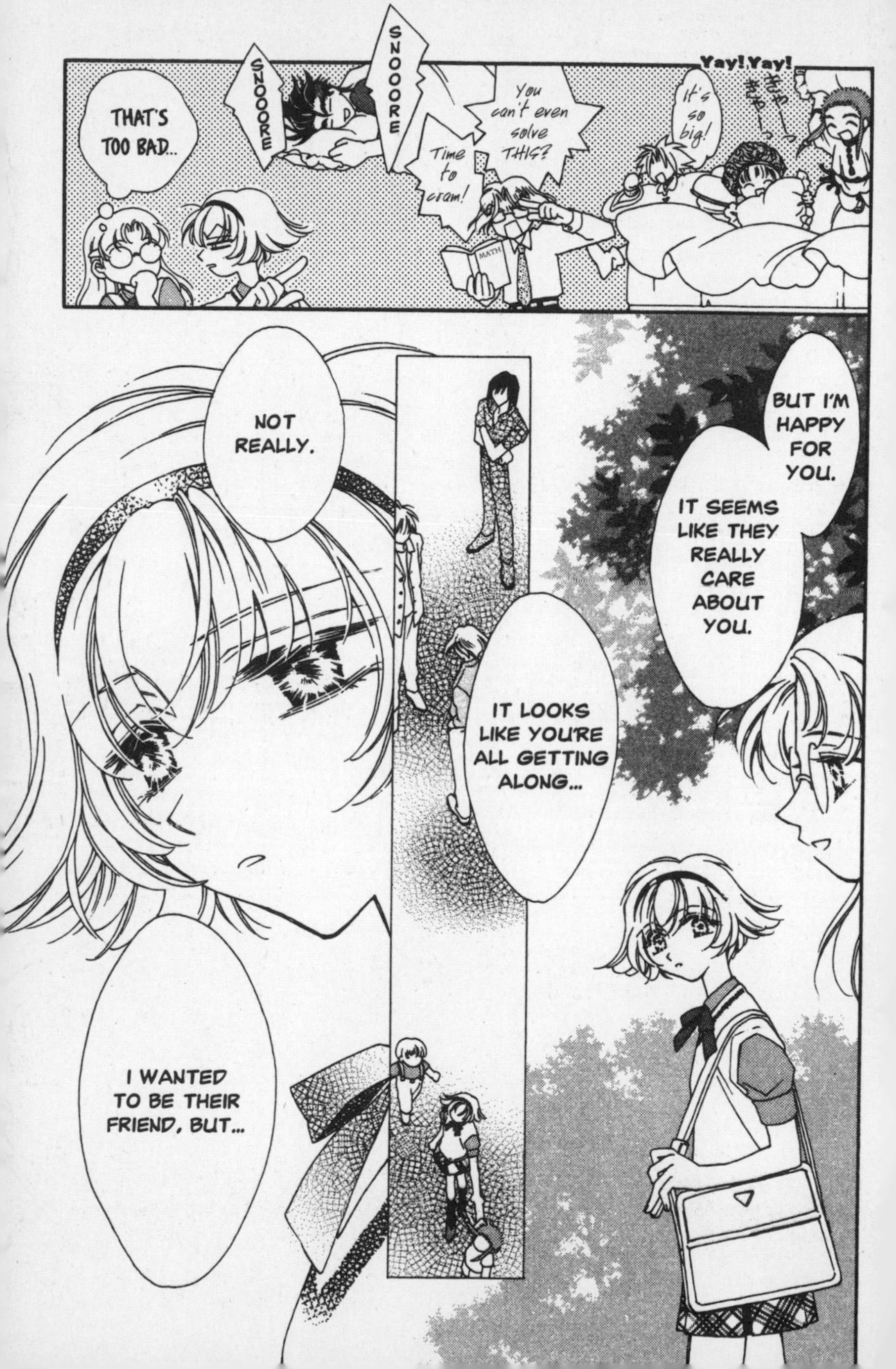
Yay! Yay!
It's so big!
You can't even solve THIS?
Time to cram!
MATH
SNOOOORE
SNOOOORE
THAT'S TOO BAD...
BUT I'M HAPPY FOR YOU.
IT SEEMS LIKE THEY REALLY CARE ABOUT YOU.
IT LOOKS LIKE YOU'RE ALL GETTING ALONG...
NOT REALLY.
I WANTED TO BE THEIR FRIEND, BUT...

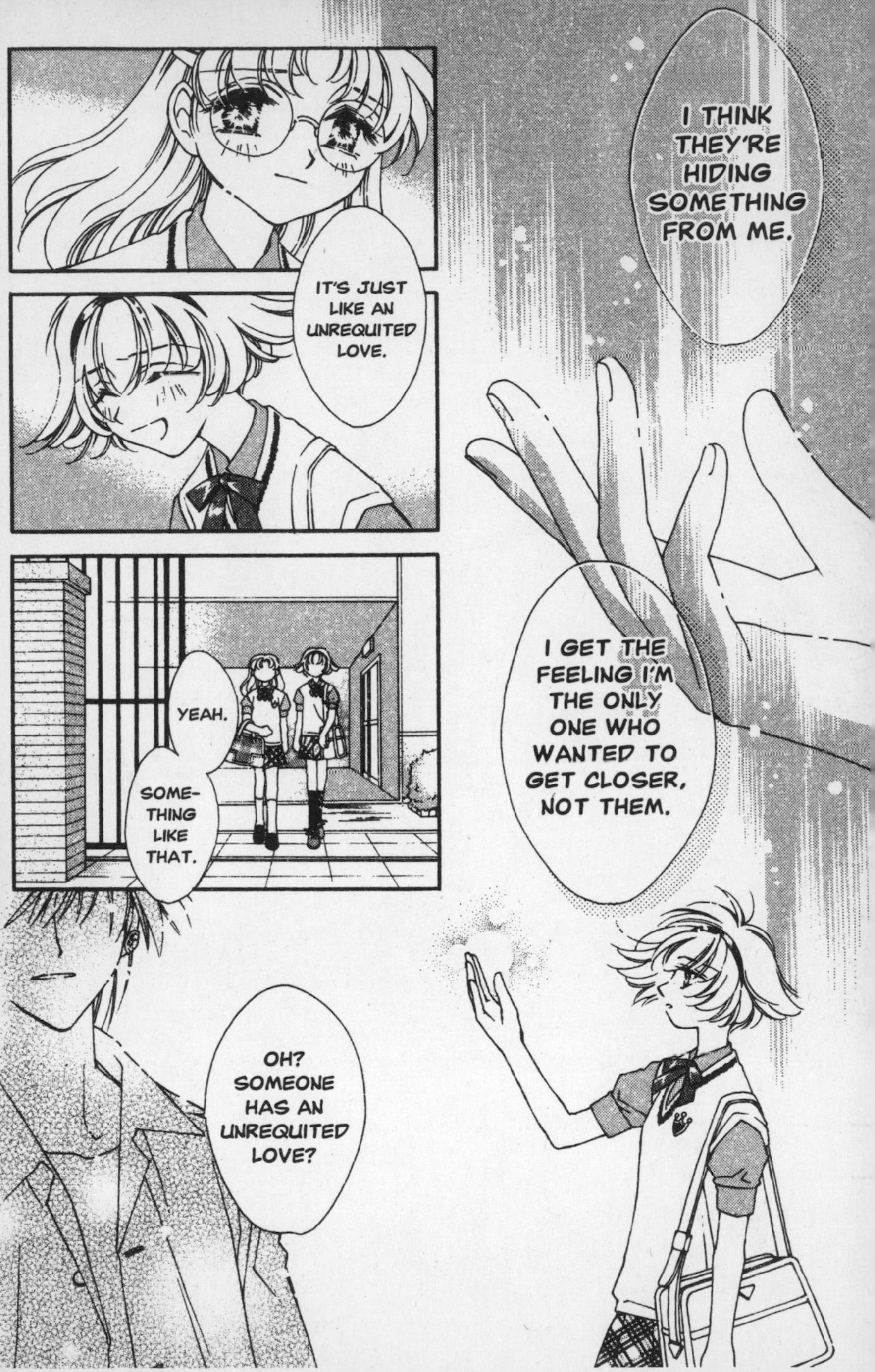

I THINK THEY'RE HIDING SOMETHING FROM ME.
IT'S JUST LIKE AN UNREQUITED LOVE.
YEAH.
SOME-THING LIKE THAT.
I GET THE FEELING I'M THE ONLY ONE WHO WANTED TO GET CLOSER, NOT THEM.
OH? SOMEONE HAS AN UNREQUITED LOVE?

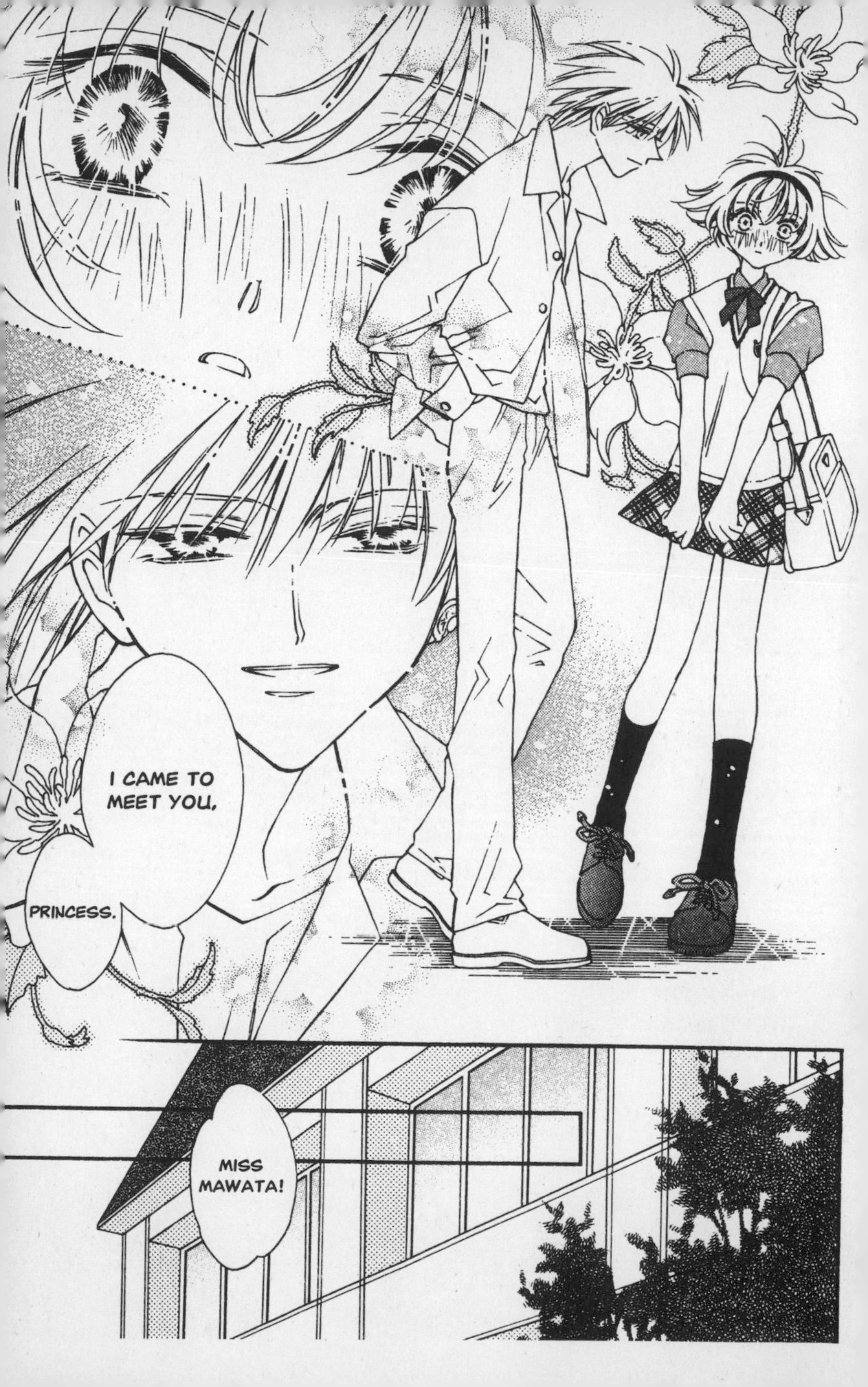
I CAME TO MEET YOU,
PRINCESS.
MISS MAWATA!

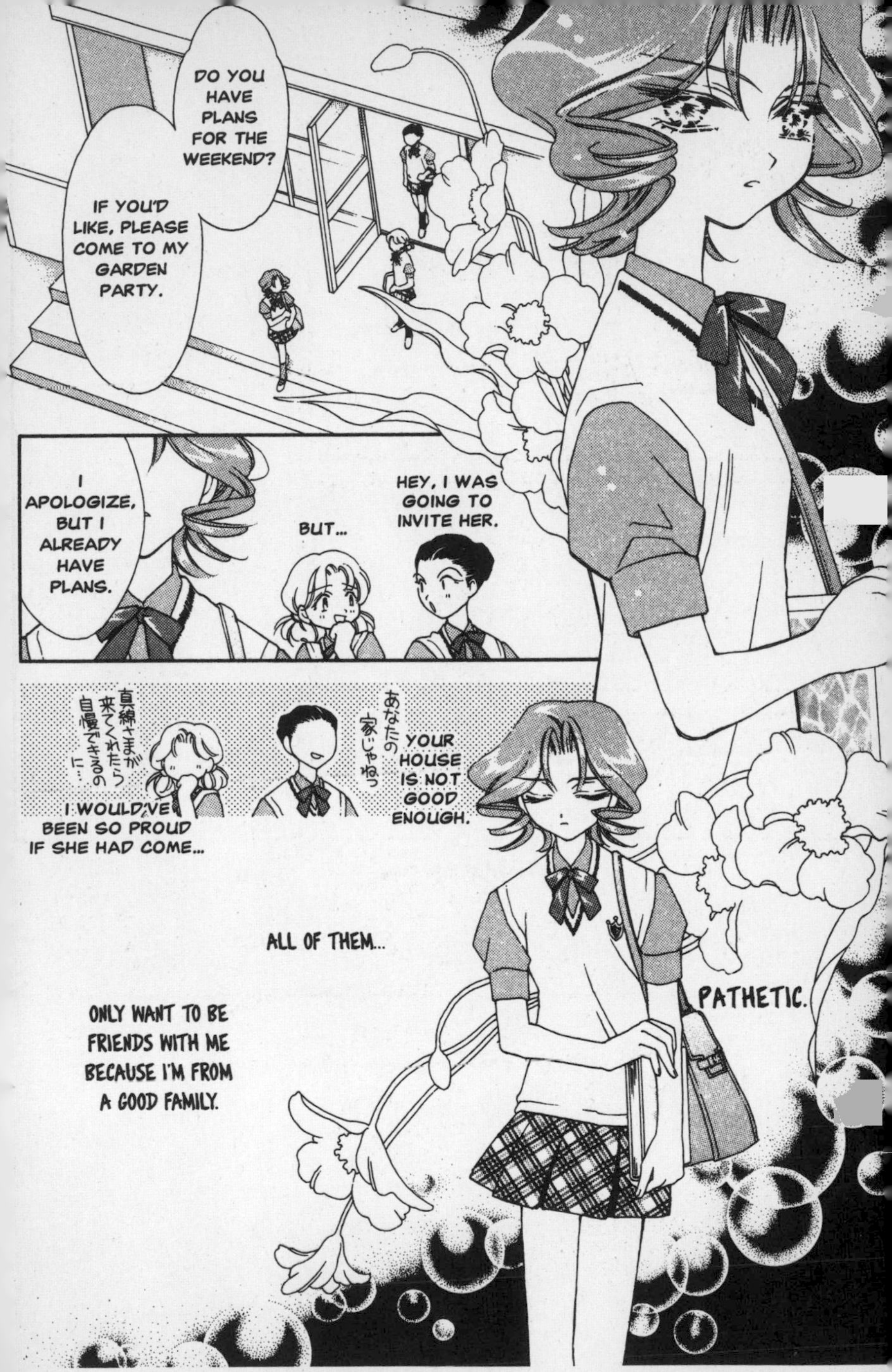
DO YOU HAVE PLANS FOR THE WEEKEND?
IF YOU'D LIKE, PLEASE COME TO MY GARDEN PARTY.
I APOLOGIZE, BUT I ALREADY HAVE PLANS.
BUT...
HEY, I WAS GOING TO INVITE HER.
あなたの家じゃねっ
YOUR HOUSE IS NOT GOOD ENOUGH.
真綿さまが来てくれたら自慢できるのに…
I WOULD'VE BEEN SO PROUD IF SHE HAD COME...
ALL OF THEM...
ONLY WANT TO BE FRIENDS WITH ME BECAUSE I'M FROM A GOOD FAMILY.
PATHETIC.

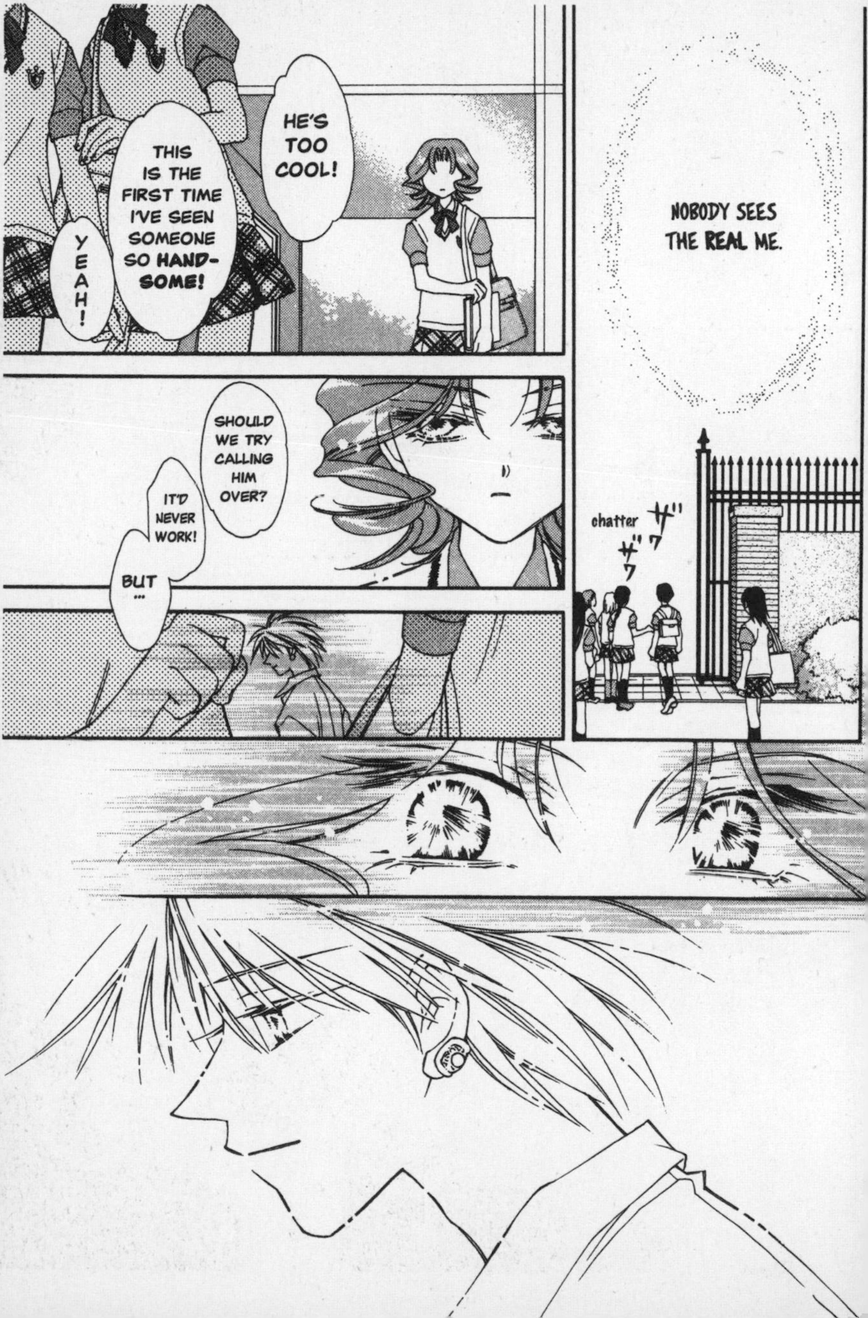
NOBODY SEES THE REAL ME.
chatter
ザワ
ザワ
HE'S TOO COOL!
THIS IS THE FIRST TIME I'VE SEEN SOMEONE SO HANDSOME!
YEAH!
SHOULD WE TRY CALLING HIM OVER?
IT'D NEVER WORK!
BUT...

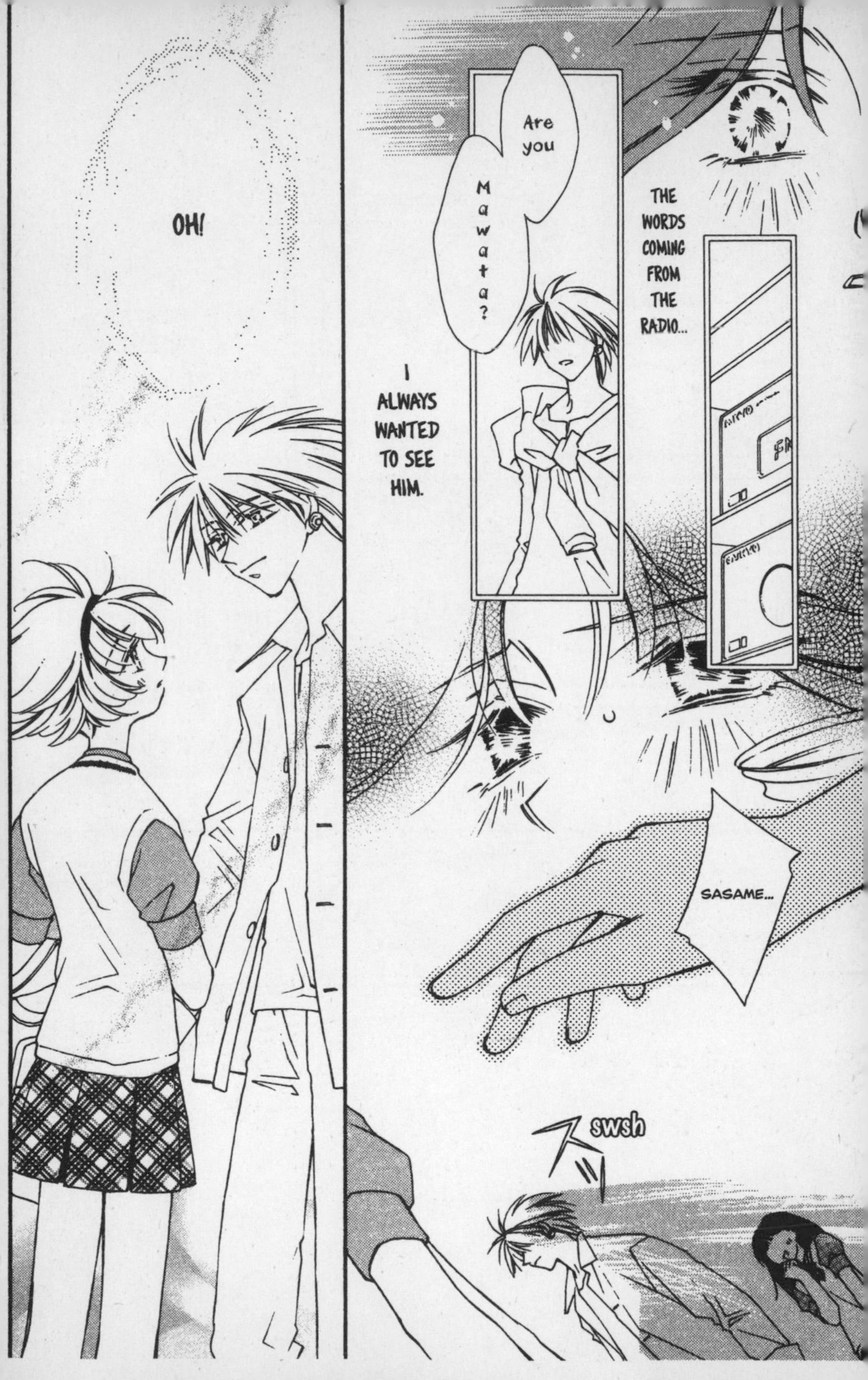
THE WORDS COMING FROM THE RADIO...
Are you Mawata?
I ALWAYS WANTED TO SEE HIM.
SASAME...
swsh
OH!

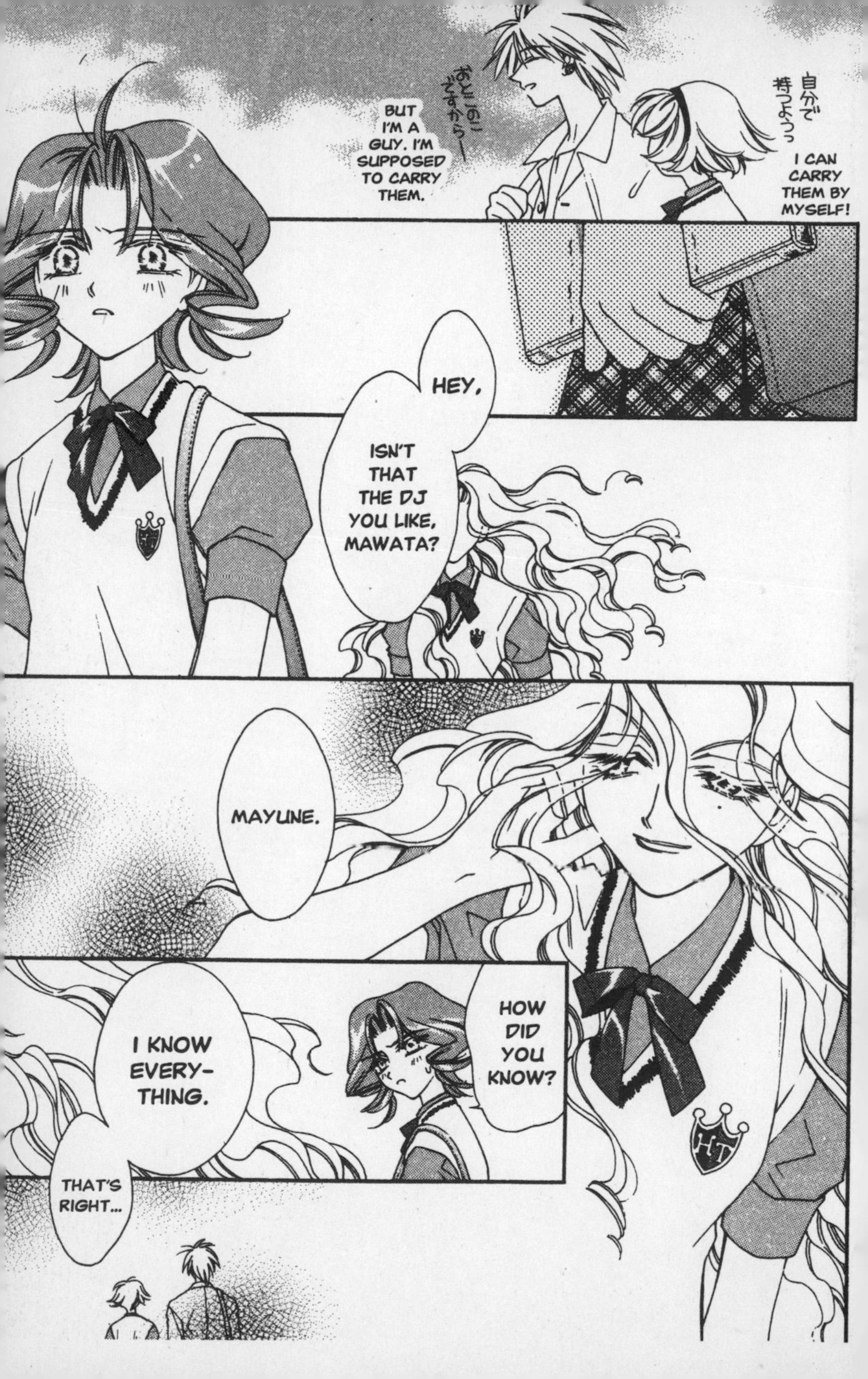
自分で持つよぉっ
I CAN CARRY THEM BY MYSELF!
おとこのこですから—
BUT I'M A GUY. I'M SUPPOSED TO CARRY THEM.
HEY,
ISN'T THAT THE DJ YOU LIKE, MAWATA?
MAYUNE.
HOW DID YOU KNOW?
I KNOW EVERY-THING.
THAT'S RIGHT...

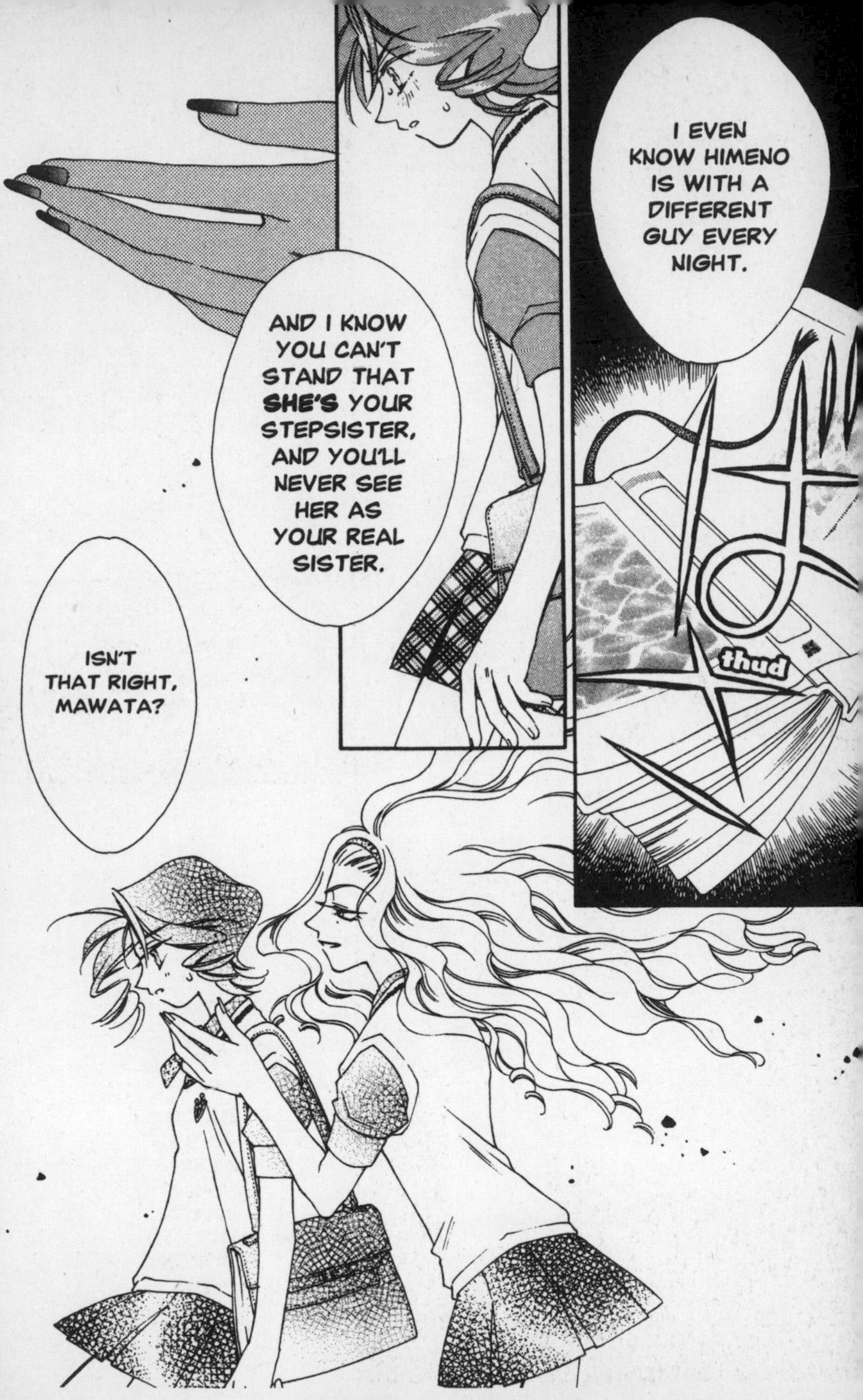
I EVEN KNOW HIMENO IS WITH A DIFFERENT GUY EVERY NIGHT.
thud
AND I KNOW YOU CAN'T STAND THAT SHE'S YOUR STEPSISTER, AND YOU'LL NEVER SEE HER AS YOUR REAL SISTER.
ISN'T THAT RIGHT, MAWATA?

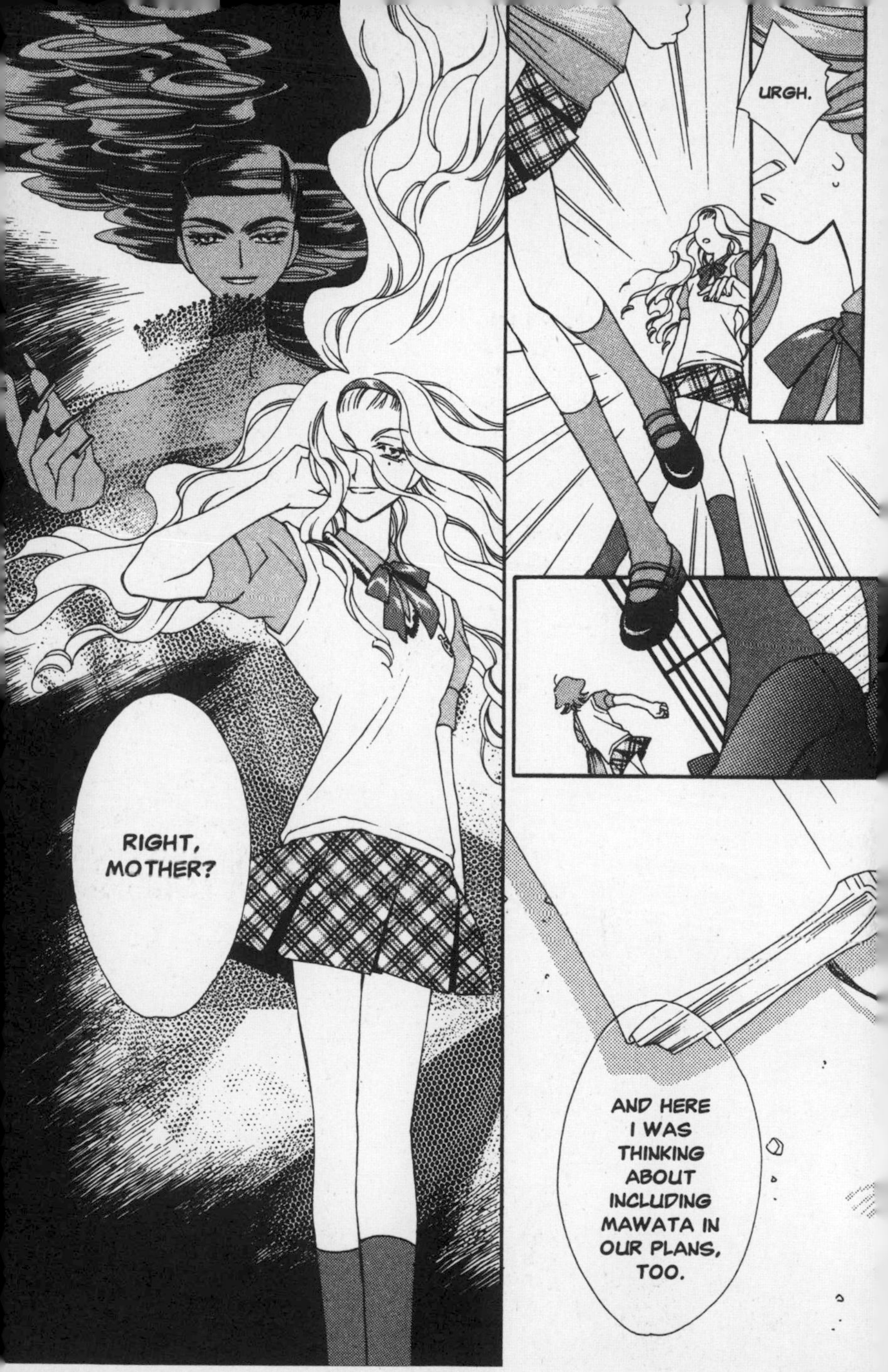
URGH.
AND HERE I WAS THINKING ABOUT INCLUDING MAWATA IN OUR PLANS, TOO.
RIGHT, MOTHER?

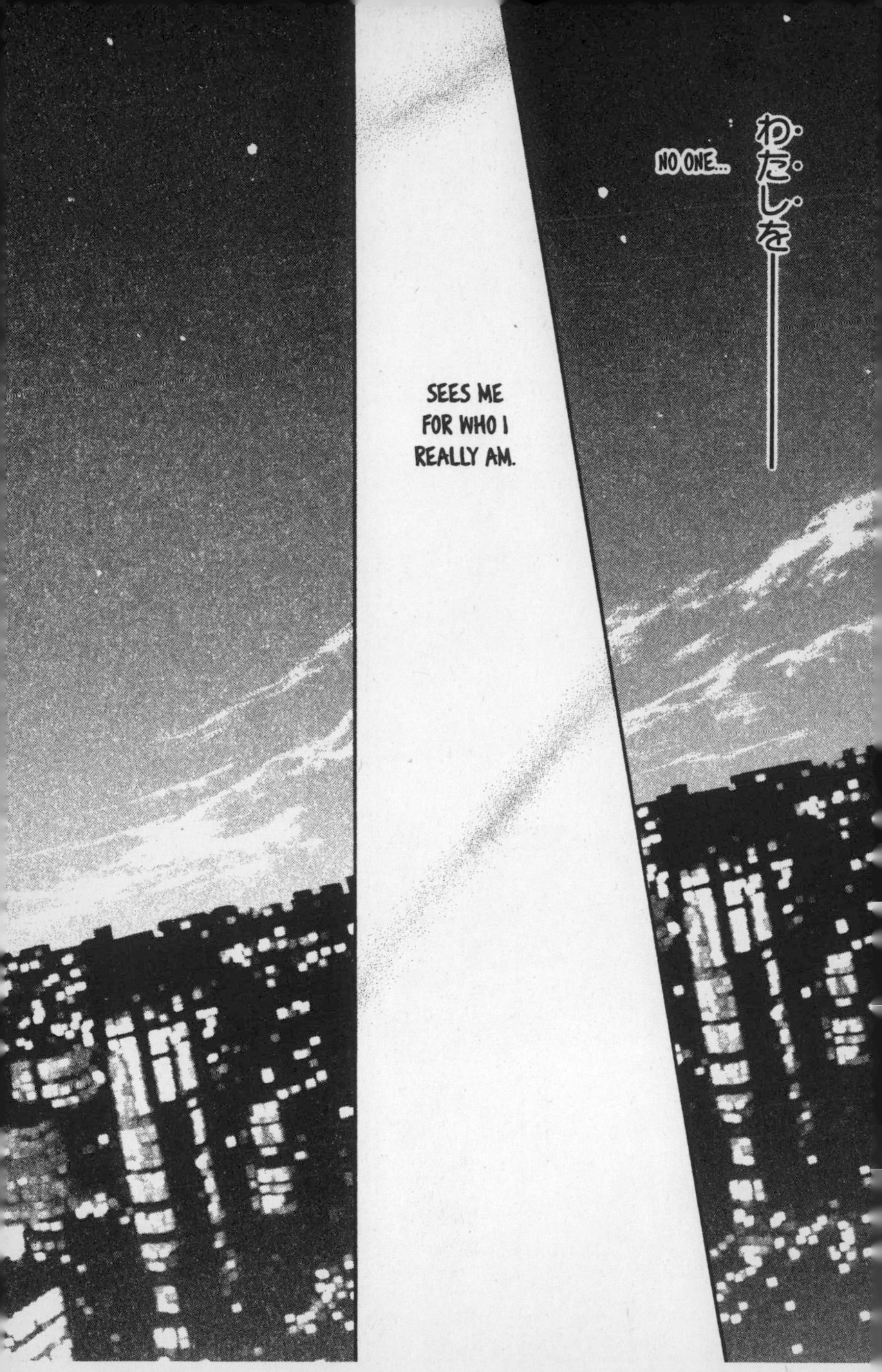
わたしを――
NO ONE...
SEES ME FOR WHO I REALLY AM.

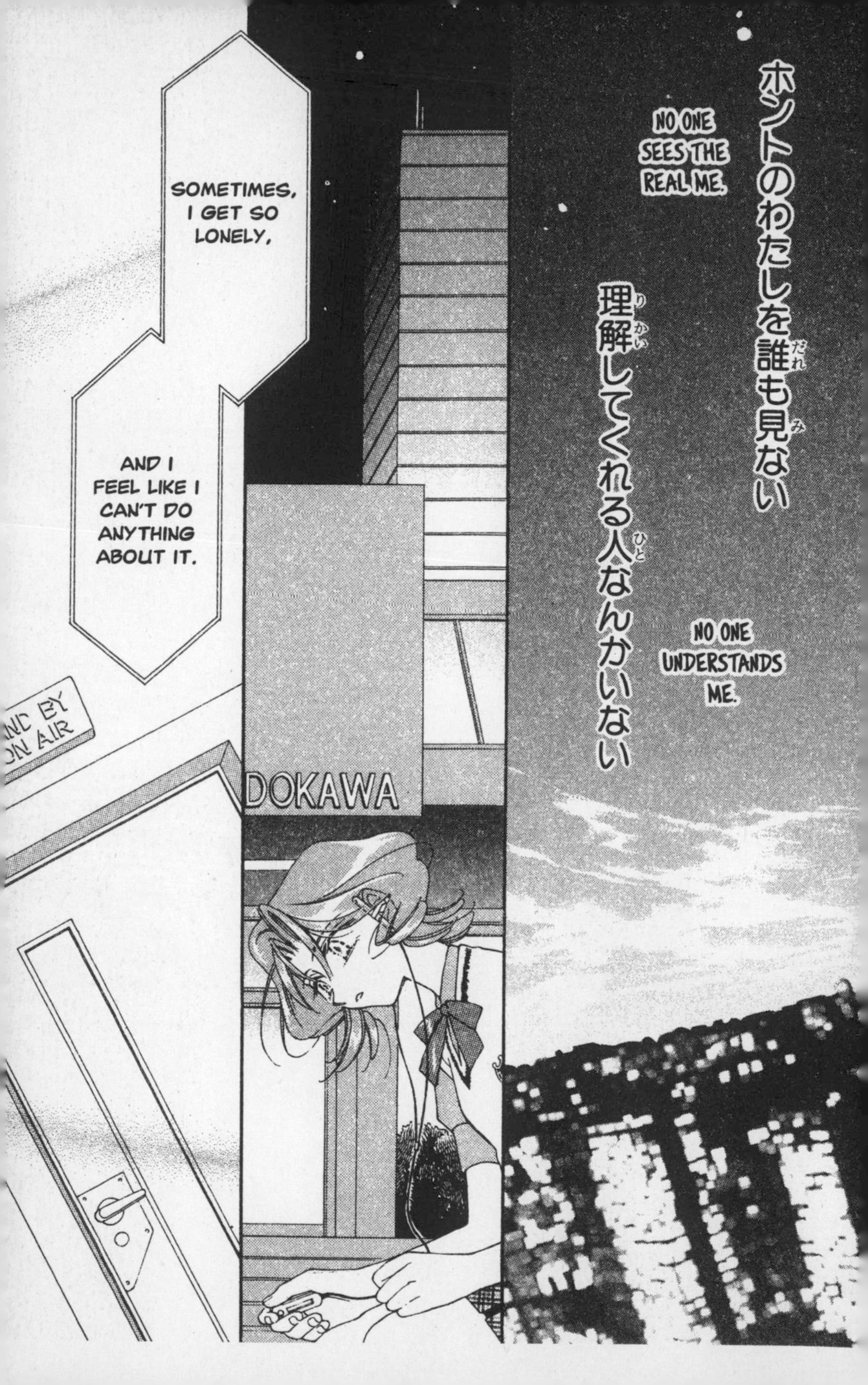
ホントのわたしを誰も見ない
NO ONE SEES THE REAL ME.
理解してくれる人なんかいない
NO ONE UNDERSTANDS ME.
SOMETIMES, I GET SO LONELY,
AND I FEEL LIKE I CAN'T DO ANYTHING ABOUT IT.
DOKAWA

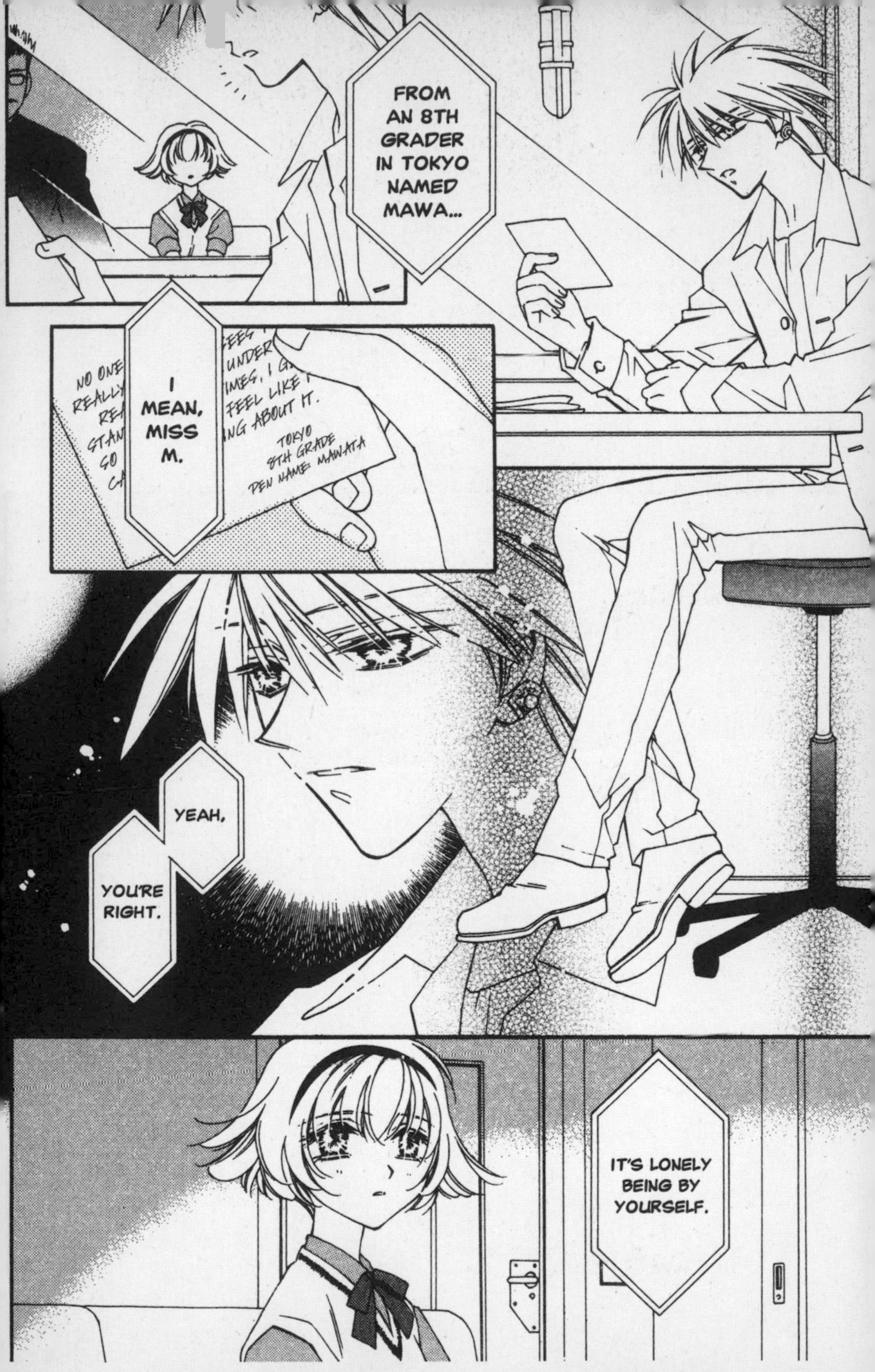
FROM AN 8TH GRADER IN TOKYO NAMED MAWA...
I MEAN, MISS M.
TOKYO
8TH GRADE
PEN NAME: MAWATA
YEAH,
YOU'RE RIGHT.
IT'S LONELY BEING BY YOURSELF.

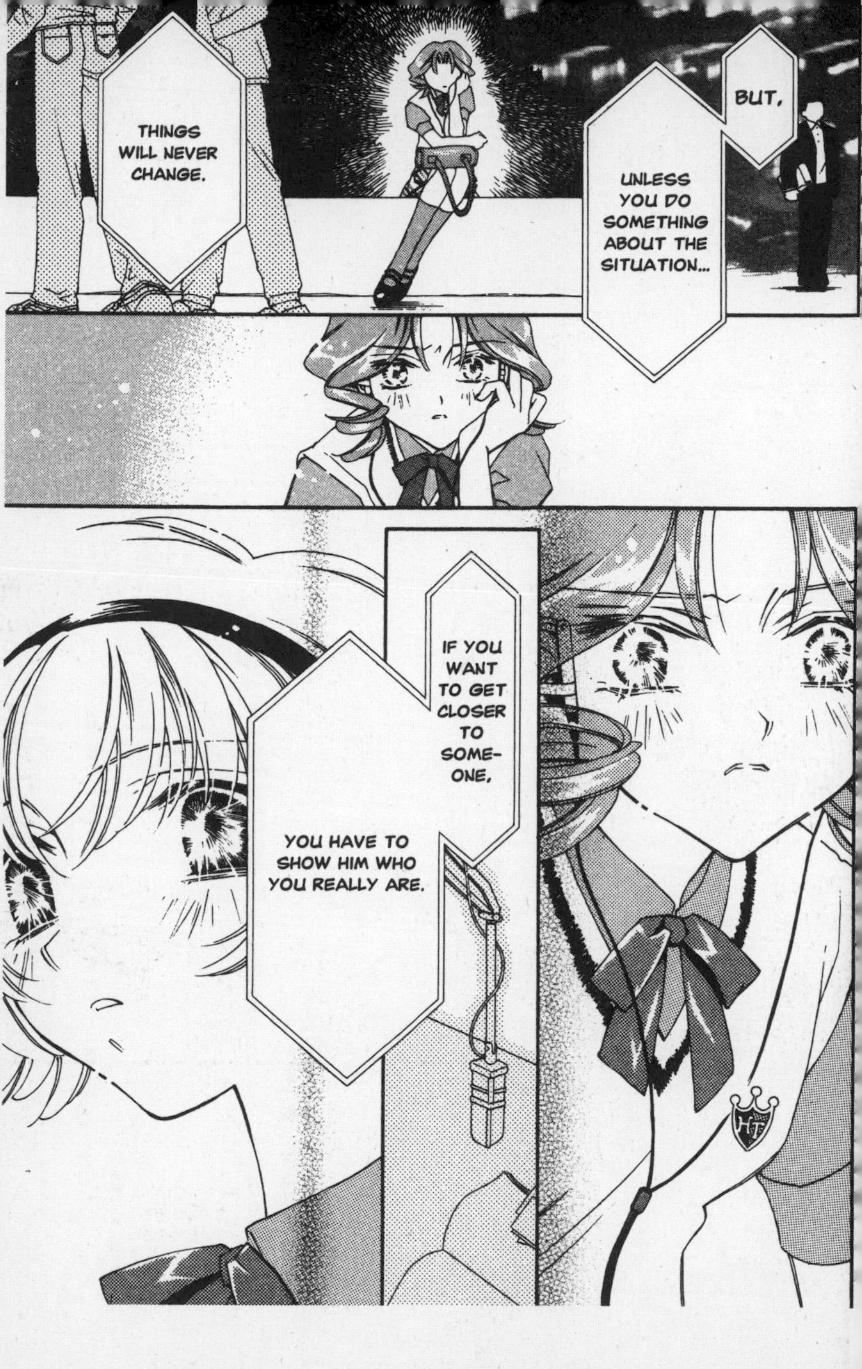
BUT,
UNLESS YOU DO SOMETHING ABOUT THE SITUATION...
THINGS WILL NEVER CHANGE.
IF YOU WANT TO GET CLOSER TO SOME-ONE,
YOU HAVE TO SHOW HIM WHO YOU REALLY ARE.

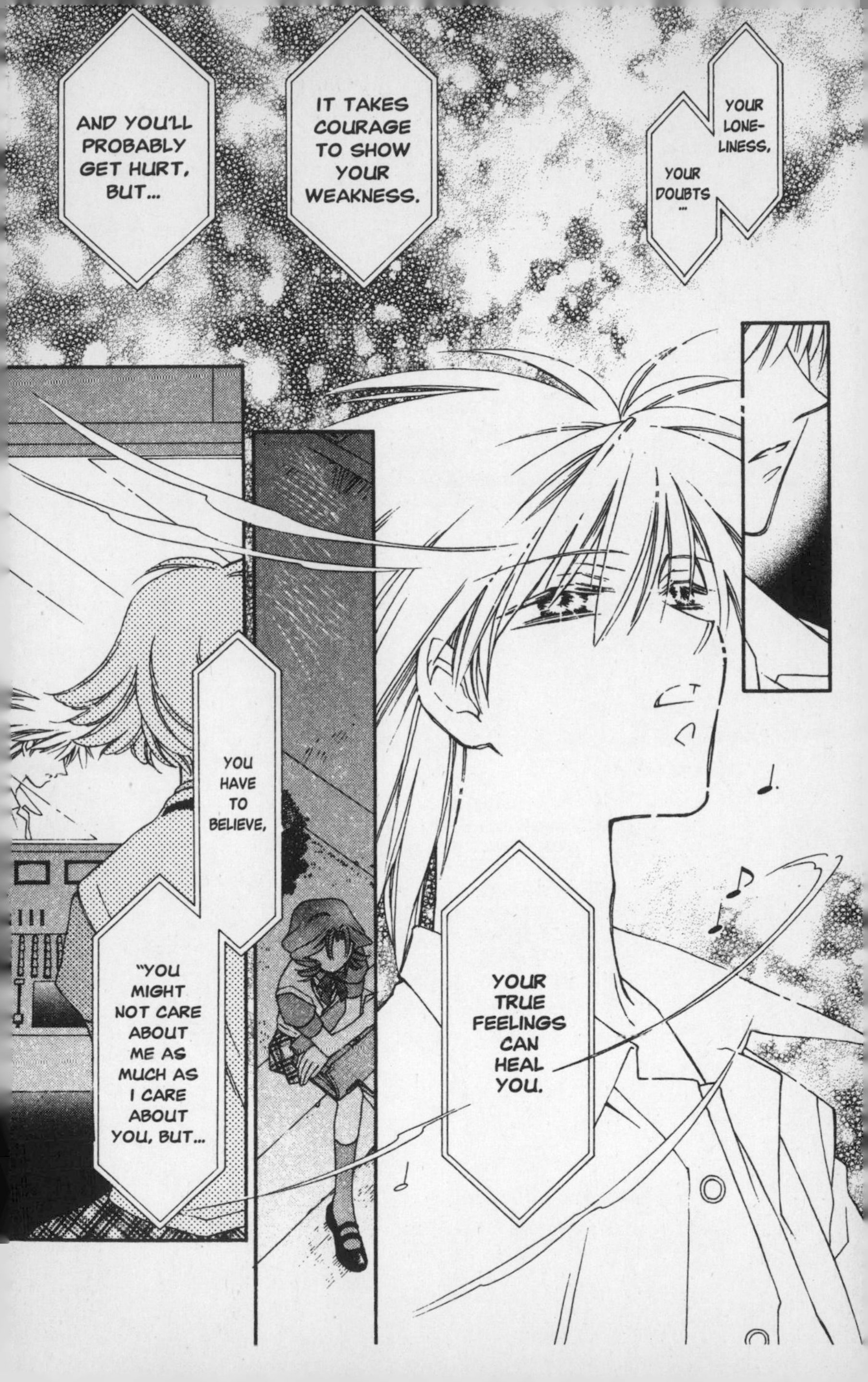
YOUR LONE-LINESS, YOUR DOUBTS...
IT TAKES COURAGE TO SHOW YOUR WEAKNESS.
AND YOU'LL PROBABLY GET HURT, BUT...
YOUR TRUE FEELINGS CAN HEAL YOU.
YOU HAVE TO BELIEVE,
"YOU MIGHT NOT CARE ABOUT ME AS MUCH AS I CARE ABOUT YOU, BUT...

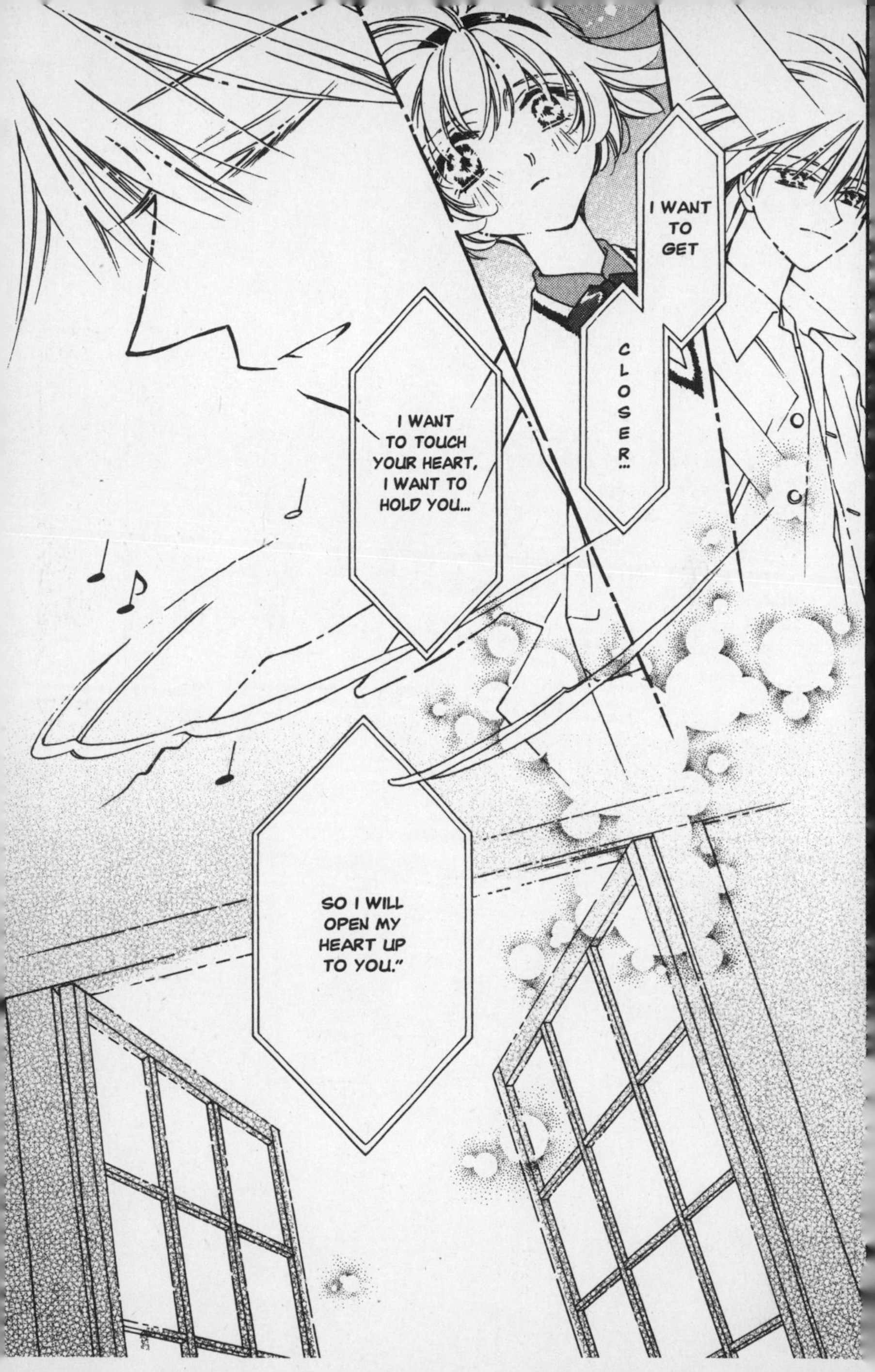
I WANT TO GET CLOSER...
I WANT TO TOUCH YOUR HEART, I WANT TO HOLD YOU...
SO I WILL OPEN MY HEART UP TO YOU."

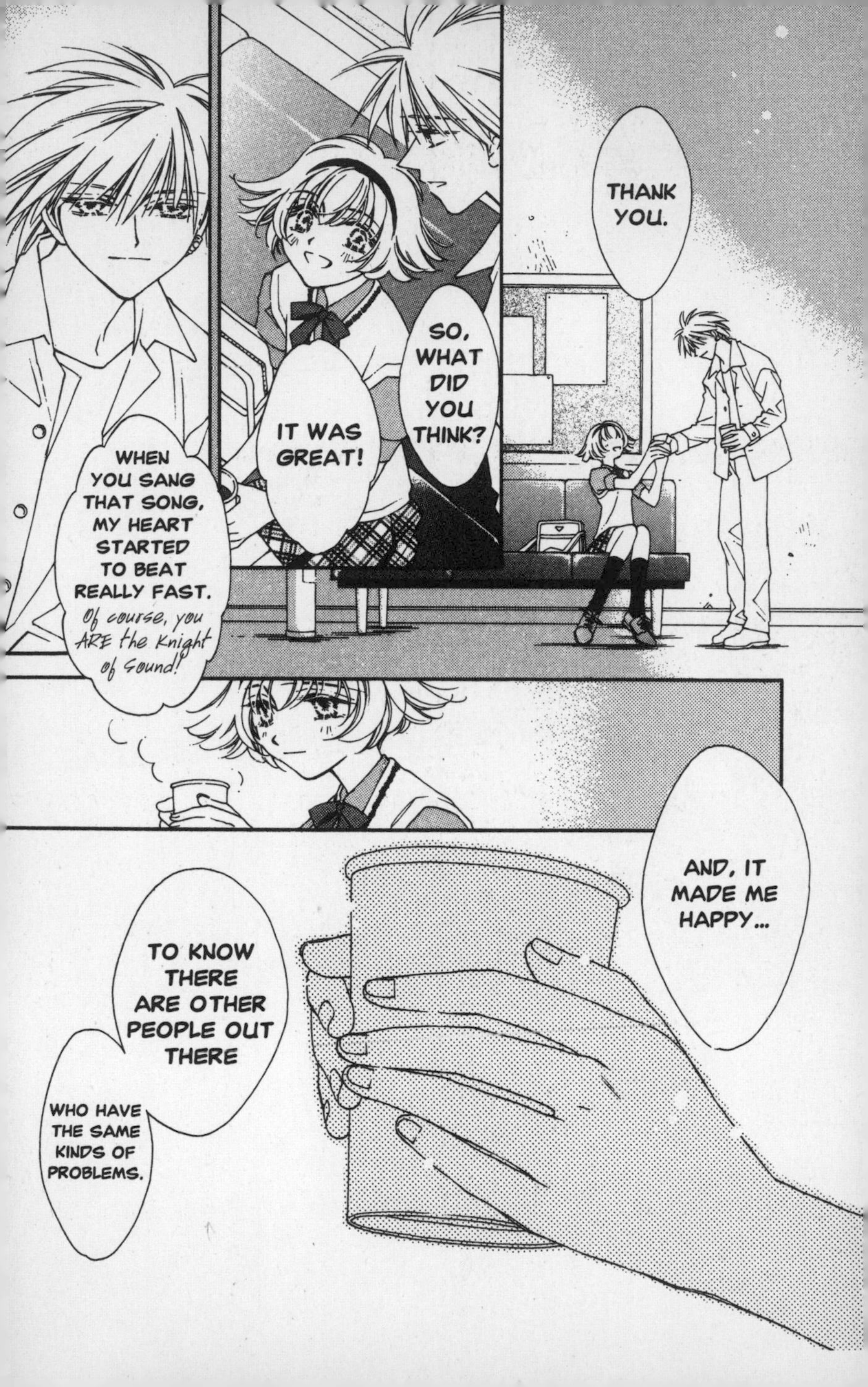
THANK YOU.
SO, WHAT DID YOU THINK?
IT WAS GREAT!
WHEN YOU SANG THAT SONG, MY HEART STARTED TO BEAT REALLY FAST.
Of course, you ARE the Knight of Sound!
AND, IT MADE ME HAPPY...
TO KNOW THERE ARE OTHER PEOPLE OUT THERE
WHO HAVE THE SAME KINDS OF PROBLEMS.

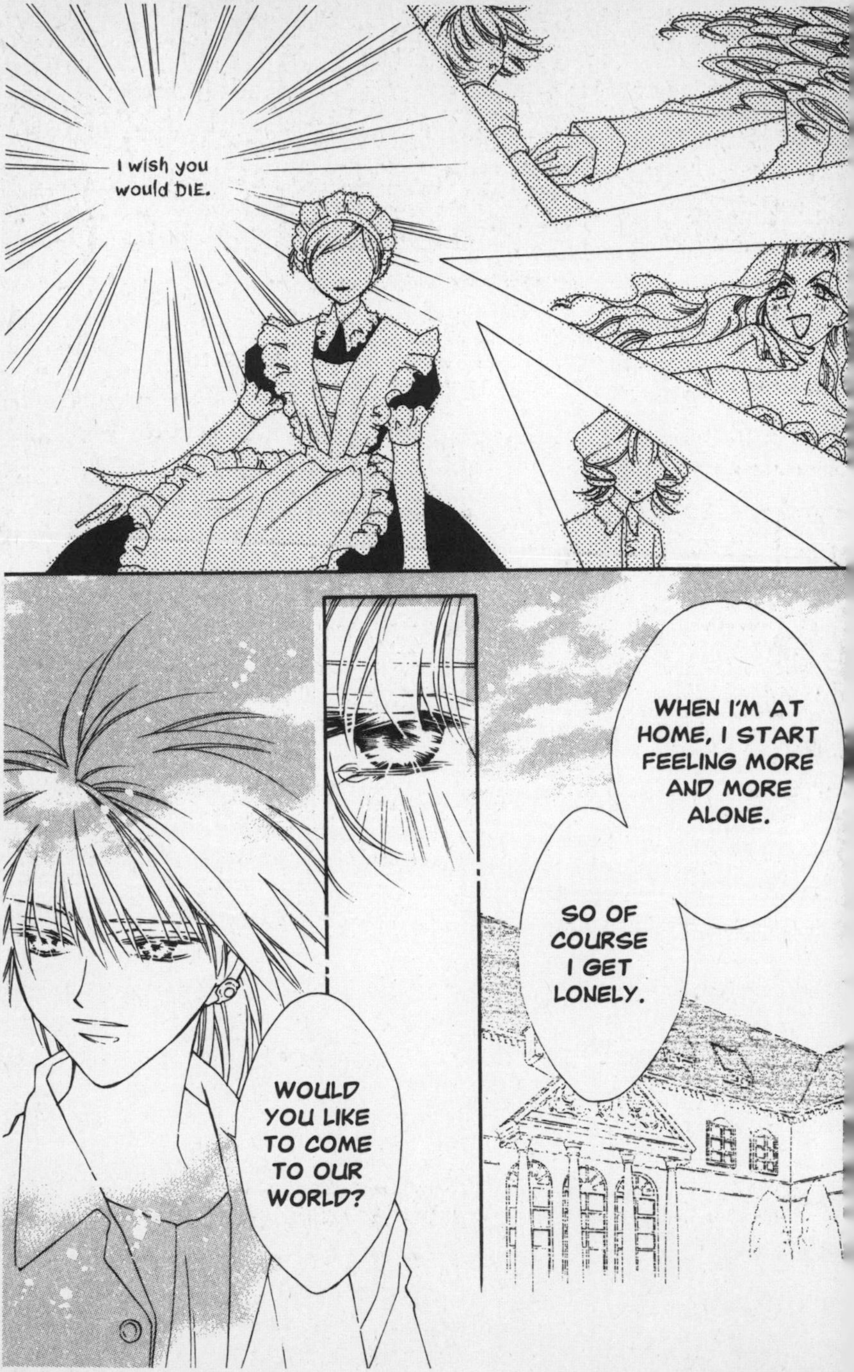
I wish you would DIE.
WHEN I'M AT HOME, I START FEELING MORE AND MORE ALONE.
SO OF COURSE I GET LONELY.
WOULD YOU LIKE TO COME TO OUR WORLD?

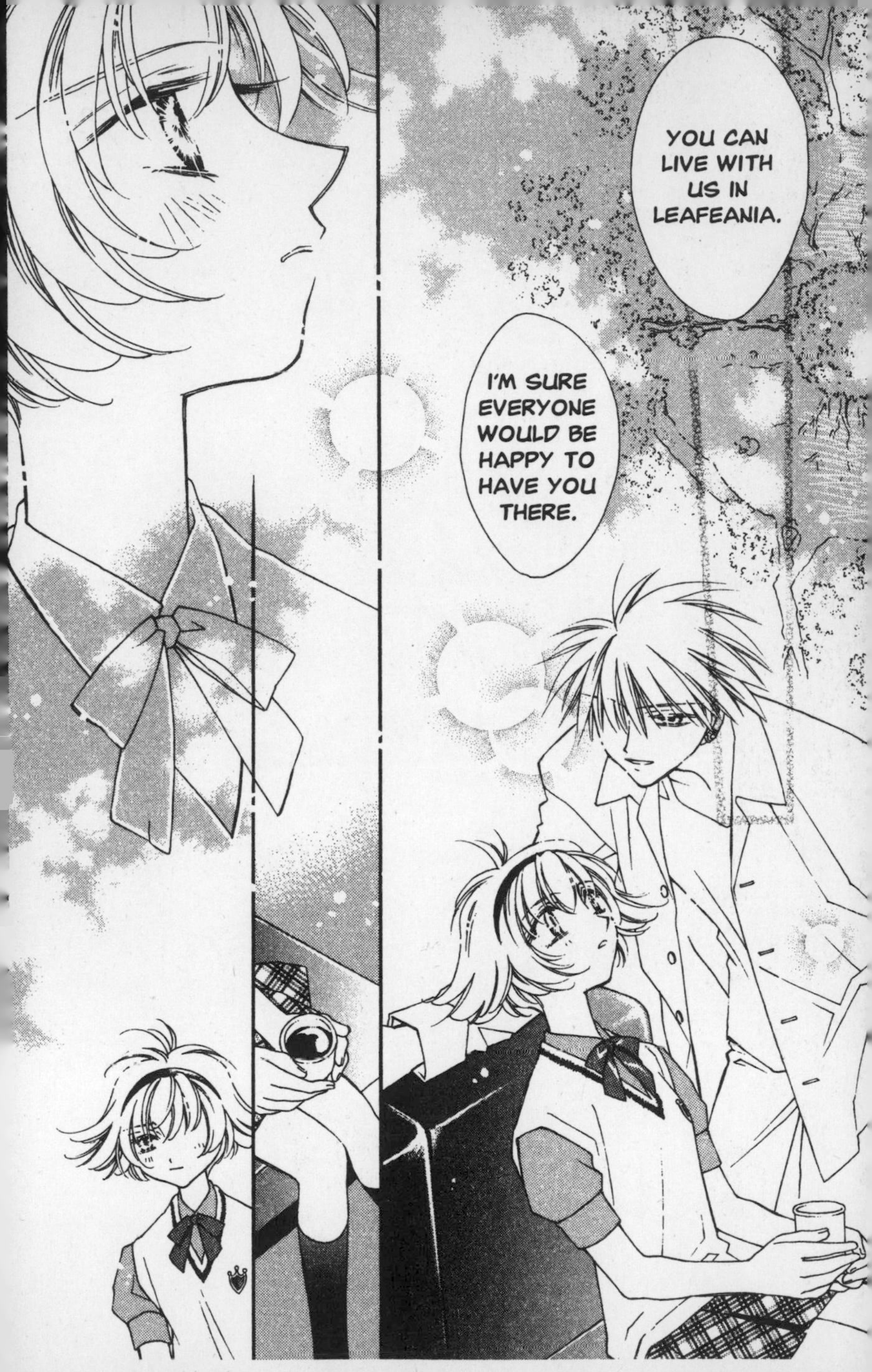
YOU CAN LIVE WITH US IN LEAFEANIA.
I'M SURE EVERYONE WOULD BE HAPPY TO HAVE YOU THERE.

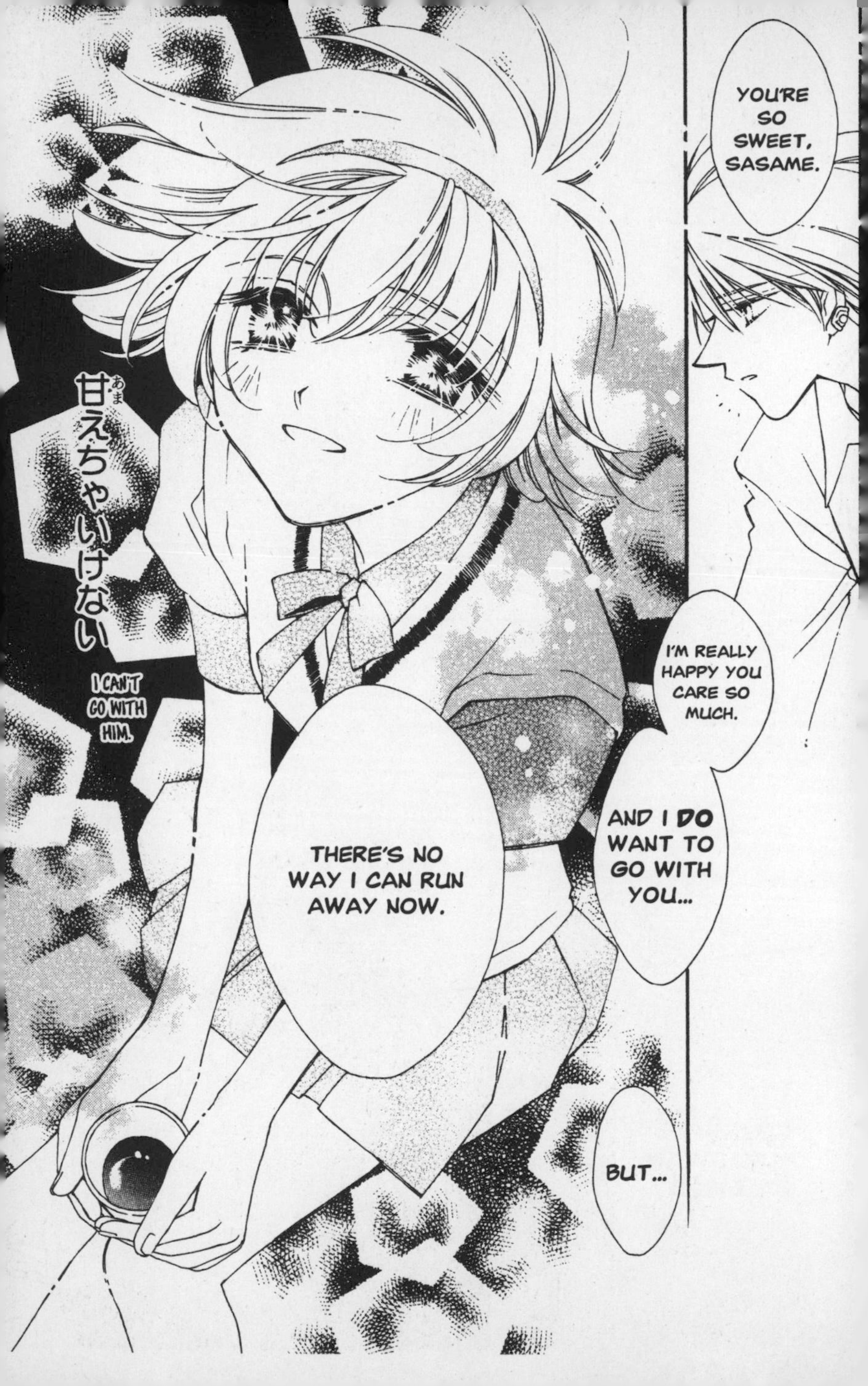
YOU'RE SO SWEET, SASAME.
I'M REALLY HAPPY YOU CARE SO MUCH.
AND I DO WANT TO GO WITH YOU...
BUT...
THERE'S NO WAY I CAN RUN AWAY NOW.
甘(あま)えちゃいけない
I CAN'T GO WITH HIM.

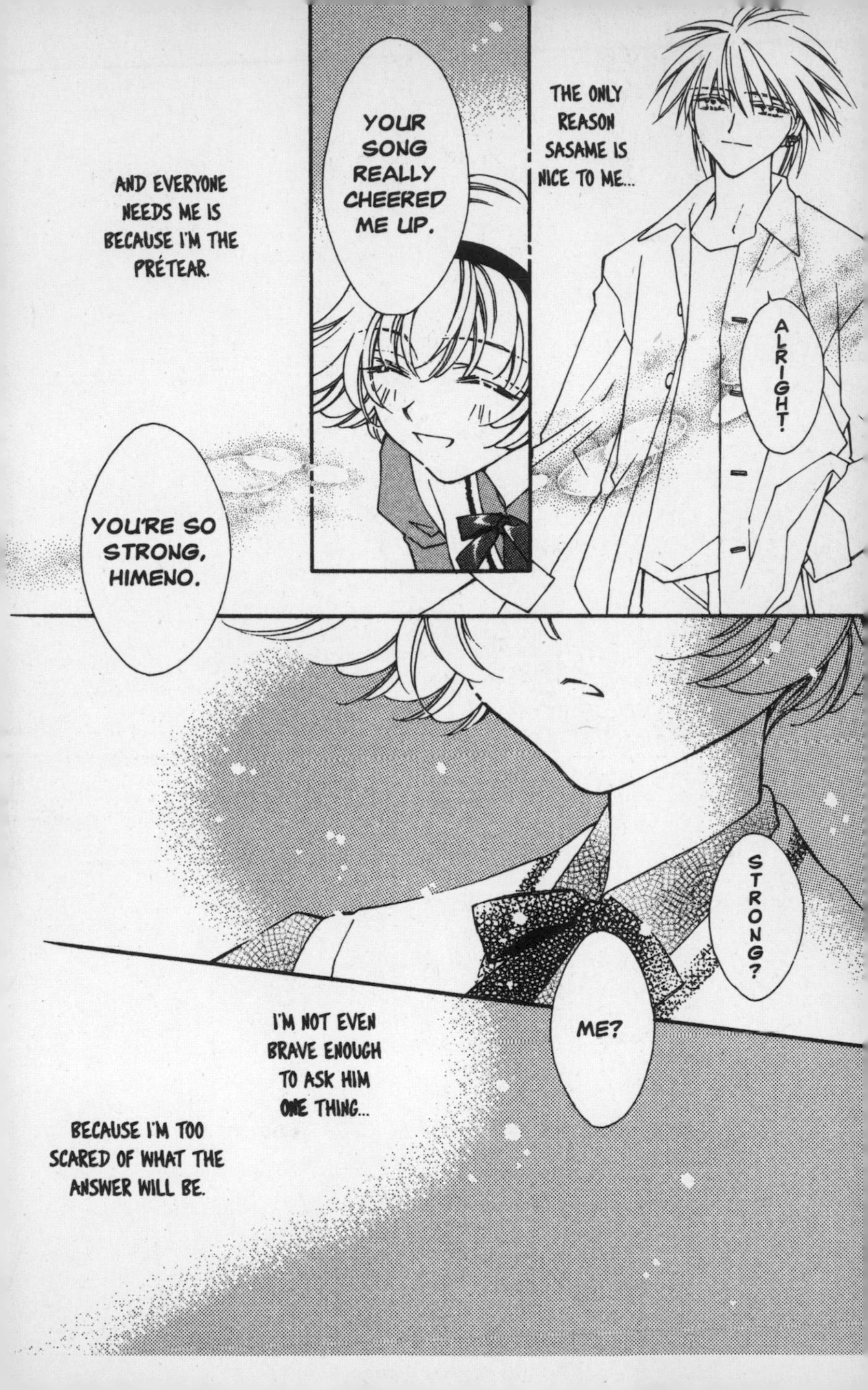
THE ONLY REASON SASAME IS NICE TO ME...
ALRIGHT!
YOUR SONG REALLY CHEERED ME UP.
AND EVERYONE NEEDS ME IS BECAUSE I'M THE PRÉTEAR.
YOU'RE SO STRONG, HIMENO.
STRONG?
ME?
I'M NOT EVEN BRAVE ENOUGH TO ASK HIM ONE THING...
BECAUSE I'M TOO SCARED OF WHAT THE ANSWER WILL BE.

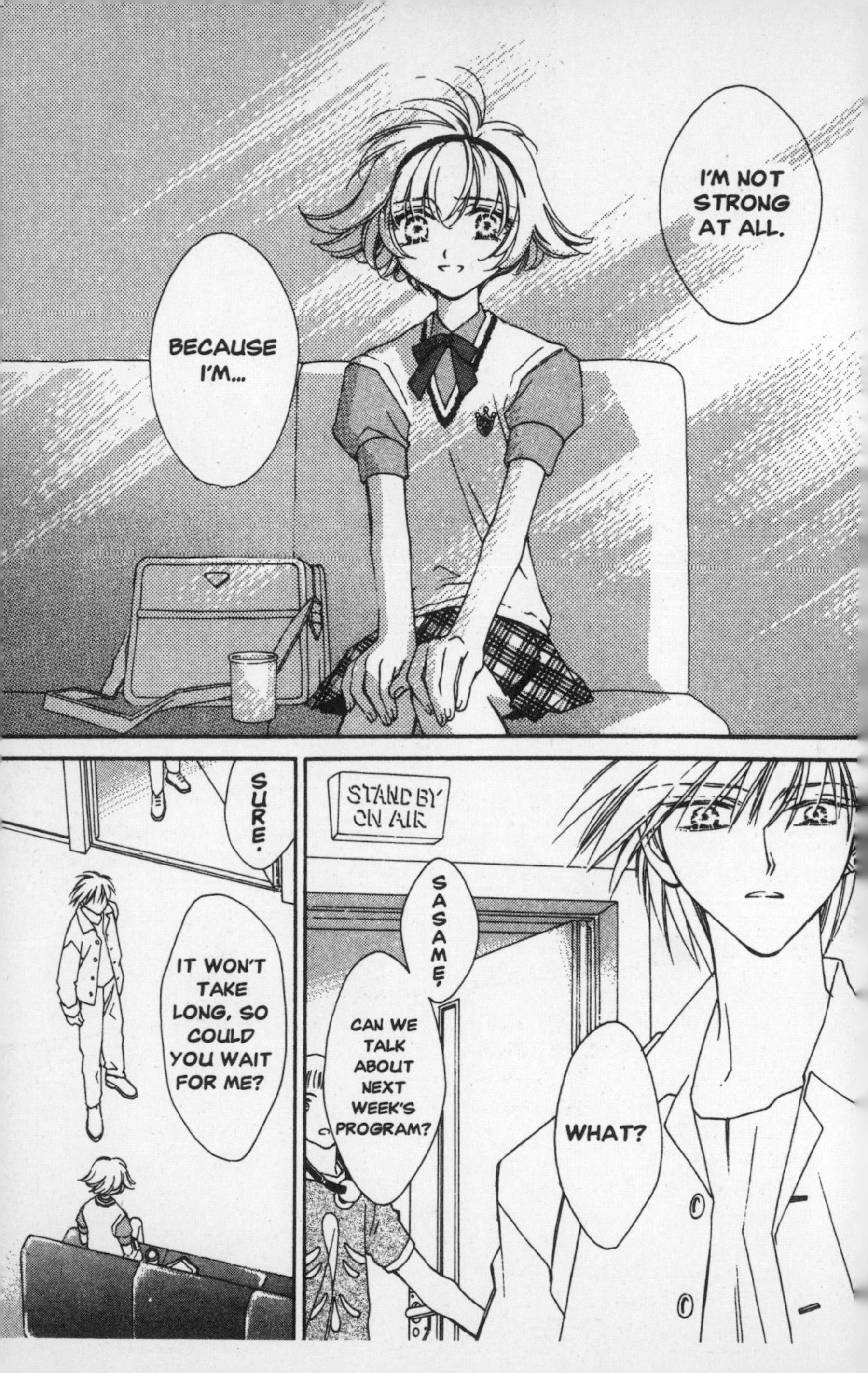
I'M NOT STRONG AT ALL.
BECAUSE I'M...
STAND BY
ON AIR
WHAT?
SASAME,
CAN WE TALK ABOUT NEXT WEEK'S PROGRAM?
SURE.
IT WON'T TAKE LONG, SO COULD YOU WAIT FOR ME?

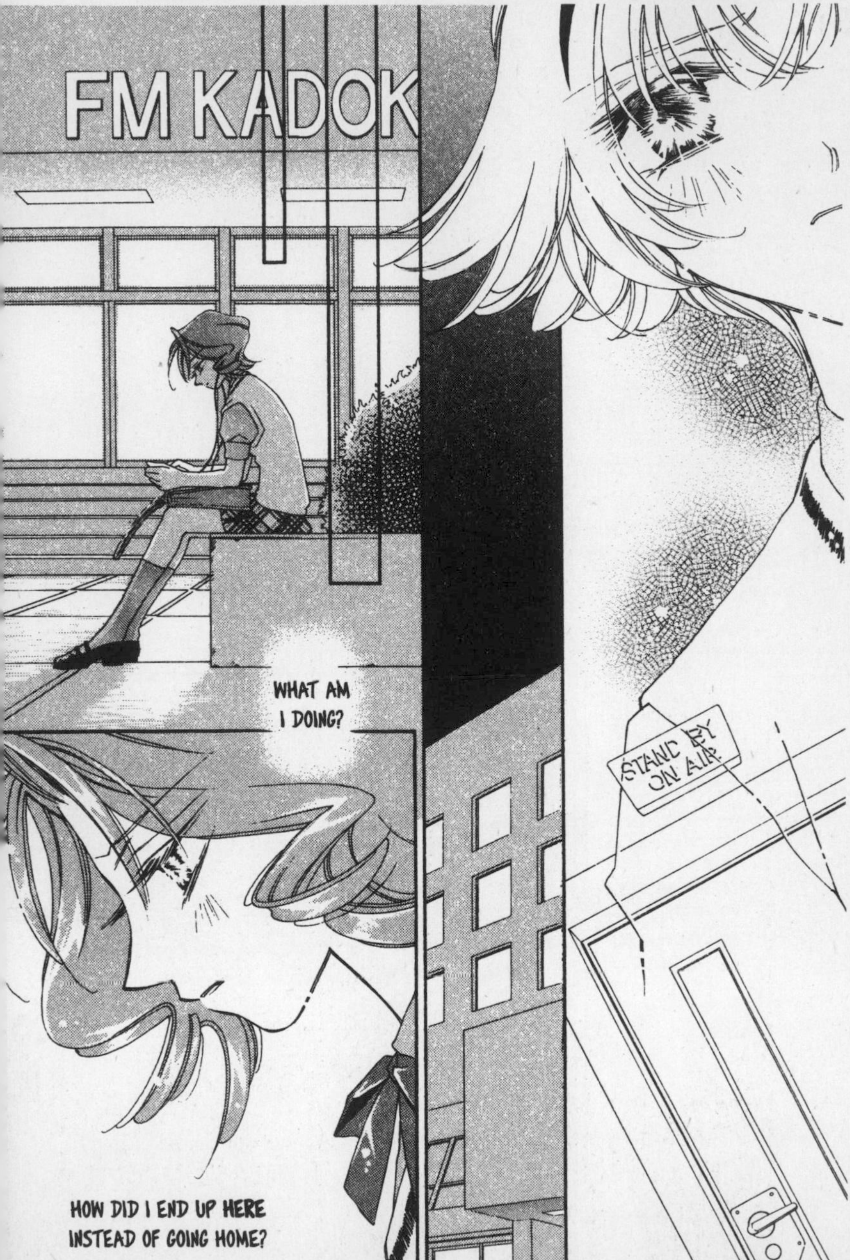

FM KADOK
WHAT AM I DOING?
HOW DID I END UP HERE INSTEAD OF GOING HOME?
STAND BY ON AIR

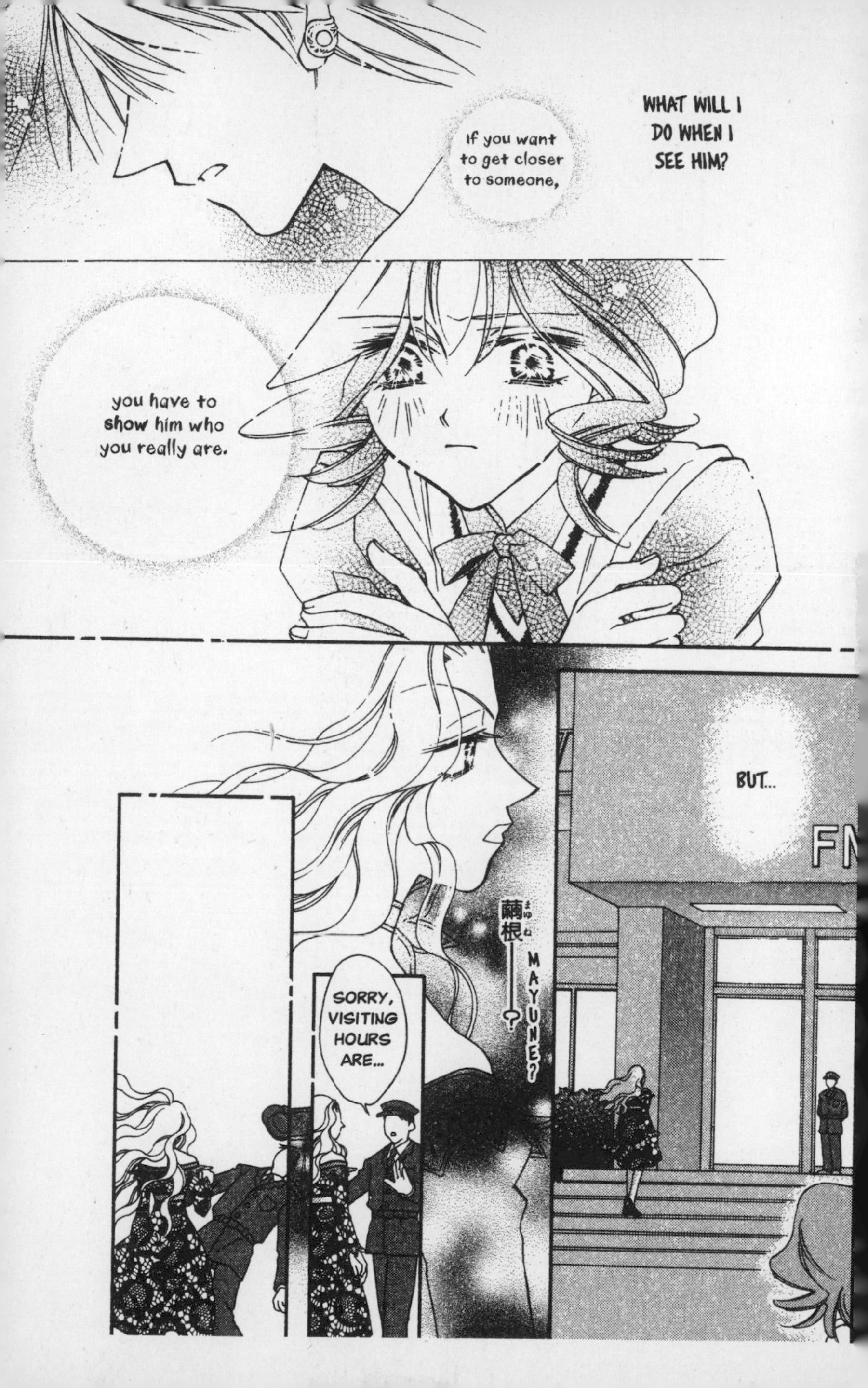
WHAT WILL I DO WHEN I SEE HIM?
If you want to get closer to someone,
you have to show him who you really are.
BUT...
FN
繭根――?
MAYUNE?
SORRY, VISITING HOURS ARE...

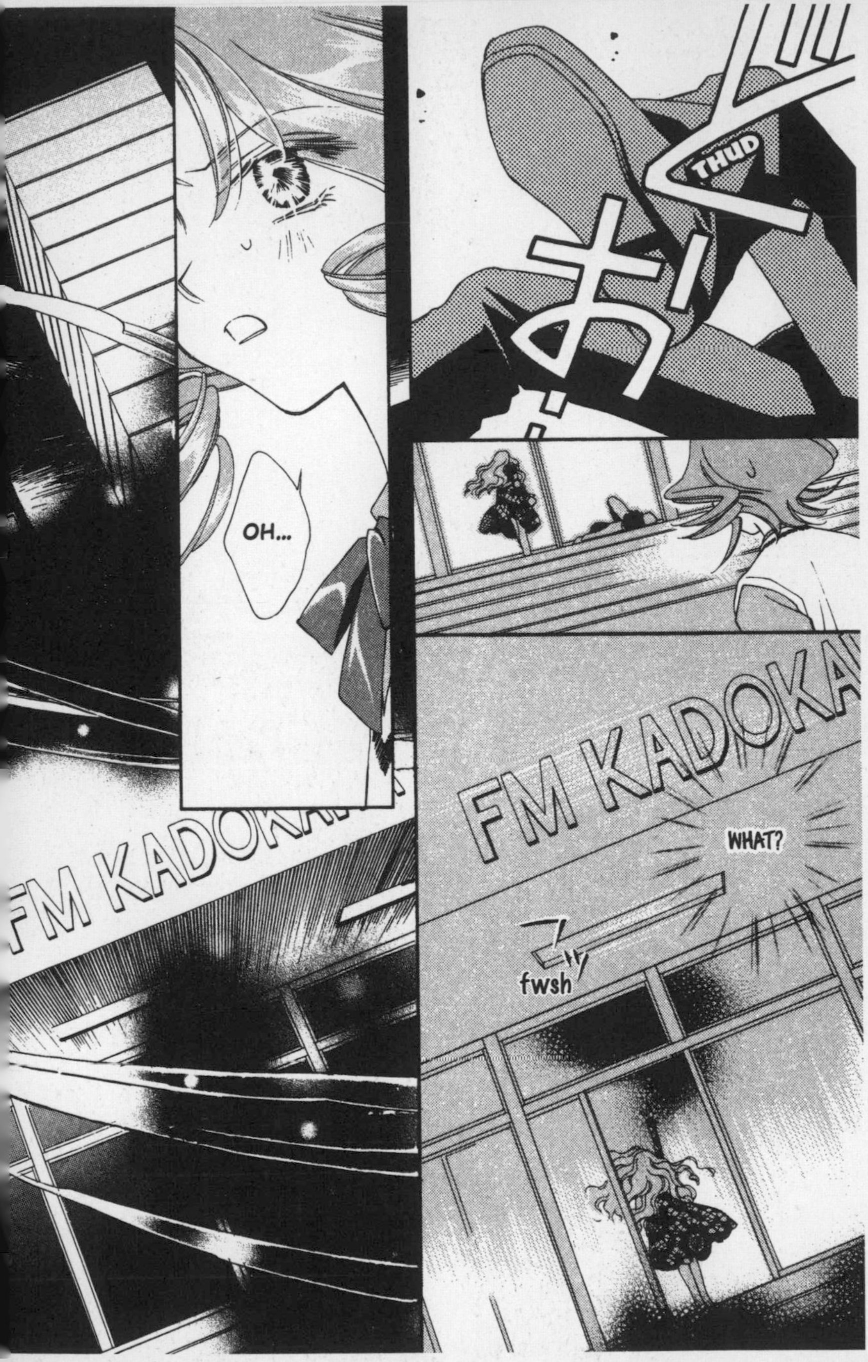
THUD
FM KADOKA
WHAT?
fwsh
OH...
FM KADOKA

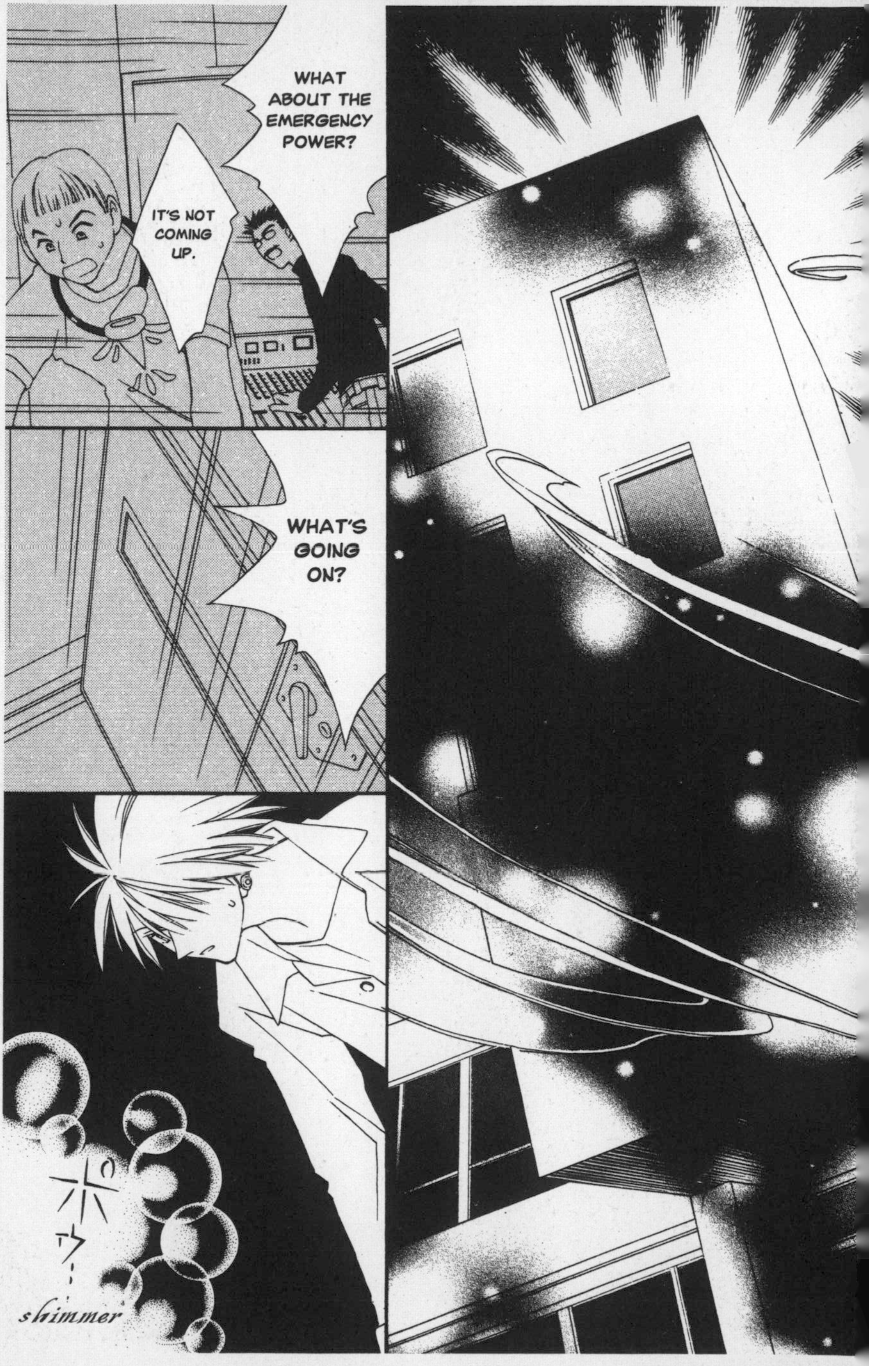
WHAT ABOUT THE EMERGENCY POWER?
IT'S NOT COMING UP.
WHAT'S GOING ON?
shimmer

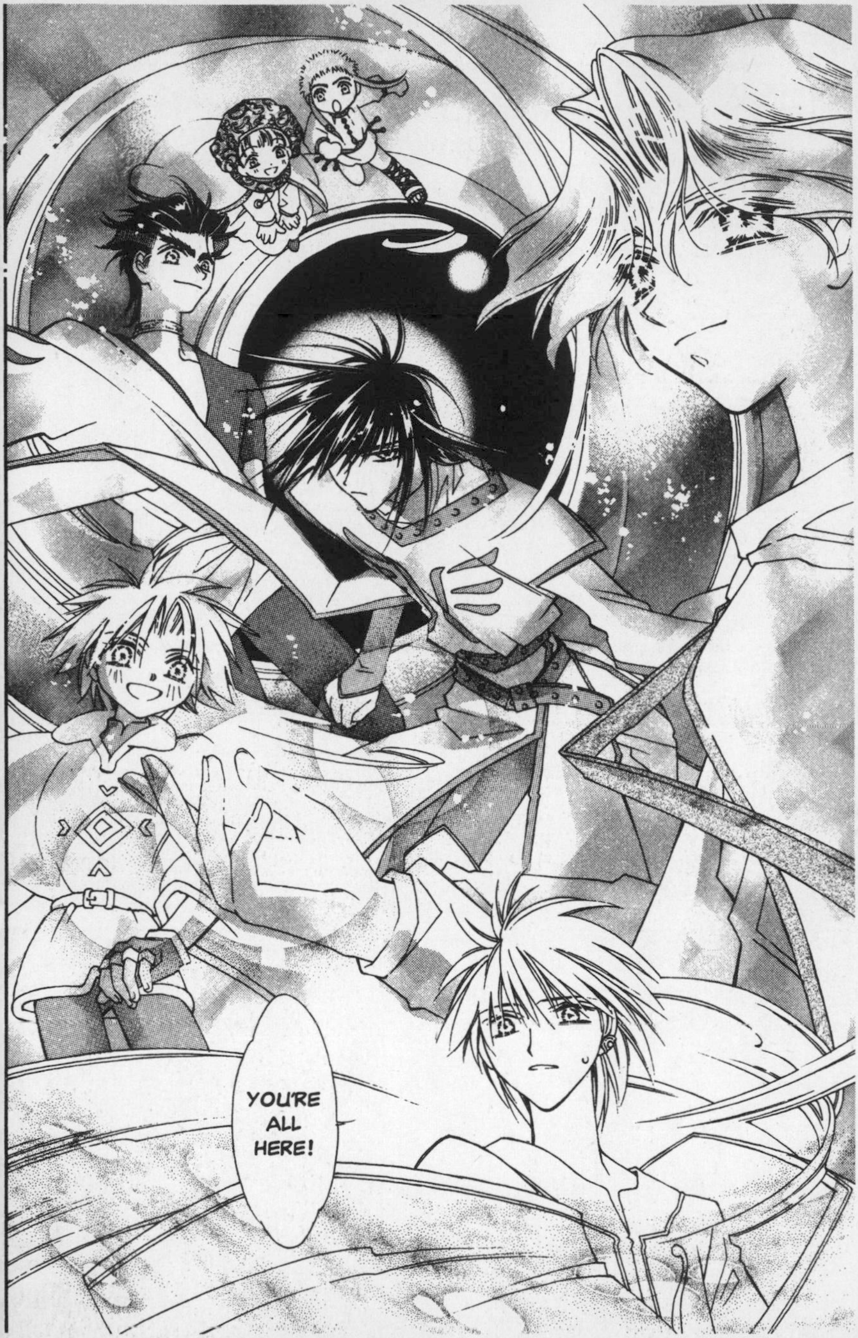
YOU'RE ALL HERE!

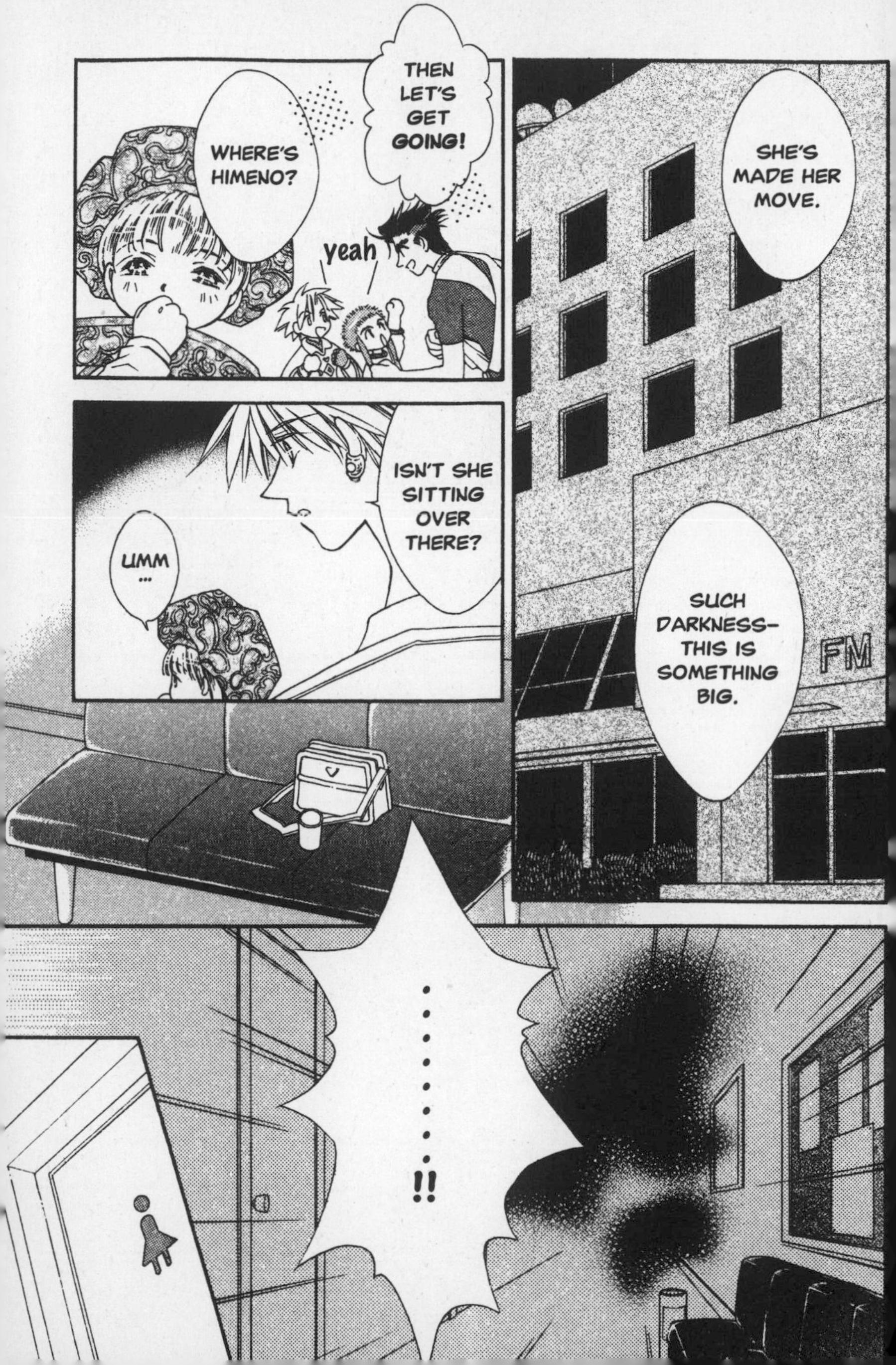
SHE'S MADE HER MOVE.
SUCH DARKNESS— THIS IS SOMETHING BIG.
FM
THEN LET'S GET GOING!
yeah
WHERE'S HIMENO?
ISN'T SHE SITTING OVER THERE?
UMM ...
......!!

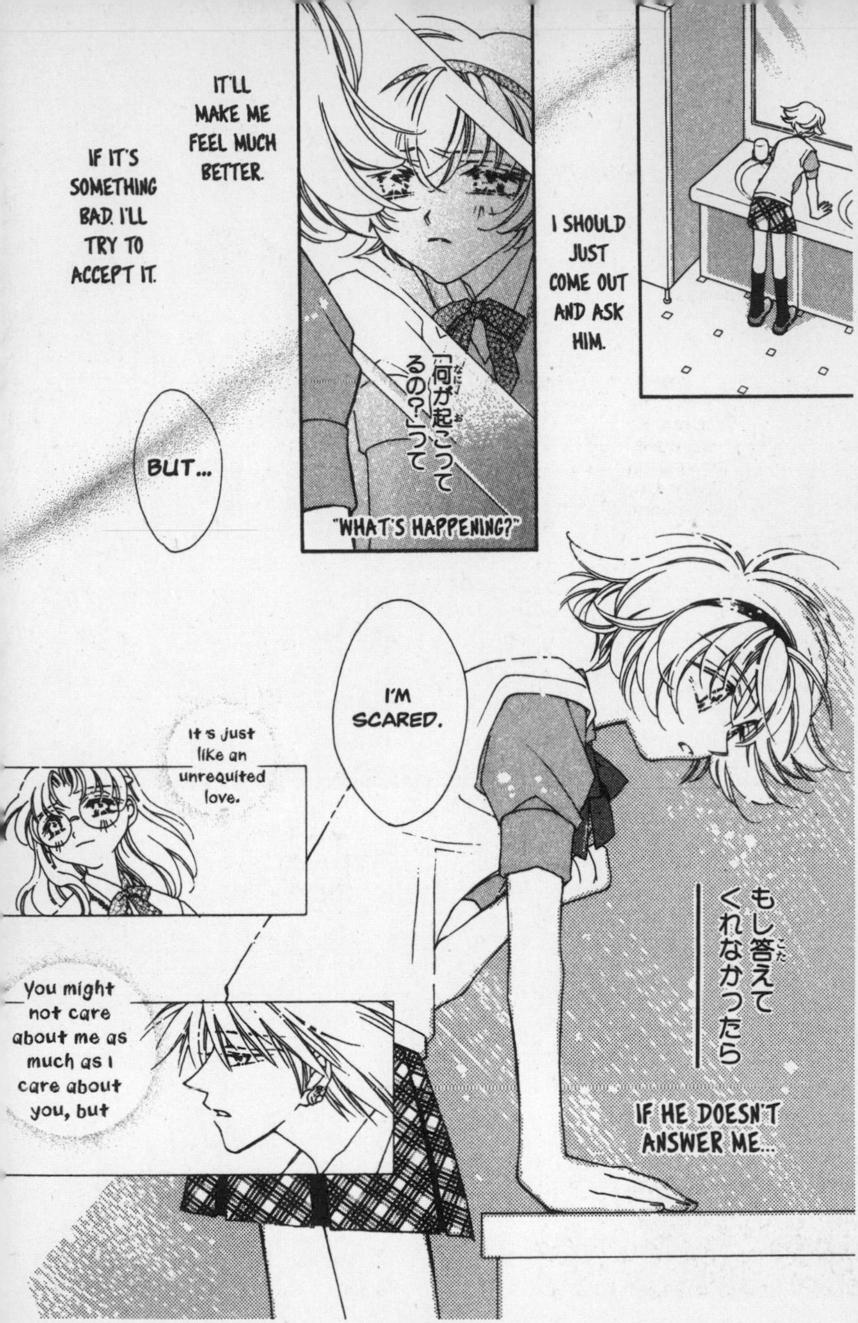
I SHOULD JUST COME OUT AND ASK HIM.
「何が起こってるの?」って
"WHAT'S HAPPENING?"
IT'LL MAKE ME FEEL MUCH BETTER.
IF IT'S SOMETHING BAD, I'LL TRY TO ACCEPT IT.
BUT...
もし答えてくれなかったら――
IF HE DOESN'T ANSWER ME...
I'M SCARED.
It's just like an unrequited love.
You might not care about me as much as I care about you, but

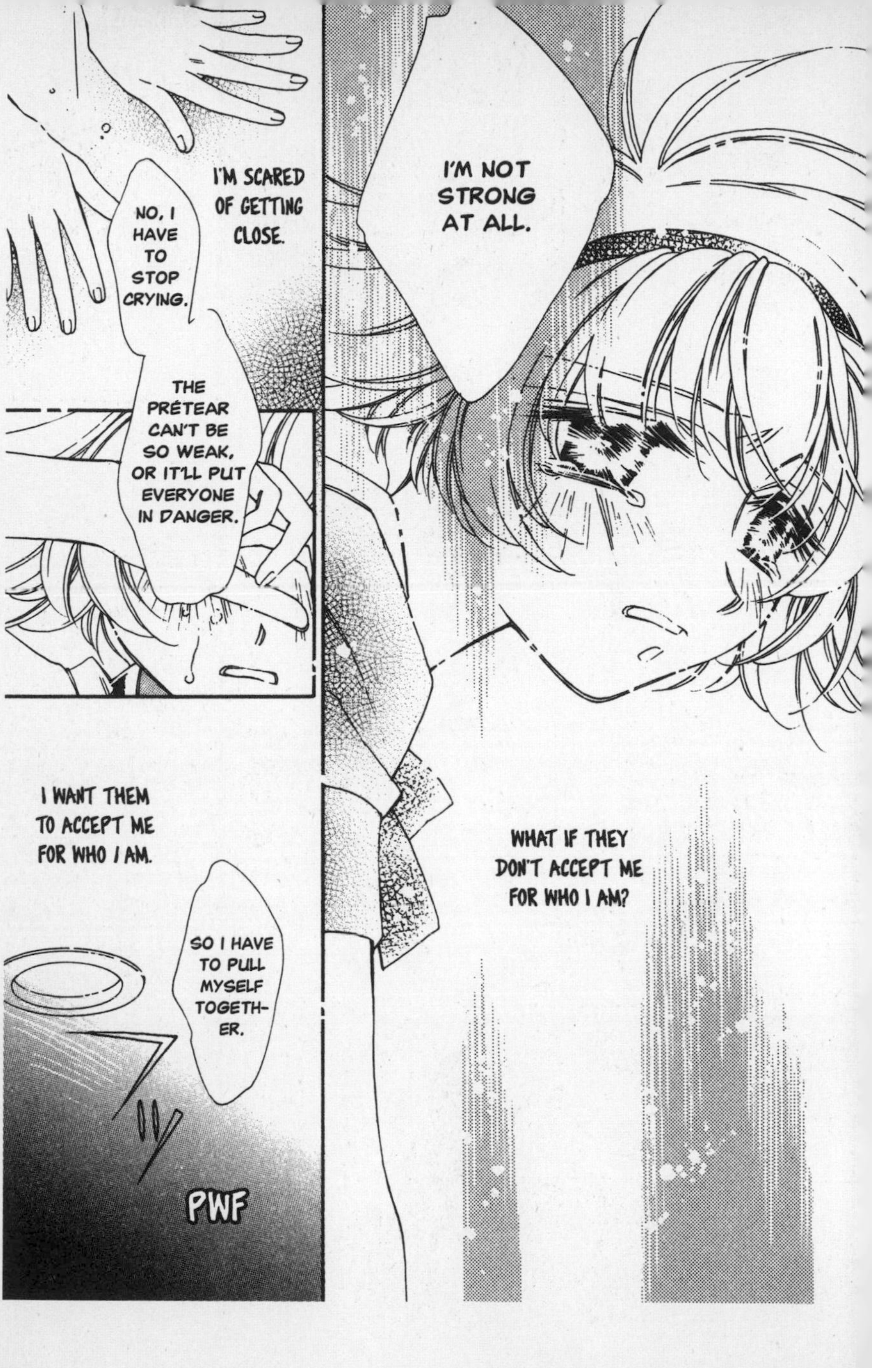
I'M NOT STRONG AT ALL.
WHAT IF THEY DON'T ACCEPT ME FOR WHO I AM?
I'M SCARED OF GETTING CLOSE.
NO, I HAVE TO STOP CRYING.
THE PRÉTEAR CAN'T BE SO WEAK, OR IT'LL PUT EVERYONE IN DANGER.
I WANT THEM TO ACCEPT ME FOR WHO I AM.
SO I HAVE TO PULL MYSELF TOGETH-ER.
PWF

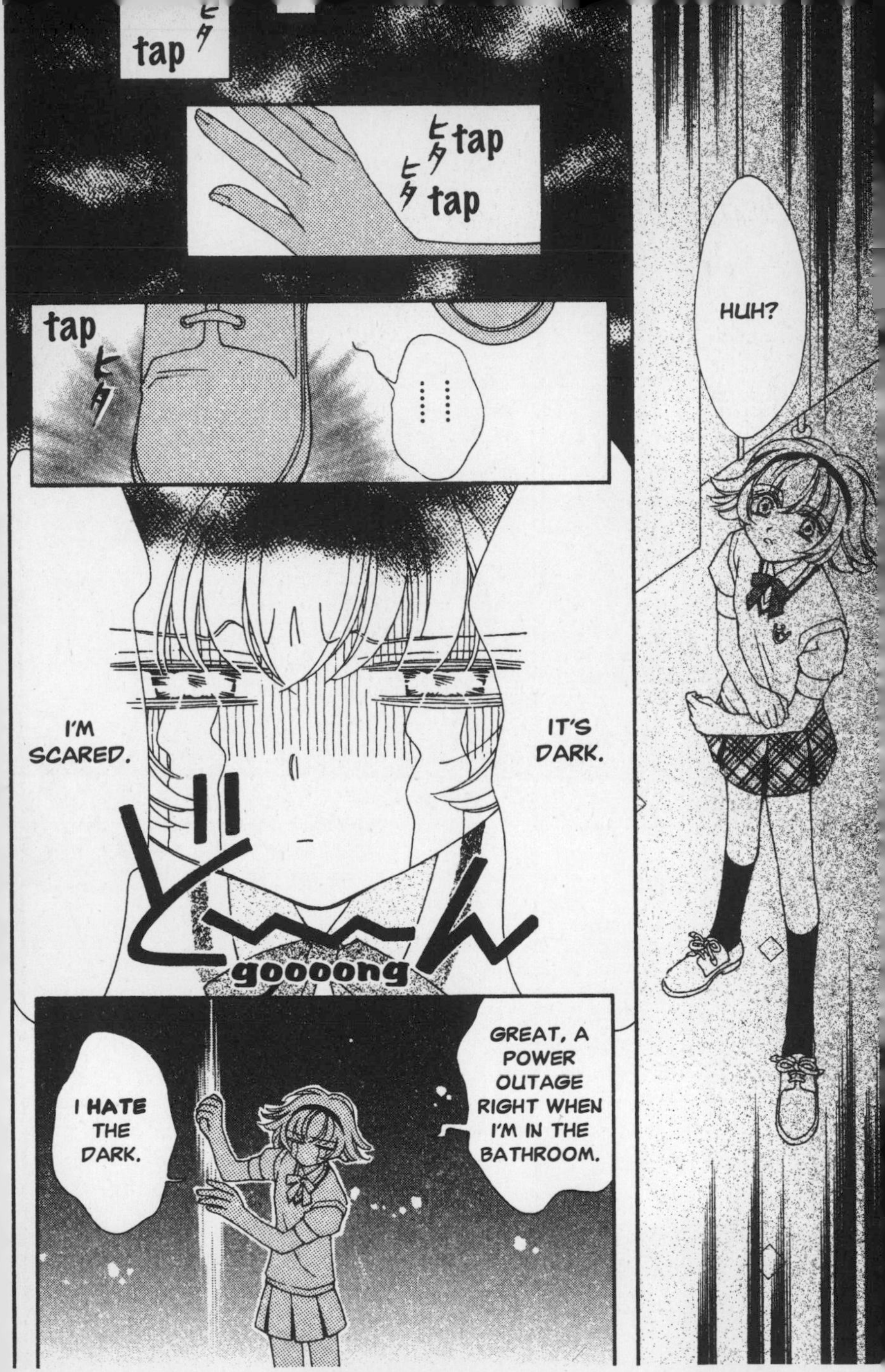
HUH?
tap ヒタ
ヒタ tap
ヒタ tap
tap ヒタ
......
IT'S DARK.
I'M SCARED.
goooong
GREAT, A POWER OUTAGE RIGHT WHEN I'M IN THE BATHROOM.
I HATE THE DARK.

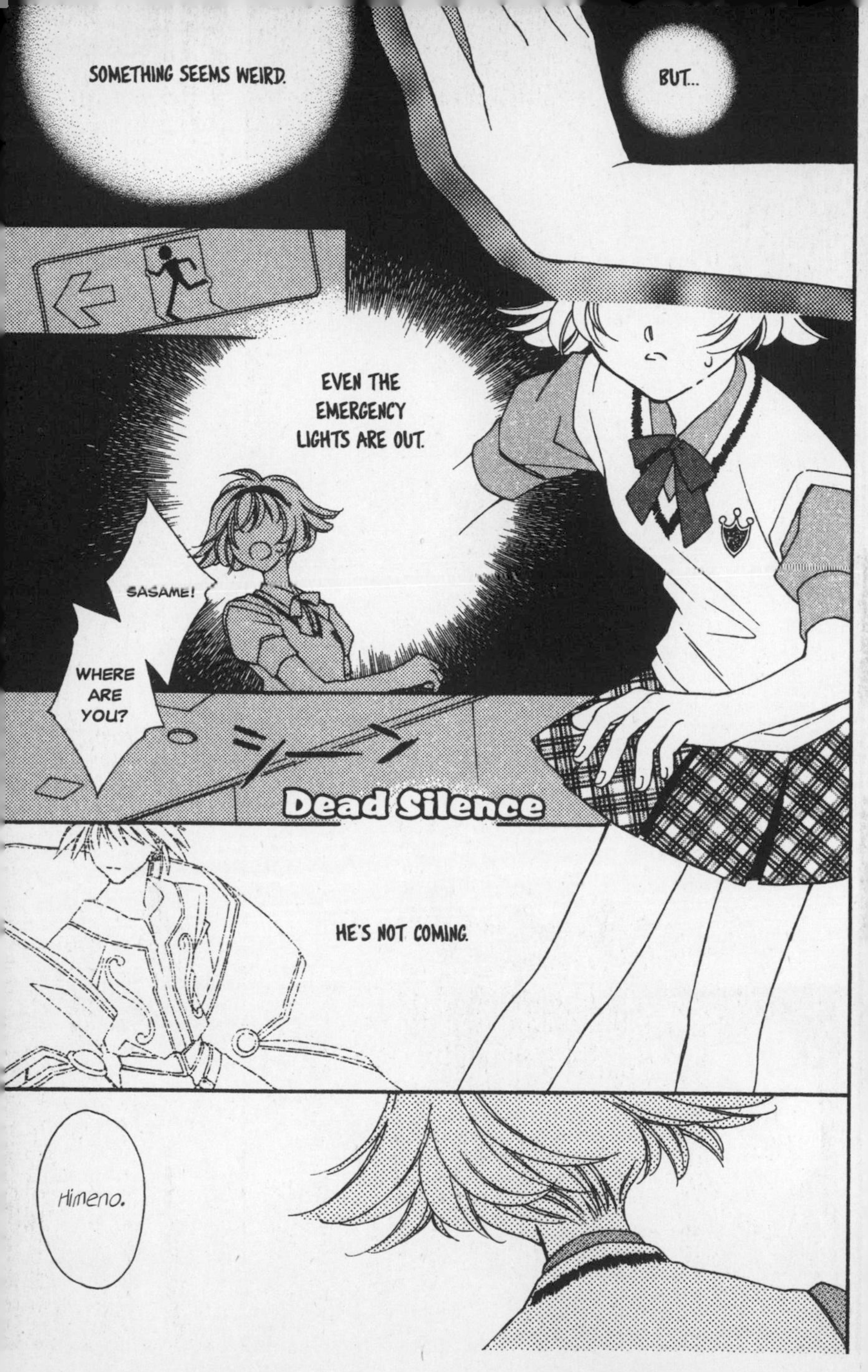
BUT...
SOMETHING SEEMS WEIRD.
EVEN THE EMERGENCY LIGHTS ARE OUT.
SASAME!
WHERE ARE YOU?
Dead Silence
HE'S NOT COMING.
Himeno.

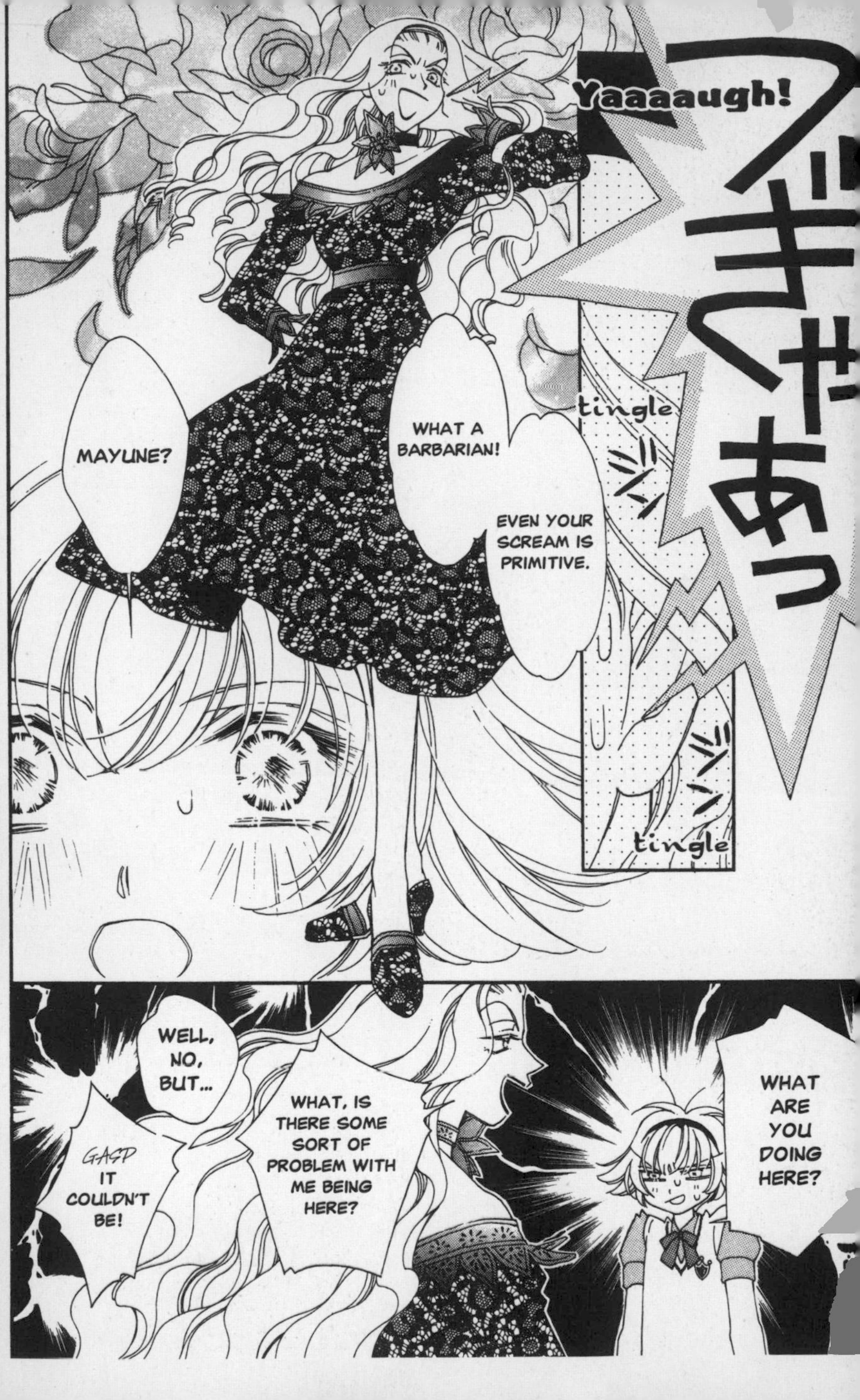
Yaaaaugh!
tingle
tingle
WHAT A BARBARIAN!
EVEN YOUR SCREAM IS PRIMITIVE.
MAYUNE?
WHAT ARE YOU DOING HERE?
WHAT, IS THERE SOME SORT OF PROBLEM WITH ME BEING HERE?
WELL, NO, BUT...
GASP IT COULDN'T BE!

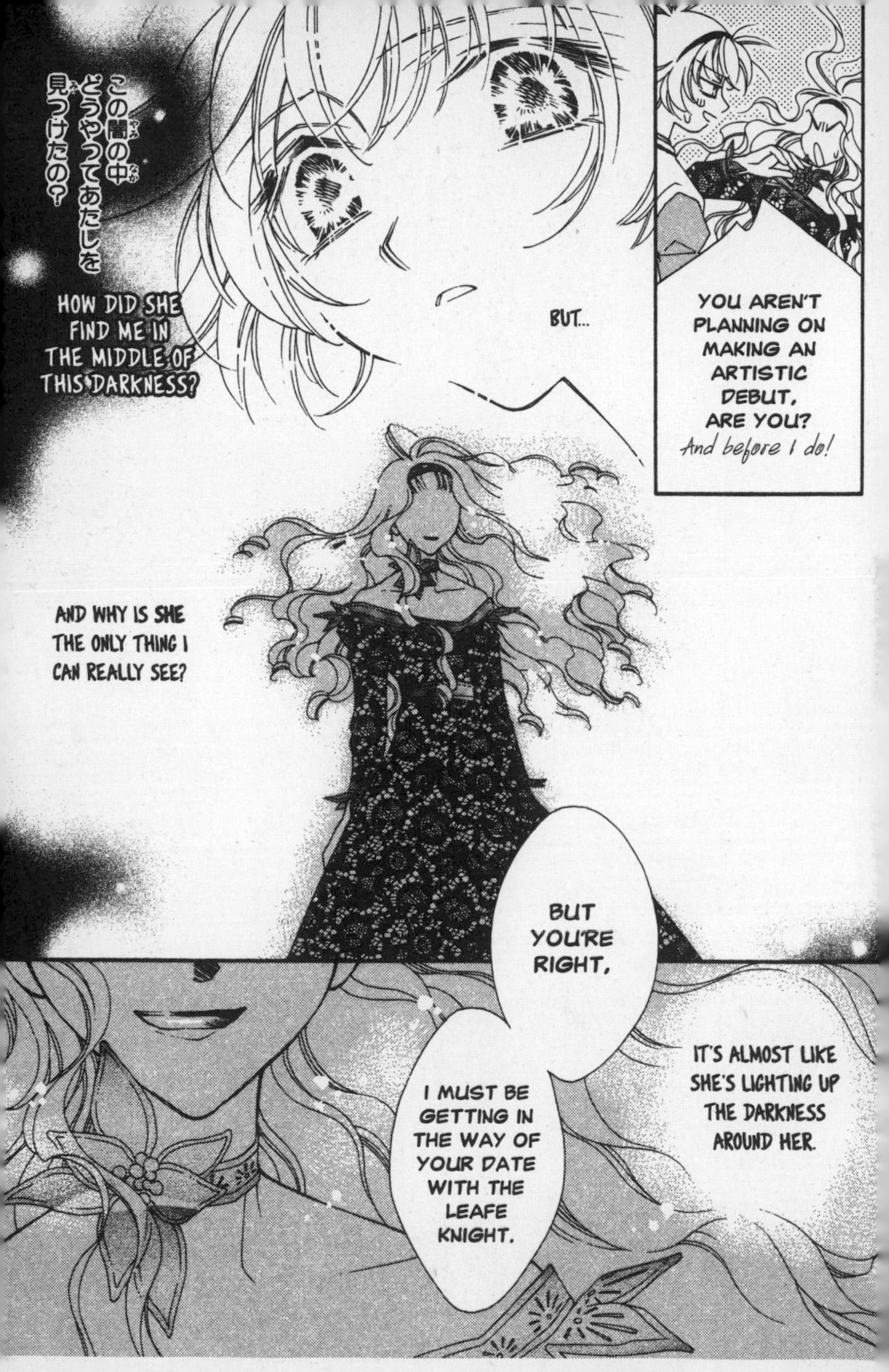
YOU AREN'T PLANNING ON MAKING AN ARTISTIC DEBUT, ARE YOU?
And before I do!
BUT...
この闇の中どうやってあたしを見つけたの？
HOW DID SHE FIND ME IN THE MIDDLE OF THIS DARKNESS?
AND WHY IS SHE THE ONLY THING I CAN REALLY SEE?
BUT YOU'RE RIGHT,
I MUST BE GETTING IN THE WAY OF YOUR DATE WITH THE LEAFE KNIGHT.
IT'S ALMOST LIKE SHE'S LIGHTING UP THE DARKNESS AROUND HER.

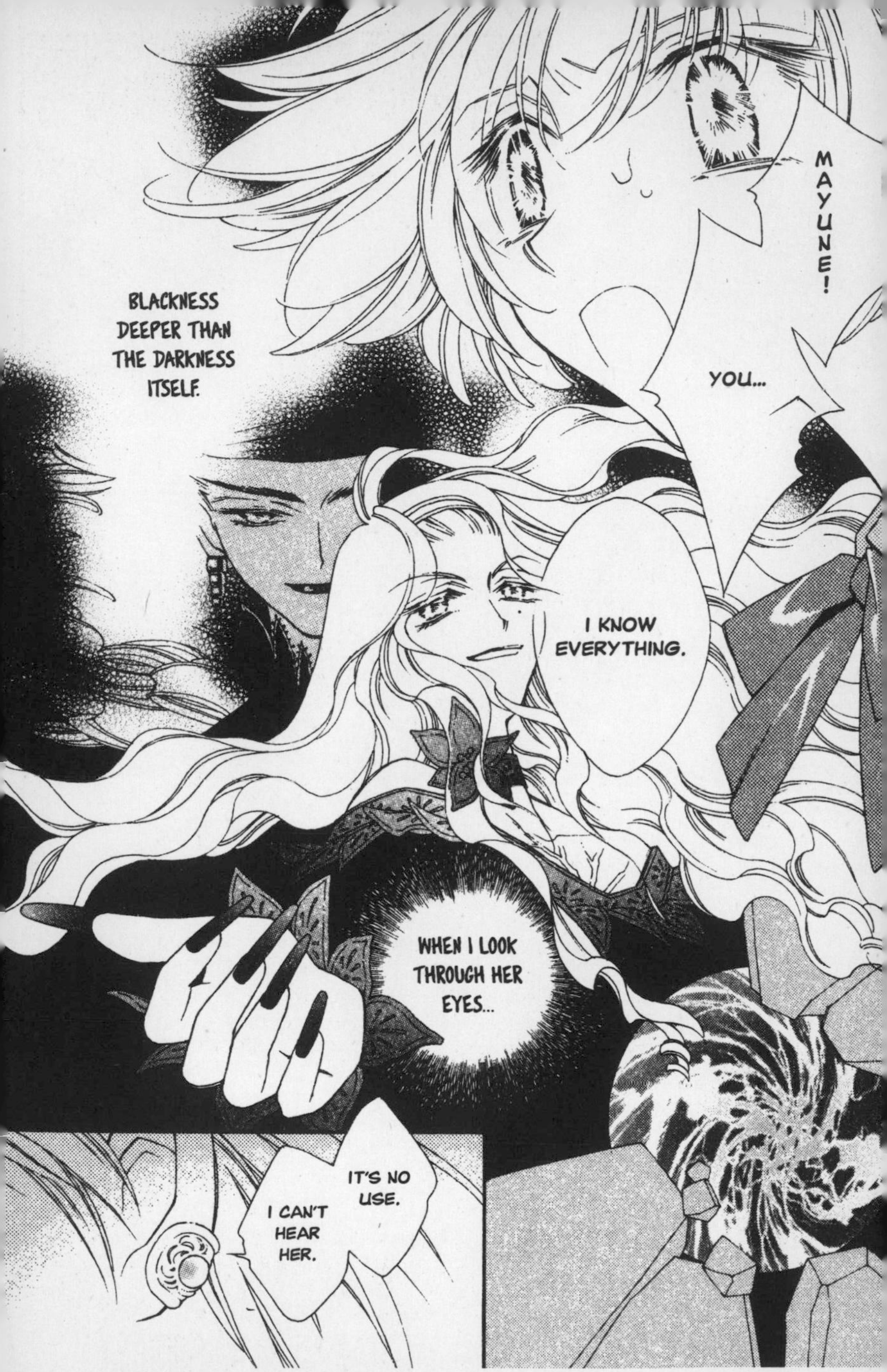
MAYUNE!
YOU...
BLACKNESS DEEPER THAN THE DARKNESS ITSELF.
I KNOW EVERYTHING.
WHEN I LOOK THROUGH HER EYES...
IT'S NO USE.
I CAN'T HEAR HER.

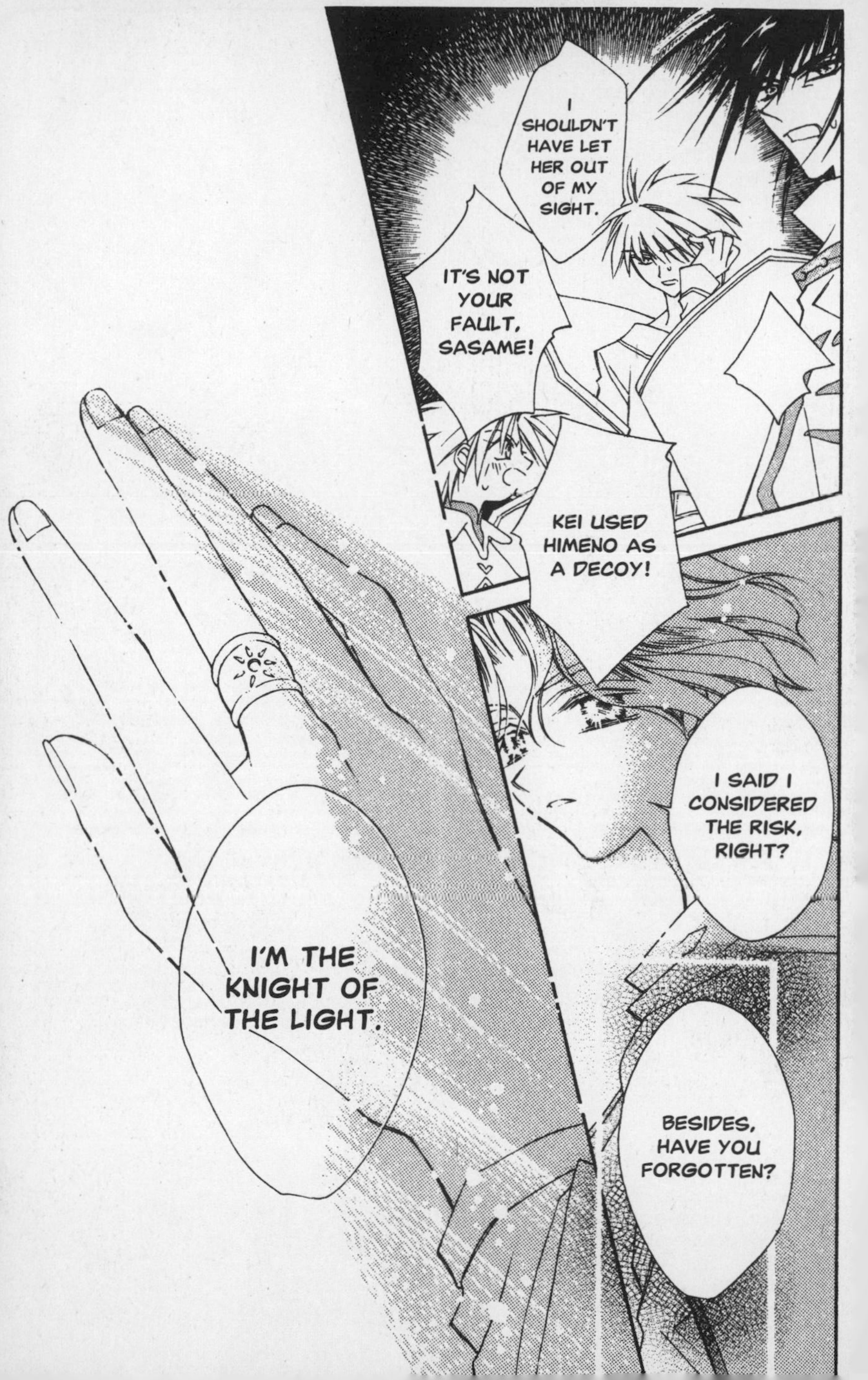
I SHOULDN'T HAVE LET HER OUT OF MY SIGHT.
IT'S NOT YOUR FAULT, SASAME!
KEI USED HIMENO AS A DECOY!
I SAID I CONSIDERED THE RISK, RIGHT?
BESIDES, HAVE YOU FORGOTTEN?
I'M THE KNIGHT OF THE LIGHT.

ABOUT THE ANIME

WELL, IF WE'RE GOING TO TALK ABOUT THE ANIME, LET'S START WITH MR. SATOU. I CONSTANTLY RELIED ON ALL OF THE ANIME STAFF, BUT...

SATOU WAS REALLY HELPFUL IN CHECKING THE SCRIPT AND STORYBOARDS BEFORE THE ANIMATION.

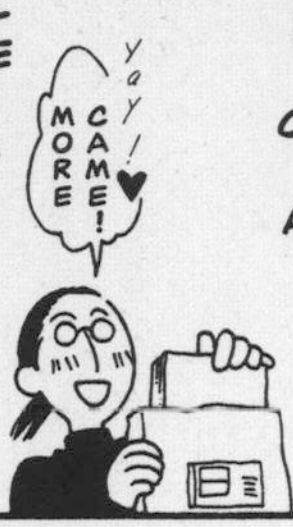

MORE CAME! ♥ Yay!

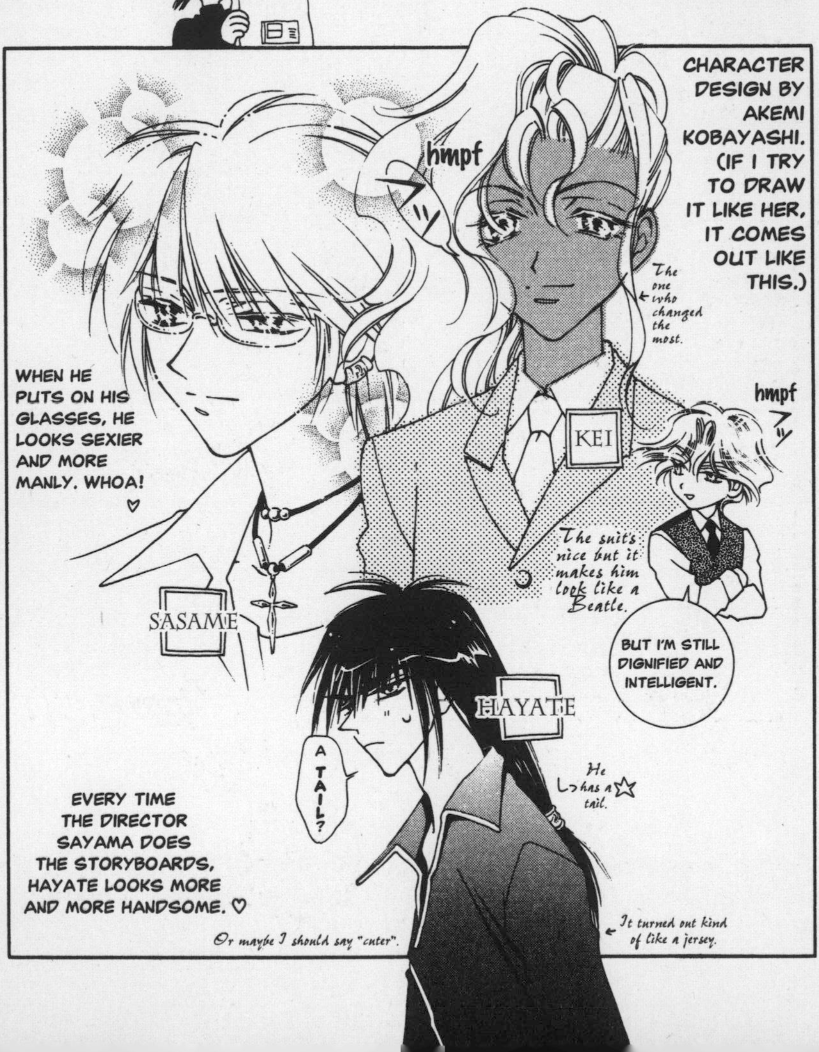

CHARACTER DESIGN BY AKEMI KOBAYASHI. (IF I TRY TO DRAW IT LIKE HER, IT COMES OUT LIKE THIS.)
hmpf
The one who changed the most.
WHEN HE PUTS ON HIS GLASSES, HE LOOKS SEXIER AND MORE MANLY. WHOA! ♡
KEI
hmpf
The suit's nice but it makes him look like a Beatle.
SASAME
BUT I'M STILL DIGNIFIED AND INTELLIGENT.
HAYATE
A TAIL?
He has a ☆ tail.
EVERY TIME THE DIRECTOR SAYAMA DOES THE STORYBOARDS, HAYATE LOOKS MORE AND MORE HANDSOME. ♡
Or maybe I should say "cuter".
It turned out kind of like a jersey.

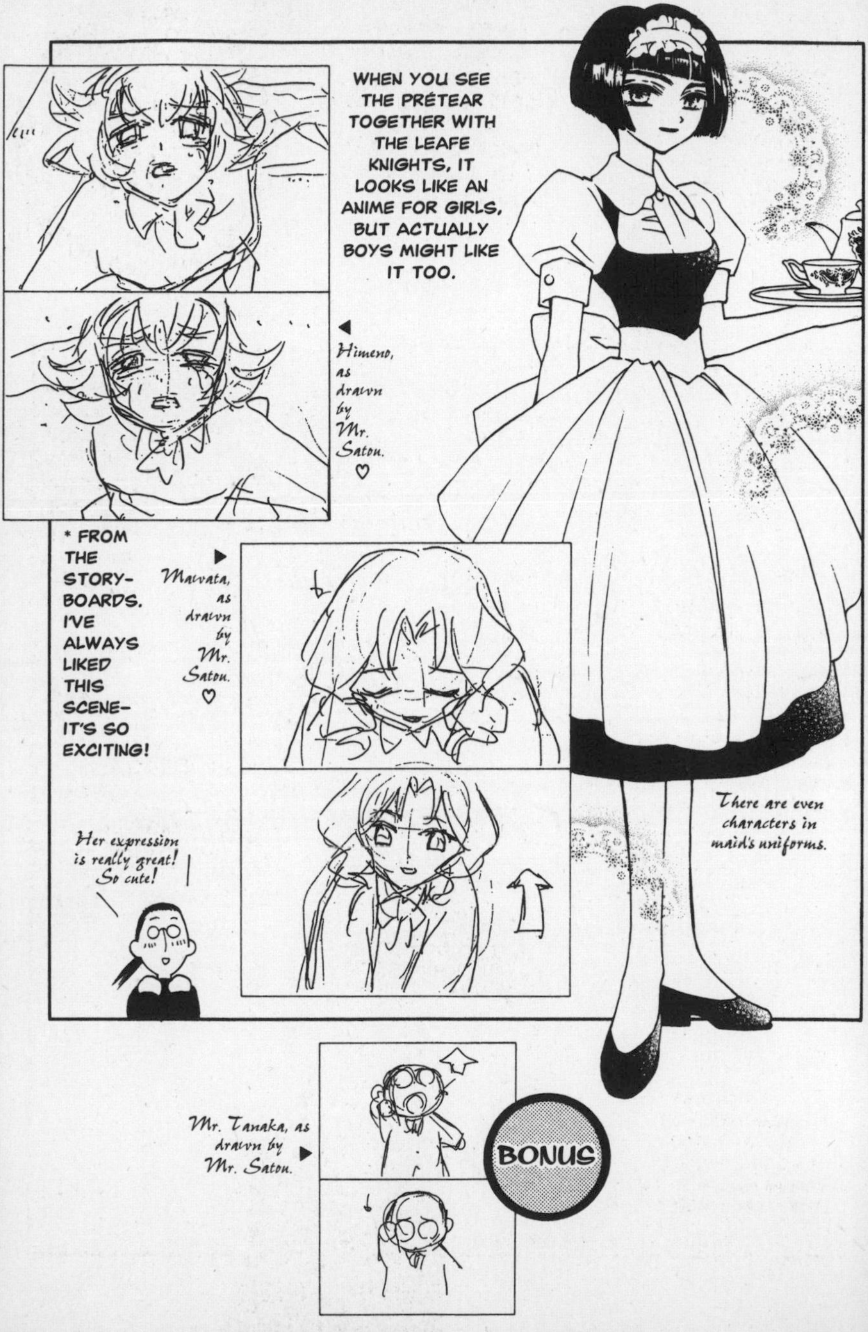
WHEN YOU SEE THE PRÉTEAR TOGETHER WITH THE LEAFE KNIGHTS, IT LOOKS LIKE AN ANIME FOR GIRLS, BUT ACTUALLY BOYS MIGHT LIKE IT TOO.
Himeno, as drawn by Mr. Satou. ♡
* FROM THE STORY-BOARDS. I'VE ALWAYS LIKED THIS SCENE–IT'S SO EXCITING!
Mawata, as drawn by Mr. Satou. ♡
There are even characters in maid's uniforms.
Her expression is really great! So cute!
Mr. Tanaka, as drawn by Mr. Satou.
BONUS

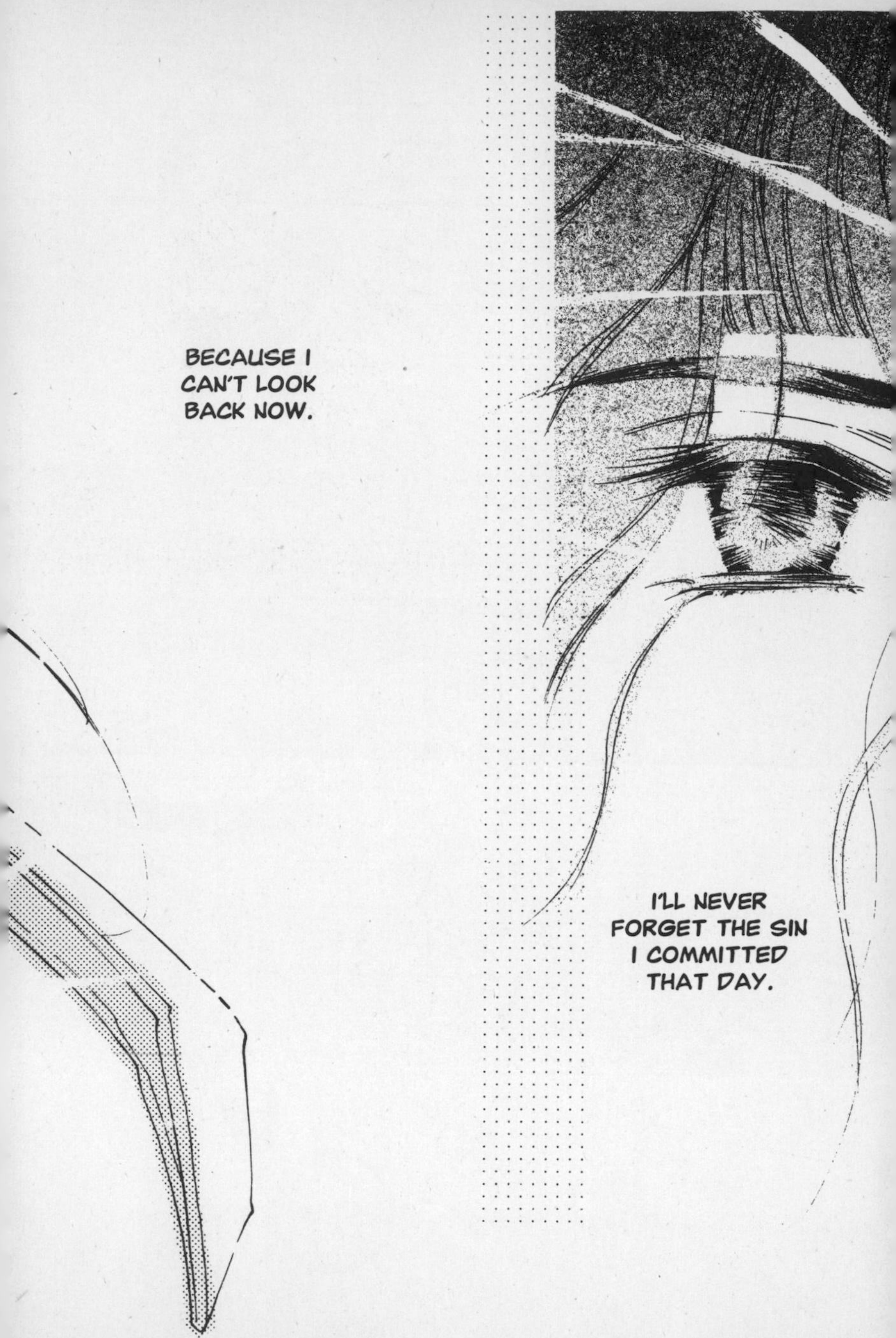
I'LL NEVER FORGET THE SIN I COMMITTED THAT DAY.
BECAUSE I CAN'T LOOK BACK NOW.

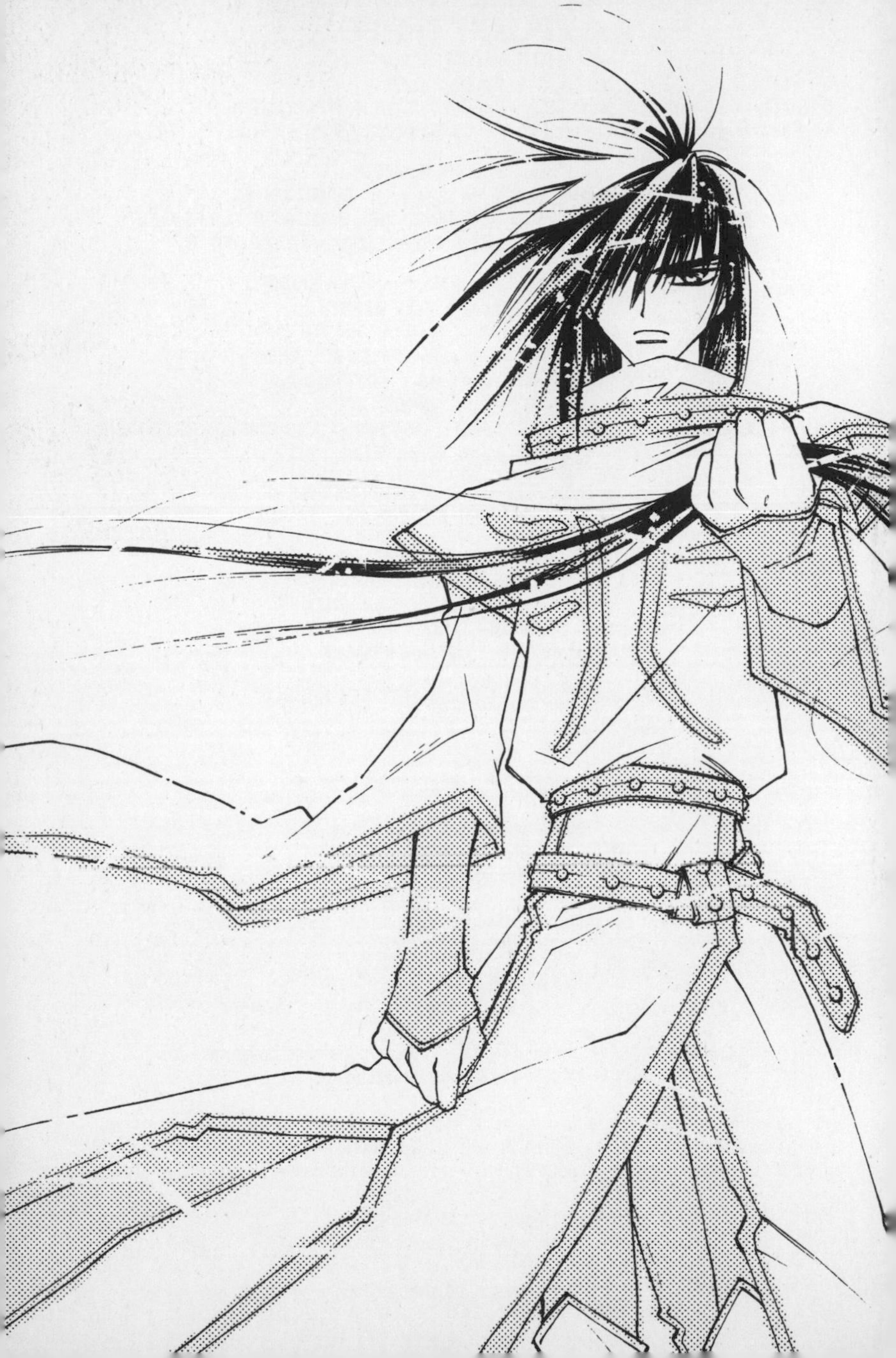

PRÉTEAR
VOLUME THREE

© Kaori NARUSE 2001
© Junichi SATOU 2001
Originally published in Japan in 2001 by KADOKAWA SHOTEN PUBLISHING CO., LTD., Tokyo.
English translation rights arranged with KADOKAWA SHOTEN PUBLISHING CO., LTD., Tokyo.

Translator **AMY FORSYTH**
Lead Translator/Translation Supervisor **JAVIER LOPEZ**
ADV Manga Translation Staff **KAY BERTRAND, JOSH COLE, BRENDAN FRAYNE,
HARUKA KANEKO-SMITH, EIKO McGREGOR AND MADOKA MOROE**

Print Production/ Art Studio Manager **LISA PUCKETT**
Pre-press Manager **KLYS REEDYK**
Art Production Manager **RYAN MASON**
Sr. Designer/Creative Manager **JORGE ALVARADO**
Graphic Designer/Group Leader **SCOTT SAVAGE**
Graphic Designer **CHRIS LAPP**
Graphic Artists **CHY LING, NATALIA MORALES, LISA RAPER AND NANAKO TSUKIHASHI**
Graphic Intern **MARK MEZA**

International Coordinator **TORU IWAKAMI**
International Coordinator **ATSUSHI KANBAYASHI**

Publishing Editor **SUSAN ITIN**
Assistant Editor **MARGARET SCHAROLD**
Editorial Assistant **VARSHA BHUCHAR**
Proofreaders **SHERIDAN JACOBS AND STEVEN REED**
Editorial Intern **JENNIFER VACCA**

Research/ Traffic Coordinator **MARSHA ARNOLD**

Executive VP, CFO, COO **KEVIN CORCORAN**

President, CEO & Publisher **JOHN LEDFORD**

Email: editor@adv-manga.com
www.adv-manga.com
www.advfilms.com

For sales and distribution inquiries please call 1.800.282.7202

ADV MANGA™ is a division of A.D. Vision, Inc.
10114 W. Sam Houston Parkway, Suite 200, Houston, Texas 77099

English text © 2004 published by A.D. Vision, Inc. under exclusive license.
ADV MANGA is a trademark of A.D. Vision, Inc.

ISBN: 1-4139-0146-8
First printing, October 2004
10 9 8 7 6 5 4 3 2 1
Printed in Canada

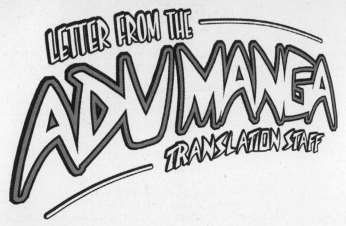

LETTER FROM THE ADV MANGA TRANSLATION STAFF

Dear Reader,

On behalf of the ADV Manga translation team, thank you for purchasing an ADV book. We are enthusiastic and committed to our work, and strive to carry our enthusiasm over into the book you hold in your hands.

Our goal is to retain the spirit of the original Japanese book. While great care has been taken to render a true and accurate translation, some cultural or readability issues may require a line to be adapted for greater accessibility to our readers. At times, manga titles that include culturally-specific concepts will feature a "Translator's Notes" section, which explains noteworthy references to the original text.

We hope our commitment to a faithful translation is evident in every ADV book you purchase.

Sincerely,

Javier Lopez
Lead Translator

Madoka Moroe

Haruka Kaneko-Smith

Eiko McGregor

Kay Bertrand

Joshua M. Cole

Brendan Frayne

Amy Forsyth

ADV Manga™

The New Legend of Snow White

Prétear 4

Himeno's father, a drunken novelist who's given up on writing, decides to run away from his family, and Natsue's vengeance rains down upon Himeno in a disastrous whirlwind of screams and accusations. As a final insult, Himeno is kicked to the curb, abandoned by her wicked family. Her new family of Leafe Knights and protectors vows to journey with the homeless Prétear to Leafeania, but a showdown with the Princess of Disaster will serve as more than a slight detour.

The Prétear is forced to make a horrible sacrifice to save the Leafe, but the trauma could lead her to discover the true identity of the Princess of Disaster in *Prétear* Volume 4.

COMING 2005

EDITOR'S PICKS

IF YOU LIKED *PRÉTEAR* VOLUME 3,
THEN YOU'LL LOVE THESE!

PICK 1

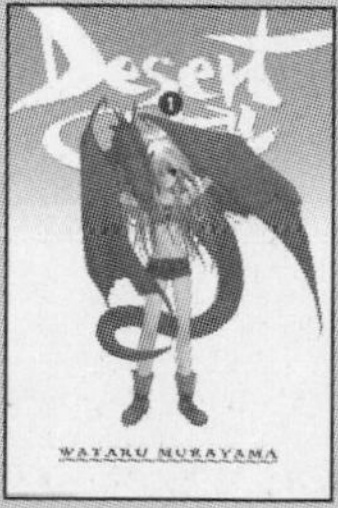
WATARU MURAYAMA

©WATARU MURAYAMA 2002

DESERT CORAL

Naoto Saki has an imagination so far-reaching that he has found an entire world within his dreams, filled with fascinating creatures and longstanding rivalries. After days and nights of escaping reality, he is summoned into this illusory land and into a battle between the Elphis and the Sand Dusts. Pain is real here, but the risk of certain injury and even death will not stave his eventual attachment to this world of fantasy. Ultimately, Naoto will be put to the test as he is forced to make a decision that will forever change him and the fate of *Desert Coral*.

PICK 2

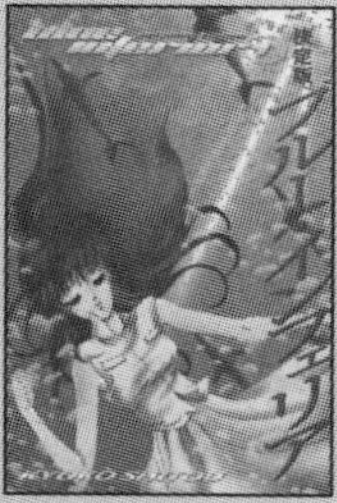

© 1999 Kyoko SHITOU

BLUE INFERIOR

In a post-apocalyptic world, whatever life has survived subsists only in small pockets throughout the world. Existence is somewhat carefree, but certain fears obstruct complete happiness—fear of the outside world, the unknown, the stories about the subhumans. These creatures threaten entire populations, making the people quite unwelcoming to newcomers. A young girl with amnesia—Marine—who washes up on shore one day, is no exception to their apprehension. It is only through the kindness of a boy named Kazuya that Marine will be able to escape the hostile town and find out who she really is.

PICK 3

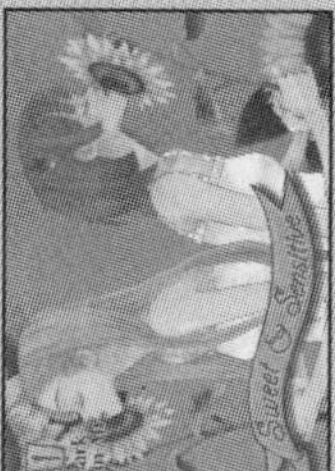
Sweet & Sensitive

© 1999 Park Eun-Ah / DAIWON C.I, Inc.

SWEET & SENSITIVE

Life is tough for lovesick teenagers! Meet Ee-Ji, a high school freshman suffering from—or is, perhaps, the cause of—an adolescent love triangle. Torn between two men, she is racked with grief over her own indecision. The first man in the running is Han-Kyul, a classmate since elementary school and Ee-Ji's longtime lovable crush, or the safe bet. But, his competition is a far cry from his sweet and sensitive demeanor. Sae-Ryun is crude, offensive and constantly bullies Ee-Ji and her friends, but he has managed to catch her eye anyway. To make matters worse, these two contenders are best friends. This situation has the potential to explode into a sordid mess, but Ee-Ji will have to pick her favorite man first!

THE NEW LEGEND OF SNOW WHITE CONTINUES IN *PRÉTEAR* VOLUME 4. COMING SOON FROM ADV MANGA!

CHECK'EM OUT TODAY!

ADV Manga™

www.adv-manga.com

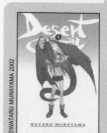

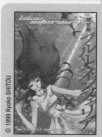

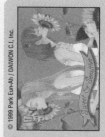

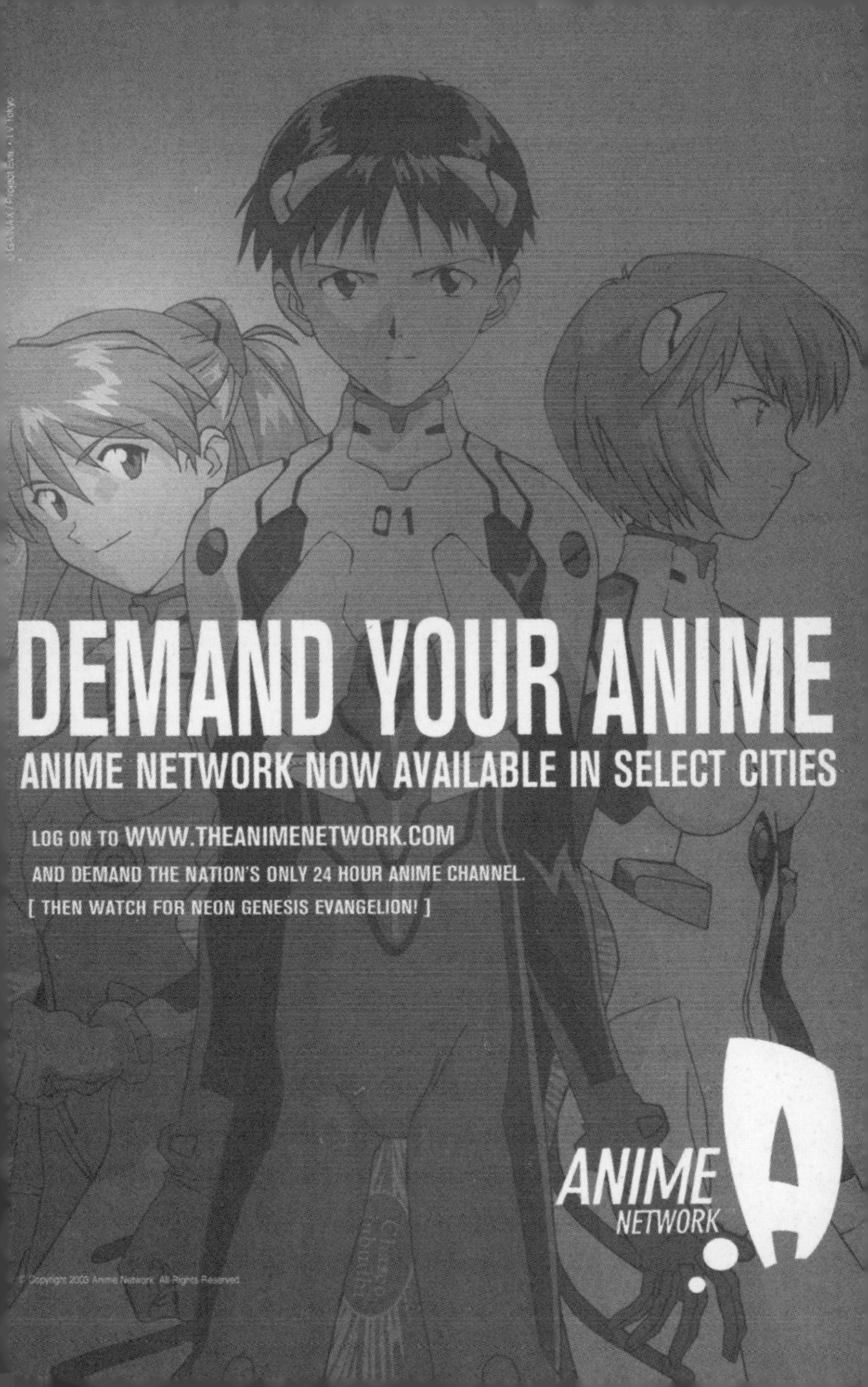
DEMAND YOUR ANIME
ANIME NETWORK NOW AVAILABLE IN SELECT CITIES
LOG ON TO WWW.THEANIMENETWORK.COM
AND DEMAND THE NATION'S ONLY 24 HOUR ANIME CHANNEL.
[THEN WATCH FOR NEON GENESIS EVANGELION!]
ANIME NETWORK
© Copyright 2003 Anime Network. All Rights Reserved.

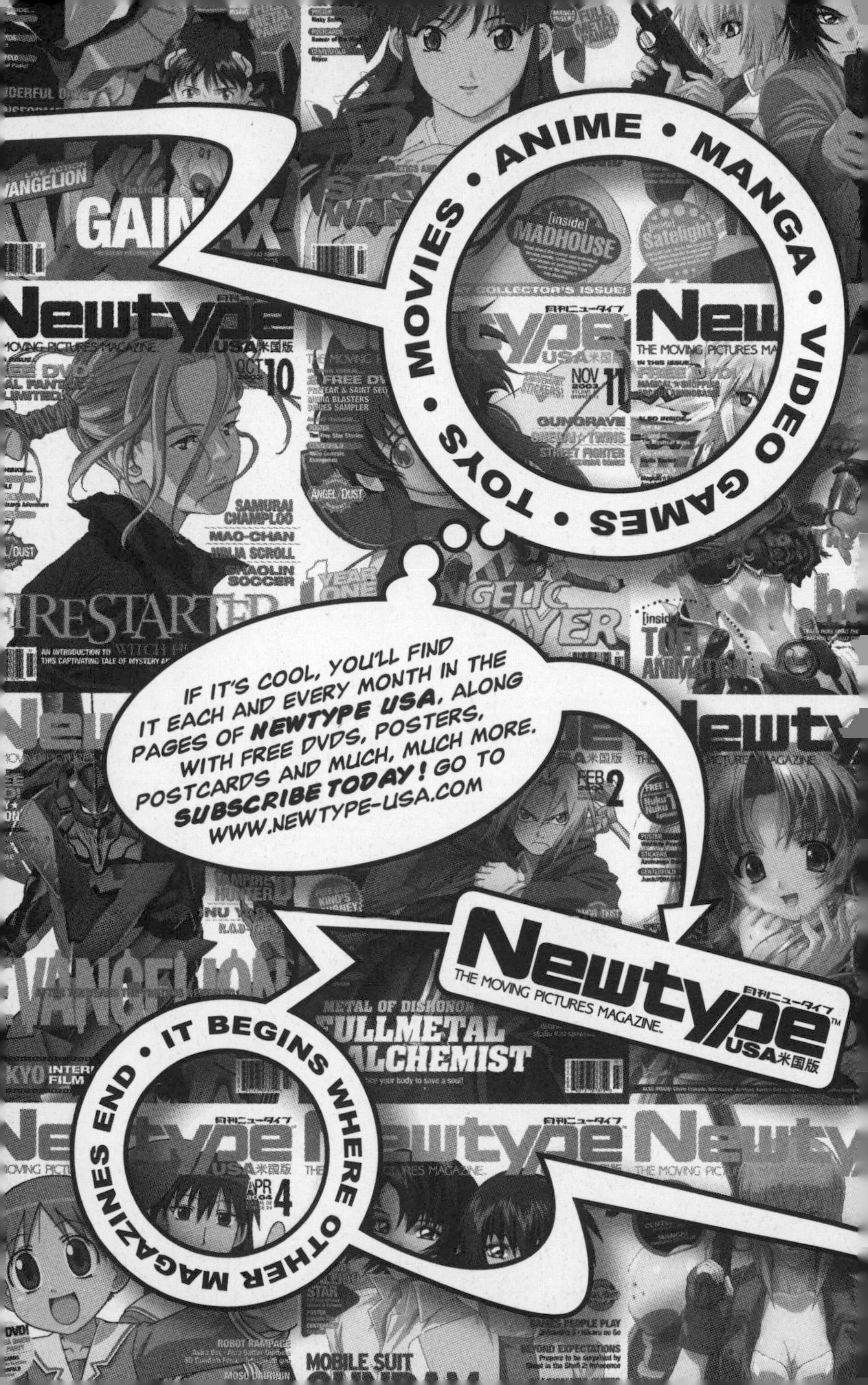

ANIME • MANGA • VIDEO GAMES • TOYS • MOVIES •
IF IT'S COOL, YOU'LL FIND IT EACH AND EVERY MONTH IN THE PAGES OF NEWTYPE USA, ALONG WITH FREE DVDS, POSTERS, POSTCARDS AND MUCH, MUCH MORE. SUBSCRIBE TODAY! GO TO WWW.NEWTYPE-USA.COM
Newtype™ THE MOVING PICTURES MAGAZINE. 月刊ニュータイプ USA 米国版
IT BEGINS WHERE OTHER MAGAZINES END •

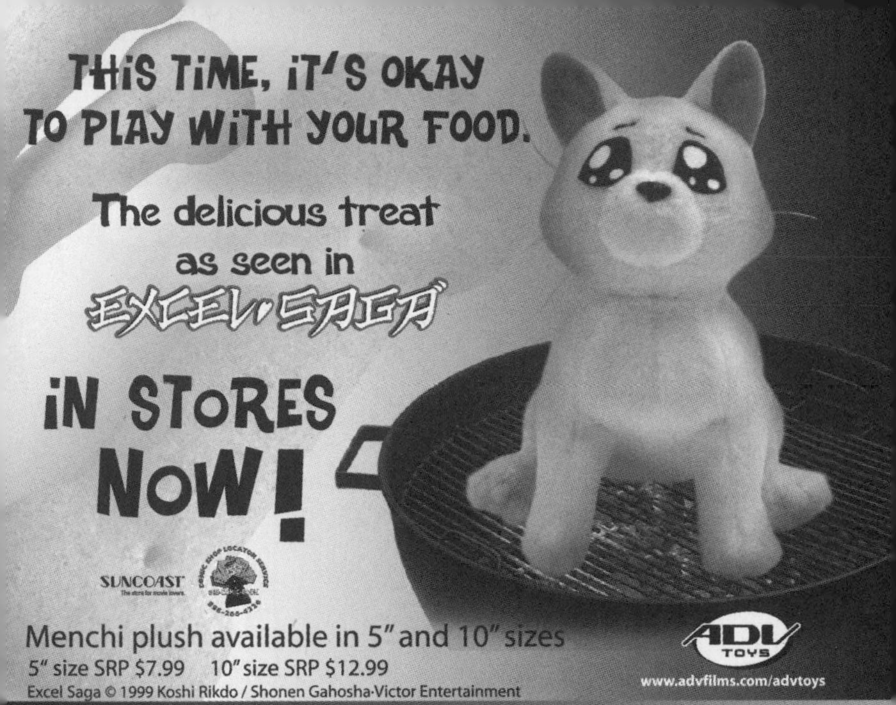

THIS TIME, IT'S OKAY
TO PLAY WITH YOUR FOOD.
The delicious treat
as seen in
EXCEL SAGA
IN STORES
NOW!
SUNCOAST
Menchi plush available in 5" and 10" sizes
5" size SRP $7.99 10" size SRP $12.99
Excel Saga © 1999 Koshi Rikdo / Shonen Gahosha·Victor Entertainment
ADV TOYS
www.advfilms.com/advtoys

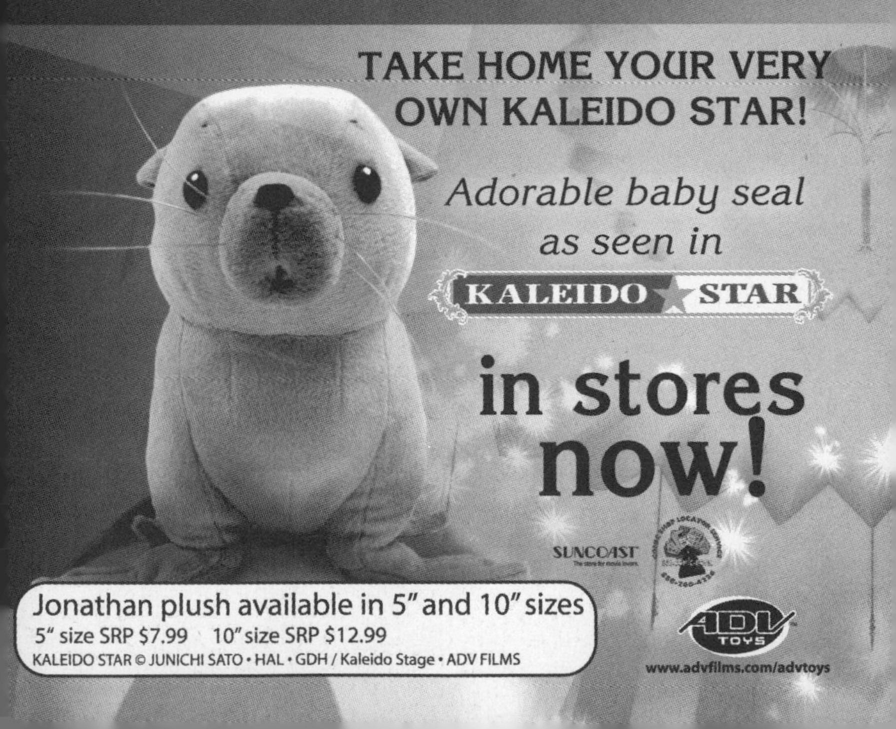

TAKE HOME YOUR VERY
OWN KALEIDO STAR!
Adorable baby seal
as seen in
KALEIDO STAR
in stores
now!
SUNCOAST
Jonathan plush available in 5" and 10" sizes
5" size SRP $7.99 10" size SRP $12.99
KALEIDO STAR © JUNICHI SATO • HAL • GDH / Kaleido Stage • ADV FILMS
ADV TOYS
www.advfilms.com/advtoys

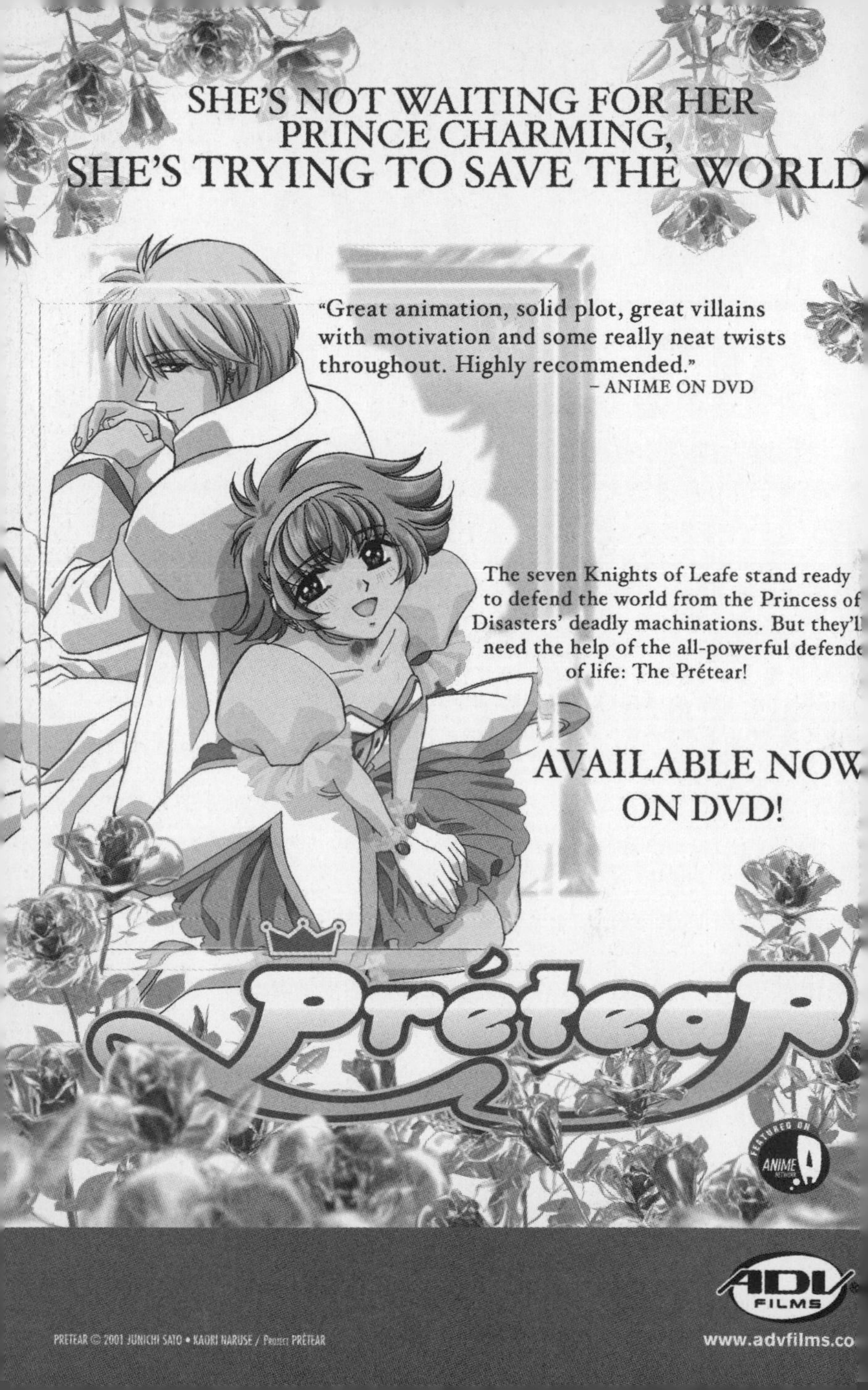
SHE'S NOT WAITING FOR HER
PRINCE CHARMING,
SHE'S TRYING TO SAVE THE WORLD
"Great animation, solid plot, great villains with motivation and some really neat twists throughout. Highly recommended."
– ANIME ON DVD
The seven Knights of Leafe stand ready to defend the world from the Princess of Disasters' deadly machinations. But they'l need the help of the all-powerful defende of life: The Prétear!
AVAILABLE NOW
ON DVD!
Prétear
ADV FILMS
PRETEAR © 2001 JUNICHI SATO • KAORI NARUSE / Project PRÉTEAR
www.advfilms.co

FROM THE CREATOR OF MYTHICAL DETECTIVE LOKI RAGNAROK!

TACTICS VOL. 01

Sakura Kinoshita and Kazuko Higashiyama

IF YOU'RE A PERSON WITH A GOBLIN PROBLEM-OR A GOBLIN WITH A PERSON PROBLEM — WHO CAN YOU CALL?

Kantaro is a boy who can speak to ghosts and goblins. Called on by people on both sides of the spirit world to fix problems and mediate disputes, Kantaro keeps relations between flesh-and-blood types and supernatural folks friendly. From helping a young woman whose husband has become a cruel goblin, to freeing a house of ghosts and goblins forced to be on display for paying customers, even orphan goblins can find a helping hand from Kantaro!

Volume 1 available October 2004

www.adv-manga.com